T0230049

Lecture Notes in Computer Science 916

Edited by G. Goos, J. Hartmanis and J. van Leeuwen

Advisory Board: W. Brauer   D. Gries   J. Stoer

Nabil R. Adam · Bharat K. Bhargava
Yelena Yesha (Eds.)

Digital Libraries

Current Issues

Digital Libraries Workshop DL '94
Newark, NJ, USA, May 19-20, 1994
Selected Papers

Springer

Nabil R. Adam   Bharat K. Bhargava
Yelena Yesha (Eds.)

Digital Libraries

Current Issues

Digital Libraries Workshop DL '94
Newark, NJ, USA, May 19-20, 1994
Selected Papers

 Springer

Series Editors

Gerhard Goos
Universität Karlsruhe
Vincenz-Priessnitz-Straße 3, D-76128 Karlsruhe, Germany

Juris Hartmanis
Department of Computer Science, Cornell University
4130 Upson Hall, Ithaca, NY 14853, USA

Jan van Leeuwen
Department of Computer Science, Utrecht University
Padualaan 14, 3584 CH Utrecht, The Netherlands

Volume Editors

Nabil R. Adam
Computing and Information Systems, MS/CIS Department, Rutgers University
180 University Avenue, Newark, NJ 07102, USA

Bharat K. Bhargava
Department of Computer Sciences, Purdue University
West Lafayette, IN 47907, USA

Yelena Yesha
Computer Science Department, University of Maryland Baltimore County
Baltimore, MD 21228-5398, USA

CR Subject Classification (1991): H.2-5, C.2, E.4-5, I.4.1, J.1

ISBN 3-540-59282-2 Springer-Verlag Berlin Heidelberg New York

CIP data applied for

© Springer-Verlag Berlin Heidelberg 1995
Printed in Germany

Typesetting: Camera-ready by author
SPIN: 10485799   06/3142-543210 - Printed on acid-free paper

Preface

Recently, digital libraries are receiving considerable attention from researchers in universities, industries and government agencies. A workshop was held at the Newark campus of Rutgers University on May 19-20, 1994, the purpose of which was to offer a forum for international experts to discuss a vision for organized and logical future developments in digital libraries. The workshop, publicized primarily through electronic mail, brought together more than 150 experts from government agencies (e.g., ARPA, NASA, National Institute of Standards and Technology, National Science Foundation, Naval Research Laboratory); commercial research laboratories (e.g., AT&T Bell Laboratories, Bellcore, IBM); industries (e.g., General Motors, GTE, Merck & Co., MITRE, Morgan Stanley, Price Waterhouse, Xerox Corp.); and from universities within the country and abroad (e.g., Australia, France, Germany, Great Britain, Italy, Japan, New Zealand, Singapore, Spain). The workshop was sponsored by Rutgers University, Purdue University, Bellcore, and AT&T, in cooperation with the National Institute for Standards and Technology and the National Science Foundation.

Nabil R. Adam, Bharat K. Bhargava and Yelena Yesha served as the program co-chairs. The program committee included R. Ashany, NSF; N. Belkin, Rutgers University; T. Finin, UMBC; H. Hirsh, Rutgers University; P. Kanellakis, Brown University; P. Kantor, Rutgers University; S. Naqvi, Bellcore; G. Schlageter, FernUniversitaet; S. Su, UFl-Gainesville; B. Wah, University of Illinois-UC.

The workshop resulted in several papers that were reviewed and their final versions are included in this book. We would like to express our deep personal thanks to the program committee members and the reviewers for their constructive comments and suggestions. We also would like to thank Dr. Linda L. Hill, University of Maryland College of Libarary & Information Services, USRA/CESDIS and IWGDMGC, for her comments on the manuscript. We are grateful for the support we received from AT&T and Bellcore. In addition, Nabil Adam would like to thank Dr. Shamim Naqvi of Bellcore for his support and help in this project, and also acknowledge the support he received during the preparation of this book from the Center of Excellence in Space Data and Information Sciences (CESDIS) at the Goddard Space Flight Center of NASA.

Nabil R. Adam
Bharat Bhargava
Yelena Yesha

February 1995

Contents

II Administration/Management   31

4 Which Way to the Future? The Control of Scholarly Publication   33
by Michael Lesk

5 Networked Information Systems As Digital Libraries   51
by Jacob Slonim and Lisa BaronLaurie

III Information Retrieval/Hypertext   63

6 Automatic Hypertext Conversion of Paper Document Collections   65
by Andreas Myka and Ulrich Güntzer

IV Classification And Indexing   163

10 Corpus Linguistics for Establishing the Natural Language Content of Digital Library Documents   165
by Robert P. Futrelle, Xiaolan Zhang and Yumiko Sekiya

11 Compression and Full-Text Indexing for Digital Libraries   181
by Ian H. Witten, Alistair Moffat and Timothy C. Bell

V Prototypes/Applications   251

15 A Video Database System for Digital Libraries   253
by HongJiang Zhang, Stephen W. Smoliar, Jian Hua Wu, Chien Yong Low and Atreyi Kankanhalli

16 Developing The Scientific-Technical Digital Library at a National Laboratory   265
by Laurie E. Stackpole, Roderick D. Atkinson and John Yokley

Chapter 1

Overview

Nabil R. Adam*, Bharat K. Bhargava† and Yelena Yesha‡

There exist large depositories of databases and old versions of software at most organization. For example, NASA has data on earth and space science, DOD has data for all events of Gulf war, and a long distance company has data for all the phone calls made during the last few years. In the same vein, a professor has collection of all her lecture notes, transparencies for talks given, handouts, old examinations, slides/videos of colloquia visitors, a list of questions asked by the audience and a large set of research papers, figures, tables, films, bibliographies etc. The type of data involved ina digital library consists of texts, figures, photographs, sound, video, films, slides etc.. In some sense a digital library encompasses all that is needed in terms of storage, processing, and communications for applications such as multimedia, video servers, and video conferencing.

The technical issues to be addressed by the digital libraries initiative are formidable. distributed processing, gigabyte networks, optical storage, resource discovery, data mining, user-interfaces, and scaling in terms of size of databases, number of users, number of sites, geographical distribution etc. Related issues deal with copyrights, security, quality of presentation, and availability. This book provides a perspective of various research issues and presents some insight into the current state-of-the-art. The book is organized into five parts: Introduction and Background, Administrative/Management, Information Retrieval, Classifications/Indexing and Prototypes/Implementations.

In the first part of the book, we discuss the issues of introductory nature. The first chapter provides an introduction and background discussion on digital libraries.

The second part of the book includes work that addresses the administration, management and socio-economic issues of digital libraries. One of the related issues is "Who will run online scientific communication?". The traditional pub-

*Rutgers University, Newark, NJ 07102, Email: adam@adam.rutgers.edu

†Department of Computer Sciences, Purdue University, West Lafayette, IN 47907, Email: bb@cs.purdue.edu

‡Computer Science Department, University of Maryland Baltimore County, Baltimore, MD 21228-5398, Email: yeyesha@cs.umbc.edu

lishers are adding electronic searching, screen display, and rapid communication to their paper journals; while the operators of computer bulletin boards are adding archiving, refereeing, and regular appearance to their systems. Each is thus converging on the same goal: an electronically available high quality digital publication. But they represent two entirely different communities: the publishers wish to charge, the bulletin board operators normally don't. They are taking slightly different technical paths: the publishers lean towards CD-ROM and to image display; while the bulletin boards are normally ASCII, with images used as hypermedia items, most commonly on Mosaic. The publishers use full text search; the bulletin boards lean towards hypertext.

In the first chapter in this section, Lesk shares the findings of some of his related experiments. His experiments show that people can use either form of display; that computer searching is an enormous gain on paper searching; and that the technology is here now to do electronic journals in either form. The questions now are administrative and economic: how can we organize scientific publication to preserve quality and openness while gaining the advantages of electronics? The site license concepts which appeal to the software industry are less popular with the information industry, which prefers large database systems that dole out little bits of information not worth stealing. Another answer might be an increased use of the equivalent of page charges: if institutions paid to publish rather than to purchase, copying would not disrupt the system.

The next chapter summarizes discussions within the IBM Academy Digital Library Study and presents some of the human and socio-economic challenges and opportunities in the creation and application of the digital library.

Part 3 of the book focuses on issues related to information retrieval and hypertext. Digital libraries should include all the enhanced search functionality that can be provided by using state-of-the-art electronic tools. With respect to this main goal, the support of intuitive searches by means of employing hypertextual features is important. In order to include these features into the browsing functionality for image representations of documents, the underlying implicit and explicit hypertext structure of library objects has to be modeled and detected. This internal conversion of real library objects into hypertext objects has to be done automatically as far as possible in order to make it feasible. Yet, this conversion has to be flexible enough to cope with the whole range of library objects. In order to do so, it has to use explicit information, such as words, phrases, paragraphs etc., as well as all the implicit information contained in fonts and layout. The first chapter in this part of the book includes a description of the automatic hypertext conversion of printed articles based on a description language for link types. The description language provides for a means of describing a whole set of links by indicating characteristics they have in common instead of specifying single links. The usage of a description language also hides problems of the optical character recognition at specification time.

In the second chapter of this part of the book, it is argued that hyperdocuments administered by digital libraries have to be structured according to standardized storage and exchange formats in order to allow for the manipulation functionality required in digital library construction, maintenance and use. A discussion of how SGML and its extension, HyTime, can play this structuring role; and how multimedia documents structured accordingly can be stored, changed, and maintained in the object-oriented database system VODAK is presented. Using the dynamic semantic extension facilities of VODAK, it is illustrated how the document structuring dynamics offered by SGML and HyTime can be accommodated in the database. In addition, the chapter includes a discussion of how this facility can be combined with other system components to provide a relevant portion of the functionality required for digital libraries.

Paper documents in a typical library have a variety of layouts, print quality, and multiple pages — which are not easily transformed into an appropriate digital form by utilizing the present technology. The next chapter discusses research towards a Document Image Understanding System that results in overcoming the limitations of current technology. It involves analysis and recognition of scanned paper document images, so they can be converted into an electronically searchable text form. An adaptive approach is used to deal with a variety of document layouts. The text recognition process converts text regions of the document image into ASCII text; contextual information is used to improve OCR performance on degraded images. To provide for intelligent information retrieval, different document elements are linked together, e.g., figure call-outs, bibliographic references. In a testbed implementation, several document types have been dealt with– including newspapers, technical journals, and books, in both English and Japanese language publications.

The last chapter in Part 3 presents and analyzes efficient algorithms for the automated recognition and interpretation of layout structures in electronic documents. The key idea is to use the patterns in the distribution of white space in a document to recognize and interpret its components. The recognition algorithm divides the document into a hierarchy of logical elements; the interpretation algorithms classify these divisions as base-text, tables, indented lists, polygonal drawings, and graphs. Experimental data and a discussion of an information access application is included in this chapter. The suggested methodology allows the automatic markup of documents for instance in the SGML format and the creation of multi-level indices and browsing tools for electronic libraries.

Part 4 of the book includes five chapters dealing with the issues of classification and indexing. Digital Libraries will hold huge amounts of text and other forms of information. For the collections to be maximally useful, they must be highly organized with useful indexes and intra- and inter-document linkages. This brings with it a demand for ever-better methods for automated analysis of text to build the indexes and links. It requires turning implicit information "encrypted in natural language" into explicit information. The first chapter focuses on word classification as an example of the utility of corpus methods (part-of-speech tagging and semantic clustering). Results are presented for the syntactic and semantic classification of words from a biological corpus. A new approach to word classification and other language structure analyses, the *balanced entropy principle* is described. Because it is a totally unsupervised classification procedure, it can be applied to a variety of domains, even when machine-readable dictionaries are not available for a domain. The word classes identified can then be used for indexing, query expansion, syntactic analysis and for linking separate library collections by aligning word senses. The chapter also discusses derivative objects, diagram analysis and authoring tools.

Recent advances in compressing and indexing information have yielded a qualitative change in the feasibility of large-scale full-text retrieval—a technique that can also be used for pictorial and other non-textual information. Comprehensive full-text indexes have traditionally been expensive in storage and computationally demanding to create. However, it is now possible for volumes of text equivalent to an entire library bookstack to reside in an office workstation and be accessed in one or two seconds through either boolean or ranked queries. This chapter examines these trends, reviews the technology involved, and exposes the potential of contemporary workstations for coping with the information explosion using fully-automatic indexing of large information bases.

This chapter looks at aspects of communications and multimedia that impinge upon the creation and organization of the digital library. Models of multimedia communication and data provision are described along with the implications for the organization of the digital library. Also, the access methods used by home based users are considered and the implications this has for the structure of information storage and access methods. Finally the chapter briefly discusses methods for navigation around the complex web of information that forms the world-wide information resource.

A query to a large data repository can easily produce so many possible sources that the user's ability to ferret out the highest quality and most appropriate information is impaired. This chapter reports on an effective visualization technique for managing this information overload. It also demonstrates how natural language processing, including both understanding and generation, can be tightly integrated with the visualization system for improved human computer interaction.

In areas as diverse as earth remote sensing, astronomy, and medical imaging, image acquisition technology has undergone tremendous improvements in recent years. Unfortunately, advances in our ability to deal with this volume of data in an effective manner have not paralleled the hardware gains in storage technology and data gathering instruments. While this has led to an explosive growth in the amount of image data available for creating digital image archives, the problems of automated analysis and useful retrieval methods stand in the way of creating true digital image libraries. In order to perform query-by-content type searches, the query formulation problem needs to be addressed: it is often not possible for users to formulate the targets of their searches in terms of queries. The chapter presents a natural and powerful approach to this critical problem to assist scientists in exploring large digital image libraries. We target a system that the user trains to find certain features simply by giving it examples of features to be located. The learning algorithms use the training data to produce a classifier that will detect and identify other targets in the digital image library.

This forms the basis for query by content capabilities and for library indexing purposes. This paper presents two such applications at JPL: the SKICAT system used for the reduction and analysis of a 3 tera byte astronomical data set and the JARtool system to be used in automatically analyzing the Magellan data set consisting of over 30,000 images of the surface of Venus. The chapter covers important problems and issues that must be addressed if a learning approach to the query formulation problem is to provide a general and effective solution.

The chapters included in the last part of the book discuss some initiatives in developing a digital library and some prototype implementations.

The digital libraries of the future must be able to accommodate multimedia source material as readily as current libraries accommodate text. The first chapter in this part of the book discusses efforts to develop a prototype video library system for the purpose of achieving this goal. Software tools for parsing the content of video sources, generating index structures, and enabling both focused query retrieval and casual browsing were implemented. Case studies have provided the primary means for testing the results.

The Ruth H. Hooker Research Library and Technical Information Center meets the information needs of Naval Research Laboratory (NRL), consisting of about 3,500 Federal staff and about 1,500 contractors at the Washington, D.C. facility. NRL, which provides the Navy with an in-house research capability, occupies as its principal site a 130-acre campus of 152 buildings located on the Potomac River in Southwest Washington, D.C. The Library facilitates end-user access to a range of scientific and technical information resources through the development and implementation of networked information systems and the conversion of print-based information to digital formats. The Library's networked information capabilities extend to other NRL research facilities located in Orlando, Florida; Bay St. Louis, Missouri; and Monterey, California; and to NRL's parent organization, the Office of Naval Research in Arlington, VA. Three library initiatives that lay the foundation for the "digital library" are discussed. The first two of these, the InfoNet Campus-Wide Information System and the Research Reports Imaging System, are fully mature and operational. The InfoNet, introduced in August 1992, allows users to query local and remote information systems and enables them to request Library materials and services without leaving their offices; from a single menu users can select a wide variety of information resources including: library-mounted CD-ROM databases; "electronic books" downloaded from the Internet; other Laboratory databases including the Library catalog; and resources located throughout the world through preprogrammed access to selected Internet hosts. The Research Reports Imaging System stores major portions of the Library's collection electronically as page images; almost 100,000 reports, about 5 million pages, are seemlessly linked to an online catalog, enabling users, seated at in-library workstations, to perform bibliographic searches, and by use of a "hot key," to view the entire contents of reports online. The third effort, called TORPEDO (The Optical Retrieval Project: Electronic Documents Online), builds on experience gained and lessons learned in the other two initiatives. TORPEDO is being developed to provide researchers with networked images for access to all the information contained in a document – graphs, charts, scientific characters, and equations. The NRL Library has signed a cooperative agreement with the American Physical Society to use TORPEDO to disseminate current issues of two of its journals, *Physical Review Letters* and *Physical Review E*. Design considerations for NRL's networked imaging system are set forth, and system plans, featuring the use of NCSA Mosaic to launch commercial software with freely distributable clients, are discussed.

The last chapter in the book discusses the development of a digital library prototype called DL-Raid at the Raid laboratory in Purdue University. The prototype is used to study the feasibility and sensitivity of various retrieval schemes for digital library data in distributed environments. The architecture of the DL-Raid and the data model supported by this prototype are presented. The chapter investigates the issues in partial content-based retrieval scheme in this prototype and presents the results and the associated analysis of various communication experiments with large data objects. Since the user may not know where what data is available, an interactive dialogue is shown to be communication intensive.

Part I

Introduction

Chapter 2

Some Key Issues in Database Systems in a Digital Library Setting [*]

Nabil R. Adam[†], Bradley S. Fordham[‡] and Yelena Yesha[§]

The goal of the National Information Infrastructure (NII) project is to allow universal access to distributed stores of information and to provide this access at a reasonable cost to every citizen. If this technical program succeeds, one can easily visualize a country-wide Digital Library environment in which every citizen can access many different kinds of information and use that information for pleasure, education, science and business. In anticipation of this possibility, large amounts of historical information is being digitized and new information is being created in digital form. This tremendous storehouse of information will be made available to *any* American citizen with any level of technical sophistication via a collection of highly intelligent network interface programs. This chapter will introduce several technical issues involved in the various DL research projects in order to provide some understanding of the scope and complexity of this work as a whole. We will define some issues and raise the questions regarding the scope of database systems in a didital library setting.

2.1 Motivation

The National Information Infrastructure (NII) is intended to be the means for interconnecting every home and organization in the United States, and the enabler of faster and easier ways to perform many daily tasks. Digital libraries will be among the applications which will take advantage of this nationally accessible network. Other application areas planned for this nationally accessible network

---

[*]We are grateful to Shamim Naqvi for his invaluable comments on an earlier version of this paper.

[†]Rutgers University, 180 University Avenue, Newark, NJ 07102, Email: adam@adam.rutgers.edu

[‡]Center for Applied Information Technologies, Computer Systems Laboratory, National Institute of Standards and Technology, Gaithersburg, MD 2 0899, Email: fordham@speckle.ncsl.nist.gov

[§]Computer Science Department, University of Maryland Baltimore County, Baltimore, MD 21228-5398, Email: yeyesha@cs.umbc.edu

include manufacturing and concurrent engineering, electronic commerce, health-care, education, environmental monitoring, and government service provisioning. It follows, then, that the NII and especially it's DL systems should be fast and efficient. In the digital library setting, an overwhelming amount of information of extraordinarily diverse types need to be collected, organized, and made available, in an efficient and user-friendly manner, to a large number of users with diverse technical backgrounds and interests. Some of this information may also be constantly undergoing change and the user may need to ability to see each of the many versions.

For this to be a reality, several issues need to be addressed, including the following.

- The ability in a digital library setting (DLS) to store, compare, manipulate, and then distribute design specifications for many industries, e.g., aircraft industries and plastic pencil cases, in order to improve U.S. marketplace competitiveness.

- The ability in a DLS to track large number of product vendors, product buyers, and products as well as the information required to actually effect the sales/purchases of products.

- The ability in a DLS to store, compare, manipulate and then distribute medical patient-files which could each be hundreds of pages long containing x-rays, ultrasounds,standardized forms, hand-written notations, and many other information formats.

- The ability in a DLS to collect, analyze, and present in a *usable* form pieces of environmental information from major geographical locations in the U.S.

- The ability in a DLS to store and provide efficient access to images, sound-bytes, videos, books, newspaper articles, government documents, and so forth.

- The ability in a DLS to store information on government services and then make those services electronically accessible to *only* those persons who are qualified to receive them.

In such an environment, database systems (DBSs) represent an essential component. DBSs are responsible for collecting and pumping the information over the network, examining the data to answer questions and structure knowledge. There are several major characteristics which make the database management problems of digital library environments unusual, and these new wrinkles necessarily force modifications to the way we approach the database problems in a digital library setting. These distinguishing characteristics are: the overwhelmingly large scale, the inherently multi- media nature of the data, the extreme dynamics of the user access patterns, the vast – although perhaps not predominant – numbers of primarily read-only data items, and the need to make query statements *ruthlessly* precise in order to limit the search space to some reasonable size. It is the purpose of this chapter to provide some understanding of the scope and complexity of database systems in a digital library setting. We define the issues and raise the questions that researchers have already been asking and exploring or will have to face in the future.

2.2   Meta-data vs. Data and Self-Description

Database management systems have always drawn a clear distinction between the structure and relationships that we intend to represent and the actual data set (integers, strings, binary images) that are physically stored and which should embody the information intent. This separation between meta-data and data has proven extremely useful as it allows us to query not only the currently stored information but also the structure of that information. In a DL setting this self-descriptive property will become increasingly more critical. Now that we are moving to multi-media in the DLS there will be an arbitrary collection of text, digitized sound, binary images, and totally new data classes such as digital encodings of tactile information readable by special output devices, all stored according to their own peculiar characteristics. In the DLS it will be imperative that application programs be able to sort out this seemingly random jumble of bits in the information storehouse by asking these information storehouses to clearly and efficiently describe their own structure, as database systems can.

Given, then the need to have meta-data to define the structure of the DL system the issue becomes one of deciding what that meta-data should look like. The purpose of meta-data in a DB is to describe the content of the DB for the benefit of the user. In a DL setting, one expects a variety of data types and within those data types a number of sources of information. There will thus be a great need for just finding out what information is contained in a DL. The act of retrieving some information may actually be secondary. To support such "what all is out there" kinds of queries, DL will need an advanced concept of meta-data that can be queried. Indeed new ways will have to be invented to present all the information in a DL to the user in a concise manner. It may not be possible to "browse" and discover what all is available on our own. It is like walking into a huge bookstore and having to browse it to discover what all it contains – a fun exercise but time consuming. What is needed are ways to construct digests and directories on the fly of the information contained in the DL, perhaps based on user preferences cited in a user profile. To carry on with the book store example, we can imagine a user walking into a bookstore, and being given a map showing what books of his/her interest are available and where they are located.

This means that the DB concept of meta-data will need to be extended by information models that present meta-information in concise and meaningful ways, and from which the user may decide what to retrieve. Another possible extension to the DB concept of meta-data is by building on and making use of the agents concepts [206, 152].

A related notion in database management is that of data independence. Most DBMSs work on some version of the 3-schema architecture which provides two levels of data-independence.

Logical Data Independence States that application programs need not be altered when the system self-description (also know as the conceptual-level schema) is changed. This allows one to alter the system structure without affecting the application programs running against the original information content.

Physical Data Independence States that the physical storage structures may be altered without making any change to the conceptual-level schema. This allows one to physically store information in more efficient ways, as they are discovered, without changing the logical structure of the system and thereby altering the way in which application programs must ask for data.

These features highlight the critical need to use database systems and techniques as information storehouses for DL systems. New information will constantly be added to the DL's and new and better ways to manage the physical layer where the data is stored will constantly be uncovered. The DL's, then, must be flexible enough to easily extend their own self-description and improve their retrieval and update performance **without** disturbing the current set of users and programs which are interfacing with it.

Also related and exceedingly important to databases are the notions of data abstraction and mnemonic naming. One would like to be able to directly request access to an image, a sound clip, or a document by some mnemonic name, i.e., through a query language, such as "Retrieve War and Peace" instead of having to browse, locate and transfer information. In DBMS environments this is possible as there exists a notion of *data abstraction*, a process that hides the details of how one stores, manipulates, and retrieves complex structures such as images, or sound clips, or highly formatted documents. Similarly there exists a notion of mnemonic naming provided by a system catalog which further hides the abstract object from the user allowing him/her to access that data, directly, by using its mnemonic name. Query languages and naming are some of the pleasant features provided by database kernels, in the DL setting they will be *requirements* for success.

There will also need to be an extension of these notions in the DL setting. The DL's will require the addition of a new level of abstraction which hides the mnemonic names of all objects related to some logically cohesive concept underneath the name of that concept. This feature will afford us associative addressing. A DL user will be able to ask for all associated information on "Tolstoy" and retrieve *War and Peace* as well as *Anna Karenina* along with other information related to Tolstoy. .

2.3   Support for Multiple Views

Database systems have long been aware that users differ in the level of information detail that they want displayed to them. Views were developed to account for this fact as well as the fact that not all users want the same presentation of data. Some users need or want to see identical data sets in dramatically different ways. This could mean seeing the data in a different order or through an entirely different interface such as a graphical user interface, a natural language interface, or a more traditional forms or command-interpreter style interface. This disparity among users will only be exacerbated in a DL setting. The database systems should present different views of the information for people with different levels of interest in the details of a given topic, with different educational levels, with different levels of background in the information being queried, with different abilities to see or hear or read, and with different security clearances. One major difference between the traditional DB environment and a DL setting is that in a DL setting there are more than just one data model and in some cases the information may not even have a clear underlying model. These represent new challenges to the DB community. Here it is advisable that we recall the past tight-coupling between database management and artificial intelligence (AI) research (e.g. Knowledge-Bases). Information visualization techniques are a growing area of interest for many researchers and there is a need to couple this area with DBMS query processing and answer presentation techniques.

2.4   DL Query Languages

It has already been noted that there should be in the DL's, as in all DBMSs, a variety of query interfaces and that most probably standards will emerge for these interfaces which will enable faster tool development. What requires more elaboration now is not so much the implementational concerns of these query interfaces but rather the general properties that DL queries, generated by **any** interface, should exhibit. The search space on the DL will be so incredibly large, that queries must be *forced* to be painfully specific just to counter the explosion of legal query responses. Somehow, users must be prevented from sending out information requests that are too general, e.g. "American Politics." Such under-specified queries can be constrained by using the emerging idea of software agents/information brokers [206]. In the example above, we can imagine defining a software agent who is knowledgeable about political queries. It will engage the user in a dialogue for the purpose of further refining and narrowing the original query "American Politics" to perhaps "What is the politicl system used to elect a President." Thus, software agents can be used to mediate under-specified queries so that they are constrained and narrowed before being presented to the DL for processing. Software agents will be needed for several common and oft-used concepts and will serve as pre-processors of queries based on those concepts or related to those concepts. Indeed, a taxonomy or hierarchy of software agents will be needed corresponding to a hierarchy of concepts and sub-concepts. The notion of concepts and concept-servers will be useful here, as concepts could be arranged in subsumption hierarchies. Software agents would also check DL queries for logical inconsistencies like, "Show me all people who are not people", as these also would waste valuable DL resource performing useless operations. In fact, it should be possible with appropriate standards to allow agent software to optimize, decompose, compile, and distribute sub-queries to DL nodes in *executable* format. This would be highly desirable, as it would save the DL information-servers some of the overhead of query-processing.

The task of locating the information in a DL setting is an information retrieval problem and will also require the use of sophisticated techniques such as information filtering agents [152]. The task of displaying the information is a user interface issue and if implemented properly, would also require built-in intelligence that would determine the appropriate format based based on the user preference, location, display media, etc. We believe that there is a need to develop different "languages" for each of these tasks. Interface and retrieval mechanisms will need to be highly adaptive on the DL. Query languages must always be based on the underlying data model and, as mentioned above, in a DL setting there is no single underlying model and in some cases there is no data model at all.

Finally, there is the issue of query by content, e.g., retreive a book on pencil manufacturing techniques. We will need to automatically extract the content from data objects of all types. We need to know what objects are displayed in an image, what themes are captured in a text or in a piece of music, and what size and weight are represented by a tactile encoding. Second, we will need to create these concepts over very large sections of the DL. There may be hundreds of thousands of references to a concept at tens of thousands of database storehouses, and yet each of those relationships must be maintained. This problem is exacerbated by the need to replicate entire concepts at a multitude of points along the network in order to ensure that user-access times are not excessive.

2.5   Database Utilities

The standard set of database utilities should definitely be extended and fully automated for use in the DL. Here we will mention just a few examples of common database utilities that will need to be given automated control. The loader module should *automatically* import new information which has been legally sent to a DL storehouse. The system monitor should *automatically* adjust buffer sizes, transaction context areas, the block counts for multi-block reads, the number of available file handles, etc. in order to provide optimal performance under highly variable system loads. The security and authorization subsystem should *automatically* approve new user accesses and select appropriate security privileges as the American public comes on-line.

On the side of new utilities, there will need to be a whole assortment of software modules to deal with the various communications and data protocols. The DL will need software subsystems to manage and access the concept and mnemonic name servers. Utility software will be required to analyze and classify all incoming data objects of every type. Specialized backup and recovery utilities will most likely be employed, and there will need to be some notion of a clerical-utility to track important events at every node so that this information can later be rolled up to more central DL sites for performance, access, failure, and other types of auditing.

2.6   Transaction Management

A DL setting is assumed to be predominantly a read-only environment. Transaction management in the DL setting will become very much a synchronization problem between subobjects, i.e., synchronizing data objects from multiple sources. for example, we may request information about Ronald Reagan, the actor. The application processes the query, sends out the requests and then the synchronization problem for the logical transaction on Reagan begins. Maybe a video slide show, the sound track for the slide show, the text to surround the slide show frames, and a few documents are retrieved. The interface now has to assemble all these subobjects into a coherent logical object subject to the subobject constraints. For example, the audio and video subobjects have presentation constraints. Notice here that we must expect the user's local application and machine to not always be capable of buffering and then managing the presentation of the entire set of retrieved information unaided. The DL will have to provide suboject presentation and synchronication constraint management facilities; thus, in this example, if the user's local application is impoverished and incapabale of handling synchronization constraints then the DL will need to provide a node where the subojects can be assembled and delivered to the user's application as a whole, i.e., in some coherent order and at some manageable rate of speed in manageably sized increments so that the user application can present it without difficulty.

Another related issue is the availability of network elements and network bandwidth. It should not be expected that the DL will need to be aware of the availability of network elements, i.e., whether the network is available for transporting information. Networking technologies have builtin capabilities to store information in case certain nodes are inoperational and, in any case, certain guarantees of delivery of information will be provided to applications in the DL setting. What will be needed is a reservation of resources such as bandwidth by the DL from the network. In other words, before delivery of information, the DL will need to ask the network for bandwidth and other resources. Thus, the DL needs to know how much information it needs to be transfered and under what constraints. There will then be a negotiation of resources and needs between the the DL and the network managment system, resulting in the network management system giving a set of guarantees to the DL application.

2.7 Files and Indexes

In the DL environment database storage structures, indexing schemes, and index files will have to take on totally new appearances. For one thing, we will now have incredibly large collections of binary data floating around be it aural, visual, tactile, or other various and assundry binary data encodings. The issue will be how are we going to **manage**, at the logical and physical level, *very* large collections of *very* diverse types of data files *very* widely dispersed over the DL nodal network? How does one decide on the data organization a DL setting? It can be argued that the success of DBMS technologies depends largely on sophisticated data placement strategies and data organization techniques. But in a DL setting with many diverse users, many and varied data types, widely varying usages, and either a lack of schema or multiple schemata, it is not clear what data placement and data organization strategies would lead to efficient query processing and information delivery. Data placement and data organization questions when answered correctly, as in traditional DBMSs, can yield significant performance increases and when answered incorrectly can yield significant performance obstacles. Database practitioners have struggled with these issues for years and solved them for very specific environments with well-defined schema and narrow classes of users. In the DL context, however, under widely varying loads, floating logical and conceptual linkages, and extremely diverse data formats we have yet to find efficient methods which will yield acceptable perfromance.

Indexing poses similar challenges. In a multi-media setting we will need to move to feature-based indexing systems that look not at information headers and labels but *inside* the data, scanning its content. Open questions abound. Will the traditional indexing schemes such as primary, secondary, clustering, hashing, and hierarchical scale up to the new challenges of the DL or will drastically new ones need to be created and adopted? Will we need to redefine the definition of an index key now that these values might be images or sound-bytes or tactile encodings? The only help that the DL will have, again, is the frequent low-volatility of many of the data sets. The traditional database problems of adjusting sorted index files as the data files are updated will largely go away in these predominantly read-only data arenas.

2.8 Security and Authorization

In the DL, some of the information will be public domain data to be made available to everyone at no charge or some very minimal charge. In this case security and authorization will most likely degenerate into more of a priority scheme for servicing requests. Even this simple case presents complications. On the DL system with so many processes trying to access so much data at once, it may be important to somehow rank-order the requests for processing. For example, should doctors and hospitals have their requests for medical records answered before a third-grader gets the encyclopedia article he/she needs for his/her school report? Also, should electronic commerce and business negotiations be handled before the servicing of book requests made to the digital library. One possibility for the authorization system, then, is to be based on the class of the users, i.e., knowing who is asking for the information in order to decide how high a priority the request should receive and consequently how soon the database will be given the request for processing. If there is billing for information involved in this process, then the priority scheme can not be based solely on the authorization of classes of users because whoever pays for information needs to be serviced promptly.

In those cases where the information is proprietary, the security and authorization problem presents difficult problems for a DL setting. On the one hand, a DL is meant to allow uuniversal access to all citizens to all kinds of information. But proprietary data means that only certain individuals can be allowed access. Thus, a security and authorization mechanism is needed that can authenticate users. If a user accesses a DL system, the security system has to ensure that the person is indeed who he/she claims to be and what levels of information he/she has access to. The open environment of a DL setting lies in sharp contrast to the restricted environment of proprietary data environments.

Digital data can be infinitely copied. The intellectual property of proprietary data needs to be enforced in a DL setting. If an information provider makes certain information available, the provider needs to be ensured that his intellectual property will be preserved by the DL. Copyrights need to be enforced and authorized users only are to be allowed access to information.

2.9 Database Design

Database design will be markedly different in the DL as well. Database design typically progresses from the entities and relationships captured in an ER or EER diagram, through the implementation-level primitives of the chosen data model, down to the files and records of the physical layer. A critical issue is always, how "good" is the design being created. A good design will *enable* database use and future development work on top of the system. A poor design will definitely *impede* future progress.

The quality of a database design is normally established by comparing the *intended* data interrelationships transferred from the "real world" through the high-level data model, ER or EER formalism, to the *explicit* interrelationships in the system design. The closer these two are to each other, the better the design. This, in practice, means that all logical functional dependencies (FDs) which exist in a data set should each be captured in a *single* primitive. In the relational model, each FD should be contained in a *single* table. In the hierarchical and network models each FD should be contained in a *single* record type. In the objéct-oriented model, each FD should be contained in a *single* object type. This rule prevents the database designer from *forcing* the system to reconstruct connections or paths *between* primitives every time an update is effected and the FDs must be validated.

The logical question, then, is what does an FD look like in the DL environment? In a standard DBMS environment, an FD looks like *ssn → name* and indicates that any given ssn value functionally determines a name value. In layperson's terms, if you give the system someone's *ssn* then it can look up the person's name value without any difficulty since the FD guarantees that there will be no ambiguity in the mapping. Certainly, these standard relational FDs will still exist in the DL context. However, we will also have new extensions of these FDs to capture content-based information. Examples might be *image → setting* or *song → mood*. These FDs are semantics-oriented. They tell us what logical meanings – portrayed by the data values – are derivable from objects of a given type, either in the more general (e.g. for all images) or in the more specific (e.g. for all images of presidents) cases to which they are applied. Good designs will need to heed these new twists on the old notion of FDs. If this is ignored then the old problems of unnecessary redundancy, NULL-space, spurious and dangling tuples, insertion anomalies, deletion anomalies, and modification anomalies will again plague the DL's DBMS systems.

Another database design notion, that of view integration, will also need adjustment to suit the DL. It is common practice to take a large set of diverse user data and functionality requirements and then stepwise synthesize them into a single, coherent global picture. In the DL, the full set of data and functional requirements will **never** exist, but rather they will forever remain a dynamic property. The challenge, then, is to design **dynamic** view-integration techniques that allow for evolutionary, real-time data and function design. In addition to the aforementioned automatic loaders and application writers there will need to be a notion of a global design watchdog which ensures that the "goodness" properties of the system structure are not unduly eroded by the processes of incremental change and extension.

2.10   Query Processing and Optimization

As aforementioned, the more query processing activities that local query sites can do, the better for the DL. The biggest costs in DL query processing, however, will probably not be the standard ones which exist today of query decomposition, compilation, and re-assembly. We expect the biggest cost in DL query processing to be in the resource location and synchronization processes. There will be a requirement to bind concepts to mnemonic names and then to (redundant) physical site addresses. There will be a need to select one site address from the list of many, hopefully based on performance metrics, for each object. Then there will be the need to enforce multi-point to multi-point synchronization rules between all querying sites and all involved information sources. Also, access to some objects may require the intervention of the payment mechanism.

The old problems of distributed join optimizations and so forth have been well studied at this point. It will be the new DL challenges of optimizing queries in spite of the overwhelming scale (in terms of the number of nodes, the number of objects, the huge sizes of objects, the number of distinct data types, the number of conceptual mappings, and the number of mnemonic mappings), billing verification, and multi-media delivery synchronization that will have to be focused on.

2.11   Database Constraints

Even database constraints will need to evolve to meet the DL challenge. Many of the restrictions that had previously fallen into the class of *semantic constraints* and which were largely ignored will now need to be rigorously enforced. For example, requiring that the meaning of a picture (i.e. the objects captured in the image) be related to the DL database representations of *all* of those pictured objects and to *no* others will be critical. Enforcing sequence constraints over data objects, like the various images in a slide show, will be required.

In addition, all of the standard integrity constraints will necessarily require broadening. How is the uniqueness constraint defined over images? For example, are two pictures of the same thing with two different backdrops the same or different key values? How is entity integrity defined over music? Is a long pause for a number of measures considered to be a NULL value? How is referential integrity formally specified over tactile information? Do we achieve a successful reference based on texture or weight or some combination? Perhaps even more critically, are we going to permit our integrity rules to move from the the world of hard and fast requirements to the universe of fuzzy logic?

In the DL, it now seems to make some sense to have varying degrees of matches between objects and hence varying degrees of conformance to integrity constraints. That being said, the tremendous problems are now manifestly obvious. We want to allow a certain range of variation among the data elements which will be considered to satisfy our DBMS constraints, however, all computer systems must eventually reduce any such determinations to a deterministic boolean value. Either the datum does satisfy the constraints or it does not. Again we appeal to the field of AI which has built up a wealth of experience in the areas of machine sensing and fuzzy-value processing to make the claim that although this is a new reality for database environments it is not an unsupportable reality.

Chapter 3

Promising Research Directions in Digital Libraries

Nabil R. Adam*, Milton Halem[†] and Shamim Naqvi[‡]

3.1 Motivation

The idea behind the emerging technology of Digital Libraries (DL) is to provide a Jeffersonian style universal access to digitized information (content). The fuel driving this engine is the recent phenomenal growth in networking. It is a commonplace now that researchers and educators, with access to electronic mail and other network programs, consider this access to be essential for their day to day activities. Networks have made it possible to interact and collaborate with one's peers and enhance one's productivity tremendously. In addition, current trends in business include global integration, pressure to intensify partnership with other companies within the states as well as abroad. As a result, more and more, commercial organizations find it essential to be linked by world-wide networks. Commercial Internet usage is growing at approximately one million new users per month.

Global networking has prompted wide-scale digitization of information. Digital content is infinitely malleable and globally deliverable across networks. As more traditional content such as books, magazines and popular fiction become digitized, users of electronic information will change from educators, researchers and businessmen to the laity. Anticipating this move, several publishers have shown interest in producing and owning the digitized content of their traditional information. Government agencies such as NASA have shown interest in providing their content to wider sections of the public.

These trends and technological advances have resulted in the emerging notion of Digital Libraries. A digital library may be viewed as electronic (digital) collections that cover a wide range of interests such as art exhibits, music, medical records and images, video, books, newspapers, and companies' brochures and catalogs. These collections are linked together by a world-wide network and are available electronically to the public in all media such as voice, video, images,

*Rutgers University, 180 University Ave., Newark, NJ 07102, Email: adam@adam.rutgers.edu

[†]Goddard Space Flight Center, NASA, Greenbelt, MD

[‡]Bellcore, Morristown, NJ 07960, Email: shamim@bellcore.com

and text. The basic idea is that individuals with electronic access can "check out" any library material. The two basic issues, thus, in this area are the nature of the content and access to this content. It is now believed that the first content to be made available in digital libraries will be scientific journals because this is the economically beneficial part of the publishing business. This will be followed by rare and old books and manuscripts which in turn will be followed by more difficult material such as maps [157].

Current estimates for the cost of digitizing an average textbook is about $50 per book. If we can assume that the pages of the book can be fed automatically then this cost reduces to less than $10 per book. Disk space for storing a book is about $10. A typical library spends about $50 to store and maintain a book. This assumes storage at the university or city library in contrast to warehousing the books at a remote location and providing overnight access. In the case of warehousing of books, the cost drops to about $10 per book [157]. It is reasonable to assume that the cost of digitizing and storing a book is roughly equivalent to storing a paper version of the book in a traditional library. Thus, the two costs—digitizing and providing electronic storage for content, and keeping the content on paper in a traditional library—are roughly the same.

Given that the costs of the traditional and digital libraries are similar, and that there are several open issues in law, copyright and intellectual property, not to mention concerns of authors, librarians and to some extent the publishers (who want to continue to own content), it seems unlikely that a national infrastructure for digital libraries can be effectively supported by the financial community. For example, the fact is that a very large percentage (almost 90%) of all books ever published are out of print. In a digital library the equivalent of being out of print is to be taken off a server. One of the open questions is, What does that mean? Where does the content go and who is responsible for it? In the scientific journal business, if a library decides to drop its subscription to a journal, will they lose all the previous issues of that journal as well because they no longer have access to the server that has that journal? Note that the library in question can not make copies of the content that they paid for because presumably the users are going to be charged per access by the journal publishers. As newer technologies come online that would drop the cost of a digital library infrastructure, traditional libraries will find innovative ways to drop their costs. Why should the financial community invest in digital library technology? We claim that there are three basic reasons that will motivate investment in digital library technology:

- DL will provide access to hitherto inaccessible information. This includes maps, schematics, architectural drawings, rare books, etc. This information is either difficult to access or extremely rare. For example, getting all the forms and information together for a public works project is New York City is so difficult that special companies offer this service.

- DL will provide access to information that changes rapidly, e.g., scientific journals that change every few months. For example, subscriptions to medical journals cost thousands of dollars per individual and very few people get all the journals.

- DL will provide new ways to use the stored content that is not provided by traditional libraries. We shall have more to sday on this issue later.

Thus, economic and technical reasons exist for assuming that DLs will be most productive if they provide new ways to use content, rather than just replace traditional access to content. In other words, DLs have to be different than traditional libraries. Otherwise, the economics are not favorable for supporting a new DL infrastructure.

Digital access to content in lieu of traditional access is based on convenience that may or may not be economically justifiable[§]. For example, access to content may mean access to digitized books from a number of bookstores, say Barnes and Noble and Book Scientifica in New York City. From the comfort of our home, we can browse these two book stores and determine what book we need. This is surely a convenience that many of us will use. What we will miss in this exercise are the reasons why we physically visit these two bookstores. Those reasons include such things as spending a day away from home, the smell of bookstores, a lunch or snack in New York City, seeing other people in the book-stores, etc. We know that we can do network equivalents of some of these social activities also (e.g., we can meet people on the network) but until virtual reality is indistinguishable from reality, there will always be certain social aspects that we miss on cyberspace that are only available in the real world. So, network access to these bookstores eliminates some of the problems with physical access; it adds some features and it deletes some features. It will always be a tradeoff. The interesting business question is, How much we are willing to pay for the features we get as opposed to the features we miss?

New uses of content does not have such an obvious tradeoff. If we need to use the content in some new and novel way, it will not help us in going to New York City and having network access to the bookstores is not enough. We need to use the content in some new way and if we need to do so badly enough we will pay for that use. In this paper we examine new uses of content that will distinguish DL from other information technologies such as Distributed Databases and Networked Information Systems.

3.2   Digital Libraries As Distributed Databases

The dominant information technology of today is (distributed) database technology [73]. The relational database market which is a subset of the full database market is about $4 billion annually in the US. The natural question is, What role will database technology play in DL system. At first glance many database features seem to apply to DL as well. The basic reasoning goes like this: a digital library will have large amounts of data, it will provide access to this data for a diverse group of distributed users, data will need to be updated and kept consistent, user interfaces will be provided to browse, find and locate information

---

[§]A friend who is not a computer user to whom we once explained the idea of DL said, "I see; you want to make people lazy."

and indexes will have to be built and maintained, and data transmission and compression techniques will have to be used. All of these topics, in one guise or another, and to varying degrees, are present in database system research. A database system stores large (but not as large) amounts of data albeit DL will have more diverse types of data. Database systems provide interfaces, build and maintain indexes, worry about data migration, etc. So a DL can be thought of as a database system which emphasizes and exercises certain traditional areas of database systems. Research proposals in this context are based on extending database ideas or techniques and have a flavor of database system research.

Database technology has certain features that weaken its position as a base technology for implementing DL systems. For example, database technology uses the principle of non-interpretation of data as a basic axiom. The database system does not interpret the data that resides in it. Every piece of data is a black box. The database system manipulates the data objects in purely syntactic terms and bases retrieval, storage and optimization decisions on this axiom of non-interpretation. In a DL system, a very large number of (different) objects are expected to be stored. Users will have very little idea of what the DL contains. So, necessarily, the user will base retrieval requests on the content of the objects. In DL terms this is called querying by content and is entirely unsupported in database systems. In a database system we would be required to retrieve an object based on meta-data and external properties of the object, and then examine its content through some application program. Contrast this with the approach of asking for a book on the behavior of Alaskan Wolves. In a DL one would expect the system to retrieve only those objects that have the specified content.

Some partial solutions are possible for this problem. In one set of proposals, the idea of extractors has been put forward [240]. Extractors are programs that examine the content of objects and construct meta-data and external properties of objects based on their content. These properties and meta-data can then be queried through a conventional database system. In other words, extractors build up the meta-data part of a database system with content from the data objects. How smart do the extractors have to be? Consider, for example, a database system containing C-program objects and we wish to retrieve programs (objects) dealing with sorting. A good extractor for this database system would have to have the knowledge of a C compiler. In order for extractors to be useful, we will need to expend considerable programming effort in constructing these extractors.

Another fundamental aspect of database technology is the central role played by the schema. A database system starts with a schema and data comes later in the sense that the database is populated with data after the schema has been designed. DL on the other hand will collect data objects incrementally. Therefore, the concept of a schema for a DL will be one in which the schema changes over time and accommodates new types of objects. In database systems only minor changes to the schema are tolerated. In DL sweeping changes to the schema are expected; indeed, multiple schemata will need to be simultaneously supported. And some data may not have a schema as we define it in databases. This also naturally leads to the notion of multiple query languages which will need to be supported by the DL system.

3.3 Digital Libraries As Networked Information Systems

The second main information systems technology is the networked information systems such as WWW/Mosaic on the Internet [74, 38, 68]. Documents containing multimedia data are provided to distributed users through a network of interconnected servers. Tools are used to organize, search, filter, navigate ("surf") the information servers around the network. All kinds of new information is rapidly being digitized and made available to the denizens of the network. Indeed, not a day goes by when some new information source comes online and its information is surfed voraciously by the user community. This area is seeing explosive growth both in servers and users. The numbers of users on the Internet is growing by 150,000 users each month, and the number of hosts is growing exponentially, currently about 3 million hosts. This model is necessarily based on "anarchy" because the Internet is based on "anarchy" in the sense that administration, documentation, security and other such features that the "database approach" takes seriously up front, take a back seat to coming online and providing the content.

The anarchist nature of the Internet poses serious problems for the avid DL provider/user. The traditional information content is possible because of a balance between the rights of three groups of people: the authors, the publishers and the readers. This balance has been reached over several decades and is embodied in complex legal decisions. The roles of the authors, publishers and readers and their rights in the world of Internet are entirely unclear and will need to be sorted out very quickly before anything can be accomplished.

Apart from the political and legal issues in this area, several technical challenges remain to be solved. Significant effort is being devoted to improving the transmission capacity of twisted pair networks to the point that existing twisted pair telephone network can deliver VCR quality video information today. Fiber optic networks will basically make bandwidth irrelevant in the equations of applications. The fact that the Internet is slow is not due to the limitations of networking to the current implementation of the Internet.

An important class of problems to be solved in this area (if it has to serve as a foundation for a DL system) is the area of finding information. Currently, networked information systems such as WWW provide limited directory services. In the case of WWW this could be the directory of home pages of various servers. But there is no categorization or classification of this information based on the needs of users. If a user is interested in finding opportunities as a mechanical engineer where should that person start looking? Allowing more powerful navigational facilities that allow users to "surf" servers seamlessly only goes a part of the way to solving the problem. The more general question is, How do people find relevant information in a networked environment of service providers?

Another important class of problems is the area of security and privacy of information. Not all the content available on a network should be made available to all the users. Even traditional libraries and video rental stores have subsections with specialized access. How do networked information systems authenticate users and assign user rights? Issues in intellectual property need to be resolved. Outdated information archiving needs to be examined.

3.4   New use of Content

We think that both database and network information systems technologies provide some technical solutions to the task of constructing DL systems. However, the motivation for universal use of DL systems can not stem from these technologies. DL will be completely different from WWW-style Wide Area Information Services and from Database Systems. Every new technology spawns its own services. DL will coexist with these other information technologies. For example, TV programming is completely different from radio programming even if we add video to it. TV is not radio with pictures. Desktop publishing is not publishing made cheaper. Desktop publishing is distinct from the traditional publishing business, from content preparation, to copy editing, to printing. In this sense DL will not be libraries with digitized traditional content. Databases will serve their clients, as will networked information systems. DL will foster a new set of services that will not be offered or competitively offered by other technologies.

What new services will be offered by DL and who will use these services? We claim that the traditional use of information is quite satisfactorily handled by traditional systems for that information, see Figure 3.1. For example, in the case of books, publishers will continue to publish books on paper for people who want to read books, etc. We do not know anybody who reads books on computer monitors. Where is the action? The action is in providing new usage for old and new content. We claim that "Old use and content" makes no business sense because it is already satisfactory for the general public, and "New content and old use" is fundamentally opposed to the idea of DL. We have argued that the economic incentive is to work in new use of old and new content. In fact, one can argue that what makes DL interesting will be the new ways in which content can be used, and this will not only drive DL but will be the distinguishing feature of DL from distributed databases and networked information systems. This is not to say that DL will not use distributed database technology and networked information system technology. It certainly will. But it will not be either one of these applications. DL must provide new ways of using content. This is why the most important thing is to digitize content. But the reason why digitizing content can be economically justified will be the new uses that one can allow on content.

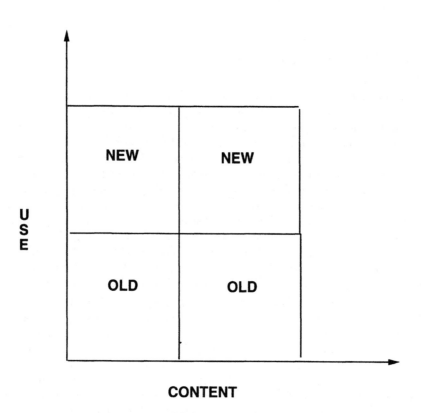

Figure 3.1 Matrix of use versus content

3.5   New Uses

We postulate three main areas which can provide new uses for the content of DL.

3.5.1   Multimodal Presentations

The basic idea behind multimodal presentations is that the user determines how the content is to be presented to him/her and not the DL object. For example, if a user is interested in a newspaper, the user determines whether he/she reads the newspaper by printing it on paper, reads it by viewing it on a display device, or hears it when it is read by a speech synthesizing program. The content of an information object should be amenable to multimodal presentations, i.e., the content should be described in ways that correspond to the various presentation platforms.

The current situation is that library objects come with a fixed presentation. Books for instance can only be read. Video can only be viewed on display devices, etc. At the moment there is no way to listen to the contents of a video clip or to listen to a book while one is otherwise occupied. Transcoding a multimedia object so that it can be presented in multimodal dimensions will be a powerful new way to use content in DL.

The presentation issues also have a bearing on user interfaces. When an object is transported to a user's environment, it forces the user's interface to change. For example, if we receive a "latex" document, we can only apply certain methods to it. Our interface has changed because the object does not support certain methods in our interface. What is needed is that the object should change and not change our interface. The "latex document" should be able to support our local methods and not vice versa. For example, displaying the document should be a generic and local method that applies to all objects that come into our environment. Of course it will mean different things for different objects but the objects come with the intelligence (read: interface definitions) to understand the action/method "display" in our environment so that the correct things happen. The basic issue is that our interface remains essentially the same, the imported objects assume intelligent interpretations of our interface. The imported object should adapt itself to our environment. DL objects should adapt to our environment rather than the alter our interfaces.

3.5.2   Adaptive/Opinion indexing

People retrieve information based on different criteria. In particular, people often select objects based on what others say or write about the objects. For example, people select movies and books based on reviews. DL should provide not only the information objects (e.g., books) but also the opinions, reviews and product information associated with that object. Thus, a DL object can be thought of the basic content plus the reviews, commentary and other information related to that object.

Users may now use the information associated with an object in many ways. In one case, a user may retrieve an object and then inquire about the reviews and comments associated with that object. In another instance, a user may retrieve objects based on the review criteria, e.g., display movie that received "two thumbs up" from Siskel and Ebert. In other words, the reviews become the retrieval criteria (there are obvious legal and fairness of advertising issues here that will need to be resolved).

The idea of using information associated with an object as a retrieval criteria is interesting from a query language point of view. With multimedia objects there is no single retrieval criteria. For example, take an image. How many ways are there for selecting the image? Based on features in the image, what one feels when sees the image, what one saw last week, experts see things that novices do not in the image, etc. What is needed is to adaptively update indexes associated with multimedia objects in such a way that these indexes are available for querying to the user community.

3.5.3   Generating New Content

A powerful and exciting new use of DL objects is in generating new objects by composing other objects in a DL. For example, combining image and audio objects to generate a new video clip, generating a new image by combining two or more images, etc. We can use the idea of multiple indexes as identifying subobjects. These indexes could be integrated as a part of the content for a number of reasons.

- Indexes can be associated with subobjects of an object. This will allow us to compose new objects from parts of other objects. For example, we can take an image, associate different indexes with some of the subobjects of the image, and then compose a new object from the constituents, for example, a more aesthetically pleasing image of a scene.

- We can retrieve objects based on subobjects, e.g., retrieve picture containing a mountain. Thus allowing querying by content.

Note that if an object is transmitted to the user's environment, the various indexes will also have to be transmitted to the user's environment along with the object. Otherwise, how is the user going to manipulate the object and its subobjects? For example, we retrieve an object from a DL and then we want to examine its subobjects and compose them with some other object. But to examine the subobjects we need the indexes. So, conceptually the indexes must be a part of the object itself.

Part II

Administration/Management

Chapter 4

Which Way to the Future? The Control of Scholarly Publication

Michael Lesk*

4.1 Introduction

Many groups are manoeuvring for a place in a new system of technical and scholarly publishing. At the same time that libraries are unable to keep up their buying power, electronics is holding out the hope of an alternative. But it is not at all clear what the mechanism of the future for scholars will be. As Sir Peter Swinnerton-Dyer said, speaking in reference to UK higher education, there is not enough money for university libraries to keep up with journal price inflation; the publishers can either help design a cheaper and more efficient system, or the universities will be forced to do something cheaper and worse.

Almost every group associated with universities is trying to stake a claim in the new area of electronic communication. At meetings ranging from those of university phone administrators to librarians to college bookstores to publishers to wholesalers to academic departments, people explain why their group should be the one to deliver information to students and faculty.

There is one summarizing distinction: those who wish to charge and those who don't. The people who wish to distribute information for free are typically from academic departments or libraries, and constantly ask why universities should pay publishers to sell them back the same information they generate. Those who wish to charge are the publishers, whether commercial publishers, professional societies, or university presses. They point to the still-growing paper publication industry, the reluctance of authors to abandon paper for their really important papers, and the importance of quality and copyright.

The 'information should be free' group views the world of the future in terms of bulletin boards, Mosaic, or gopher. Information is normally in ASCII, free text search is the dominant retrieval paradigm, and the goal is to add regularity of appearance, archiving, and refereeing to a system which is already electronic and searchable. In general, this material is newly created and is being donated by the authors. Older material (generally out of copyright) is rekeyed, and the keying work donated.

*Bellcore, Morristown, NJ07960

The publisher community wishes to build on existing material. They often produce CD-ROMs containing images of the existing pages, searching is by titles, abstracts and index terms, and the goal is to add electronic speed and searching to an already professional and high-quality system. Most of the material distributed is new, in copyright, and charged for. Older material when republished is often scanned, although publishers concentrate on newer material since it is more valuable.

Many examples, of course, exist of both charged and free distribution of both images and text. For example, charged-for distribution of images include the the ADONIS project, which [234] distributes images of medical journals; the CD-ROMs of IEEE journals published by University Microfilms; Elsevier's TULIP project [173] in which about a dozen universities are receiving images of materials science journals, and the Red Sage project in which AT&T and Springer-Verlag are offering images of biomedical publications at UCSF. [127] Both Elsevier and AT&T use optical character recognition to produce data for full text searching; the other systems rely on commercial abstracting and indexing data. Of these four projects, the first two are commercial today, and AT&T is offering to sell an image system for biomedical journals (RightPages) in early 1995. The AT&T system is based on an online network, not upon CD-ROM. [235]

Publishers also are selling systems based on ASCII text. Again in CD-ROM format, these include such offerings as the *Oxford English Dictionary* and the Chadwyck-Healey database of English poetry. In addition, large-scale commercial online systems such as Lexis and Dialog have existed for about twenty years. None of these include illustrations. However, systems that include both ASCII text and pictures are appearing commercially. For example, OCLC is publishing online journals such as *Current Clinical Trials* (with AAAS) and *Electronic Letters* (with IEE). The *Chicago Journal of Theoretical Computer Science* is to be published electronically by MIT Press, and there are also smaller ventures such as *Matrix News*, a demonstration of the success of the net at supporting a very small scale publication.

Non-commercial projects are extremely numerous and hopeless to even list. There are text collections including Project Gutenberg, the Online Book Initiative, and the Oxford Text Archive. There are bulletin boards; in addition to the thousands of almost unrefereed discussion groups, there are now over a hundred attempts at traditional serials in an online format. For example, the online journals *Postmodern Culture* and *Psycoloquy* are issued by permanent organizations and refereed. Gopher and Mosaic [246] include a great deal of additional text, and also some image databases. The Library of Congress is scanning its current exhibits, the University of California has pictures from their paleontology museum, and the Census Bureau has mounted the Tiger map file of the United States.

There are even a few offerings, to finish the list, that are produced free or for nominal cost on CD-ROM. For example, the Data Collection Initiative of the Association for Computational Linguistics distributes a large collection of text intended for lexicographic and linguistic studies on CD-ROM, and the *Thesaurus*

Linguae Graecae corpus of ancient Greek text is available in this form.

Still other large projects are really data publishing, not either text or image. Such items include the enormous NASA collections of observations of the earth and the sky; the database of social science information at ICPSR (Inter-University Consortium for Political and Social Research) in Ann Arbor; and software archives such as Netlib.

With all these examples of successful electronic systems, why have they not taken over? The most important reasons are not technical, but economic and social. We do not know how to price electronic information in a way that will not provide strong incentives to cheat and yet bring in enough revenue to justify providing it. Nor are authors yet sure that electronic publication will provide the prestige and rewards (e.g. tenure) that have traditionally accompanied paper publication.

4.2   Technical issues

The major technical conflict is between the distribution of images and the distribution of ASCII text. Page image systems provide a format which is familiar to the users. They are more easily programmed, make fewer demands on the upstream document preparation system, and are harder to steal from. ASCII-based systems can provide more capabilities (including cut-and-paste, full text search, highlighting, and so on), require less network bandwidth and display capability, and can adapt the format to improve readability.

Although the idea of showing users exactly what they are accustomed to seeing makes sense, this is one of the flimsiest advantages of image systems. The ability to provide something other than what was seen on paper is a major advantage of ASCII-based systems. This is only partly the ability to make better use of the screen space and provide a more readable image. It also permits the document to contain formats which would be expensive or impossible on paper: color pictures, sound excerpts, animations, or interactions with running programs. The document can also adapt to the user's particular requests; highlighting search terms is the most familiar such adaptation, and quite popular with users. So the advantage of familiarity will wear off rather quickly.

A more serious problem with ASCII systems is lack of standardization of text formats. Although most groups that have considered the situation have plunked for SGML, that alone is not enough. First, SGML is merely a syntax, and users must agree on the specific tags and their meanings. Two standards are well-known: the Electronic Manuscript Standard (EMS) of AAP and the Text Encoding Initiative, but neither is actually used enough to remove the need to face large numbers of conversions. Instead, most documents appear in one or another word processing format, often based on a WYSIWYG model, so that the only format information available relates to the appearance of the document, and not its content. For example, something might be in italics because it is a foreign word, the title of a referenced journal or book, or for emphasis. For purposes of searching or reformatting, it is valuable to know which reason applies, and a purely WYSIWYG system does not tell you this. Unfortunately, this argument has been going on for years [140] and the lower cost of neglecting to specify *why* something is in italics usually wins out. I have heard publishers say that preparing documents in SGML rather than a conventional word processing system doubles the cost, and certainly companies in the business of converting documents to SGML often charge several dollars per page. SGML is likely to win in the long run, since many of the largest publishers have endorsed it, but for the moment building ASCII systems often involves tedious conversion efforts.

This is true on the output side as well as for input. Even if one says that all users must have workstations running X-windows, there is no standardization on exactly which fonts in which sizes are available. Installing our chemical journal system has required some degree of tinkering with each new workstation and operating system we have encountered at Cornell. Sometimes this merely means installing a few new fonts; in other cases, it has required fussing with the security configuration. Few X-windows users understand how the security works, so that all sorts of strange setups are found and rarely can the users fix problems themselves.

Image systems have more serious problems, including in particular their demands for network bandwidth and screen resolution. This is why most image systems are local CD-ROM-based operations and why they often come as a packaged system, ensuring that the users have adequate screens. To deal with screen size first, note that a typical PC screen of 640x480 can not display an entire 8-inch page width unless the resolution is 75 dpi. Now this may be quite readable, especially if antialiasing is used rather than one-bit-per-pixel images; and many people can tolerate not being able to see the top and bottom of the page at once. But many people will not like it; facsimile machines have a resolution of 200 dpi and many think that this is not good enough. Yet 200 dots per inch means 1600 pixels across an 8-inch page. I once heard a representative of National Geographic voice dissatisfaction with the format of Kodak Professional PhotoCD, which is 4096x6144 resolution. For most users, I think that 150 dpi would be ample, which requires a screen size of about 1200x1600 for a full page. Few workstations have that large a screen.

Furthermore, an uncompressed image at 150dpi with 8 bits of grey level per pixel would be over 3 Mbytes. Usually such an image would be compressed, and a typical size for the compressed image might be 30K-50K, but again the user terminal may be a problem. If the user's machine can not quickly decompress the image, the system may decide to do the decompression in the server (which may, for example, have a special hardware board, or at least a faster CPU). That will mean that the full 3 Mbytes have to be sent across the communications link to the user. If we assume that the user will desire a page flip time of one second, even a 10 Mbit/sec Ethernet can't provide that. In practice, assuming some contention on the LAN, the display time for a page in those circumstances will exceed 3 seconds, by which time most people will get annoyed. Again, having the images on the same machine is possible, but only in controlled circumstances. CDDI or FDDI is of course another solution, as well as moving the decompression to the user workstation, but in either case this is a substantial amount of work. The ASCII text of the same page is not likely to be as much as one-tenth the size of the image. It may range over 5 Kbytes for a quite dense page, but such a page in image format is likely to be more than 100 Kbytes even with Group IV compression.

Perhaps the strongest argument for image systems for new material is the extra security they offer. As mentioned before, fear of illegal copying is a major problem for the electronic publishing industry. If all the user can steal at one time is a picture of a half page, this is more of a nuisance than if an entire document can be downloaded quickly. In addition, it is easier to add cryptographic tricks to images than to text, which has less redundancy to spare. This will be discussed in a later section of the paper.

Image systems have a particularly important role in the retrospective conversion of older printed material, whether to deal with the problem of deteriorating paper as in the Cornell CLASS project, or to make widely available something which does not exist in many copies (as with the digitizations of the manuscripts of Beowulf and the Canterbury Tales). To rekey a 300 page book might cost about $800, while scanning it costs about $50. Scanning is so cheap, in fact, that the buildings for the new national libraries in both the United Kingdom and France cost more than it would have cost to scan all the books they hold. †

4.3   Our experiments

Over the last few years, Bellcore has been involved in a project to compare image and ASCII systems, the CORE project. CORE is a collaboration of the American Chemical Society, Chemical Abstracts Service, Cornell University, Bellcore and OCLC. This project uses twenty primary journals published by the American Chemical Society, which are available both in text format from their databases (available commercially via the STN service), and in image format from scanning done by the project. The scanning of current issues is done from paper and for older issues from microfilm. Indexing is also available from Chemical Abstracts; fortunately for present-day users, ACS and CAS have been involved in computer typesetting from the beginning and have worked continuously to keep records available.

Figure 1 shows the data flow in the CORE project. Two major streams of data preparation are shown, the image data on the left and the ASCII data on the right. Two full files result, and the user can then search the text and retrieve either the images or the text for any article.

There are two tricky issues in the preparation of our file. First, we convert the ACS text format into SGML. We had to extend the EMS standard, which did not cater to some of the more specialized aspects of chemical journals (e.g. structured index terms, four kinds of in-line graphics, or 3000 different character codes). For inter-article links, we have also made an effort to identify citations

---

†But note that the $50 cost is only achieved by unbinding the book, which mightn ot be considered acceptable in this context.

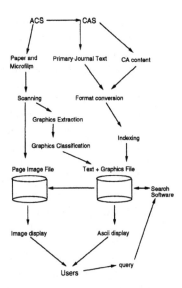

Figure 4.1 Data flow in the CORE project

which refers to another article which is in our database. These problems are actually much simpler than would usually occur in document conversion, since the ACS primary journal database is unusually thoroughly marked for content, and all twenty journals are in almost the same format (there are minor differences in areas such as reference style).

Equations and tables are the most complex data that we convert. The difficulty with semi-graphical items such as these is that our users have a wide variety of workstations, and we need each display program to operate successfully on all of them. Thus it is hard to know how much typographic facility will be available to display equations; for example, each workstation type has a different set of fonts. The solution for equations has been to convert them to bitmaps; they are reformatted for *eqn* and then turned into Postscript and then into conventional bitmaps. This means, unfortunately, that the user can not search for particular words in equations, but equations don't contain many useful search terms anyway. For tables this would not be tolerable, and so tables are retained in ASCII. To avoid the formatting problems, they are arranged for display in fixed-width characters.

Searching the text file is performed by the OCLC Newton search engine for most of our interfaces and by Bellcore software in one case. The Newton search engine is fast and supports the familiar kinds of Boolean searching. Since our text is in SGML, we can provide fielded searching as well as free-text searching. We do not, however, provide searching for numerical data or ranges of numbers (aside from some special processing for the year of publication).

The trickiest issue in the creation of the file is the identification of the graphical items. These are not in the text database and must be obtained from the scanned pages, by page segmentation. Various heuristics for segmentation have been described earlier. [158] [159] This is a very tricky problem, unfortunately. Not only do the figures have to be extracted, but they must be sorted into "Figures" and "Schemes" since the typesetting tapes distinguish these and they may be permuted relative to one another in the page makeup process. Worse yet, very high accuracy is needed. Originally it seemed reasonable that identifying a few non-existent figures would not be serious; it would simply mean that a few pieces of text were available both in ASCII and image format. However, because the count of figures is essential for linking up to the references in the text, misidentified figures can throw off the entire figure numbering in the remainder of the article, and thus confuse the readers very substantially.

Various other problems may affect the actual database. Since the three parts of the database (the scanned images, the ASCII for the articles, and the ASCII for the indexing) are coming from three different sources, they can arrive in any order. As a result, although nearly all the material is available in both formats, for occasional articles one or another format may be missing, and the software attempts to keep the users unaware of this (e.g. by suppressing from search results articles which can not be displayed).

The creation of the database is fairly tedious. Running to over 200,000 pages at time of writing, it can take weeks to make the full index for the material. The need to move everything from Morristown to Columbus to Ithaca does not help, either. Most serious is simply the very large size of the full database: a couple of gigabytes of text and 30 GB of text. This means that we are constantly shifting files around to unify empty space, and, for example, causes users Exabyte cartridges and Express Mail rather than the Internet to move material from place to place.

Once the database is ready, three interfaces have been written for the users to get at them. One is an image interface and two are ASCII based. Two were written at Bellcore; one ASCII interface is from OCLC. The availability of this database and the various interfaces have permitted us to experiment with comparisons between the two forms of display.

The first interface is the image interface, called Pixlook. It operates in two modes, searching and browsing. In the browsing mode, shown in Figure 2, the user clicks through menus for the list of journals, volumes (years), and issues, to get a table of contents for one issue. This is taken from the ASCII file, rather than being an image of the actual journal title page. The user can then click on a title to bring up the first page of that article. Additional clicks on other titles will bring up more articles. In fact, the user may have additional tables of contents or journal menus open as well, but screen space will be exhausted quickly. Each page is originally presented in 100 dpi size, so that it will fit on a workstation screen. Anti-aliasing is used if the user has a color or grey-level display screen.

Calculating the anti-aliasing is very simple. As the original 300 dpi one-bit-per-pixel image is condensed to one-third its width and height, 9 pixels become

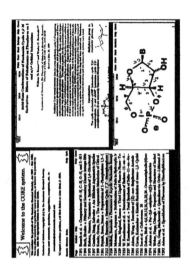

Figure 4.2 Pixlook - the browsing mode

one. We use 2 bits of grey information per pixel to gain legibility while not using much more space. To assign these grey levels (from 0 to 3), the number of dark bits are counted, and mapped as follows: no dark bits is grey level 0, 1 dark bit is grey level 1, 2 or 3 dark bits are grey level 2, and 4-9 dark bits are grey level 3. Experiment shows that it is more important to retain the differences between the light areas than the differences inside the darker areas, hence this mapping.

As can be seen in the top corner of the page display, a scrollbar indicates the number of pages in the article and lets the user move around it. Among the buttons are two that move forward and backward through the list of titles displayed, and a button to enlarge the image to the full 300 dpi scan. A portion of this page enlarged is shown in the screen dump. At one time 200 dpi was used as the larger resolution, but this was felt inadequate for reading the details within figures, for example.

Searching in Pixlook is shown in Figure 3. The user types a search string in the lookup window; this can be either a simple name or word, or a Boolean search with field restrictions. For example, "Corey/au" would request a search for articles with Corey as author; while "Corey/au & ginkgolide/ti" would search for articles written by Corey with the word *ginkgolide* in the title. The result of the search is a window showing the matching articles, and the user can click on any line to bring up the first page of that article. If there are a great many matching articles, the system informs the user how many, and estimates the time that will be required to fetch all of the titles. The user has a choice of looking at only the first fifty articles. The page display that is produced by selecting any article operates as before.

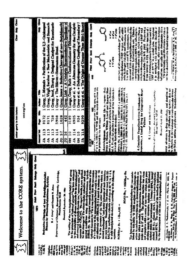

Figure 4.3 Pixlook - the searching mode

As with any image system, Pixlook presents the pages in the format to which the user is accustomed. It is unable to highlight matching search terms, since the search system is unrelated to the display system. We have considered estimating how far through the article the matching terms are, and then counting through the column inches of the display to approximately highlight them. Normally this would be accurate to within a few lines, but mistakes in page segmentation would introduce some errors, and we have felt it better to avoid an unreliable service.

Two other interfaces exist. Both are ASCII based. One is a research version of the SuperBook product Bellcore has developed, and the other is Scepter, by OCLC. In both cases, the article is completely resynthesized for presentation, based on the text and the extracted graphics. Scepter, in addition, will display the page images if the user wishes. An important difference between the systems is that Scepter treats each article as an independent item, while SuperBook acts as if the articles had been concatenated into a single long stream.

An example of SuperBook [71] is shown in Figure 4. On the left is the table of contents window, giving an overview of the entire file. In this case, the table of contents follows the subject categorization of Chemical Abstracts, which divides chemistry into five main areas, then 80 sections, and then about 240 subsections. The display can be expanded to show the complete hierarchy in any area: this goes from area to section to subsection to article title to portions of an article. To the right is the text window, which shows the current bit of text that fits on the screen. By clicking in the table of contents window, the text window will jump to that place in the collection. There are also controls in the text window to move to the previous or next page. In the right margin of the text window are icons indicating the presence of footnotes, tables, or graphics. At the top of the text window is the set of headings leading down to this location, thus orienting the user in the collection.

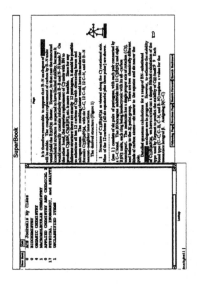

Figure 4.4 An example of SuperBook

Below the table of contents window is the lookup window, in which the user can type words to be sought; in this example, the word "buckyball" is the query. SuperBook uses its own search system, rather than a Boolean system. The basic search is for words appearing together within the same paragraph. There is no way to search for adjacent words or a direct specification for fielded searches. The reason for refusing adjacency searches is that the typical user may not understand that a search for the adjacent words "character recognition" (for example), will not find the phrase "character or word recognition" or many other slight reorderings that are likely to be considered relevant. Fielded searches can be done by hunting for special terms (arti) and (auth) that are added to the title and author paragraphs respectively. We are not sure that more elaborate procedures would actually be more effective in our context (although some users who are familiar with other searching systems have asked for them). In addition to typing words in the lookup window, a search can also be done by clicking on a word in the text window; this does a search on that word. The search system interacts with the table of contents window by indicating to the left of each section title how many hits are in that part of the document. Thus, after doing a search the user sees how the matches are distributed in the document, providing more information than just a count of hits.

Supplementary material, including footnotes, tables, equations and figures, are indicated by icons in the right margin. Clicking on these items brings up an example; in Figure 5, for example, an enlarged figure is shown. For chemistry journals, this may be a suitable way to present footnotes, but it suffers as a way to handle graphics, since they are easily ignored. Graphics are so important to the use of the journals that they need a more prominent position. What has been done since our experiments with CORE has been to use thumbnails rather than merely icons to indicate the presence of graphics, and to provide an option to insert these thumbnails in the middle of the text, not just out in the margin.

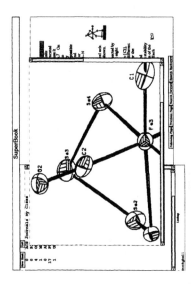

Figure 4.5 An example

The OCLC interface, Scepter, is shown in Figure 6. Scepter is also an ASCII-based interface and is more tailored to the specific chemistry journals in use here. It presents a specific menu for searching, for example, in which the user can check off which journals and years to search, as well as entering search terms, Boolean operators, and field restrictions. The result of searches is again a title-author list, and the user clicks on it to bring up new journals. A key feature of Scepter is that each article comes with its own list of contents, telling the user what parts of the article exist, and giving the user a choice of what to look at first. The list of figures is given as a set of thumbnails showing the user at a glance what kind of figures exist. Clicking on any of them, of course, brings up an enlarged version of the figure.

Dennis Egan of Bellcore took advantage of the CORE project to run a measured comparison of ASCII and image display systems. The results of this experiment have been presented elsewhere [71] and will only be briefly summarized here. In these experiments 36 students were given about six hours of tasks to do, covering five different categories of library research. One third of the students

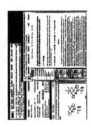

Figure 4.6 The OCLC interface, Scepter

used journals on paper; one third used the SuperBook ASCII interface; and one third used the Pixlook image interface. The tasks involved some requests for specific facts, and some for essays or complex synthetic pathways; also, in some of the tasks, the experimental subjects knew which articles to read and in others they had to find the relevant material.

Some quick results:

1. Any task involving searching was done much better with either electronic system than with paper Chemical Abstracts; our subjects were simply not well trained in the use of Chemical Abstracts.

2. Tasks involving just reading took about the same time, and were done about equally well in any mode. This is true even though people complained that the 200 dpi images used in this experiment was not adequate.

3. People using computer searching retrieve more material than those using paper they are more likely to make precision errors (finding more relevant material than is there) rather than recall errors (finding less relevant material that is really there).

4. In overall performance there was no clear winner between SuperBook and Pixlook; on tasks not involving searching, all the results are comparable.

5. There is no time-quality tradeoff; where there are substantial differences in the time taken to do a task, the people working more rapidly are working at least as accurately.

The user community also gets to experiment with the software in an uncontrolled mode. We have observed, for example, that when choosing what parts of an article to look at, the users look first at the figures, then at the author names, and then at the title, abstract, references, and so on; only as a last resort do they read the text.

4.4   Economic issues

Perhaps the most difficult problem holding back digital libraries is the inability to decide how to price information. The traditional Adam Smith economist believes that price should equal incremental cost, based on the models of supply and demand curves in which to increase the quantity of a product supplied you must increase the price. This may well reflect the situation in 18th century Cornish tin mines, which could only increase production by exploiting additional ore deposits that were less rich or more often flooded, and required more work per pound of tin extracted. This model has nothing whatever to do with the information business, in which the incremental cost of another copy of some piece of information is very small compared with the cost of getting the first copy. For electronic copying, the incremental cost of making another copy is almost zero.

This poses problems even for serials on paper, of course. A typical scientific society publication might incur three-quarters of its costs getting ready to print the first copy of a journal (editorial costs, composition, make-ready and so on) and only a quarter of its costs in reproduction (printing, paper, binding and mailing). Thus, the publishers are always threatened with a downward spiral; if a few libraries start to cancel their subscriptions, the rates must increase for the remainder, which encourages them to cancel. And libraries regularly consider whether their use of a journal justifies retaining a subscription, or whether they should rely on interlibrary loan. With electronic information, the delay getting something from a remote source may be insignificant and the cost minimal, thus encouraging people to try to share access if possible, destroying the financial base of the information creator.

In particular, every publisher is well aware of the destruction of the software games industry ten years ago by pirate copying, and of the amount of pirate software that exists today. The Business Software Alliance claims that software piracy amounts to $12B per year, and that the piracy rate ranges from 35% in the United States through 86% in Italy to 99% in Thailand. In Eastern Europe the situation is particularly complex. In Czechoslovakia, for example, major U.S. software vendors proposed to sell very cheap copies of their software, in order to compete with the pirates. They promptly ran into opposition from the nascent Czech software industry, arguing that it is hard enough to compete with Microsoft or Lotus when they charge U.S. level prices in hard currency, and objecting to any lower prices as dumping. At least, the rise of such a local software industry does also produce a demand to enforce anti-piracy laws.

Among the possible responses to the piracy issue can be technical tricks to try to dissuade the pirates or pricing mechanisms to make piracy less important. In the software market, for example, copy-protection was widely tried in the early 1980s as a technical fix, but failed. A pricing fix has been per-user site licensing, providing a costing system that both sides perceive as fair and that can be reasonably administered, which is also important: too much hassle translates into higher costs. Much of the trouble with intellectual property protection is in fact the lack of mechanisms for people to obtain certain kinds of use rights without excessive administrative costs.

One technical attempt which is being made to avoid information piracy is to see if it is possible to code electronic publications so that if someone starts selling illegal copies, it will be possible to identify from which legitimate purchaser's copy the pirate copies are coming. For example, the method proposed under the name "video stenography" [170] involves adding bits to ordinary pictures in a way that is not obvious to the viewer, and that does not degrade the image quality, but will permit the recovery of the hidden message from a copy. Unfortunately it looks to me as if low-pass filtering would defeat many such techniques. Bell Laboratories has invented a technique for coding messages into [27] image of pages that is more robust. It involves manipulation of spacing within the page. This technique certainly meets the condition that the average user is not going to be able to defeat it for less than the cost of buying a legal copy of the information, if the user has to write the defeating program himself. The question is whether, as with software copy-protection, the program that defeats the coding becomes widely available. One advantage of the Bell Laboratories algorithm is that the code to defeat it wouldn't appear to have any other use; whereas the video-stenogrphy algorithm is defeated by low-pass spatial filtering, a technique useful for smoothing pictures and likely to be widely available in many programs.

A simpler technical trick is the one used by the large databases today: don't let people download the entire database, but give them in exchange for their money access to a little bit of the data at a time. Even if the users make illegal copies of the information they have, they will not easily find somebody else who wants that exact piece of information.

In this context, image systems are more robust than ASCII systems. Stealing data from an image system will need more time and space than stealing from an ASCII system; there is more opportunity to hide codes in the data; and the technical difficulty of re-using the information is increased. For example, if the user is stealing by taking screen dumps, only being able to get a fraction of a page at a time in high resolution will discourage the simpler attempts at stealing document files.

A more useful answer than a cryptographic trick would be a method of pricing that made illegal copying irrelevant. For example, if the fixed costs of scientific journals were funded by page charges on the author, then copying would be irrelevant, as publishers would have already been paid. Although some journals, typically those published by professional societies, charge page charges now, these rarely cover anything like the full first cost, and they are often optional and the authors sometimes do not pay. If page charges became larger and more common, the subscription prices of journals could decrease, and the incentive to copy rather than subscribe would also decrease.

Page charges could be administered by charging institutions, rather than authors. In this model, only an incremental cost would be charged to deliver a copy of a journal to a library, but a hefty fee would be charged to any university or corporation to qualify authors from that institution. Universities might react, of course, by pressuring faculty to restrict their publications to a relatively small number of journals, and some of the more specialized or smaller journals might go out of business.

The software industry often uses site licenses as a way of avoiding the need to monitor copying within an institution. These are perceived as more fair by the users than the normal software license, which, for example, may forbid two users on different workstations from sharing a program even if both users runs it less than once a month. Site licenses are normally charged by simultaneous user, rather than by the total number of people at a site. Information has often been sold by site license; this is the normal contract written when tapes of an A&I service are delivered to a corporation, for example, since no one thinks that a corporate library would buy Inspec or Psychinfo tapes merely for use by the library staff member who signed the purchase order. Site licenses do, however, require coordination of the computing facilities which are sharing the license, and this may be difficult in a world of laptop PCs or in some university environments. Furthermore, a university may wish to bill back the use of information services to users, and exactly the same pricing issues will then arise in that billing operation. Finally, it is sometimes hard to limit the use to the university environment; aside from visiting faculty in both directions, outreach operations, cooperating institutions, and other blurring of the campus boundary, the elimination of the need to stop student copying within the university of one particular resource may also eliminate the need to learn that other kinds of copying are still illegal.

Finally, as mentioned before, complex presentation styles make downloading more complex and harder to deal with. Image systems offer less scope for downloading, and complex multi-window displays may be even worse. These restrictions conflict, of course, with the desire to allow the users as many facilities as possible, including the ability to download and otherwise re-use the information they are buying.

This whole issue is often resented by many people at universities. Many university libraries do not charge for their services, as a matter of principle, and do not like being pushed into a world in which they must keep records and bill people. Universities also often have problems with the variety of procedures wanted by the information vendors. For example, a seller of legal information may offer a special discount to a law school, but wish to offer the discount rate only to law students. This may conflict with a university's wish to treat all students equally what are they to do if they allow a student of government to take a law course, but that student can not use the library resources available to the law students?

There are also non-financial issues involved in electronic information distribution. The more freedom the user has to arrange the screen display or choose how the information is presented, the less control the author has over the presentation. Some authors resent this loss of control. Hypertext-like interfaces which allow readers to jump from one item to another may cause authors to fear that their intent has been ignored, parodied, or defaced. Consider, for example, the fuss about colorizing movies: far more dramatic license can be taken with electronic documents.

It is clear that these organizational and economic questions are posing more of a bottleneck than are technical issues. We know how to build digital libraries and print digital journals; we do not know how to arrange the industry that will produce them.

4.5   Conclusions

The technical face of the future of information can be seen more clearly than the organizational face. Many organizations feel they should be in charge of delivering information to the student desktop: people representing publishers, wholesalers, bookstores, libraries, university computer centers and university telecommunications operators all think they should have a major role. The academic departments themselves think they should have more control, and a project name CUPID has indeed proposed to take back the publishing business. [166] There are two groups which stand out, however: the publishers and the operators of bulletin boards. Both are moving towards the same world; the bulletin board operators need to add quality and permanence, the publishers need to add electronic speed and searching.

The publishers today are more likely to offer image systems, and more likely to offer CD-ROM distribution. They are, of course, more likely to charge. There is a danger that the bulletin board operators can provide additional features, since they are not tied to a presentation that must track a printed journal. Thus, they can add color, sound, and animation more readily. However, the individuality of many moderators, and the lack of institutional backing, gives the publishers an edge. Editorial quality is in the end the most valuable property of a publication. Most people do not lack as much for material to read as for time to read it, and need to be able to trust the worth of what they are getting. ASCII text formats have the advantage in searchability and selectivity, but nothing can compensate for having the right material in the beginning. So the user may indeed like the technical capabilities of an ASCII system, but want them with the organizational strengths of a publisher.

4.6   Acknowledgments

My thanks to the collaborators on the CORE project, specifically Dennis Egan (Bellcore) Richard Entlich (Cornell), Lorrin Garson (ACS), Lorraine Normore

(ACS) Jan Olsen (Cornell), John Udall (Cornell) Stuart Weibel (OCLC), and others including Peter Kirstein of University College London; and to the supporters of the CORE project, including Sun Microsystems, Inc.; Digital Equipment Corporation; Sony Corporation of America; Apple Computer. Part of the CORE research recently has been conducted using the resources of the Cornell Theory Center, which receives major funding from the National Science Foundation (NSF) and New York State. Additional funding for the Theory Center comes from the Advanced Research Projects Agency (ARPA), the National Institutes of Health (NIH), IBM Corporation, and other members of the center's Corporate Research Institute.

Chapter 5

Networked Information Systems As Digital Libraries

Jacob Slonim* and Lisa BaronLaurie†

5.1 Introduction and Motivation

As information is increasingly captured and made available in digital form and as network and communication infrastructures evolve, the traditional library is being transformed into a digital one. Simultaneously, libraries are expanding beyond the physical limitations of space and time: they will have no walls and be available 24 hours a day. The digital library will hold collections of digital information distributed from geographically separate sites and will provide access to multiple forms of information: text, image, movies, video, graphics, audio, etc. No longer time bound, the digital library will integrate information into knowledge, and use multimedia to present subject oriented material. The way users look at information and how they work will change.

Recently, western countries such as the US, Canada, and Japan have begun to take steps to realize an information infrastructure. They believe a global network is essential to economic growth. The digital library will play different roles in the overall global information infrastructure. While continuing to serve their traditional user, libraries must seek new opportunities in such areas as content vending, publishing, business information services, entertainment, environment, and health care. The library, as a repository of information and a provider of services, has an essential role in education in public schools, university, corporate settings, and life-long learning. The emergence of the digital library and its accompanying applications depends on an in-place global information infrastructure. Both the US and Japan have targeted 2010 for a full deployment of their respective national information infrastructures. The educational literature suggests that many educational applications and a working infrastructure will be in widespread use by the year 2000.

Education, its purpose, delivery methods, and consumers are changing. There are new challenges to meet. Libraries and education have always had a strong

---

*Centre for Advanced Studies, IBM Software Solutions Toronto Laboratory

†Centre for Advanced Studies, IBM Schapter was olutions Toronto Laboratory. This chapter was written as a result of a study conducted for the IBM Academy of Technology, November, 1994.

relationship with each other: a US Department of Education study [64] shows that more than 80% of the public consider education as a primary purpose of a library. We believe that this relationship will continue and become even stronger.

There are already indications that this combined evolution has begun. Educational use of the Internet and experimental educational environments are already emerging:

1. The Stars Schools program is reaching 200,000 students in 48 states with advanced placement courses in mathematics, science, and foreign language instruction using fiber optics, computers, and satellites.

2. Teachers, students, workers, mentors, technicians, and subject matter experts are using electronic mail and bulletin boards to communicate.

3. More than 12 million Americans access over 60,000 bulletin boards every day.

4. Gopher services are growing at an annual rate of over 1,000%. [190]

5. World-Wide Web use multiplied 187 times from January 1993, moving from 127th place in all network services, to 11th in December 1993.

6. Users of the World-Wide Web follow the makeup of the Internet fairly well: 49% US Educational (.edu), 20% US Commercial (.com), 9% US Government (.gov), 7% United Kingdom (.uk), and 5% Canada (.ca), and 10% other[‡].

A question that arises regularly is what is the difference between a digital library and networked systems. The consensus of our study was that there was little difference perceived, except for the added quality in the digital library, such as editing, refereeing, and expert validation. Adding value to the content and transforming the data into trusted information and then to knowledge is the key. To be successful, the digital library of the future must become a knowledge base, not just a storage and archival-based library system.

Governments are placing more importance on access to information in the global economy. As an example, the US Council on Competitiveness presented a vision of the information infrastructure:

The information infrastructure of the 21st century will enable all Americans to access information and communicate with each other easily, reliably, securely, and cost effectively in any medium: voice, data, image or video, anytime, anywhere. This capability will enhance the productivity of work and lead to dramatic improvement in social services, education and entertainment [87].

Different digital technologies are converging to support this vision: powerful processors, high-speed communication, mass-storage capabilities, and user interfaces. The technologies must converge with social and economic needs.

[‡]Statistics available from the World-Wide Web at URL: http://www.eit.com/ web/www.guide/ guide.05.html

Furthermore, major investments in capital towards this evolution are being made. Iowa and North Carolina are two examples. The state of Iowa has already spent over $100 million on its state-wide communication information infrastructure intended to link every college and high school in the state. North Carolina is now considering a $350 million proposal to fund educational technology [191]. The US HPCC effort has targeted $1 billion dollars for 1994 and $1.5 billion in 1995 for part of the research and development in the National Information Infrastructure (NII).

These commitments suggest that the information infrastructure required to take advantage of digital libraries is emerging and will continue to develop at a rapid pace. Such an infrastructure is essential for the digital library and for supporting applications that access it. In addition to the public spending, the private sector is making major investments. IBM, AT&T, Sony, Kodak, Apple, Microsoft, Xerox, Oracle, Hewlett-Packard, Sun, and TCI are some of the major players focusing on electronic information delivery services and content. Many of them, particularly IBM, Apple, Microsoft, Kodak and Xerox, are participating in projects in museums and on university campuses such as the University of Michigan at Ann Arbor, the University of California at Berkeley, and the University of Illinois at Urbana-Champaign. Each is perceived to have one or more "best-of-breed" components (for example, the AT&T, RightPage Image).

5.2   Challenges

The technological, human-centric, socio-economic, and standards issues all present challenges. Some of these issues require a multi-disciplinary approach to ensure that those working towards solutions do not work in isolation (especially the architects of the new systems). End users, enterprises, libraries, educators, publishers, and content owners must be involved in solving these problems. The major issues that concern these groups include ease of use, realizing productivity gains from investments in electronic libraries, payments and intellectual property protection, content conversion, systems management, and patron privacy.

5.2.1   Technological Issues

There are many technological challenges in the construction of a digital library. Perhaps it is only because they are more tangible that the technological issues seem easier to solve. Some of the technical issues to be addressed are accessibility, communication and networking, intelligent agent toolsets, and integration and scaling of data.

Accessibility

The success of the digital library in the future will depend heavily on accessibility issues. In our study, we argue that accessibility is more than a technical challenge. Dealing with accessibility from a technical vantage without understanding and addressing the socio-economic and human-centric issues will only lead to failure.

Accessibility depends on having available end-to-end solutions and end-user, easy-to-use, multilingual interfaces. The interfaces should contain different levels of entrance into the system, automatically accommodating varying levels of sophistication of the end-user (naive/expert, regular/occasional). These must be aided by text analysis and information extraction as well as lexicons and thesauri to automatically help users in searches. We need dynamic models of different classification schemes that will handle structured and non-structured material.

It should be possible to browse different material types such as music samples, abstracts, etc. in different ways and in different languages (for example, fast forward for music). Different methods of searching should be available: direct searches; fuzzy searches; search by example ("sounds like Jaws"); shelf browsing, which shows physical neighbors and allows for serendipity; query augmentation with personal profile; and navigation based on item content using automated reference librarian, usage history, and user feedback/reader comments. One of the functions of the "intelligent agents" will be automatic translation between different languages, or, when translation is not possible, languages not selected by the end-user should be invisible.

Hardware, systems, communications, applications, and information content must be interoperable and transparent so that the user is not aware of the source of the information he/she is using. From the user's view point, information is just there. Wireless communication will stretch the accessibility much further. It will be available to everyone everywhere; access to the network will be independent of physical or geographical location.

And finally, we must address copyright management systems. While the policies that govern copyright are a social issue, their enforcement is a technical issue of accessibility.

Copyright management systems should have the ability to exclude users from areas for which they are not authorized, either because users are not paying for the service or because the data is confidential. If users from the same or different countries are given access the system must provide for confidential, automated rights and royalty exchange. Information must be protected from unauthorized, accidental, or intentional misattribution, alteration, or misuse. The system must ensure rapid, seamless, efficient linking of requests to authorizations for information use, and there must be effective billing and accounting mechanisms [105, 70].

Communication and Networking

Networks are the components that will glue together the different digital libraries. Although the designers of the digital library do not have to be aware of the details of the enabling technologies in the area of communications, they must provide their requirements and be prepared to take advantage of the networking resources provided. Those creating any digital library strategy must consider:

1. Hybrid Asynchronous Transfer Mode technologies (ATM) with Cable Television

2. Global Wireless Networks and Communications, which will provide mobility and remote access

3. Integrated Services Digital Networks (ISDN): narrow band technology

4. Asymmetric Digital Subscriber Technologies (ADST)

5. High-bit-rate Digital Subscriber Technologies (HDST)

All of these technologies will be integrated into existing and new topologies such as ring, stars, and buses, etc.

Intelligent Agent Toolsets

We may identify the main functions of a digital library as acquiring new materials; cataloging, including indexing and document analysis; searching the catalog, navigating the full item; and circulating material or document delivery. At present, the automated library consists of circulation, cataloging, online public-access, acquisitions, and interlibrary loan and needs to be integrated into the evolving future digital library systems.

On top of the core functions, we have to add tools to customize the digital library to user needs, or working habits. For example:

1. Storage systems for document, image and records management.

2. Access control for heterogeneous large collections.

3. Systems for data capturing and digitizing.

4. Software for searching, browsing, filtering, and selecting.

5. Clustering analysis for high volume data.

6. Tools to innovatively classify, abstract, and cluster (analysis) high volume data.

7. Tools to manipulate large data collections, including models for storing them, policies for retrieving and manipulating them, and making large amounts of data available for display.

8. Sophisticated tools for textual and multimedia retrieval, including statistical and semantic methods for large data.

9. Methods for content-based search of video and image data.

10. Tools for navigating among distributed heterogeneous collections on the network, using conceptual characterizations of content.

11. Software for foraging, flagging, and delivering information tailored to users' interests.

12. Sophisticated desktop analysis tools [§] [106].

Before the tools have been implemented and deployed, they must have the properties of extensibility, adoptability, extendibility, flexibility, and smooth integration into existing systems.

Integration and Scaling of Data

We must determine how or whether to preserve information and materials for future generations. Should we be preserving the material in its original form and/or in a digital format?

Not everything in a library is concerned with text. The increasingly popular multimedia, including text, image, motion, voice and music, needs special solutions. Digitizing these separate and unstructured components for conversion and storage depends upon costs, benefits, or needs. A number of questions must be addressed regarding the digitizing of analog material. For example, how do we decide what to convert from the past 500 years of printed materials, 150 years of photographs, and 100 years of movies? Do we even want to?

There is the issue of dealing with evolving legacy library databases already stored. Information in a digital library will often originate in various formats and from many vendors. For example, the Library of Congress has the Presidents' Papers on a very early form of microfilm that used nonstandard paging and has no sprockets. How would these be converted/stored? Should they remain where they are in their present format? To ensure that material digitized today will be retrievable in 100 years, there is a need to standardize data types and formats of non-structured data (text, graphics, image, memos, music, and other multimedia). Where standardization is not practical, automatic conversion and mapping between them should be developed.

We need to extend existing data models or research new ones to be able to store and manipulate nonstructured database material. The data model must be able to handle: objects, preview, full text search, index, filtering, meta data, grouping, links, annotation, feature sets, and content class [40].

Integration issues include the names domain and cataloging, where the name domains are standardized or mapped across different systems, and catalogs or directories will be the vehicle of the end user for name resolution. With such a flexible architecture, people should be able to search across different domains. For example, meta-information in the catalog can be used to mediate between a medical database and a chemical database.

Distributed digital library networks will include hundreds of thousands of libraries, each containing terabytes of data. Users are not interested in where the information resides or how their query gets there: users just want it right, fast, seamlessly, and now [107].

[§]Byrd, R., IBM T.J. Watson Research, Personal communication; Lyons, K., IBM Toronto Laboratory, Personal Communication.

5.2.2 Human-Centric Issues

User-interface technology, so restricted by keyboards and mice, needs to be broadened and enhanced to encourage use of digital library applications by a wider, less-technical audience. Interfaces should be simple, and the dialogs must be interesting, challenging, exciting, and fun. Digital library applications for different purposes would have different interfaces including the use of integration, consistency, and metaphor(s), such as spreadsheets. Systems should be human-centric oriented, be intuitive and have a low barrier to entry, be understandable/explainable, and support expert use. They should not be disenfranchising. For example, the use of virtual reality techniques to encourage exploration of remote locales could enhance learning and use. Children should be able to explore a forest instead of reading about one. The dialogs must accommodate a wide range of users, from students in kindergarten, to university researchers, to corporate knowledge workers.

The following anecdote shows how our perceptions of users and their needs can be misleading. An Internet user with a new software program that he could not get to work sent out an E-mail plea for help on an electronic bulletin board. He received the help of an expert. After four or five messages were sent back and forth, and with the problem solved, the two exchanged personal information. The person needing help was a 46-year old university professor, while the expert was a 12-year old 7th grader [108]. We cannot take anything for granted. Users might be casual users, they might be from business, from the home, or they might be executives. However, as we see from this example, the usual predictors of how a person uses a system, such as age or job responsibility, no longer work. The ultimate goal of human-centrics is to make it possible for users to take the components and set up the systems as they want them, according to how they work. Developers cannot do it as they tend to preselect categories and groups that don't necessarily work.

Another area of human factors is more content oriented. Electronic books represent a shift from packaging information in a single form to one that incorporates multimodal information sources and encourages a human-oriented exploration based on need and interest [89].

We need to be concerned with how users will get to the information. A mediator or intelligent agent, whether it be a person or a system or a combination of both, is needed between the vast information network and the user. It must be able to cross platforms and databases. Today a user must be an expert in both the operation of the system and the knowledge area. In future, the user will expect to be an expert only in the knowledge area. Tools and interfaces will have to make the system transparent.

Collaboration with real-life experiments being set up around the world, such as the Blacksburg Village Project ¶, [121] or Intercom Ontario [90], can help researchers and developers gain insight into many of the factors and issues present in developing human-centric solutions to end-user needs.

¶Fox, E., Blacksburg, VA Project, Workshop Comments

5.3   Socio-Economic Issues

The participants in our study believe that the social aspects of digital libraries are much more likely to slow down progress. Regulations, such as copyright, privacy and security, anti-trust laws, carrier liability, competition policies, etc., will affect the progress made in the development of digital libraries. These are areas that government tries to address. Because each country has different regulatory bodies, there are problems with each of these issues with regard to global implementation of a digital library. At present, the traditional library is based on the principal of equal access. Librarians in the western world (normally supported by politicians) have always advocated "equal access," which has been widely interpreted to mean "unlimited and cost-free access", but the access was predominantly limited to the local population. With a global network, will governments be as concerned that non-citizens have free access? A more pragmatic approach is needed.

There is so much information now, that without methods of filtering information, and disseminating it to those who need it, relevant information will be hidden or lost and all that will be left will be bits and bytes. Without a way of charging and generating revenue, companies will limit their investment in research in the field. However, if the library is changed to an online environment, and the provision of information is changed to a value-added service, how can people be stopped from charging? We believe that current models of charging for similar types of value-added services should be investigated before diving into new schemes, which might be unfamiliar and confusing to users. Examples of such services include cable and telephony services. A parallel to the cable industry would be the addition of more channels such as the movie channels, or to the phone industry, with different rates for local and long distance calls, or of added services such as call waiting.

We need a socio-economic model that will address how accessible information will be. Who will pay for the infrastructure; how will usage be charged: on a per request basis or as a service fee or both; and how will it be determined? To make the model work, we must shop around for the best value instead of believing that the public funds can continue to subsidize the libraries to make their use free.

The economics must work. The fax machine was known for years, but it did not become successful until it became a commodity. Likewise, the digital library will not become successful until it is affordable. Questions of affordability and funding remain complex.

Current and potential problems with privacy and security must be solved. Security is more of a technical problem, while privacy needs government regulations to provide protection. For example, some readers do not want their reading tastes known by others, or investors do not want others to know which companies they are researching. In the US, these are already protected by the first amendment and must be enforceable in any system. If the anonymity of users is to be maintained, how does a distributor charge? The most likely medium of payment for electronic services is electronic billing. If the anonymity of the user is maintained, how does the distributor know who to bill? Electronic billing has other problems associated with it. For example, what currency will the user pay in?

The information infrastructure will not be limited to within a single country. Global interconnectivity is required to move data between countries. Interoperability will be affected by different countries' decisions affecting standards and policies. Users would not necessarily be aware of the regulatory details existing in another country. As well, regulations will need to be enforced. Disks, tapes, books, etc. used to go through customs when travelling to another country. Electronic shipping no longer has officers checking content.

Workshop participants from the publishing and music industries believe that copyright holders feel the need to control the management of the environment and access to data, the setting of price, the closing down of certain users, and copying. However, they indicated that the best approach to overcome the threats was to understand the costs of electronic versus traditional services and to work with the existing industry and market structures. They felt the main issues that copyright owners needed to address were still to ensure the material delivered to customers is the genuine article and the "brand" or quality of information. The issue of surety can be extended to other groups and includes certification, approval, giving credit, citation counts and voting/rating. Other issues related to surety include confidentiality, security, signatures and ownership, trusted data, payments and denials, rebuttals, and criticisms.

5.4   Conclusion

Despite the many challenges involved, the study saw the emerging digital library giving value-added service to the customers by providing speedier and more efficient delivery of materials in the most cost-effective manner possible. To achieve these goals, we need better search/find capabilities, 24-hour access, the ability to define end-user needs, both as individuals and as categories, growth of the user base via trade/professional users, and pricing for different markets.

In the study, we identified potential opportunities in the digital library market: hardware, storage, communication and networks, and value-added services. The greatest area of opportunity in the short-term lies in the integration and value-added services. New services will help information providers, such as libraries and publishers, create, maintain and manage the content of digital libraries, which will help them provide better services to their customers.

There are at least three stages in the development of the digital library. Currently, we have automated libraries linked to local networks (university libraries). We are in the midst of building the national and global digital library concepts and infrastructure that will link the existing and future libraries and customers into the network. The third stage will entail the integration of the libraries, museums, customers, and information bases globally. Ideas, components, and systems need to be tested in proof-of-concept experiments and projects such as

Intercom Ontario [91] and the Blacksburg Village Project [122].‖ They provide an opportunity to gain first-hand experience and improve the technology. National libraries, such as the Library of Congress ** and the British Library ††, have massive projects and concerns that need the co-operation and collaboration of other institutions and enterprises.

Many of the participants' concerns during this study were limited to our understanding of text. Yet multimedia is emerging as the most powerful part of the digital library of the future. To take full advantage of the multimedia, we will need to move out from the world of text and focus more on multimedia storage, indexing, retrieval, and high resolution display.

The authors strongly feel that the customers' problems must first be identified (from their viewpoint). Once they are identified, we should engage in a multi-disciplinary approach to solving them. Undoubtedly the technical challenges will be central to the solution, but acceptance of the solutions will depend on our resolving of the human-centric, s ocial, and economic issues.

5.5   Acknowledgements

The IBM Academy Digital Library Workshop was held in Briarcliff Manor, New York on Sept. 12-13, 1994. Forty leaders from the field of digital libraries participated: 17 external guests and 23 IBM researchers. All came from diverse areas and backgrounds. We would like to thank these participants without whom the workshop would not have been a success: Fran Allen, Herbert Becker, Alan Bell, Michel Bezy, Mike Blasgen, Steve Boyer, Roy Byrd, Jim Corgel, Jeffrey Crigler, Bruce Croft, Edward Fox, Henry Gladney, Benjamin Grosof, Luther Haibt, Donna Harman, John Heidbreder, Andy Hill, Richard Hulser, Karen Hunter, Frank Licata, Clifford Lynch, Kelly Lyons, Alan Marwick, Margot Montgomery, Norm Pass, Tony Prior, Marilyn Redmond, Jim Reimer, Heinz Sagl, William Scherlis, Willem Scholten, Hans Schwartz, Dave Sebring, Neil Smith, Heiner Sussner, Mark Thompson, William Walker, Katherine Willis and Kevin Wolf. And thanks to Ann Gawman and Mike Bauer for their technical assistance.

5.6   Trademarks

The following are trademarks and/or codemarks in the United States and/or other countries: IBM, AT, XT, and OS/2 are trademarks of International Business Machines Corporation. DECNET is a trademark of Digital Equipment Corporation. AT&T and RightPage are trademarks of American Telephone and Telegraph Company. Sony is a trademark of Sony Corporation of America. Kodak is a trademark of Eastman Kodak Company. Apple and Macintosh are

---

‖ Fox, E., Blacksburg, VA Project, Workshop Comments.
** Becker, H., Director, ITS - Library of Congress, Workshop Comments
†† Smith, N., Head, Network Services - British Library, Workshop Comments

trademarks of Apple Computer, Inc. Microsoft is a trademark of Microsoft Corporation. Xerox is a trademark of Xerox Corporation. Oracle is a trademark of Oracle Corporation. Hewlett-Packard is a trademark of Hewlett-Packard Company. Sun is a trademark of Sun Microsystems. TCI is a trademark of TCI Software Research, Inc.

Part III

Information Retrieval/Hypertext

Chapter 6

Automatic Hypertext Conversion of Paper Document Collections

Andreas Myka[*] and Ulrich Güntzer[†]

6.1 Introduction

Digital libraries possibly have a lot of advantages over ordinary libraries. These advantages include the independence from location, the minimization of restrictions with regard to availability, the speed of access, the possibility of annotating without annoying succeeding users, and the enhanced search functionality. Especially the last point extends the functionality, as provided by ordinary libraries, by far. Yet many of the digital libraries rather try to copy the search functionality of ordinary libraries instead of enhancing it appropriately. While full text search mechanisms are part of most of the systems, hypertextual searches are either not supported at all or only to a small extent, e. g. as implemented in the RightPages system [235]. Of course, the common retrieval by means of a fixed retrieval language, for example Boolean retrieval, can be very helpful. On the other hand, supporting intuitive searching without forcing the user to put his information needs into an explicit query is necessary, in case the user either does not exactly know what he is looking for or how to formulate his information needs [56]. Thereby, implicit connections between documents or document parts, respectively, may be of great help. In addition to implicit links, many documents contain explicit references to other parts of the same document or to completely different documents. Linking these references to the referenced document part supports the controlled navigation of a user who, otherwise, would have to browse sequentially through the images of pages or by means of formulating queries in order to get to the desired destination. By means of both implicit and explicit links, a set of separate documents is converted into a large hypertext web.

Besides directly supporting user navigation, the introduction of hypertext links may have other benefits as well. With regard to alerting functionality,

---

[*]Wilhelm-Schickard-Institut, Universität Tübingen, Sand 13, D-72076 Tübingen, Germany, email: myka@informatik.uni-tuebingen.de

[†]Wilhelm-Schickard-Institut, Universität Tübingen, Sand 13, D-72076 Tübingen, Germany, email: guentzer@informatik.uni-tuebingen.de

users may be informed in case new documents have been inserted in the digital library that are highly linked to documents, the user has inspected several times before — thus, implicit profiles are used in addition to explicit profiles [235]. Links may also be exploited in order to support information retrieval purposes by means of using the additional information that is attached to the link [97, 128].

The common lack of linking in digital libraries is mainly due to the two facts that the manual hypertext conversion of a real-world library is not feasible and methods for automatically converting paper documents have been missing. In contrast, our system called HYPERFACS enables the automatic generation of sets of links by means of describing the features of all links within a specific set. It is based on the processing of paper documents, because today most of the objects that are stored within real-world libraries are paper documents. At the same time, paper documents are more difficult to handle than electronic documents, because the conversion from non-coded information to coded information produces errors, the hypertext generation unit has to cope with. Thus it can be stated that the methods for processing paper documents may be applied — of course in a modified and to a certain extent simplified form — to electronic documents, e. g. Postscript or LATEX documents, as well.

Using HYPERFACS, links within a certain library object (e. g. an article) may be generated as well as links that connect different objects. Thereby, characteristics of link types are specified and examined that include layout, syntactic, and/or statistic criteria. Links do not necessarily connect one part of a document to another, but may also connect a document part to an action: thus, the traversal of links may trigger actions such as full text searches or the execution of UNIX shell commands. Furthermore, tools may be generated that link virtual nodes, e. g. a system generated list of definitions, with real nodes, i. e. images of pages.

Links are specified by means of a link type description language. This usage of an abstract level has two main advantages. First, links are specified by means of describing the features of all links of a certain type. This link type description then may be re-used throughout all matching documents. Second, on an abstract level, the special problems of working with the raster images of paper documents may be hidden from the user who delivers the link type description. These problems arise from the work of HYPERFACS with so-called non-coded information and comprise errors with regard to character recognition, determination of zones, or classification of structure elements.

In order to create all the sensible links for a special document type, several distinct link type descriptions are combined within a description module. This module together with the preliminary recognition of basic structure elements forms the basis for the link generation. The preliminary recognition of basic structure elements, such as headings and paragraphs, is based on the output of an OCR software.

Browsing through the library after the conversion process, the user works with the facsimile pages that resulted from optically scanning the original paper document at the beginning of the processing. Using facsimiles has two advantages over a pure ASCII representation of documents: First, the user may work with the kind of representation he is accustomed to, leaving his common navigation and orientation habits unchanged. Second, the system can cope with OCR errors on the link generation level, whereas these errors are more annoying on the representation level: presenting OCR errors to the reader directly leads to decreasing trust in the overall system. On the link generation level some kind of fuzzy evaluation can be integrated that, in most cases, preserves recall and does not lead to a substantial loss of precision. Thus, the facsimile representation is helpful, additionally using ASCII information in order to satisfy full text queries. Underlying hypertext nodes are stored within the system's data bases and are used in order to locate relevant passages. However, in contrast to ordinary hypertext systems, these nodes are not used as completely independent representational units. Instead, they are presented to the user only indirectly as link anchors.

In section 6.2, we will start with a description of preprocessing steps that are necessary in order to enable link recognition. This preprocessing includes the recognition of characters and basic structure elements. Section 6.3 deals with the generation of links: subsection 6.3.1 gives an overview of the language that is used for link description as well as tool specification. The processing of such descriptions, that takes into consideration possible errors of the preprocessing steps, is shown in subsection 6.3.2. Thereby, also the interconnection of separate documents by means of using a central data base is described in addition to the generation of intra-document links. Due to the fact that the automatic hypertext conversion of a linear document cannot be perfect, the results of conversion have to be evaluated by means of monitoring the interaction of users with the system. The conclusions that can be drawn by means of analyzing this data, are described in section 6.4. A description of the user interface of HYPERFACS is given in section 6.5. This section also contains aspects of converting the data stored in HYPERFACS into other formats. The chapter concludes with some final remarks in section 6.6.

6.2 Preprocessing of Documents

Library objects such as books, journals, or articles have to be preprocessed first in order to be integrated in an electronic information system. Typically, this comprises optical scanning and OCR processing (figure 6.1: 1-2). Because our system focuses on the recognition and generation of hypertext structures based on matching specified criteria, a preliminary analysis of layout is done at preprocessing time, too (figure 6.1: 3-4). Preprocessing may include other steps as well, e. g. correction of skew or reduction of noise. These steps can be integrated into such a system easily. However, since our own tests with regard to further preprocessing did not show any promising results — with regard to skew correction, overall readability even deteriorated —, these steps are omitted in HYPERFACS at the moment. In order to support flexible and fast analysis, the results of the preprocessing phase are stored within a relational data base system.

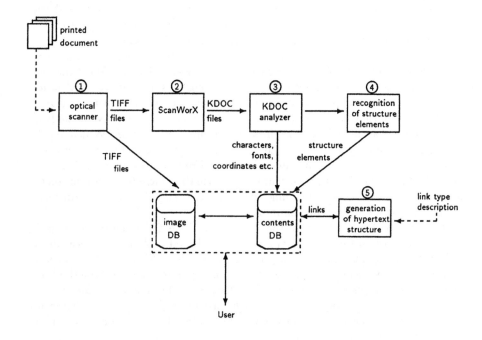

Figure 6.1 Architecture of the HYPERFACS system

6.2.1   Optical Scanning and OCR Processing

Optical scanning is, of course, a prerequisite for digital processing of any paper document. As already stated, the raster images are then stored in order to enable subsequent analysis of them as well as using them for representation purposes. After scanning, the detection and classification of primitive objects, i. e. characters, is started. Thereby, SCANWORX 2.1 for Motif is used. The importance of optical character recognition in any kind of digital library is due to the fact that full text retrieval is based on this information. Besides, clues with regard to structure elements may be encoded using certain character patterns, e. g. *"figure n"*, where *n* is a number, hints at a figure caption or a reference to a figure. Thus, character recognition is also important with regard to structure element and link recognition.

According to tests of the UNLV Information Science Research Institute and our own evaluation, SCANWORX 2.1 performs well compared to other OCR packages: depending on the quality of the paper original, the fonts and the scanned resolution used, the character accuracy can be approximated to 98%, whereas the word accuracy varies between 94% and 97% [205].

In contrast to the architecture of HYPERFACS , OCR processing of course may also follow layout analysis, as implemented in other systems, cf. [186]. However, in HYPERFACS the sequence of preprocessing steps as stated above is taken for two reasons. First, the preprocessing steps that are required for optimising OCR results, like internal skew correction, noise reduction, and basic layout analysis (distinction between text and graphics zones), are done by SCANWORX on its own. Second, our layout analysis, to a certain extent, is based on the outcome of the the OCR package. This analysis uses information that is provided from SCANWORX in addition to pure character information including information on word coordinates, fonts, and zoning. However, the reliability of a certain piece of information highly depends on its type.

In order to further improve the reliability of the OCR output automatic methods of post-editing can be applied [239]. Thereby, supposed misspellings are clustered around high-frequency terms (centroids). With regard to our system, the improvement that can be achieved by applying this basic method depends on the processed document: HYPERFACS at the moment is directed to the processing and management of scientific articles in the areas of mathematics and computer science. Many of these articles contain large portions of formulas which lead to a failure of such a clustering, as the recognition of term boundaries and characters varies highly within one library object. E. g. a mathematical term "$N_i^j * k$" may be recognized as a single term "$Nij * k$", as a single term "$Nji * k$", as separated terms "Nij" and "$*$" and "k" etc. Instead of trying to achieve a 100% correct character recognition, which does not seem to be feasible at the moment [205], we propose the integration of error-tolerant methods at the processing level (see section 6.3.2) and the presentation of scanned raster images (see section 6.5).

The image files are stored in the UNIX file system, because no further manipulation of raster images is done. The information delivered by SCANWORX is stored within a data base in order to support flexible evaluation.

6.2.2 Layout Analysis

In general terms, links can be regarded as relations between two or even more nodes. Therefore, the recognition of nodes is a prerequisite for describing and generating hypertext links. With regard to scanned paper documents the recognition of nodes is equivalent to the recognition of the logical structure by means of analyzing the document's layout and classifying the recognized elements accordingly.

Within a hypertext conversion system like HYPERFACS, the recognition of structure elements may be rather coarse. That means, only those elements that are common to any kind of scientific document, e. g. in our case scientific articles, have to be classified: title, authors, headings, paragraphs, figures, tables, pages' heads and feet. Of course, the system may also handle a finer output of the preliminary layout analysis. Thus, the work with regard to describing (section 6.3.1) and recognizing links (section 6.3.2) can be made easier. This is due to the fact that the more detailed the output of the preliminary layout analysis is, the less work has to be done during the phases of link generation.

The methods for segmenting documents automatically can be usually classified according to the following two approaches: *Top-down approaches* start at the highest level. The document is first segmented into distinct blocks, e. g. on a page level by means of alternating horizontal and vertical cuts; cf. [186]. These blocks are then used as input for the next stage of segmentation. Finally, segmentation stops at the lowest level (e. g. the level of words or characters). In many cases, top-down segmentation is done without any involvement of previous or intermediate OCR analysis [65]. *Bottom-up approaches* start with basic regions that are combined and thus form larger regions. Thereby, the detection of connected components on the first stage may be the starting point for recognizing characters on the second stage. Characters are the basic units of words, words are then combined to paragraphs etc., going up to the highest level [225]. Bottom-up segmentation often involves OCR on the second stage, i. e. connected components are combined and evaluated by means of trying to match them with characters.

Taking into consideration larger documents (e. g. software manuals [184]), a slightly modified approach has to be taken, because the problem of segmenting such documents is different from the more often analyzed problem of segmenting a single document page: First, separate segments of the document are determined which organize their contents differently, e. g. table of contents, glossary, ordinary text etc. Afterwards, single document pages are processed according to the document segment they belong to and according to the directly preceding and succeeding pages. With regard to scientific articles, the first segmentation phase is not as important, because generally no fundamental differences during the evaluation of the different article segments have to be made. Thereby pages are processed as follows:

1. Horizontal segmentation in order to recognize page head, foot, and body.

2. Vertical segmentation in order to detect different possible columns of text.

3. Again, horizontal segmentation in order to detect section headings, paragraphs, figures, tables, captions etc. During this phase, context information (previous and succeeding pages) is taken into consideration, too, in order to treat separated parts of one and the same logical element appropriately.

Thereby, information that is delivered from the OCR software, is used in almost any step. Due to specific aspects of reliability, mainly character information and part of the font information are used. As examples, the recognition of headings and paragraphs will be shortly described in the following.

The recognition of headings is based on the analysis of the average line distance and three possible characteristics: First, the height of the font used normally exceeds the height of the font that is used most often within the document. Second, the horizontal alignment may indicate headings if lines are printed left-justified (or right-justified or centered), whereas ordinary paragraphs use lines that are justified on both sides. Third, headings are numbered in many documents. The latter two criteria are rather weak, but they have to be applied in order to recognize headings that cannot be distinguished using the first criterion only. Thereby, weaknesses with regard to the recognition of fonts, especially with regard to the recognition of bold printing, may be overcome.

In most cases, paragraphs may be distinguished from other segments (which may be paragraphs as well) by means of analyzing the distance to the following/preceding segment, by means of analyzing indentation, or by means of recognizing the beginning or the end of a different segment, as illustrated above. According to common accepted rules, the distance between a paragraph and its successor/predecessor either exceeds the average distance of lines within paragraphs or the first line of the paragraph is indented (except for the line following a heading). Special care has to be applied if tables or figures appear within a document: such elements do not necessarily have to mark boundaries of different elements, but may also be inserted in the middle of one and the same element.

The preliminary layout analysis works well within the environment for which it was developed: the processing of scientific articles in the areas of computer science and mathematics. This is due to the fact, that the basic rules for assigning layout characteristics to special logical elements within such documents are rather standardized.

6.3   Link Generation

The generation of links consists of two phases. During phase one, i. e. at specification time, certain types of links are described making use of a link description language (section 6.3.1). This description is used during phase two, i. e. at generation time, in order to automatically evaluate the data base that was filled during preprocessing and generate hypertext links accordingly (section 6.3.2; see figure 6.1: 5).

6.3.1   Link Description

In order to be able to connect different document parts, criteria have to be specified for selecting appropriate parts. The selection of these parts can be regarded as a kind of low-level structure recognition [42]. The filtering of the data is done by means of analyzing the data base entries that are created during preprocessing. With regard to pure ASCII files, filtering by means of ad hoc formulated SQL queries is sufficient [219]. However, with regard to scanned documents, certain specific aspects cannot be dealt with sufficiently using this approach. That means that i. a. layout criteria and possible OCR errors have

structure element		possible subordinate elements
article	:	title_env chapter* head* foot*
title_env	:	title author*
chapter	:	c_heading c_content section*
section	:	s_heading s_content subsection*
subsection	:	ss_heading ss_content
c_content	:	c_paragraph* c_figure* c_caption*
s_content	:	s_paragraph* s_figure* s_caption*
ss_content	:	ss_paragraph* ss_figure* ss_caption*
head	:	page_heading page_number
foot	:	foot_text

Table 6.1 Possible structure elements.

to be taken into consideration. In order to achieve these goals, it is useful to provide for descriptions on a more abstract level. Thus, specific hypertext problems can be considered as well, such as the problem whether nodes have to be connected if their subordinate nodes are connected. In addition, the abstract level hides certain problems from the user/administrator, taking care of them at the interpretation level automatically.

The developed link type description language LıTHP (Link Type description language for HyperText Processing) is based on experiences with a prototype for the processing of a software manual [184]. In order to cope with different types of input, structure elements, as detected during preprocessing, are taken from a structure element description file that can be either specified by the administrator or extracted automatically from the data base; part of such a file is shown in table 6.1. By means of this file, the administrator declares, which structure elements may be used for link description purposes and which possible hierarchies may be formed by these elements.

Ordinary Links

In most cases, the description of ordinary link types is based on the description of a specific type of information. Specific types of information include definitions, captions, explanations, or bibliography entries. In many cases, specific pieces of information are characterized by means of specific character patterns. Within paper documents however, an author may have used layout properties in addition to pure textual information in order to encode the type of information. Therefore, the specification language has to be flexible enough to take into consideration possible layout characteristics as well as specifications of character patterns. Of course, these characteristics may vary from document to document for one and the same type of information.

Basically the specification of ordinary link types comprises the name of the link type, optionally some constants and variables, the characteristics of the link source, the characteristics of the link destination (in most cases the information

```
NAME      "definition"
EVAL      BACK 1
VAR       term      SYNTAX   "\S+" END;
          def_term SYNTAX   "\S+" END;
          def_dest SYNTAX   "[^\.]+\." END;

SOURCE    REGION   s_paragraph, ss_paragraph END
          SYNTAX   term END
          MARK     term;

DEST      REGION   Paragraph END
          FONT     def_term NORMALSIZE BOLD ROMAN
          SYNTAX   "Definition:" def_term "(::=|is a|is an)" def_dest,
                   "Def.:" def_term "(::=|is a|is an)" def_dest
                   END
          MARK     def_dest

RELATION  String(term) = String(def_term) AND
          Directly_Preceding(def_term, term);

EXPORT    DEST
```

Figure 6.2 Example of a link specification.

unit), the characteristics of the relationship between the source and the destination of a link, and possibly some information about exporting or importing link parts. As already mentioned, the destination of a link does not necessarily have to be a text area.

Table 6.2 shows the example specification of a definition link. Thereby, each occurrence of a word "term" or phrase within the specified region (PARAGRAPH) is connected to its definition "def_term", preceding its occurrence. The relationship is mainly based on the syntactical equality of "term" and "def_term". This relationship is stated in the RELATION part where other kinds of binary predicates can be used as well.

The NAME of the link type is indicated as "definition". This name is used after the link generation in order to inform users of the library's browser, which kind of information can be reached by means of traversing the link. Also by means of this name, data from this specific type of link can be referenced during the processing of a different link type.

Constants may be declared by means of using a C preprocessor-like syntax, i. e. "#define ...", resulting in a pure textual replacement of a constant by its definition. The concept of variables in LITHP is important with regard to the description of link types. By means of specifying variables, the user lays down some characteristics of text parts, that have to be fulfilled in matching anchors and destinations appropriately. In the given example for a definition link type, three variables "term", "def_term", and "def_dest" are used. In the variable declaration only the basic syntax characteristics are specified (see below). In addition, variables can also be characterized with regard to fonts, possible regions, positions, and their context.

The description of possible anchors (SOURCE) and destinations (DEST) of ordinary links is similar to the description of variables with some extensions. By means of specifying certain criteria, parts of nodes are described that qualify as candidate link parts. In case, all the specified criteria are fulfilled, a link can then be established.

The SYNTAX part defines a list of possible strings that characterize a link source or destination, respectively. A string may contain fixed components as well as variables. In table 6.2, the specification of destinations contains variables for the term that is defined, "def_term", and for the definition as such, "def_dest". The variable "def_term" can then be referenced within the RELATION part. In addition, fixed components contain key words and key symbols that characterize that certain type of information, cf. [141].

By means of FONT font descriptions for complete link sources/destinations may be given. Besides, also fonts of parts of sources/destinations may be specified using variables. E. g., in our example the font of "def_term" is indicated, whereas no restrictions with regard to the other terms of a definition exist.

In order to ensure plausibility as well as efficiency, the search for link sources/ destinations or variables is restricted to those areas, i. e. structure elements, that are mentioned in the appropriate REGION parts.

The absolute position of a link source/destination may be specified with regard to the page layout. Thereby, the approximate vertical position is indicated by means of key words such as, e. g.,TOP or HEAD. The horizontal position may be indicated similarly, including the adjustment of lines containing source/destination candidates.

In contrast, the relative position of a link part may be specified in the context part of a link specification. There, criteria for contextual structure elements may be specified: preceding or succeeding structure elements (according to the linearity of the original document), parent structure elements or subordinate structure elements (according to the hierarchy of structure elements; cf. table 6.1). Again, the specification may refer to characteristics of syntax, font, and position. By means of these constructs, also those problems of hypertext conversion may be addressed individually for single documents or document types that cannot be solved on a global basis: e. g. whether a link between passages implies the necessity of links between nodes that are directly related to the linked ones.

The relationship between the link source and the link destination is described by means of the RELATION part. There, unary predicates are used to characterize specific aspects of a link's source or destination, respectively (e. g. "SYNTAX(...)"). Binary predicates have to be given in order to specify the kind of relationship that has to be evaluated. These binary predicates may be connected by means of operators (AND, OR); in the example given, only those links are generated that connect an anchor with the immediately preceding definition. Thus, all definitions following the occurrence of a defined term and all definitions

```
NAME      "class_expl"
VAR       class_term SYNTAX "\d\d[A-Z]\d\d" END;
          class_dest IMPORT ALL FROM "classification"
                     WHERE doc_title = "Mathematics Subject Classification 1991";

SOURCE    REGION  Paragraph END
          SYNTAX  "^Mathematics Subject Classification: (\d\d[A-Z]\d\d,)*"
                                               class_term "[,\n]";

          END
          MARK    class_term;

DEST      MARK    class_dest

RELATION String(class_term) = String(class_dest);
```

Figure 6.3 Example of a link specification with import.

ahead of the immediately preceding one are ignored.

The essence of the whole link is laid down within the two **MARK** specification parts. There, it is determined which document parts are marked as the source and destination of a specific link. In our example, the position of "def_term" will be marked as the source of a link (this extends the possibilities of anchoring links as described in [52]).

EXPORT is used if the gathered information shall be stored in a central data base. This central storage allows the access from succeeding generation runs (covering different documents), thus allowing the specification and creation of inter-document links. Since the main information part of definition links is located in the destination parts, only these are exported in our example in fig. 6.2.

On the other hand, it is possible to IMPORT that information in different ways depending on the information that is wanted.

First, the import of information may be local or global. This distinction has to be made, because processing of a whole library is done incrementally. Local imports only affect information that is generated for one and the same document, thus allowing only intra-document links. In order to do so, only the link name has to be specified, e. g. IMPORT FROM "definition". Global imports may comprise information from all documents that have been processed before. In this case, additional selection methods by means of document names and key words are useful. For example, in fig. 6.3 the explanations of subject classifiers are imported from the document "Mathematics Subject Classification 1991" (as published, e. g., in "Zentralblatt für Mathematik und ihre Grenzgebiete — Mathematics Abstracts", Springer-Verlag) and connected to the appearances of such terms within the classification line of a mathematical article; cf. figure 6.9. Conceptually, it would also be possible to model a library as a single document consisting of all library objects. Thus, inter-document links could be specified by means of appropriate REGION specifications. In contrast, we haven chosen the mentioned approach, because we consider library objects, e. g. articles, as objects that should not be mixed with ordinary structure elements: doing this, the incremental processing of a digital library is possible by means of taking each library object as an entity that can be processed without being forced to take into consideration other library objects. If different objects have to be taken into consideration as well, access to these objects has to be supported by means of additional information retrieval tools [183].

Second, information may be imported completely or reduced to parts that are used as parts of local links. I. e. with regard to the destination part of definition links, all possible destination parts (all definitions) could be imported or only those definitions for which links have been established locally. Importing all local information is similar to a textual replacement of a link part description by the description of the imported link part. However, using the IMPORT functionality is more efficient, because the results of an earlier processing can be used instead of starting the processing once again from the very beginning.

Partially Virtual Links

Partially virtual links are similar to ordinary links with regard to the fact that again a specification of layout or textual information is given in order to detect some kind of information unit. Partially virtual links are different to ordinary links with regard to the fact that either the link source or the link destination is not part of the original document collection.

Virtual link sources have to be created in order to generate textual tools. Such tools, as e. g. table of contents, list of figures, list of abbreviations etc., may already be contained in the original document. In case they are not, they may be modelled and created using LiTHP. An example for the description of a list of definitions is given in figure 6.4. The list of definitions is specified similar to the description of definition links (figure 6.2). The main difference is that all the link sources are grouped on a newly created node that is not part of the scanned original document. The order of the virtual node's entries is indicated in figure 6.4 as ascending lexicographical order (LEX ASC). Another difference is that for each definition (as specified in the destination part) there exists exactly one link. Of course, the information needed to create these virtual links could also be imported from definition links if that type of link had been processed before.

Virtual links also include links that connect text with actions. Thus, the traversal of a link may trigger the execution of a UNIX command or the execution of a full text search. By means of this mechanisms, a great variety of features may be included: e. g. the integration of executable examples in software manuals or the establishment of connections to completely different hypertext systems, thus creating an open hypertext system.

```
NAME       "definition_list"
TITLE      "List of definitions"
VAR        term     SYNTAX   "\S+" END;
           def_term SYNTAX   "\S+" END;
           def_dest SYNTAX   "[^\.]+\." END;

ENTRY      SYNTAX   term END
           ORDER    LEX ASC
           MARK     term

DEST       REGION   Paragraph END
           FONT     def_term NORMALSIZE BOLD ROMAN
           SYNTAX   "Definition:" def_term "(::=|is a|is an)" def_dest,
                    "Def.:" def_term "(::=|is a|is an)" def_dest
                    END
           MARK     def_dest

RELATION String(term) = String(def_term)

EXPORT   DEST
```

Figure 6.4 Example of a tool specification.

Statistical Links

Statistical links are based on the similarity of two different structure elements, mostly paragraphs, with regard to statistical measures. The steps towards the computation of a numerical similarity value are equivalent to the process for ASCII documents described in [219]:

1. filtering of the relevant structure elements by means of a negative list in order to exclude stop words (like "the", "and", "a" etc.),

2. term reduction in order to achieve a common word form for words of the same stem,

3. weighting of the remaining terms in order to describe the relevance of a term with a regard to a specific text passage,

4. computation of the similarity.

Thereby, the granularity of text pieces which is used in order to generate statistical links is fixed by the user's definition of such links (see figure 6.5): there, the structure elements "s_content" and "ss_content" (cf. table 6.1) are indicated as nodes, i. e. as possible sources and destinations of links.

In addition to the flexible selection of structure elements, it is also sensible to enable flexibility with regard to characterizing the contents of a piece of text. Usually, the characterization of a text piece is restricted to the set of terms that appear in the relevant hypertext node. In HYPERFACS, however, the user may indicate that super-ordinate/subordinate titles and/or paragraphs should be included in the characterization of a hypertext node, too (see CONTEXT attribute in fig. 6.5). Doing this, the extended context of a structure element may be taken into account in addition to its textual content. Basically the weighting of terms is based on the pure frequency distribution, at least with regard to the "HyperMan" weighting as indicated in figure 6.5. In many cases, the weights of terms should be modified if they are not taken directly from the element under concern, but from its context. Therefore, the user may also specify modification rates for this context in order to specify the relevance of a certain structure element with regard to the structure element under concern. An example of such a link type description is shown in fig. 6.5: there, terms of the relevant heading "s_heading" are modified with rate 1.4 (in comparison to a fictive rate of 1.0 for "s_content" itself) in case they belong to the context of "s_content".

In addition to contextual aspects, font information may be taken into consideration, too. This is due to the fact that the author of the original document may have used font characteristics in order to assign special relevance to a term, e. g. by means of using bold printing. This aspect may be integrated into the link type description as well: according to fig. 6.5, terms of "s_content" that are printed in bold face, are modified by a rate of 1.5.

Normally, the modification rate should not be cumulative, because experiments with our system have shown that rates should not leave a very limited interval around 1.0 in order to produce good results. In case cumulative rates are desired with regard to a special link type description, this has to be stated explicitly.

In addition, several modifications can be triggered with regard to the computation of statistical links, some of them are given in fig. 6.5: the weighting function may be indicated as well as the similarity function; also, the user may indicate how many links should be created either by means of giving the total number of links, by means of giving the number of links for each structure element, as done in the given example, or by means of giving a minimal similarity threshold.

6.3.2   Link Recognition

In order to recognize and generate links, the description of a link type, as described in the previous section, has to be interpreted. This is done by means of a LEX scanner and a YACC parser. How the evaluation of the processed document with regard to a link's parts (anchor and destination) is done, depends on the type of information: character pattern information (section 6.3.2) or layout information (section 6.3.2). The final generation of links depends on the fact whether linking is done locally (section 6.3.2) or globally (section 6.3.2).

```
NAME   "statistical"

NODES s_content
          CONTEXT
                    s_heading          1.4
                    ss_heading         0.7
                    ss_content         0.5;
          FONT
                    BOLD               1.4;
      END

      ss_content
          CONTEXT
                    ss_heading         1.3;
      END

WEIGHTING  HyperMan
SIMILARITY Cosine
NUMBER     Local 5

EXPORT
```

Figure 6.5 Examples of a statistical link specification.

Treatment of Character Pattern Information

Most of the information in documents is, of course, stored as patterns of characters. Furthermore, specific types of information are encoded using specific character patterns as cues. In printed documents, these cues may be based on (additional) layout characteristics as well. The automatic detection of such cues within original electronic documents can be solved in a straightforward way by means of matching two fixed patterns exactly, thereby ignoring only typing errors. However, even locating the occurrences of character patterns only within an optically scanned document is more difficult. This is due to the fact that today's character recognition systems cannot provide for completely correct output [205]. Though this situation gradually will improve, the fact that output of OCR systems contains errors will foreseeably not change during the next few years. Thus errors, such as confusion of characters and incorrect insertion or deletion of word delimiters, have to be taken into consideration during link generation.

Our approach towards approximate pattern matching is mainly based on three phases. During phase 1 (see numbers 1–4 in figure 6.6), a preselection of source and/or destination candidates is done. In order to achieve this, the character pattern as specified within a syntax description is analysed and digrams are formed accordingly. For example, the digrams " d", "de", "ef", ..., "n " are derived from the term "definition". Whether n-grams with n>2 perform better, depends on the size of the document. Of course, n-grams can only be used if the syntax specification under concern contains appropriate fixed patterns, such

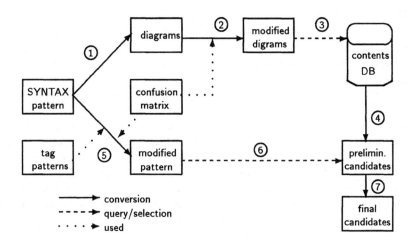

Figure 6.6 Processing of Character Pattern Information

as "definition" or an already instantiated syntax part of a variable. If patterns with regular operators are specified only, no such preselection is possible. These digrams (n-grams) are further modified by means of involving a confusion matrix that lists confusions that are common within the output of a specific OCR software: characters belonging to a set of characters that are often mixed up are mapped to one character, e. g. 0,O,o are mapped to O. It has to be clearly stated that this step may be imprecise as long as the recall, resulting from this kind of preselection, is preserved. Finally, the modified digrams are used for querying the data base in which the analogously extracted digrams (n-grams) of all the document's recognised terms are stored. As a result, preliminary candidates are received (fig. 6.6, no. 4).

In phase 2 (numbers 5–7 in fig. 6.6), these preliminary candidates are further evaluated. Thereby, not only the fixed patterns within the syntax description are used, but the whole description, i. e. the whole regular expression. This expression is modified by means of the confusion matrix (cf. [205]) and tagging patterns. The confusion matrix is created by means of specifying the most common confusions of characters or character patterns with regard to the OCR software under concern. Because errors of an OCR package may as well depend on the fonts that are used, the global confusion matrix has to be evaluated and modified once for every new document type in order to achieve optimal results. With regard to the first part of the link destination's syntax definition in fig. 6.2, the expression ``Definition: \S+ ::='' is possibly transformed into

```
([DOO][ \.',]?[ecao]?[ \.',]?[ftl][ \.',]?[iltI]?[ \.',]
?(ii|ri|[num])[ \.',]?[iltI]?[ \.',]?[tcl][ \.',]?[iltI]
?[ \.',]?[ocaO][ \.',]?(ii|ri|[num])[ \.',]?:)[ \.',]?
?[ \.',]?(\S+)[ \.',]?  ?[ \.',]?(:[ \.',]?:[ \.',]?=).
```

After complete structure elements, e. g. paragraphs, have been filtered by means of these regular expressions, the exact location of variables within these elements is found by means of using tagging patterns. Thereby, the structure elements are modified by means of putting the data base key of a term ahead of its occurrence, e. g. ''...<43565>Definition:<43566>TransBase<43567>is<43568>a...''. Now the closest tag to each variable instance can be extracted, using the string analysing mechanisms of PERL.

By means of using PERL for this kind of pattern matching, it is evaluated whether a candidate matches the prerequisites laid down in the syntax specification. If it does, the relevant variables are instantiated. Using PERL provides for a more appropriate means of analysing patterns than direct evaluation of the document by means of data base queries. E. g. in order to take into consideration incorrect word delimiters only, the selection of the term "Definition" would extend to an SQL expression containing search conditions like

```
WHERE (term1 = "Definition") OR
      (term1 = "D" AND term2 = "efinition") OR
      ...
      (term1 = "D" AND term2 = "e" AND ...  AND term10 = "n")
```

The same condition may be formulated as a PERL expression

$$/D[ ]?e[ ]?f[ ]?i[ ]?n[ ]?i[ ]?t[ ]?i[ ]?o[ ]?[ ]?n/$$

which is processed faster for single documents. More complex expressions, as the one given above, cannot be evaluated by means of SQL queries anymore.

Finally, the reliability of the filtered candidates is rated. This is done by means of computing the number of errors that have been located within the candidate, divided by its length: there, the number of errors is determined by means of counting the minimal number of confusions that could have occurred if the original expression – as printed on paper – did match the syntax template. Instead of this approach, the distance between a candidate and the syntax template could also be computed by means of using the Levenshtein measure. There, a certain distance d is computed if d insertions, deletions, or substitutions of characters are necessary in order to transform a candidate to match the given regular expression [160]. However with regard to the specific problems of OCR errors, we consider the first approach more appropriate. The reliability rate is either used in order to delete a candidate link part from the set or to enable computation of an overall reliability rate with regard to the whole link, including its source part, its destination part and its relation part.

Treatment of Layout Information

The treatment of layout information, to a certain extent, is even more difficult than the treatment of information concerning character patterns. This is due to the fact that certain types of layout information are more vague. With regard to the SCANWORX software this is especially true for information about fonts and zoning. Other software packages (like e. g. Omnipage) may perform better with regard to the recognition of basic printing modes such as bold face, italics and ordinary mode, but do not provide for information on font families. Therefore, the relevance of this kind of information, today, has to be estimated and handled appropriately. For example, with regard to statistical links, the inclusion of font information (see table 6.5) seems to be reasonable, because it contributes to the improvement of such links in most cases. Other kind of layout information normally will not be included in the generation of statistical links.

With regard to ordinary links, different pieces of layout information may be included. There, the analysis of layout information takes into consideration only those candidates that result from the filtering by means of information about character patterns. Only if no information about syntax was specified, the whole data base is evaluated. Font information only leads to an increase (in case the specification is met) or decrease (in case it is not) of an ordinary link's rate. Unfortunately, it cannot be used as a primary source for link generation yet. In contrast, information about position and region of a link's source or destination is more reliable and thus may lead to a stronger modification of a link's reliability rate.

In summary, it has to be stated that the reliability of some of the layout information, especially font information, at the moment is not sufficient. However, this will change foreseeably in the near future and the designed link type description language LITHP already provides for means of using layout information not only additionally as a means for plausibility testing of hypotheses based on other information.

Generation of intra-document links

Considering the generation of links, again a distinction has to be made between the generation of ordinary links, partially virtual links, and statistical links.

With regard to ordinary links and partially virtual links, the anchor and destination parts of a link type specification are processed sequentially, starting with the part that is specified more precisely, i. e. in most cases the destination part. During the processing of the first part, all possible assignments to variables are stored for each candidate (cf. fig. 6.2: "def_term" and "def_dest"). How much information is stored depends on whether the part under consideration will be exported. If it will not be exported, only that amount of information has to be stored that is needed locally. In case the destination part in figure 6.2 would not be exported, the storage of the string values for both "def_term" and "def_dest" as well as the storage of the coordinates (including page references) for "def_dest" would be sufficient. The storage of e. g. font information for "def_term" would not be necessary, because this information is only needed during the processing of the destination part. The stored information is then used for identification or creation of matching counterparts (i. e. sources or destinations). If such a counterpart can be found/created, a link is established.

If the processed link part is exported, all the available information with regard to candidate parts has to be stored in a central data base. Doing this, succeeding access to the already analysed data during the processing of a different link type or a different document is possible. Additional information therefore also has to include information about font, position, and region. However, context information cannot be stored centrally as the aspects/parts of context that will be needed for future references cannot be foreseen (see section 6.3.2 below).

With regard to statistical links, anchor and destination parts of a link type are not processed during different phases. First, for each node a set of specific terms and their weights are determined. Afterwards, the degree of the (bidirectional) relationship between two nodes is computed by means of the cosine coefficient. Each node is then connected to the nodes for which the highest similarity value has been computed.

Generation of inter-document links

The generation of inter-document links is analogous with the generation of intra-document links. Again, with regard to the generation of ordinary or partially virtual links, the detection of counterparts to a piece of information is based on the information given by the user. However, in this case the specified part belongs to a different document. The information that is needed in order to process the specification can be retrieved from a central database. Only in case of context information a different approach is needed: within the central data base only references to the data bases containing the context data are stored. By means of these references the relevant data bases can be addressed and the appropriate context can be evaluated.

In contrast to intra-document links, it may be necessary to apply some pre-processing to the imported information before it may be used. This is true e. g. if documents are combined that use different languages. In this case, an intermediate usage of a thesaurus could bridge the gap between the two languages. Possibly, a dictionary could also be useful for creating statistical links between such documents. An intermediate processing is necessary e. g. with regard to bibliographic references: on the one hand, they can be found in almost any scientific publication. On the other hand, they vary from publication to publication. Therefore, it may be useful to do some preprocessing in order to work with normalised representations of references.

With regard to the generation of statistical links connecting different documents within a digital library, another problem has to be addressed: let us assume that statistical links should be generated for a set of documents that contain n nodes. Then, the complexity of generating such links would be $O(n^2)$. Therefore, a processing of all objects of a real-world library is not feasible this way. As a solution we propose two methods. The set of candidate documents for the construction of new statistical links may be restricted by means of manually ascribed key words or classification entries. Or this assignment of key words to the document under concern is done automatically by means of taking those terms for which the highest weights have been computed together with the recognised subject classifiers if they exist. The advantage of the latter approach is that different sets of key words may be assigned to documents, and structure elements of documents. Thus, a more selective specification of link types can by made on the level of library objects and the level of structure elements. Both ways, the computation of statistical links for a new library object and therefore the incremental processing of a whole library is feasible [183].

6.4   Hypertext Evaluation

After the generation of links has been finished for a specific set of library objects, the set of links could be regarded as static, because the involved objects are static, too. However, it is better to allow modifications of this web at the time the system is used for browsing. Besides the obvious feature that links may be inserted manually, monitoring user actions may provide for additional benefits: thus, new links may be learned by the system and already generated links may be evaluated.

6.4.1   Link Learning

The learning of links within hypertext environments can be approached by means of looking for paths within a user's interaction with the system. A link can be created by means of connecting the starting point with the end point of this path. Such links can then provide for shortcuts to succeeding users. Thus, the set of automatically generated links is dynamically enlarged. Of course, there are two main problems. First, not every string of actions is goal-directed and/or reasonable. Second, not every sequence of actions can be transformed into a link.

As a partial solution to both problems, a rule-based system has been implemented. The rules that form the basis of the system have been established manually according to an evaluation of previously collected monitoring data [182]. There, common patterns within action sequences were determined and transformed into rules. Of course, only those patterns could be taken into consideration that provided for sensible locations of link sources and destinations. One obvious example for such a rule is:

`If the user sequentially traverses links` $l_1, \ldots, l_n$ `without interrupt,`
`then connect the source of link` l_1 `with the destination of` l_n.

In order to establish sensible links, several preconditions for action sequences have to be fulfilled. Some of them are given in the following. In contrast to other hypertext systems, our link model is not based on disjoint nodes that form the only entities that can be interconnected by means of links. Instead, nodes may be overlapping and link anchors do not necessarily have to be complete nodes. Therefore, other data has to be taken into consideration in order to validate the connection between the traversal of link l_i and l_{i+1}. E. g. the time of a break between the two link traversals is considered as well as the local distance between the destination of l_i and the source of l_{i+1}. In addition, the user has to indicate that he is contented with the result of his search. This may be the signalled if he makes a print-out of the final node or if he does not initiate further searches. If a sequence of actions matches one of the templates defined in the rule-base completely, then the link base is updated.

6.4.2   Evaluation of Introduced Links

Automatic hypertext generation may introduce wrong links as well. These errors most often are due to OCR errors, wrong classification of structure elements, and/or inconsistencies within the original document. Therefore, it a mechanism is integrated in the system that evaluates links and modifies the set of links accordingly.

The evaluation of links is done by means of analysing implicit and explicit feedback from users. Implicit feedback can be collected by means of evaluating the action that directly succeeds the link traversal. Positive implicit feedback may be the printing of a link's destination node. Negative implicit feedback can be given by means of dismissing the viewer that contains the link destination. Explicit feedback is given by the user by means of rating the link under concern explicitly using a special rating window. However, this window is only displayed if the user agrees to such kind of questioning.

Using the explicit and implicit feedback, the rate of affinity (or reliability) that is stored with each link, is modified accordingly. I. e. in case of a positive feedback, the affinity rate is increased, otherwise it is decreased. After the modification, two thresholds may trigger additional action: if the link rate exceeds the higher one, the link is established as permanent, disabling further evaluation of user feedback with regard to this link. If the link falls beyond the lower one, it is recognised as irrelevant or wrong and is therefore deleted.

6.5   User Interface

According to our point of view, a user interface to a digital library should preserve the look-and-feel of the original paper documents with regard to the display of library objects. At the same time it should add facilities for ordinary full text and key word searches, intuitive searches, creation of (private) links and annotations. Furthermore, the usage of a hypermedia environment is desirable that is open with regard to the integration of different types of media [94]. This makes sense, because different types of media are already integrated into ordinary libraries.

In the following description of user interfaces, we will concentrate on the hypertext/hypermedia functionality. However, the "ordinary" information retrieval functionality is, of course, necessary in order to navigate within a large web such as a digital library. Thereby, the delivery of useful entry points can decrease the possibility of getting lost in the web. Thus, the integration of hypertext and common IR functionality is advisable and feasible [183].

6.5.1   HyperFacs

In our system HYPERFACS, we have chosen to present raster images of paper documents to the user instead of pure ASCII for several reasons:

- Authors have encoded specific information by means of layout that would be lost in a pure ASCII representation.

- Readers have learned how to navigate and orientate themselves in paper documents by means of using visual information.

- Errors of the OCR software are hidden.

In order to be able to combine raster image representation with hypertext navigation, the common hypertext model had to be modified. With regard to the common model, the user is free to find his way through a document by means of choosing appropriate links (figure 6.7). Sometimes paths through the document are proposed by the system based on personal information needs and/or a user's profile. Within the modified model (fig. 6.8), a certain path through the document is always strengthened: the one that follows the linear structure of the original document. Apart from this emphasis on a special path, the user is free to choose his own way through the document collection. Therefore, he may either navigate by means of browsing page-by-page or by means of traversing links.

A screendump from a HYPERFACS session is shown in figure 6.9. There, part of an article as published in the journal "Numerische Mathematik", Springer-Verlag, is presented. The viewer on the left side displays a page from an article containing eight different link sources and one highlighted link destination. The sources are marked by means of surrounding boxes which may be turned off by the user. The destination is marked by means of highlighting. In the given example the destination (footnote starting with '*') was reached and therefore highlighted by clicking on the framed asterisk ('*') following the first author's name. Additional information on a link (besides indicating the existance of a link by means of boxes) is presented to the user if he moves the cursor into the framed boxes: then, the type of information that is contained in the link destination is shown as well as the type of action that is triggered. On the right side of the figure the central control window is shown. There, different kind of actions may be initiated, e. g. full text searches, selection of objects or sets of objects, manual link generation and manual link deletion, generation and deletion of annotations, selection of the display type for showing search results, and indication whether internal nodes (sections) or external nodes (pages) should be used.

Of course, it is not desirable to present each link and annotation to every user. This is true because of differences with regard to personal expertise or information needs. Therefore, access and modification rights with regard to links may be restricted to single users or groups of users. This restriction may be done either manually or by means of indicating appropriate access rights within the link type specification.

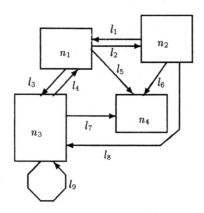

Figure 6.7 Common model

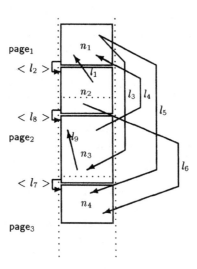

Figure 6.8 Restructured model

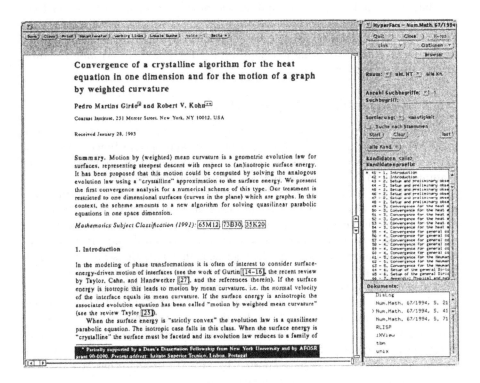

Figure 6.9 Screendump from a HYPERFACS session

Because the browser has been specifically tailored to the representation of raster images in connection with hypertext links, the hypertext functionality is completely integrated into the imaging system and works directly on top of the data base that is generated during the processing of library objects (see figure 6.1). Therefore, it can efficiently use the access structures within the data base. However, the usage of the browser again is restricted to a certain system environment, both with regard to hardware (SPARCSTATIONS) and software (data base management system TRANSBASE).

6.5.2   Conversion of hypertext bases

In order to achieve availability across a variety of platforms, it is possible to make use of existing systems that may offer an appropriate functionality. In the following we will illustrate the usage of external systems by means of two examples: the MOSAIC browser and the Adobe Acrobat Reader.

The MOSAIC browser is a World-Wide Web client that can handle documents as delivered by a hypertext transfer protocol daemon (HTTPD ; see [20, 165]). Mainly marked-up text nodes are delivered by a HTTPD, but it may also deliver clickable images that are embedded within a marked up document node. For each clickable image a map has to be specified, that tells the server what kind of action to trigger in case a specific region within the image is clicked upon. This map may be generated from link data that is stored within the HYPERFACS data base system. Thereby, the interconnection of library objects may be implemented, too. Conventional search mechanisms like full text searches may be integrated by means of using WAIS (Wide Area Information System) or by means of connecting any kind of full text data base. Thus, both conventional searches and intuitive searches may be supported by MOSAIC or any other World-Wide Web client that supports clickable images [181].

Problems arise if an enhanced functionality has to be implemented in the system. E. g. if the sources of links have to be marked by means of boxes, these boxes must be inserted into the clickable image before the image is transferred from the server to the client. Therefore, these images have to be changed if a new link is introduced, if the user does not have access permit with regard to a specific link, or if the user wants to turn off the link boxes. In contrast, the HYPERFACS browser adds link boxes to raster images dynamically, based on the current entries of the link relations within the relational data bases. Thus, images do not have to be changed, but only the relevant relations.

In contrast to MOSAIC that may provide for access to the digital library from anywhere across the internet, the Adobe Acrobat Reader is designed for local use. It is based on portable document format (pdf) files that may contain links. Making use of the pdfmark operator (cf. [6]), PostScript 2 files can be enhanced by means of introducing information on links. These files may then be transformed into pdf files. Again, this link information can be gained by means of converting the HYPERFACS link base. Using the newest version of Adobe Acrobat, links across different documents can be created (which is mandatory for digital libraries) and efficient full text searches can be started. One of the biggest advantages of using Adobe Acrobat is the quality of its display that is based on PostScript. However, this dependency on PostScript is also the disadvantage with regard to digital libraries: library objects have to be available in PostScript format in order to make use of Acrobat.

6.6   Conclusion

The automatic generation of sensible and supportive links both within and between documents is feasible. With regard to the processing of paper documents the hypertext generation has to be fault tolerant in order to take care of errors that may occur during the whole processing phase. The availability of these hypertext structures does not necessarily conflict with the display of a document's raster image that is sometimes desired and sometimes even needed. Thus, an enhanced digital library can be build that provides for the best of both worlds: the look of paper documents and the functionality of electronic documents.

Apart from providing mechanisms for associative navigation, these links can also be used for query options: e. g. queries like "show me all library objects that contain a bibliographic reference to *Numerische Mathematik*" or "give me all explanations for the acronym *OCR* that are stored within the library" can be supported.

With regard to the creation and selection of link type descriptions, work still has to be done. While an automatic creation of such descriptions is not feasible at the moment, tools can be created that select matching descriptions or description modules automatically from a set of previously created ones. This could be e. g. based on the number and/or the overall quality of generated links.

Of course, other problems than the technical ones that are addressed in this chapter have to be solved, before such a digital library can be implemented in a real-world environment. These problems foremost include questions of copyright that arise from the fact that a single library object that is stored in a digital library can be easily copied and transferred across long distances. Also the questions whether copyrights for the creation of hypertext structures within existing documents can be granted and whether such an enhancement may conflict with the copyright of a document's original author, still have to be answered.

Nevertheless, because the number of published documents and also the number of published paper documents is steadily increasing, all kinds of methods should be included into digital libraries that help the reader to cope with this flood of information.

Chapter 7

Administering Structured Documents in Digital Libraries

Klemens Böhm*,Karl Aberer [†] and Erich Neuhold[‡]

7.1 Introduction

The exponential growth in the amount of published information has led to a crisis in many of today's libraries. On the one hand the choice of what to keep, even in a limited field, is becoming harder and harder, on the other hand the selection of relevant information for a specific library user also becomes more difficult. The old idea that a library provides its readers with the right information in the right amount for an acceptable price at the right time is about to fail. In a nutshell, a solution to these problems can be seen in transforming the contents of a library to digitalized electronic form and thus gaining advantages in producing, selecting, storing and offering information. However, next to the growth in the amount of information two other phenomena have occurred. The information to be handled by libraries is increasingly becoming multimedia. In addition to texts, also images, videos, audios, even animation- and simulation programs, e.g. computer games, have to be kept. Second, this multimedia information is increasingly becoming interconnected, resulting in hypermedia documents. Inter- and intra-document links have to be created between distant storage locations and maintained sometimes over long periods of time. One of the frequently cited examples of this information interlink is the World Wide Web, the world-spanning "hyperdocument". However, the idea of essentially offering the worlds information as a single "document" containing innumerable pieces of information interconnected by an innumerable amount of links does not solve the crisis mentioned above. It rather aggravates the problem. To offer the user the right information in the right amount at the time of need is becoming

*GMD-IPSI
Dolivostraße 15, 64293 Darmstadt, Germany
E-mail:kboehm@darmstadt.gmd.de
[†]GMD-IPSI
Dolivostraße 15, 64293 Darmstadt, Germany
E-mail:aberer@darmstadt.gmd.de
[‡]GMD-IPSI
Dolivostraße 15, 64293 Darmstadt, Germany
E-mail:neuhold@darmstadt.gmd.de

more difficult as the World Wide Web is continuing to grow in an uncontrolled way. Anybody is now free to produce and offer arbitrary "information" to the whole world. The human being, however, who needs information for his work, his decision making or entertainment planning is actually the loser as many people have observed. Browsing, i.e. not searching (!), the Internet we have found the following characteristic description of the situation.

> From: rocky@cadence.com (Rochelle Grober)
> "The Internet is already an information superhighway, except that you have to be a full-fledged computer nerd to navigate it. I have been there. It's like driving a car through a blizzard without windshield wipers or lights, and all of the road signs are written upside down and backwards. And if you stop and ask someone for help, they stutter in Albanian."
> Columnist Mike Royko

In this chapter we cannot possibly discuss all these aspects of the electronic information age, and the new roles all players in the information chain have to assume. We will concentrate on the document infrastructure that we are developing as a basis for the creation, interchange, storage and offering of digital multimedia interlinked documents. The multitude of other services in the "digital information world" will basically be ignored for now. But, as we believe, they can be added easily to the framework we are discussing here. Two large experiments at our research laboratory are currently used to evaluate this assumption. An electronic house-magazine, the MultiMedia Forum [237]§, evaluates concepts and ideas of distributed electronic authoring, cooperative editing, and releasing information in digital newspapers or digital magazines. A project centered around the Dictionary of Art [209], a digitized encyclopaedical information store, is focusing on the interoperation of authors, editors, publishers and eventually of information brokers, a possible new role of libraries and librarians, together with a variety of users. The individualization of the information offered to the end users is the principle goal - and added value - of this information store.

To handle documents electronically a digitized format for all documents is necessary. They may already be produced in digitized form - an approach that does hold true for texts, images, audio, video or any other representation medium of information. On the other hand, they may also be produced in a "traditional" way and then have to be converted into a digital format. In both cases individuals using different hardware, software and other machinery platforms are involved in handling large or even huge amounts of information. In order to create, exchange, control and use this information it has to be structured into manageable pieces using certain conventions or at least conversion mechanisms that are agreed upon between the many different representation and interchange formats available. When not considering a document to be 'atomic' but rather structured, more flexible access mechanisms to documents are possible [11, 46, 23].

---

§A public version of the MultiMedia Forum is available on WWW under http://www.darmstadt.gmd.de.

Next to documents' classification by subject, a traditional task of publishers and libraries, structured information can be used to locate and retrieve documents more effectively. For example, it is possible to retrieve only the abstract of "full text" documents, to retrieve all chapter headings, or to use full text search mechanisms to retrieve those chapters or sections only containing specific information. In an interlinked hyperdocument such "scope" restrictions will be needed to limit the size of the document pieces selected, transported, stored and displayed in response to an information retrieval query. Limiting the size of the retrieved documents through navigation along intra- and inter-hyperdocument links leads to the "driving" phenomena encountered in the WWW or observed as "getting lost in space" [51] in hypertext systems.

Problems related to documents' internal structure have become more acute due to the increasing supply of information. Hence, the demand for concepts and technologies has also risen. SGML ('Standard Generalized Markup Language') [ISO86, Her90] is within the center of interest. With SGML the logical structure of documents of arbitrary types¶ can be described. In a nutshell, this is accomplished by identifying logical document components such as sections, subsections, definitions, listings, figures, etc. within the document. SGML documents need not be text documents. Rather they may be composed of basic components of arbitrary types, e.g. pixel graphics or audio. - However, in SGML document-type definitions the semantics of document components are not recorded. As a consequence, rules for handling the different datatypes are not part of SGML.

In more detail, on the one hand, there is the processing semantics, e.g. how to handle a video, an audio, or a simulation program. Besides that, there is the 'real world' content semantics of document components, i.e. the role of document components such as title, abstract or conclusions. Other examples are the name of a letter's sender or in a book the information about the publisher or author, together with the knowledge how to handle this information. For example, one may store the sender's address in an address register, or one will pay the publisher royalties when accessing the electronic version of the book.

Processing semantics have now been included into SGML via the HyTime standard. It contains a number of templates to define canonical hypermedia elements such as (time-)schedules and hyperlinks. These semantics, but also the content semantics, must be reflected before full manipulation functionality can be achieved. Capturing the content semantics is closely related to the field of document content description by authors, editors, publishers, librarians, etc. or document content analysis by computer linguists, indexers, document relevance analyzers, etc. Standardization of content semantics in the form of knowledge nets is currently out of reach by much. Content semantics will not be further considered in this chapter.

Even though approaches for the identification of logical document components are subject to these restrictions, we make a strong point for the use of such formats when administering documents in digital libraries: The dividing

---

¶ At a rudimentary level of analysis, examples of document types are letter, technical manual, newspaper, biography, novel.

line between intra-document relationships and inter-document relationships is not clean-cut. As an example, consider a document of type 'conference proceedings' consisting of several articles. On the one hand, these articles are parts of the document of type 'conference proceedings'. On the other hand, they can be seen as documents in their own right. The impact of these different views is that the same portion of the digital library may be referenced in different ways.

Another consequence of structuring documents in digital libraries is that search and delivery size of information can be limited.

The equation of 'libraries' with 'archives', that can be encountered in the literature occasionally, leaves aside certain subtleties. Archives are static, i.e. documents that have been archived are normally not altered. In order to modify them in general they need be dearchived. To support this rather static view, less sophisticated architectures tend to be sufficient. With libraries, however, reorganizing the document stock, modifying individual documents, and annotating them by the original author, by readers, or by other authors must be possible. Database management systems (DBMSs) should be applied to meet the requirements imposed by this more sophisticated functionality. Databases allow for concurrent use and update, for user protection, for recovery and persistence of the information stored. If database technology was not used, these properties would have to be provided by the individual application systems accessing the digital library.

The approach taken in this chapter is to describe first our way on how to store SGML documents in an object-oriented database. An extension towards HyTime is sketched afterwards as it has not yet been implemented completely. Subsequently we illustrate, by a number of sample applications, how the hyperdocument base may be combined with other system components to cover the integral handling of documents in various applications in a more complete way. Our application framework stores documents using the object-oriented database management system (OODBMS) VODAK [144, 142]. As described above, the documents that are particularly well-suited for storage in object-oriented databases are highly structured and are repeatedly edited or annotated by several persons. Typical examples are newspapers changing dynamically ("partial news-update-strategy") or encyclopediae with many authors and editors and individualized or annotated versions for different user groups.

Conventional file-oriented systems without databases [224] lead to many difficulties in handling this kind of documents. For example, by leaving document-file objects intact multi-user mode is not supported. The granularity is on the document level. Concurrently authoring different parts of the same document is cumbersome at least. Besides that, if versioning is to be supported then each task has to have a copy of the entire document even if only a small fragment of the document will be modified. On the other hand, fragmentation of documents in database applications, as practised so far [58, 262, 57], also has a number of shortcomings. For example the question how documents are fragmented in an optimal way cannot be generally answered. Either a very generic document structure has to be chosen, or only a few predefined specific document types can be supported. From our point of view, this is the main distinction between the notions to be presented in this article and other approaches to store documents within databases. While others limit themselves to design database schemata for just one or a few document types our system can handle documents of arbitrary types. Furthermore, by designing database schemata for individual document types, it is implicitly assumed that document types do not change over long periods of time. If the system is based on a very generic document type, this view might actually be sufficient, but this is not sufficient for a more refined approach to document handling [7].

In our approach logical document-component types of SGML correspond to classes in the database. To be capable of handling arbitrary document types and of incorporating document-type changes into the system these classes are created dynamically and may in principle be modified at runtime. The underlying OODBMS VODAK provides the relevant system support. SGML document-type definitions (DTDs) introduce the logical components of a document of a particular type. Hence, with this approach the decision how the documents are fragmented in the document base is shifted to the designer of the DTD. In this article we will describe the kernel structure of our application framework and the functionality it offers to the applications illustrated. Another facet, dynamic DTD handling, has already been discussed in [3].

The remainder of this article is organized as follows: In the following section SGML concepts are briefly reviewed in brevity. Section 7.3 contains a short overview of the VODAK Modeling Language. Both Section 7.2 and Section 7.3 form the basis to describe our database application framework. This description is given in Section 7.4. Section 7.5 deals with the integration of HyTime semantics. In Section 7.6 the additional functionality which may be obtained by coupling the framework with other systems components is documented. Conclusions are contained in Section 7.7.

7.2   Review of Basic SGML Concepts

SGML (Standard Generalized Markup Language) has received considerable attention, because it provides the means to tackle some of the problems related to document handling. In the SGML context, the distinction between a document's *logical structure* and its *layout structure* is fundamental: Italicizing or boldsetting a word is on the layout side. Identifying the reason why a word should be italicized, e.g. because it is introduced right there, is on the logical level. This identification can be accomplished by *marking up* the document. In the document fragment in the upper right of Figure 7.1 `<title>` and `<body>` are examples of *start tags*, `</title>` and `</body>` are the corresponding *end tags*. With SGML a document's logical structure can be predefined. A document consists of document elements, e.g. `title, body, new_term`. The relationship between them is specified by a set of production rules called *document type definition (DTD)*. Figure 7.3 contains a fragment of the DTD of the document instance from Figure 7.1. A section consists of a title followed by a body. A

```
Specific markup
To get a feeling for what markup is, consid-
er the traditional processing of texts...
```

```
...<section author="Eric van Herwijnen">
<title>Specific markup</title>
<body><paragraph>To get a feeling for what
<new_term>markup</new_term> is, consider the
traditional processing of texts...</paragraph>
</body></section>...
```

Figure 7.1 SGML Example: Markup

Misuse of SGML concepts: Markup does not capture the logical structure

```
<bold>Specific markup</bold>

To get a feeling for what <italic>markup</italic>

is, consider the traditional processing of texts...
```

Figure 7.2 SGML Example: Misuse of Markup

paragraph's content is a list whose components are either **CDATA** elements or new terms. Lists are defined using "*", alternatives by using "|". In a nutshell, **CDATA** is a "plain data type" comparable to STRING. Sections have an attribute author of type **CDATA**. - From another perspective, DTDs are machine-independent document-interchange formats.

Using SGML inter alia has the following advantages.

- Authors can concentrate on the document content rather than its layout.

- We call the fact that the same layout is used for the same logical document components *document consistency*. It is fostered by using markup instead of "private" layout conventions. If big documents are composed without using markup it can easily occur that one author, say, underlines new terms and another one italicizes them. Document consistency is an issue both within documents as well as among several documents. It is a contribution to corporate identity.

```
<!ELEMENT document  section*>
<!ELEMENT section   (title, body)>
<!ATTLIST section   author          CDATA>
<!ELEMENT title                CDATA>
<!ELEMENT body                 paragraph*>
<!ELEMENT paragraph (CDATA|new_term)*>
<!ELEMENT new_term  CDATA>
```

Figure 7.3: SGML Example: Fragment of an SGML Document Type Definition

- A marked-up document bears more information than one without markup. With markup authoring is eased especially if there are several authors or other persons involved in the process, e.g. reviewers.

- Queries making use of the document structure can be formulated, e.g. "Select all new terms." or "Select all sections whose title contains the word: markup.". SGML is most useful to identify logical document components whose function is not evident even to a human reader. In a big reference work there may be two dozens of reasons why, say, a word might be italicized.

- Attributes for document elements can be introduced (see Figure 7.1 and Figure 7.3 for attribute `author`). This further eases (multi-)authoring and querying.

SGML Terminology. In SGML a document has a tree structure: the nodes, i.e. the logical document components, are called *elements*. The subelements of an element are its *content*. The leaves contain the *data content*. In Figure 7.1 there are elements `section`, `title`, `body` etc. There is a differentiation between *generic* and *specific document descriptions*. For instance, the specification that a section contains a list of paragraphs is generic. On the other hand, stating that a section consists of a particular paragraph p1, followed by paragraph p2, is specific. An *element-type definition* is the generic description of an element, i.e. the set of rules specifying its content and attributes. The element-type name is also called *generic identifier*. The generic description of the content of elements of a particular type is its *content model*, the one of the attributes the *attribute model*. In SGML there exist six *constructors* to construct a content model from other element types, three *connectors* and three *occurrence indicators*. For instance, the *sequence connector* (,) introduces an order of the content-element types, '*' is the *optional and repeatable occurrence indicator*.

`CDATA` and `#PCDATA` being examples of *terminal element types* contain textual data. - Aside from SGML there is the standard ODA [131] and various proprietary formats to describe documents' logical structure. The concepts that are discussed in the sequel can quite easily be applied to other formats.

7.3 Key Concepts of the VODAK Modeling Language (VML)

Applying OODBMSs has turned out to be advantageous with regard to various application domains. Because there exist conceptual and terminological differences between different OODBMSs and OOPLs the terminology of the VODAK Modeling Language (VML) is reviewed in brevity. With object-oriented models the data and the procedures that process them tend to be grouped in autonomous

```
CLASS PARAGRAPH METACLASS METACLASS
    INSTTYPE
        PARA_INSTTYPE;
END;

OBJECTTYPE PARA_INSTTYPE
    INTERFACE
        METHODS
            retrieveTextualContent(): STRING;
            ...
    IMPLEMENTATION
        PROPERTIES
            content: STRING;
        METHODS
            retrieveTextualContent(): STRING;
            ...   //method implementation omitted
END;
```

Figure 7.4 VML Code Fragment

entities, the *objects*. We call the constituents of an object *properties* and *methods*. Properties are the variable-like containers for the data, methods the procedures capturing objects' semantics. In our terminology, the object's *type* is its property- and method definitions. As usual, objects' unique identifiers are given out and administered by the system. In the VML conception, *classes* are sets of objects of the same type. In VML, it is possible that instances of different classes are of the same type. The separation of the structural and the extensional aspect is called *dual model*. With main-stream OODBMSs this differentiation is not made. In VML classes are first-class objects. With the OODBMS VODAK both data and operations on it are administered by the system. The advantage is that the application semantics is within the database system. A sample code fragment is given in Figure 7.4. The INTERFACE-part is the public part, the IMPLEMENTATION-part the private one. The metaclass of the class is preceded by the keyword METACLASS. METACLASS is a metaclass provided by the system that does not furnish a particular semantics for its instances and metainstances.

Metaclasses are a special feature of VODAK. A metaclass is a class whose instances are themselves classes. Symmetrically, a *metainstance* is an instance of a metaclass's instance. As a rule, a class definition contains the definition of its instances' types. In VML terminology, this type is the *insttype* of that class. In addition, it is possible that an object has properties or methods the other instances of its class do not have. (This is a relaxation of the principle that all instances of a class are of the same type.) Those individual properties and methods are part of an object's *owntype*. Furthermore, the properties and methods in a metaclass's *instinsttype* are the ones of its metainstances. Hence, an object has the properties and methods defined in its owntype, in its class's insttype and in its metaclass's instinsttype.

Inheritance. In VML there is a distinction between three kinds of *inheritance*. Two of them are mentioned here: *type inheritance* and *inheritance via metaclasses*. It is possible to factor out a portion of an object-type definition and

```
CLASS CATSPEC METACLASS METACLASS
    //This metaclass is metaclass of both gener-
    //alization and specialization classes. Namely,
    //in multi-level inheritance a class can be both
    //generalization and specialization class.
    INSTTYPE CATSPEC_INSTTYPE
    INSTINSTTYPE CATSPEC_INSTINSTTYPE
END;
```

Figure 7.5 VML Code Fragment of a Metaclass

to reuse it in other object-type definitions. This mechanism is called type inheritance or *subtyping*. On the other hand, the definition of a metaclass contains properties and methods of their instances and metainstances. The phenomenon that an object or an application class has properties and methods that are neither part of the object definition nor the class definition but instead part of a metaclass definition is referred to as inheritance via metaclasses.

Semantic Relationships. A reason why metaclasses are in use is to model semantic relationships between classes. Examples of semantic relationships are *aggregation ("partOf")* or *specialization*. For example, a section may be an aggregation of subsections, a subsection an aggregation of chapters, and a chapter an aggregation of paragraphs. Some OODBMSs offer hardcoded mechanisms to describe relations between classes (cf. IS-A and IS-PART-OF relationships [18]). However, semantic relations have a variety of facets. Furthermore, some facets, which are called dimensions in [119], impinge on the interface. E.g. within an aggregation the order of the components may be relevant (as with the chapters of a book) or not (as with the ingredients of a fruit salad). With hardcoded mechanisms the opalescence of these relations cannot fully be taken into account. We are convinced that a flexible mechanism such as freely definable methods for VML metaclasses' instances and metainstances is mandatory to come up with an appropriate modeling. - Once a kind of aggregation has been modeled and implemented on the metaclass level it need not be repeated in the individual cases, e.g. between classes SECTION and SUBSECTION, between classes SUBSECTION and CHAPTER, and so on. An integrity constraint to be verified by an aggregation-metaclass method is that there are no cycles in the aggregation hierarchy, such as SECTION - SUBSECTION - CHAPTER - PARAGRAPH - SECTION, to give an example.

The approach to specialization is basically the same. To introduce our terminology, consider bibliographical entries that can be categorized into independent publications (books), dependent ones (articles), special publications (dissertations, proceedings etc.) and journals. We call an individual bibliographical entry a *generalization instance*, an individual journal and the like *specialization instances*. One real-world object is represented by different database objects. In VML there would be a class BIBENTRY on the one hand and classes INDEPPUB, DEPPUB, SPECPUB and JOURNAL on the other hand. The class BIBENTRY is called *generalization class*, classes such as JOURNAL *specialization classes*. The real-world features all objects being categorized have in common are modeled

```
OBJECTTYPE CATSPEC_INSTTYPE
    INTERFACE
    METHODS
        defHasSpecCls(specCls: OID): BOOL;
            //This method is applied to a generalization class to specify that the class
            //'specCls' is one of its specialization classes.
        defHasGenCls(genCls: OID): BOOL;
            //Symmetrically, the target is the specialization class, and the parameter
            //('genCls') is the generalization class.
        ...
    IMPLEMENTATION
    PROPERTIES
        hasCatSpecClasses: {OID};
            //This property contains the specialization classes.
            //The property values are the OID of the specialization classes.
        GeneralizationClass: OID;        //symmetrically...
        ...
END;
```

Figure 7.6 VML Code Fragment of a Metaclass's Insttype

```
OBJECTTYPE CATSPEC_INSTINSTTYPE
    INTERFACE
    METHODS
        initHasSpec (specInst: OID): BOOL;
            //This method is applied to a generalization instance to specify that the object
            //'specInst' is one of the specialization instances.
        initHasGen(genInst: OID): BOOL;
            //Symmetrically, the target is the specialization instance, and the parameter
            //('genInst') is the generalization instance.
        ...
    IMPLEMENTATION
    PROPERTIES
        genOfObjs: {OID};                //spec. instances
        specOfObj: OID;                  //gen. instances
        ...
END;
```

Figure 7.7 VML Code Fragment of a Metaclass's Instinsttype

as the generalization instances' properties and methods. We call this principle *generalization principle*. The example is one of *category specialization*. While category specialization reflects the objects' structure, *role specialization*, on the contrast, reflects the objects' behavior, e.g. **STUDENT** or **PATIENT** are role-specializations of **PERSON**. A relevant fragment of a metaclass for category specialization is given in Figures 7.5, 7.6, and 7.7. OID ('object identifier') is the type of objects of arbitrary types.

In this context it is important that in VML instances of metaclasses can be created at runtime. Their type and the metainstances' type is part of the metaclass definition.

7.4 A VODAK Application Framework for SGML Documents

7.4.1 Modeling Issues

This section describes the core structure of a prototypical VODAK application framework for the storage of structured documents. It seems to be a straightforward option to model element types as VML classes being part of the schema. SGML attributes would be just properties. In that case, however, the requirement that DTDs must be modifiable dynamically would not be met. System shutdown every time a DTD is altered or a new one is introduced would not be acceptable.

Overall Structure. We differentiate between document-type-independent features, document-type-specific ones and HyTime-specific ones. On the one hand, elements have element-type-independent or document-type-independent characteristics, e.g. the fact that they make up a hierarchical structure with other elements. On the other hand, attributes, to give an example, are element-type- or document-type-specific. Correspondingly, the schema consists of a *document-type-independent layer*, the *document-type-specific layer*, and the *Hy-Time layer* as in Figure 7.8.[||] HyTime-related issues are part of the following section. Classes are represented by ellipses. Objects that are not classes are just dots. The fact that an object is an instance of a class is displayed by a plain line arrow between them.

The distinction between 'document-type-specific' and 'document-type-independent' is according to the generalization principle. For every SGML-element type there is a corresponding application class in the document-type-specific layer . In the sequel, we refer to these classes as *element-type classes*. Each element-type class is a specialization class of the class DOCUMENT_ELEMENT in the document-type-independent layer. For every real-world document element there is an instance of the corresponding element-type class and another one of the generalization class DOCUMENT_ELEMENT.

Document-Type Independent Layer. The objects in the document-type-independent layer have the element-type-independent features, due to the generalization principle: The structural information is part of this layer, as well as, say, methods to navigate through the tree.

In the previous section metaclasses modeling aggregation and specialization have been described. The class DOCUMENT_ELEMENT and its instances take part in more than one semantic relationship: First, the category-specialization relationship with element-type classes as specialization classes, second, the aggregation relationship. In this particular partOf-relation parts and wholes are instances of the same class, namely DOCUMENT_ELEMENT. Because document elements may take part in the partOf-relation independent of their type, the partOf-relation is between generalization instances, due to the generalization

---

[||]The diagram includes the class system 'metaclass - (application) class - instances'. The rungs of this hierarchy will be referred to as levels. Levels and layers are orthogonal.

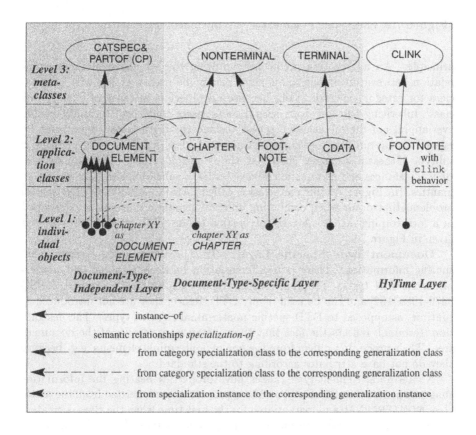

Figure 7.8 Overview of the Modeling

```
CLASS Document_Element METACLASS CP
    INSTTYPE
        INTERFACE
        METHODS
            getUp(): OID;
            ...
                //Method to navigate through the document tree
                getElementTypeName(): STRING;
                    //Method that can be invoked for SGML elements of arbitrary types
        IMPLEMENTATION ...
    END;
```

Figure 7.9 VML Code Fragment of the Document-Type Independent Layer

principle. An aggregation metaclass capturing the semantics of the partOf-relation between document components cannot be used together with a metaclass for category specialization, because an object is instance of exactly one class: Inheriting features from several metaclasses could lead to unforeseeable overlappings of the metaclasses' types. Instead the metaclasses' types must be related via the subtype mechanism. A new metaclass is defined: The insttype is subtype of these metaclasses' insttypes; the same holds true for the instinsttypes. Hence, instances and metainstances have both specialization and aggregation semantics. (In Figure 7.8 this metaclass is called **CATSPEC&PARTOF**.) The special problems that occur when combining different semantic concepts are described in a forthcoming article. A relevant portion of the VML-code for this layer is given in Figure 7.9.

Document-Type Specific Layer. This layer bears the element-type-specific information. There is a differentiation between *terminal* and *nonterminal element types*. Terminal element types such as **CDATA** are part of ISO 8879-1986 [132] and can be used in any DTD. Hence, they are not introduced at runtime, as opposed to DTD-specific nonterminal element types. The designation 'terminal' reflects the fact that their instances are leaves of the document tree. Their processing differs from the one of nonterminal elements, e.g. because they do not have attributes according to the standard.

Nonterminal element-type classes have properties bearing the information that constitutes the element type. These properties are inherited from the metaclass **NONTERMINAL** and instantiated for the first time when the class is created. Likewise, the properties and methods of the element-type classes' instances are inherited from that metaclass. The dual-model conception facilitates the creation of element-type classes without defining new types. Element-type classes are containers for SGML elements of the same element type. - In Section 7.2 it has been implied that SGML DTDs are essentially grammars defining the documents' structure. The semantics of document components does not follow from the element-type definitions.** The effect is that no element-type-specific processing is necessary. Element-type classes' instances are of the same VML

***

** An exception are SGML types ID, IDREF, IDREFS. These types, however, need not be used in connection with documents having a tree structure only. Therefore, they have not been introduced.

```
CLASS TERMINAL
METACLASS METACLASS
    INSTTYPE
        INTERFACE METHODS
            createElem(): OID;
                //returns the OID of newly created terminal elements,
                //e.g. instances of PCDATA
            IMPLEMENTATION ...
```

Figure 7.10: VML Code Fragment: Metaclass for Terminal Element-Type Classes

```
CLASS PCDATA METACLASS TERMINAL
    INSTTYPE
        INTERFACE METHODS
            getContent(): STRING;
            setContent (newContent: STRING): BOOL;
        IMPLEMENTATION PROPERTIES
            content: STRING;
        ...
```

Figure 7.11 VML Code Fragment: Class Comprising **#PCDATA** Elements

type. In the database, the content of an SGML element is a list of instances of the generalization class DOCUMENT_ELEMENT. The attribute values are, according to the SGML standard, a sequence of characters. The interpretation of user-defined attribute types is not part of SGML. The code fragments in Figures 7.10 through 7.12 serve as an illustration. '|[...]|' are list delimiters. The method setContent is element-type-specific because it is only meaningful for non-terminal element-types. Furthermore, the method may check the new content's conformance to the element-type's content model. Hence, the method performs differently for different element types.

Type-to-Class Mapping. Figure 7.13 is a fragment of Figure 7.8: The boxes next to the objects indicate from which types the objects inherit their properties and methods. An instance of DOCUMENT_ELEMENT, for instance, has the properties and methods defined in the instinsttype of CATSPEC&PARTOF and the ones from the insttype of DOCUMENT_ELEMENT. The line between types within a box display the subtyping relation: CP_INSTINSTTYPE is subtype of CATSPEC_INSTINSTTYPE and of PARTOF_INSTINSTTYPE. The plain lines outside the boxes connect the types with the classes where they are defined.

7.4.2   Functionality and Experiences

Querying Documents. With our approach queries may refer to documents' structure. This is accomplished by introducing appropriate methods both for the document-type independent objects and the element type classes' instances. The following queries based on the document-type definition in Figure 7.3 serve as illustrations.

```
CLASS NONTERMINAL
    OWNTYPE
        INTERFACE
        METHODS
            createElementType (elemTypeName: STRING, ...): NONTERMINAL;
            ...
                        //returns the newly created element-type class
    INSTTYPE SUBTYPEOF CATSPEC_INSTTYPE;
        INTERFACE
        METHODS
            setContentModel (newContentModel: STRING);
            setAttributeModel (newAttributeModel: STRING);
            createElem(): OID;
            ...
        IMPLEMENTATION
        PROPERTIES;
            elementTypeName: STRING;
            contentModel: STRING;
            attributeModel: STRING;
            ...
    INSTINSTTYPE SUBTYPEOF CATSPEC_INSTINSTTYPE;
        INTERFACE
        METHODS
            setContent (newContent: I[OID]I): BOOL;
            ...
```

Figure 7.12: VML Code Fragment: Metaclass for Nonterminal Element-Type Classes

1. "Select all sections whose author is Neuhold".

   Using the VODAK Query Language VQL this query can be expressed as follows:

   ```
   Q1 :=ACCESS s
        FROM s IN section
        WHERE (s − > getAttributeValue ('AUTHOR') == 'Neuhold')
   ```

   In this query the typing of SGML elements is exploited. **section** denotes the object identifier of the class object corresponding to the element type **section**. In query 4 it is shown how to obtain the object identifier of a particular element-type class.

2. "Select all new terms being contained in sections selected in Q1."

   ```
   ACCESS d
   FROM d IN DOCUMENT_ELEMENT, s IN Q1
   WHERE (d− > isContainedIn (s − > categorySpecializationOf()))
           AND (d − > getElementTypeName() == 'NEW_TERM')
   ```

   In this case the tree structure of SGML documents is referred to. Note that s is in the document-type specific layer, but d is in the generalization layer. categorySpecializationOf is used to shift between these layers. The method isContainedIn makes use of documents' tree semantics.

3. "Select the first elements of the documents."

```
ACCESS d − > getFirst()
FROM d IN DOCUMENT_ELEMENT
```

This query makes use of document contents' ordering. From the DTD we can infer that the elements selected represent elements of type **section**. getFirst is a method to return the first content element.

4. "Select all element-type classes representing element types with content model: **paragraph***."

```
ACCESS n
FROM n IN NONTERMINAL
WHERE n.contentModel == 'PARAGRAPH*'
```

The query illustrates that in our framework DTDs can be accessed in a natural way.

We claim that with this approach document querying is as expressive as with other approaches currently discussed in literature [46, 236]. The sample queries could now be optimized by using application-specific semantics [4].

Concurrency Control. Extended functionality, as compared to previous approaches to document handling, is our objective. Multi-authoring (i.e. multi-user mode) and versioning have been mentioned. - In VML there exists the possibility to brace a sequence of operations to a transaction. Then the DBMS inter alia ensures that no interleaving with other operations occurs. Multi-authoring need not be realized as part of the database application, but instead built-in features can be applied. The code fragment in Figure 7.14 is part of a sequence of operations generating an instance of the DTD in Figure 7.3. The meaning of BEGIN_TRANSACTION, COMMIT_TRANSACTION and ABORT_TRANSACTION is canonical. BODY is the object identifier of an instance of NONTERMINAL, i.e. an element-type class. The method createElemType creates a new instance of the class NONTERMINAL. Because in VODAK classes and metaclasses are first-class objects they can receive method calls. The second operation sets the content model of the element-type class BODY to '(Paragraph)*'. Now an instance of BODY can be created: The method createElem actually creates two objects: An instance of the target-element-type class and the corresponding generalization instance. The first one is returned; the variable body is instantiated with it. In the next step, the content of body is instantiated with a list of paragraphs: para1 and para2 are instances of DOCUMENT_ELEMENT that must have been created

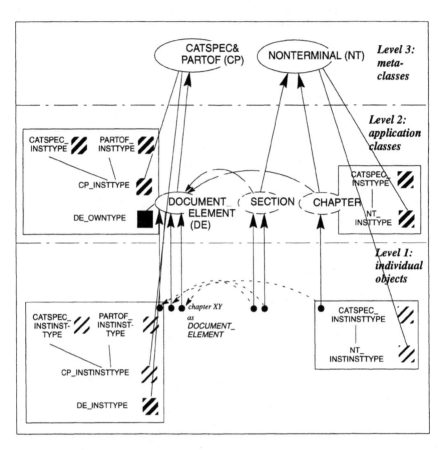

Figure 7.13: Dual Model: Document-Type Independent and Document-Type Specific Layers

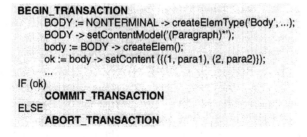

Figure 7.14 Example Using VML Transactions

before. ok is a variable of type BOOL. setContent returns TRUE iff it executed as foreseen.

Versioning. For versioning it is necessary to break down the authoring process into so-called tasks. As a rule, each task's end corresponds to a version of the document, the result of the task. With our approach granularity for versioning is on the SGML element level: If within a task a small portion of the document is altered, it is not necessary to generate a copy of the entire document, but only copies of the elements that have been modified. They are generated automatically by operations being part of the versioning metaclasses if within the current task a copy of the element being modified has not yet been generated. Hence, the interface of edit-operations (e.g. setContent) needs not be altered. On the other hand old document versions can be read and new versions can be derived from them. In the world of non-versioned objects, for example, there is a method printDocument. In the world of versioned objects it has a counterpart printDocument (task: taskType) displaying the state of the document at the end of the relevant task.

Coupling with SGML Parser. To insert documents as a whole into the system, the SGML parser ASP ("Amsterdam Parser") [250] is coupled with the database application. The ASP has been extended to invoke the methods creating the database objects that represent the logical document components. This is already part of the parsing process. On the other hand, the parser also checks the document's conformance to its DTD. Because after the parsing process it is known that the document is correct certain verifications can be omitted that are part of the operations in the general case. For instance, one axiom states that the aggregation relation is cycle-free. This is checked within the corresponding operation of the metaclass PARTOF every time a new relation is introduced. Because of the documents' correctness after parsing, i.e. the document has a tree structure, checks of this kind can be omitted when inserting documents the way just described. This is advantageous for performance reasons. The metaclass PARTOF provides another version of that operation without that check. It is to be used within the coupling with the ASP. This is feasible because of the extensibility of the data model, i.e. the freely definable methods in metaclasses. Application-specific knowledge is not only necessary to model semantic relationships. It is also advantageous with regard to efficiency.

Experiences. Setting up the hierarchical structures representing documents in the database naturally results in an overhead for storage with regard to time and size. Documents stored in OODBMSs according to their tree structure naturally occupy more disk space than stored as a file: First experiments indicate a growth in size by a factor of ten for "structure-only" documents as compared to an ASCII file representation. Because "normal" documents exist, to a large degree, of text, which does not lead to any enlargement of the tree, the average factor to be expected is substantially lower.

Previously, our applications have been based on an SGML document base which, in turn, is based on a relational database system. It seems that updates for small document sets (i.e. both number and size of documents are small) are comparable in duration to our current system. For large document sets relational systems reportedly tend to cause problems. The reason is that systems based on this technology have to stick to a fixed schema. Hence, relational tables inevitably grow. This effect is not to be expected with a dynamic approach such as the one presented in this article. Besides that, with the relational paradigm access requires a large number of join operations. Thus one would expect that an object-oriented system behaves superior already for small document sets. With our implementation this experience has actually been made. In addition, frequent access operation schemes can easily be accelerated both in a general or SGML-specific manner. An example of an access scheme with optimization potential would be the search for the content of elements of a particular element type. Another example are pointers from document elements to the root element speeding up that kind of navigation.

7.5 Extending the Framework with HyTime Features

The objective of a significant portion of the concepts and technologies that are commonly subsumed under the term 'digital libraries' is the processing of multimedia documents. For multimedia documents the internal structure of the documents must be taken into account, as explained in Section 7.1. At a naive level of analysis, the HyTime standard is seen as an extension of SGML to deal with documents' hypermedia content. However, a more differentiated view is necessary because SGML documents may already be multimedia documents with hyperlinks. The objective of the HyTime standard is to capture the document elements' semantics. With SGML, it is only the structure of documents that can be defined. The element's interpretation is left to the reader and, hence, is not uniform in general. With hypermedia documents where document components need actually be processed this is not sufficient. Thus, the HyTime standard essentially is a list of element-type definitions together with an informal, but binding specification of these elements' processing semantics. Element-type definitions with a fixed semantics are referred to as *architectural forms*. The architectural forms provided by the HyTime standard are classified into modules according to their function: in addition to a basic module there are the measurement module and the location module, whose architectural forms can be used to identify arbitrary locations in the documents or the presentation space, e.g. the seventh to eleventh word, the hyperlinks module, whose architectural forms are templates for link structures, a scheduling module, whose elements are indeed useful for (time-dependent) multimedia content, and a rendition module (that is of minor importance in this context). In most cases, in application-DTDs HyTime architectural forms are not directly included, but instead refinements of them are introduced. Refinements of architectural forms are possible in two ways,

```
<!element    clink          -- Contextual link --
                            (%HyBrid;)*>
<!attlist    clink          HyTime      NAMEclink
                            id          ID
                            linkend -- Link end --
                               ...
                                        IDREF    ...>
```

Figure 7.15 Example of HyTime Architectural Forms

```
<!ELEMENT    footnote#PCDATA>
<!ATTLIST    footnoteHyTime              NAMEclink
                            id          ID
                            linkend IDREF
                            following  ID>
```

Figure 7.16: Example of Element-Type Definition in HyTime Application DTD

1. by introducing additional attributes,

2. by confining the range of content or attribute types.

For illustration purposes consider the example taken over from [3] with slight modifications. The name of the architectural form clink (see Figure 7.15) is short for 'contextual link'. An instance of clink is a reference together with content, such as footnotes (see the element-type definition being part of an application DTD in Figure 7.16). With regard to '(%HyBrid;)*' in this content it suffices to know that '#PCDATA' is a specialization of it (cf. item 2 from above). It may be helpful to have a reference from a footnote to the following one. To this end, the attribute following that is not part of the architectural form clink has been introduced (cf. item 1). The attribute HyTime in Figure 7.16 specifies that footnote is a specialization of a HyTime architectural form, namely clink.

With regard to the realization of architectural forms the following observation is fundamental. The (HyTime-)aspect is a role specialization of the corresponding SGML element. However, a metaclass ROLESPEC for role-specialization classes and instances cannot be applied in a straightforward way: Analogously to SGML element-type classes the corresponding role-specialization classes need be created dynamically. Hence, they themselves as well as their instances need to inherit property- and method definitions from their metaclass. A metaclass provides both the role-specialization semantics and the semantics of a particular HyTime architectural form. Again, the type definitions are related via subtyping (see Figure 7.17). A relevant fragment of the metaclass corresponding to clink is contained in Figure 7.18. getReferencedElement is a fairly simple example of a method reflecting the semantics of the architectural form clink. To summarize, an SGML element with HyTime semantics is represented by three database objects: A generalization object bearing the element-type-independent semantics, a specific one with element-type-specific features and one with properties and methods modeling the HyTime semantics.

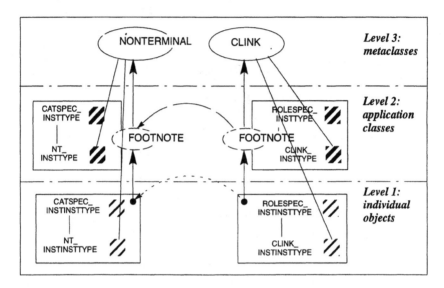

Figure 7.17 Dual Model: HyTime Layer

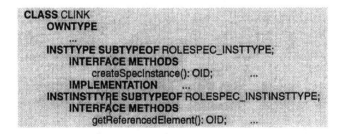

Figure 7.18 VML Code Fragment: Metaclass for Architectural Form clink

7.6   Embedding the Application Framework in Various Scenarios

In this section an integral scenario is described that may rely on the database application framework presented in the previous section. Extensions such as the ones that will be described are meaningful in order to offer typical services of digital libraries. Some of these extensions have been, others are currently realized as part of the project HyperStorM ('Hypermedia Document Storage and Modeling') at our institute.

7.6.1   Coupling with Information-Retrieval Systems

Combining content orientation with structure orientation in queries on documents is an issue of current research. Examples for queries of that kind are 'Select all documents whose introduction deals with the information highway.' or 'Select all section headers about the World Wide Web.'. On the one hand, we are aware of systems being able to handle documents of arbitrary structure [35]. However, instead of content-based search there merely exists the possibility to search the text for patterns. On the other hand, with state-of-the-art information-retrieval systems a fixed set of document types is allowed at best. In [57], to give an example, there is a limited set of document-component types such as paragraph or section which may be referred to in queries on documents' content.

When coupling information-retrieval systems with database applications there is a principal distinction between loose coupling and tight coupling. With tight coupling the information-retrieval functionality is part of the database application. With loose coupling data is not shared. There is merely communication on the documents between the database application and the information-retrieval system. Tight couplings in general are more efficient and less space-consuming. However, with tight coupling one is confined to a certain approach towards information retrieval.

Recently, at our institute a loose coupling between our database application and the information-retrieval system INQUERY [39] has been realized. INQUERY index structures are set up for elements of certain types. These element types can be chosen arbitrarily. If an element's content is modified or an element is created or deleted the index structure is altered accordingly. It is not advantageous to set up INQUERY index structures for elements with little textual content (less than 30 words as a rule) because meaningful content-based queries are not possible. On the other hand consider queries referring to document elements with INQUERY index structures existing only for their components. Experience shows that relatively good results are obtained by sending the query to the components and combining the results, e.g. by using the maximum-function or sum-function, whatever is appropriate.

7.6.2 Combining Documents' Content with Knowledge Bases

With the extremely large amount of data to be administered in digital libraries the assumption that access can be accomplished without additional knowledge is not realistic. Consider the query 'Select the descriptions of all German universities.'. In order to evaluate this query the names of these institutions are first retrieved from a database. These names are inserted into the query to the document base. Furthermore, independent from a particular application scenario the knowledge base may also contain fuzzy terminological knowledge that, analogously, may be called upon to evaluate document queries [147]. - To model knowledge semantically rich data models are advantageous. The possibility to make a broad variety of modeling primitives available has been an objective when developing VODAK.

7.6.3 Handling HTML Documents

While the primary structure of conventional documents is a tree, as described in Section 7.2, hypertext documents have a graph structure. The World-Wide Web (WWW) [192] is such a hypertext structure whose nodes may be physically distributed without restrictions.†† The nodes are conformant with an SGML-DTD, the HTML-DTD ('Hypertext Markup Language'). In addition to this DTD there is a universal naming scheme for documents so that the WWW can be browsed as one large document. With HTML, SGML concepts are, to a degree, misused. The strict distinction between logical and layout structure has been dissolved because in this special context it is supposedly more convenient. E.g. there is an element type 'Line Break', and element type 'Paragraph' has attributes 'align', 'indent' etc. Another interesting feature is that actions, i.e. how to process the document together with some user entries, can be specified. In this context it is important to notice that HTML documents are SGML documents, and, thus, can be stored using our database-application framework. When accessing WWW documents through a database typical database-integration problems can be encountered. Namely, WWW servers can be seen as external multimedia databases. According to [143] one can distinguish two different stages in database integration, the *syntactic transformation phase* and the *semantic integration phase*. In the syntactic transformation phase the external databases' representation is transformed so that it can be accessed and manipulated by the database serving as the integration platform. In our case, this is VODAK. To this extent two approaches may be considered.

- With regard to the first approach it is assumed that a relatively small number of external documents is accessed frequently. Under this assumption physically importing the document is a reasonable approach. A WWW document can in principle be considered as a pair (location identifier,

---

†† The WWW is another example for the phenomenon that the boundary between intra- and inter-document processing is not clean-cut. On the one hand the WWW can be seen as one large document, from another perspective the individual nodes are documents in their own right.

SGML document as file). Hence, importing the document into the database only needs internet access via the location identifier and consecutive parsing of the SGML file. Parsing is possible due to the coupling with the ASP. However, a restriction in this context is the fact, that the majority of HTML documents is not conformant to the DTD. Presentation of these documents in principle is possible, storage according to the logical structure, on the other hand, is subject to restrictions.

- With regard to the second approach there is the assumption that large numbers of documents will be queried rather seldomly. In that case physical import does not make sense. It is necessary to provide an appropriate view on the documents according to their virtual logical representation. This can be facilitated by allowing parsing operations on the documents in query evaluation [5].

Once access to WWW documents is provided in one way or the other, the semantic integration phase begins. Several ways of semantic enrichment and integration are feasible with regard to WWW documents: The most obvious option is to support the particular HTML-semantics. In particular, supporting the semantics of HTML's world-wide links, e.g. by resolving them explicitly to physically imported documents, is conceivable. Furthermore, in many cases WWW documents are in accordance with some implicit editorial conventions. To make this implicit structure and semantics explicit, e.g. by transforming the documents to more application-specific document-type definitions, is subject to current research [7]. Consider conference proceedings in HTML format available only via WWW (cf. [2]). It might be necessary to transform these proceedings from HTML to proceedings conformant to a DTD in another format. A third item that may be subject to further work is overlapping information in the WWW. Different approaches for providing an integrated view (on this potentially contradicting information) would have to be developed. Schema integration is a related issue in the database area [143].

Different issues with regard to the integration of WWW document bases in an SGML database have been discussed. They reflect a particular kind of architecture: The database is on the consumer side. This might be particularly relevant to improve access for special interest groups in the WWW. It may be known that they regularly access a certain fragment of the WWW. Improving access has two facets: First, by caching frequently accessed documents access is substantially accelerated. Second, by enriching the documents syntactically and semantically, retrieval capabilities are enhanced in a nontrivial way. Such a "consumer server" will be used by several users. To this end, DBMS functionality is mandatory.

Another topic remaining to be explored is the use of SGML database technology on the document producer side. This will be particularly significant with a large number of users contributing to a WWW documents' "archive". Without database technology this can only be accomplished by an archiver's manual intervention. Otherwise consistency of the archive is at stake. Conventional database updates would correspond to the insertion of documents that are completely new.

7.6.4 Coupling with DFR-Archive

With the current version of the database application framework documents are apportioned to pools. Pools are merely sets of documents. For some applications this classification is appropriate. To meet the requirements arising in connection with digital libraries a more sophisticated approach is imperative. The DFR-standard is a platform to define the documents' classification. There is a primary structure, which is hierarchical: The root is referred to as *DFR root group*, the internal nodes are *DFR groups*. A document or a DFR group may directly be contained in one DFR group. Besides that, there are DFR reference objects that model a containedIn-relationship between DFR groups that are not directly related in the tree. Names and attributes for the individual DFR objects are freely definable thus reflecting the concrete application semantics. Documents' internal structure likewise is not part of a DFR specification. A DFR archive that has been realized on top of VODAK is described in [179]. - The combination of a DFR archive with our database application for SGML documents is advantageous if a large number of SGML documents is to be administered. Consider a DFR structure for travel guides classifying documents by the location they describe. Furthermore, assume that these travel guides are SGML documents having an introduction. Then queries such as, say, 'Select the introductions of all documents about Heidelberg' can be formulated and evaluated.

7.6.5 Architecture

The disposition of the individual components of the digital library for structured documents we envision is displayed in Figure 7.19. Arrows reflect the flow of data between the components. In more detail, arrows labeled with A stand for documents' insertion into the document base. Arrow B reflects the fact that SGML documents can be generated from the database content in a straightforward way. - The MultiMedia Forum is an interactive online journal published by our institute. An issue of the journal consists of a number of articles, but the reader is free to look only at the documents he is interested in. Articles are SGML documents conformant to an SGML-DTD with inter-document references. From a different perspective, it is the entire issue of a journal that might be seen as a document in its own right. Then these links become intra-document references.

7.7 Conclusions

Starting point of this article has been the observation that both a documents internal structure as well as the relations between documents should be properly reflected when documents are stored in digital libraries. The phenomenon that

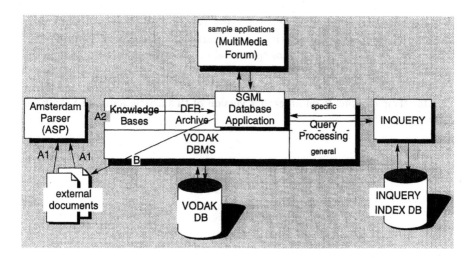

Figure 7.19 Proposed Architecture for SGML-based Digital Library

the dividing line between inter-document relationships and intra-document relationships is not clean-cut has been hinted at by means of examples, such as the WWW. Describing documents according to their internal structure is advantageous with regard to the various services offered by digital libraries. Within our database application framework documents of arbitrary types can be handled. Querying documents according to their structure is an issue currently attracting researchers' attention [11, 46, 23]. The queries given there can also be formulated using the VODAK Query Language VQL. Some sample queries have been formulated to sketch the expressive power of VQL. We have briefly explained how to amalgamate the system with the extension toward HyTime semantics. Besides that, the coupling with other modules for enriched functionality has been explained. The systems that have been mentioned in this context are an information-retrieval system, knowledge bases and a DFR archive. An interface to the WWW has also been discussed.

The main issued of this chapter has been that storage of SGML documents of arbitrary types is possible with VODAK. The VODAK data model differentiates between types and classes. If the necessary types are defined, classes may be generated at runtime. This feature is exploited both for the dynamic creation of element-type classes and for role-specialization classes bearing HyTime semantics. In the application framework there exist metaclasses reflecting the semantics of the different HyTime aspects. The corresponding types are combined using the subtyping mechanism of VODAK to provide the necessary types for the HyTime-oriented classes created for the different applications. Using an OODBMS has the general advantage that the application semantics - in this case the SGML and HyTime semantics - are part of the database.

Leaving aside the completion of the integration of the components mentioned in Section 7.6, an issue that may be part of future work is to improve the efficiency of retrieval operations. With documents stored in accordance with their hierarchical structure optimization of tree structure retrieval is an important topic. There will also be even more potential to optimize access by including the other system components that will contribute to an integrated digital library.

Acknowledgements. We thank Peter Muth, Thomas Rakow and Marc Volz for their comments on an earlier version of this article and Ute Sotnik for correcting mistakes.

Chapter 8

Document Recognition for a Digital Library

Sargur N. Srihari*, Stephen W. Lam† and Jonathan J. Hull‡,

8.1 Introduction

An important part of the development of a digital library [DL] is the transformation of digital images of documents into an ASCII representation. Although newer entries in a conventional library may be in electronic form already, the majority of library archives is still in printed form. The latter needs to be automatically recognized, represented in a form suitable for information retrieval [IR], and integrated.

The transformation of digital images of print documents into text-searchable form is popularly known as document image understanding [DIU], and includes the processes of *document layout understanding, text recognition* and *logical linking*. All of these steps are crucial for IR.

Document layout understanding [DLU] includes the processes of *segmenting* multiple page documents into text, graphics, and halftone images, *labeling* these elements into meaningful entities (such as title, author, section header, etc.), and *grouping* these entities on the same page or from different pages into logical units. The text regions are processed by an optical character reader [OCR] which produces ASCII. A DLU system which uses an adaptive approach can be applied to a variety of documents.

An important part of document recognition is the recognition of the images of text. Current OCRs operate mainly on a character-by-character basis and at times a lexicon is used to postprocess the results. This provides reasonable accuracy. However, OCR performance can suffer when the input images are degraded, for example, when microfilm is processed. We have developed a new

---

*Center of Excellence for Document Analysis and Recognition (CEDAR), State University of New York at Buffalo, 520 Lee Entrance, Suite 202, Amherst, NY 14228, USA, Email:srihari@cedar.buffalo.edu

†Center of Excellence for Document Analysis and Recognition (CEDAR), State University of New York at Buffalo, 520 Lee Entrance, Suite 202, Amherst, NY 14228, USA, Email:lam@cedar.buffalo.edu

‡Center of Excellence for Document Analysis and Recognition (CEDAR), State University of New York at Buffalo, 520 Lee Entrance, Suite 202, Amherst, NY 14228, USA, Email:hull@cedar.buffalo.edu

method for interpreting the results of a text recognition algorithm based on concepts from IR.

The logical linking of document elements is important for IR. Figures, tables, equations and bibliographies can be automatically retrieved when the text that matches a user query has explicit or implicit references to those elements. This is difficult when the images are degraded, since the figure and table numbers may consist of only a single digit, probably of poor quality. Our solution to the linkage problem detects the reference links in the text and locates the referenced elements. This will allow the user to retrieve specific areas of the document which are related to the query rather than retrieving the entire document.

The following describes the three areas mentioned above in more detail.

8.2   Adaptive Document Layout Understanding

Recognition problems occur when there are a variety of page layout, print quality and contextual differences. This research focuses on improving the methods used to process large volumes of documents which are found in a typical library. The DLU process consists of four stages: (i) skew correction, (ii) block segmentation, (iii) block classification, and (iv) layout understanding. Block segmentation and classification can be broadly grouped into a single stage called zoning. Since most of the techniques developed for zoning require content of a document with proper alignment, a skewed document image has to be corrected prior to the zoning stage.

8.2.1   Skew Correction

A fast skew correction algorithm based on the estimation of the projection profile complexity [130] has been developed. Projection profiles on the foreground pixels are generated at several orientations ($\pm10°$ are used). It detects the orientation of the white gaps between text lines (see Figure 8.2.1). The orientation of the profile with the largest variance will be selected as the skew angle of the document. A document image is first partitioned into several small regions. Only those text regions will be used to determine the document orientation. It can also process documents with text printed in a vertical direction such as Chinese and Japanese documents (in this case, $80° - 100°$ are used). It can accurately estimate the skew within 0.5 degree and takes 3 CPU seconds on a SUN SPARC2 for a letter-sized document.

8.2.2   Block Segmentation and Classification

Layout analysis starts with block segmentation which decomposes the digital image of a document page into regions. The process locates large streams of white space (background analysis) running horizontally or vertically. Streams that are considered region boundaries are used to partition the image into regions.

a tilted axis. The recognition result is shown in Fig. 21(b). (We overlayed a grid of the range image of the model, which was transformed by the resulting transformation on top of Fig. 21(a).) In Fig. 21(c) and (d), we show the final hypotheses, which lead to the result in Fig. 21(b). Hypotheses 2 and 3 and 18 and 19 are overlaid.

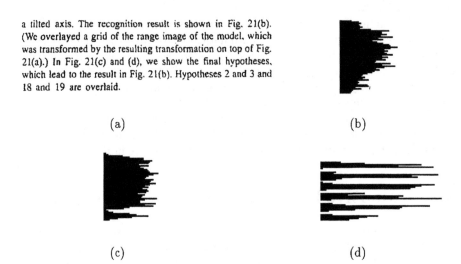

(a)   (b)

(c)   (d)

Figure 8.1: Profiles of a text block generated at different projection orientations: (a) image contains skewed text, (b) profile projected at -3°, (c) profile projected at 0°, and (d) profile projected at 3°.

A region must be bound by two horizontal and vertical background boundaries. Criteria of considering a white stream as region boundary are derived from the analysis of all the white streams in the page image. Non-boundary white streams, which are usually smaller in size, separate elements of the same region such as those between text lines. This global statistical approach does not need to predefine the size of the white streams, which varies from page to page. This local adaptive method increases the robustness of the segmentation process. Figure 8.2.2 shows the regions of a document after block segmentation.

The next step is classifying a region into one of the structural categories such as text, line drawings, tables and photographs. The classification of a region is performed by matching a set of features extracted from the region against the predefined reference features of a category. This approach allows the addition of new categories only if they contain distinctive features. Therefore, it has great flexibility in handling various types of documents.

8.2.3   Layout Understanding

Region labeling is to assign a region a document specific semantic tag. Different documents have different sets of tags, *e.g.*, a text region on a technical journal is labeled as title while a text region on a newspaper page is labeled as headline. Therefore, this process is knowledge-driven. The knowledge contains information about all possible semantic tags on a page and their spatial relationships.

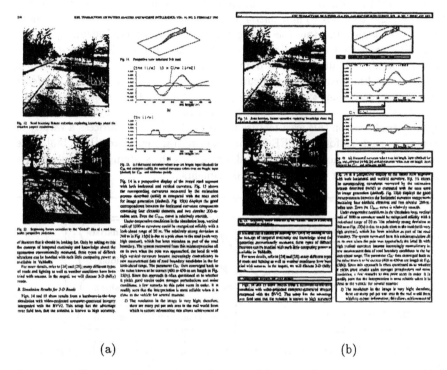

(a)   (b)

Figure 8.2: Result of block segmentation. (a) Original document image. (b) Regions located by the block segmenter.

Logical grouping is invoked when all the pages of the document have gone through the previous stages. The physical partition of document elements becomes transparent to the grouping process. The grouping is guided by the knowledge about the content of the whole document. For example, the knowledge for analyzing a technical publication defines all the essential components of a journal. The group process locates all these components according to given specifications. The results of the grouping process contain the logical units and their physical locations represented in SGML format.

The tasks of labeling and grouping can be combined into a single process called layout understanding. A system can be categorized as either "closed" or "open", depending on whether it is designed for a particular class of document. Most systems in use today are closed systems, *i.e.*, they are designed for some specific documents (such as forms, specific journals and business letters). They cannot easily be adapted to other types of documents.

An open system architecture has been developed at CEDAR. It is designed for processing multi-page documents, *i.e.*, it generates a logical interpretation of a document by combining information on different pages of the document. The architecture, (see Figure 8.2.3), consists of three components: control, knowledge base and tool box. The *Control* possesses some general purpose document analysis strategies and the *Tool Box* contains a set of generic document image processing tools that are applicable to different documents. The system has no prior knowledge about document domain. The use of strategies and tools relies solely on the knowledge of the document of interest defined in the *Knowledge Base*. Since document-specific knowledge is not part of the system, it can be viewed as input (in addition to the document images) to the system. A prototype system based on this architecture has been developed to process a variety of documents such as forms, IEEE journals and postal mailpieces [154, 153]. The research focus is on how to use knowledge to adjust the system reading strategies for handling different types of library documents.

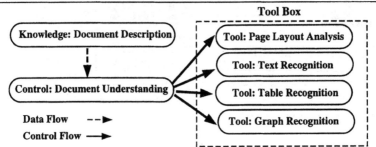

Figure 8.3 Components of an adaptive document understanding system.

8.3 Text Recognition Using Document Context

The recognition of word images is a solution to text recognition in which images of text are transformed into their ASCII equivalent. Word recognition algorithms are an alternative to traditional character recognition techniques which rely on the segmentation of a word into characters. This is sometimes followed by a postprocessing step that uses a dictionary of legal words to select the correct choices.

Errors in the output of a word recognition system can be caused by several sources. When a noisy document image is input, the top choice of a word recognition system may be correct relatively infrequently. However, the ranking of the dictionary may include the correct choice among its top N guesses ($N=10$, for example) in nearly 100% of the cases.

Solutions for improving the performance of a text recognition system have utilized the context of the language in which the document was written. An observation about context beyond the individual word level that is used here concerns the vocabulary of a document. Even though the vocabulary over which word recognition is computed may contain 100,000 or more words, a typical document may actually use fewer than 500 different words. Thus, higher accuracy in word recognition is bound to result if the vocabulary of a document could be predicted and the decisions of a word recognition algorithm were selected from that limited set only.

This chapter discusses a methodology to predict the vocabulary of a document from its word recognition decisions. The N best recognition choices for each word are used in a probabilistic model for information retrieval to locate a set of similar document in a database. The vocabulary of those documents is then used to select the recognition decisions from the word recognition system that have a high probability of correctness. Those words could then be used as "islands" to drive other processing that would recognize the remainder of the text. A useful side effect of matching word recognition results to documents from a database is that the topic of the input document is indicated by the titles of the matching documents from the database. The algorithmic framework discussed in this chapter is presented in Figure 8.3. Word images from a document are input. Those images are passed to a word recognition algorithm that matches them to entries in a large dictionary. *Neighborhoods* or groups of words from the dictionary are computed for each input image. The neighborhoods contain words that are *visually* similar to the input word images.

A matching algorithm is then executed on the word recognition neighborhoods. A subset of the documents in a pre-classified database of ASCII text samples are located that have similar topics to the input document. The hypothesis is that those documents should also share a significant portion of their vocabulary with the input document.

Entries in the neighborhoods are selected based on their appearance in the matching documents. The output of the algorithm are words that have an improved probability of being correct based on their joint appearance in both the word recognition neighborhoods as well as the matching documents. These are words that are both visually similar to the input and are in the vocabulary of the documents with similar topics.

8.3.1   Experimental Investigation

The word decision selection algorithm discussed in this chapter was demonstrated on the Brown corpus[151]. The Brown corpus is a collection of over one million words of running text that is divided into 500 samples of approximately 2000 words each. The samples were selected from 15 subject categories or genres and the number of samples in each genre was set to be representative of the amount of text in that subject area at the time the corpus was compiled.

Testing Data

One of the samples in the Brown corpus was selected as a test document to demonstrate the algorithm presented in this chapter. This sample is denoted

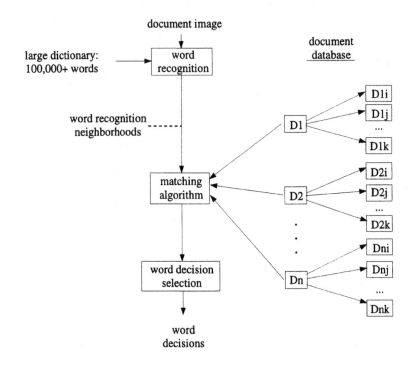

Figure 8.4 A proposed word matching algorithm.

G02 (the second sample from genre G: *Belles Lettres* and is an article entitled *Toward a Concept of National Responsibility,* by Arthur S. Miller that appeared in the December, 1961 edition of the Yale Review.

There are 2047 words in the running text of G02. After removing stop words and proper nouns, there were 885 words left. Raster images were generated for those words with a postscript-to-bitmap generation technique. This was done to provide test data for a recognition algorithm that would compute neighborhoods of visually similar words for each of the 885 input words. The stop words and proper nouns were excluded from the test data set since it was assumed that algorithms existed to find those words in a document image.

Neighborhoods were generated for each word in G02 with a word shape calculation in which a feature vector that describes the global characteristics of a word is compared to similar feature vectors for each word in a dictionary [125]. A ranking of the dictionary results in which words that are visually similar to an input image are ranked close to the top. For the experimentation discussed here, the approximately 53,000 unique words that occur in the Brown Corpus were placed in the dictionary.

The ten most visually similar dictionary words were calculated for each input word. This provided 8850 neighbors overall. The word shape calculation had performance of 87% correct in the top choice and 99% correct in the top ten choices.

Training Data and Results

The training data for the matching process and the word decision selection algorithm was the other 499 samples in the Brown corpus besides G02. The document matching algorithm described earlier was used to rank the other 499 samples for their similarity to G02.

The ability of the most similar samples determined by the matching procedure to select the correct word decisions from the neighborhoods was tested under three noise conditions using three selection criteria.

Noise was introduced in the word recognition output to test the tolerance of the decision selection procedure to imperfect input. A uniform random number generator was used to select a given number of neighborhoods from among those that had the correct decision as the first choice. The second choice was substituted for the first, thus providing a neighborhood that contained a visually similar, but incorrect, word in the first position. A 24% error rate was simulated by applying the above procedure to 93 of the 769 neighborhoods that were correct (i.e., the top choice of the recognition algorithm was correct). A 30% error rate was introduced with a similar method.

The top choices of the recognition algorithm were filtered by comparing them to the most similar samples and retaining the words that occurred in those samples. The three selection criteria that were tested included *overall* performance in which all the top recognition choices in G02 that occurred anywhere in the similar samples were retained.

The *G02-nouns* condition refers to the case where only the top choices for the nouns in G02 that matched any of the nouns in the similar samples were retained. The application of this selection criteria in a working system would assume the presence of a part-of-speech (POS) tagging algorithm that would assign POS tags to word images.

In the *matching-nouns* condition, only the nouns in the similar samples were used to filter the top recognition choices. This case was explored because nouns may be considered carrying more information about the content of a text passage rather than verbs or words with other parts of speech. Thus, the co-occurrence of nouns in two documents about similar topics should be due less to chance than other word types.

The results of word decision selection when applied to the original word recognition output (with 13% error at the top choice) are summarized in Table 8.1. When all the words in the most similar sample (J42) were matched to the top recognition decisions for G02 (top left entry in Table 8.1), it was discovered that 251 of those top decisions also occurred in J42. Of those, only nine words were erroneous matches. This corresponds to an error rate of about 4%. In other words, the correct rate for 28% of the input words was raised to 96% from the 87% provided by the word recognition algorithm alone.

The other results show that as more of the similar samples are used to filter the word recognition output, a progressively higher percentage of the eligible neighborhoods are included and the correct rate remains stable. For example, in the *overall* condition using the four most similar samples, 441 of the 885 (50% input words were effectively recognized with a correct rate of 97%. The results for the *G02-nouns* matching condition show that up to 26% of the input can be recognized with a 99% correct rate. In the *nouns-matching* condition, 29% of the input words can be recognized with a 97% correct rate.

Samples Used	Decision Selection Criteria								
	Overall			G02-nouns			Nouns-matching		
	M	E	C %	M	E	C %	M	E	C %
1	251	9	96	130	2	98	187	6	97
2	345	11	97	177	2	99	206	6	97
3	393	12	97	199	2	99	241	6	98
4	441	12	97	229	2	99	257	8	97
5	451	12	98	234	2	99	258	9	97
6	459	13	97	248	2	99	272	9	96
7	474	16	97	254	3	99	280	11	96
8	483	16	97	254	3	99	284	11	96
9	498	16	97	261	3	99	288	11	96
10	526	22	96	300	4	99	296	12	96

Table 8.1: Word selection performance on the original 885 neighborhoods (with 87% correct at the top choice). M=number of matches. E=number of errors. C=correct matches in percentage.

8.4 Logical Linking

An important step in logical linking is to detect the locations in the recognized text where linkings to other document elements are needed. There are two types of references: explicit reference and implicit (contextual) reference. The explicit references include the figure and table callouts, chapter and section references, and footnote and bibliography indices. The contextual references include keywords, key phrases and the domain of discourse of a text paragraph.

The explicit references are located by using graphical cues from the recognized text. The graphical cues provided by font change, case, point size, and underlines are used to locate the possible references. Figure and table callouts are indicated by upper cased words. Parenthesized text often contains figure and table callouts and bibliography indices. The system locates strings of characters delimited by an open and closed parenthesis. The objective is to to find text that has a high probability of being a reference. Footnote indices can be detected by the sudden change in point size and character baseline position of the characters at the end of a word.

The implicit references are located based on the content of caption of the figures and tables and the data entries of the table. Keywords or key phrases are extracted from these text areas and are used to find text where these keys are found.

8.5   Conclusions

Our work concerns three major processes which help to build a DL database for IR. Several components of the system are shown to be useful for creating a DL database. The design of these processes stresses the importance of robustness and ease of adaptation to the processing of different documents. Output generated by these processes facilitates the IR mechanism to produce intelligent response to user queries. An adaptive approach to document understanding was presented in this chapter. Its robustness was shown to be crucial to the success in processing varied library documents. This chapter also presented an adaptation of the vector space model for information retrieval to improving the performance of a word recognition algorithm. The neighborhoods of visually similar words determined by word recognition are matched to a database of documents and a subset of documents with topics that are similar to those of the input image are determined.

Chapter 9

Using Non-Textual Cues for Electronic Document Browsing

Daniela Rus[*] and Kristen Summers[†]

9.1 Introduction

The proliferation of information in electronic form, the development of high-speed networking and the evolution of digitized audio and video, make the flexible browsing and retrieval of electronic documents one of the grand challenges of computer science. Many word-based tools have been proposed in response to this challenge [61, 120, 138, 215]. Our methods use non-textual cues to complement the linguistic approach to information retrieval, as well as to provide more versatility for indexing and browsing. By *non-textual cues* we mean layout-oriented document components like figures, fonts, marks (such as bullet points), indentation, *etc.* For example, we can retrieve the paper in Figure 9.1 by posing a query that is visual in nature: "find the paper with a table at the top of the fourth page". Flexible and sophisticated document manipulation tools greatly increase the practical usefulness of electronic libraries. Unless users find electronic documents to be as easily manipulable as paper, they will resist the transition.

A typical browsing application in an electronic library is illustrated by the following example. Mike is interested in surveying papers on mechanical walkers. A keyword search over the Ei-Compendex database produces 936 records. Mike wants the flexibility to browse over the titles and authors of the papers. When a particular title appears interesting he wants a more detailed view, consisting of that paper's section titles. If this view continues to sustain his interest he wants to access more detailed pieces of the document, such as the full text of the abstract, all the figures that go with a particular section, or the performance tables for the mechanical walker. Current systems do not provide this flexibility; the work in this chapter leads to systems that do.

---

[*]Department of Computer Science, Dartmouth College, Hanover, NH 03755, rus@cs.dartmouth.edu

[†]Department of Computer Science, Cornell University, Ithaca, NY 14853, summers@cs.cornell.edu

We believe that the non-textual content of documents complements the textual content and should play an equal role in information retrieval. An illustrative example from the realm of speech (where non-verbal cues include facial expression, gestures, postures, tone of voice, *etc.*) is found in [214], where Oliver Sacks describes the hilarity generated on an aphasia ward by a presidential address. The patients, with no understanding of words as such but with a heightened sense of the visual and tonal aspects of communication, found the president's dishonesty so obvious as to be laughable. Their close attention to the details of the non-linguistic components of speech enabled them to see clearly the Actor's dissimulation, obscured for many normal viewers. This parallel is not just anecdotal. In our previous work [212, 213], we discuss classes of retrieval tasks that are supported by non-textual cues but not by word-based systems.

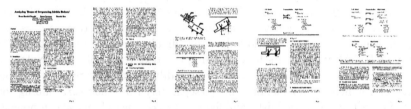

Figure 9.1: A zoomed-out view of an article on coordinated pushing with mobile robots. The first page has the title/author information represented as centered text. Page three has an itemized list. Pages three and four contain polygonal drawings of boxes. Pages four and five contain robot protocols presented in tabular form.

Structural, non-textual information can be used in the development of a variety of tools for document manipulation. Consideration of the logical locations of word occurrence (for instance, in the abstract versus a later section) can be used for improved weighting schemes in information retrieval systems. Logical structure may be directly mapped to automated markup in a format such as SGML [111]. Documents may be indexed according to the presence of (and relationships between) various logical structures. Such an index can enable flexible hierarchical browsing, based on expanding components to their subcomponents on request; it can also enable component-based queries such as "sections containing tables" or "figures from relevant sections," where relevance is determined by information retrieval techniques. Automated hyperlinking may proceed based on structural information, *e.g.*, a match between an element of the reference section in one document of a collection and the title of another might yield a reference hyperlink.

Our approach is to automate the *layout* analysis of electronic documents, in order to provide support for automated markup, intelligent document navigation, and conceptualized retrieval. Our methodology consists of developing algorithms to automatically detect and encode views of electronic documents that users might wish to request. Rather than explicitly and manually constructing all the possible models of a document, we provide flexibility by automatically building a hierarchy of partial models of the document. The layers in the hierarchy highlight different levels of detail. For example, a useful *zoomed-out* view (see Figure 9.1) reveals the presence of coarse-grained structures like figures, paragraphs, sections, *etc.*[‡], but hides the actual text.

Our algorithms are efficient, geometric in nature, and apply to *generic* documents, *i.e.*, the documents are not marked up, and nothing is known or assumed about the formatting tools that created them; we do not require even a very general Document Type Definition or grammar to define the document's representation of structure. Instead, we rely on the analysis of white space, a simple concept that we believe to be universally significant in text. The basic information consists of the quantity and location of white space in a block of text. We provide support for customizing browsing and searching in the form of algorithms for (1) segmentation, that is, discovering the topology of the logical hierarchy, and (2) classification, that is, labeling the nodes in the hierarchy with the structures they represent: paragraphs, itemized lists, sections, tables, and line drawings. The segmentation algorithm divides the document into a hierarchy of logical components by examining the text contours only. Note that our notion of logical components requires readily identifiable reasons to group together the included document elements separately from their surrounding context. Subsections, itemized lists, and figures are examples of logical components. The interpretation algorithms classify document portions as base-text, tables, polygonal drawings and graphs, and indented lists. We have implemented a prototype system based on these algorithms. Our experimental results are obtained by using the the Cornell Computer Science Technical Report electronic library and our data is presented in Section 9.4.

9.1.1 Outline

In the remainder of this section, we discuss previous related work.

In Section 9.2, we present the segmentation algorithm, which divides the document into a hierarchy of logical components by examining the text contours only (*i.e.*, the left and right white space). The algorithm itself is described in Subsection 9.2.1. In Subsection 9.2.2, we discuss the indentation language used by this algorithm to capture basic zoomed-out document views.

In Section 9.3, we describe and analyze interpretation algorithms for classifying document portions as tables (in Subsection 9.3.1), polygonal drawings and graphs (in Subsection 9.3.2), indented lists (in Subsection 9.3.3), and base-text.

In Section 9.4 we describe the implementation of our system. We present

---

[‡]The term zoomed-out refers to a document view in which only the shapes of its components are distinguishable; this corresponds roughly to the human eye perception of a paper document from a great distance. For example, the representation of a computer science technical paper includes the title and author information at the first level of the tree, the section structure at the second level, and the individual blocks of each section (text paragraphs, figures, tables, code) below.

data collected from the segmentation system, and we describe an experiment that uses our algorithms for (1) automatically marking up documents and for (2) non-textual retrieval tasks.

Finally, in Section 9.5, we talk about the implications of our results and future directions of work.

9.1.2   Previous Work

We are inspired by research in three areas: information retrieval, automated document structuring, and document processing as described in [30].

- *Information Retrieval.* In classical information retrieval [25, 33, 55, 93, 120, 215, 216], unstructured text is indexed based on its keywords. Each keyword that occurs in a collection is viewed as an axis in a large space. A document is viewed as a point in this vector space; its dimension along each axis is given by the frequency of the defining word in the document. This approach to representing documents yields an index that encodes information about document topics; we seek to supplement this with the content cues found in coarser patterns: tables, graphs, pictures, *etc.*

- *Automated document structuring.* The goals of the document structuring community are to identify the key constituents of a document image (sections, paragraphs, pictures, *etc.*) from its layout and represent the logical relationships between these constituents. This is a first step towards analyzing the contents of documents.

  Most work on document structuring applies only to documents whose format is known in advance. The systems in [134, 187, 202, 248], segment pages of one format type each. The systems in [176, 243] find a logical document hierarchy composed of paragraphs, subsections, and sections, based on knowledge of standard printers' formatting rules. In [198], hierarchies are built that also include intermediate structures; knowledge of the formatting rules for a particular document's style is required. For example, a document may be known to have been formatted with the LaTeX `article` style.

  Our approach finds document divisions at multiple levels of granularity. The algorithm is driven by the structure of the document, rather than prior knowledge of document layout rules. Thus, the height of the extracted hierarchy reflects the degree of nested structure within the document, and the algorithm performs reasonably when confronted with novel documents. Information about printers' rules can be incorporated naturally, in order to aid in characterization of the revealed structures.

- *Document Processing.* Work in document processing addresses the issue of document layout generation. In [30, 31, 84], a formal separation of document structure from its layout effects is proposed. The suggestion is that a document should be defined by its content and structure, according to a *source grammar*. Then an instantiation of the document can be formed by applying the layout rules of a *result grammar* to this defined structure. Different instantiations of the same document will be formed by applying different result grammars to the same document definition.

We support this effort; if the approach suggested in these works, together with a small set of document source grammars, becomes standard, then access to the definition of a document will make the task of finding that document's structure trivial. We do not, however, believe that the problem of finding document structure in general will disappear; paper shows no sign of becoming obsolete, and this approach will not help us to find structure in a scanned-in document. Nor is it likely ever to be the case that *all* electronically available documents are represented as definitions in a known source language.

9.2   The Segmentation Algorithm

In this section we present an algorithm that takes an electronic document and generates a hierarchy of partial models (or logical divisions.) The observation of repeated indentation structures is used to partition the document into sections, subsections, and other finer-grained divisions, including arbitrary degrees of nesting. The resulting tree is suitable for indexing, browsing, and searching: its divisions may be indexed according to information retrieval techniques, a document may be browsed by navigating through the tree, and a set of trees may be searched for documents that include components with required properties.

This layout segmentation captures the divisions of the document's logical structure. In order to generate a tree that describes the logical structure all that remains is to classify its nodes. For example, Figure 9.2 contains a miniature document with a centered title and two sections, at the coarsest level. Each section contains a structure in which the pattern *paragraph, list* is repeated; lists lie nested within these structures.[§] The document division algorithm generates the tree in Figure 9.3. This tree provides a useful document view in its own right; it also constitutes the topology of the tree in Figure 9.4. Elements of the node classification tasks needed for the construction of Figure 9.4 are addressed in Section 9.3.

9.2.1   The Algorithm for Generating the Logical Hierarchy

The algorithm works in a bottom up manner, building a tree of indentation structures from a given set of leaves. At each level, the nodes are characterized according to an *indentation alphabet*.[¶] The level is then searched for repeated indentation patterns; sets of nodes that form pattern elements are combined into new nodes at the tree's next level; then, each whole pattern becomes a block

---

[§]The two sections contain different types of lists.

[¶]Indentation alphabets provide symbols to express the indentation of blocks of text and rules for matching sequences for these symbols. They are defined formally in Subsection 9.2.2.

Figure 9.2 A miniature document

at the level above.‖ Each of the old nodes becomes a sub-block of the block described by the new node. (A node that does not participate in a repeated pattern is considered to form a pattern of length one. Thus, at the next two levels it remains a node, and each block it describes has a single sub-block: itself.) Then the indentations of the new level's nodes are characterized in the indentation alphabet, and the process repeats, until no new patterns can be found. The algorithm appears in Figure 9.5.

Our current implementation for step 1 includes two options: one divides the documents into text blocks and blank blocks, and the other divides the document into text blocks of one indentation value each. (A blank line has its own indentation value.) Each document line in such a block constitutes a sub-block. Other segmentation algorithms are possible, such as the one proposed in [213].

The hierarchical document divisions allow an arbitrary degree of nesting in

---

‖Between these stages, the current level is searched for isolated nodes that seem to interrupt patterns (such as an equation in the middle of a paragraph); these nodes are merged into surrounding nodes before the algorithm continues.

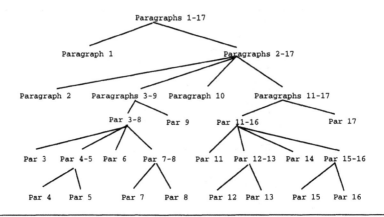

Figure 9.3 Indentation tree for the miniature document

the structure of the document. For example, in the algorithm in Figure 9.5, the enumerated list in step two forms an identifiable indentation structure, which is a part of the observable (higher-level) indentation structure consisting of steps one and two. With a carefully defined indentation alphabet (described in Subsection 9.2.2), the structure formed by the subsections and sections is also identifiable. The degree of such nesting in a given paper is arbitrary. Correspondingly, our bottom-up algorithm builds trees of arbitrary depth.

9.2.2   Indentation Alphabets

We now provide a formal specification of indentation alphabets; then we discuss the particular alphabet that our version of the algorithm uses. Finally, we offer a formal specification and analysis of the language defined by patterns in any indentation alphabet that shares the basic properties of ours.

Formal Definition of an Indentation Alphabet

Definition 9.2.1 *An* indentation alphabet *is a triple* $\langle \Sigma, D, R \rangle$, *where* Σ *is a set of symbols;* D *is a set of definitions for the symbols in* Σ, *such that, given a block of text made up of one or more sub-blocks, exactly one sequence of definitions describes the sub-blocks that make up the block; and* R *is a subsumption relation among the symbols in* Σ, *in the sense of Definition 9.2.2.*

Definition 9.2.2 *A* subsumption relation R *in an indentation alphabet* $\langle \Sigma, D, R \rangle$ *is a lattice over* $\Sigma^* \cup \top$, *where* $\top$ *is a special "top" symbol such that* $\alpha \in \Sigma^* \Rightarrow \top \succeq_R \alpha$.

If $\alpha \succeq_R \beta$, this is interpreted to mean that α represents an indentation form that subsumes the form represented by β. Thus, in the process of comparing

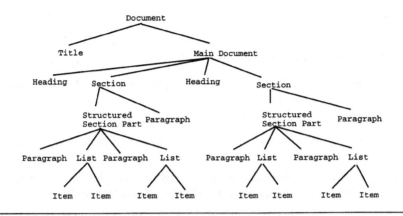

Figure 9.4 Goal tree for the miniature document

sequences of indentation alphabet symbols, an instance of β may be matched against an instance of α, yielding a pattern of α. Moreover, if $\alpha \succeq_R \gamma$ as well, then both β and γ may be matched as instances of the pattern α (without an explicit appearance of α). More precisely, the interpretation of the subsumption relation is: if the least upper bound of two sequences α and β is not $\top$, then the two sequences match, yielding a pattern of their least upper bound.

For example, *centered* $\succeq_R$ *both-justified* indicates that the form *centered* subsumes the form *both-justified*; a piece of text that is justified on both the left and the right may be a long piece of centered text. Hence, in comparing two sequences α and β, if an instance of *centered* is encountered in position i of α and an instance of *both-justified* is encountered in position i of β, with all previous symbols in the sequences matching, then these symbols are considered to match; the examined prefixes of α and β are instances of a pattern γ with *centered* in position i.

To see the effects of the least upper bound, consider an indentation alphabet containing a symbol *paragraph-start*, which represents an indentation followed by a move to the left margin. Suppose this alphabet also contains the symbols *indent, left-margin, centered, both-margins* and *right-margin*, each of which represents a single sub-block. Thus, the symbol *paragraph-start* appears instead of the consecutive symbols *indent, left-margin*. Centering that precedes a move to the left margin may also indicate a paragraph beginning, however; the appearance of centering may be an accident of line length. For example, consider Figure 9.6. The first line of the first paragraph is centered with respect to the left and right margins of the text. Similarly, right-justification may be an accident of line length, so a line that meets the right margin (but not both margins) followed by a move to the left margin may indicate a paragraph beginning. This can be seen in the second paragraph of Figure 9.6. To make the subsumption relation reflect these possibilities, it includes *paragraph-start* $\succeq_R$ *centered left-*

1. Divide the document into blocks at the lowest level by an external algorithm.

2. Repeat until no changes are generated

   (a) Represent each sub-block by an appropriate character of the indentation alphabet.

   (b) Find sets of blocks that form repeating patterns.

   (c) Group together the blocks in each element of each pattern, forming the next level of the tree.

   (d) Check for pattern interrupters; merge any such blocks into surrounding blocks. (If this generates changes, it creates another level.)

   (e) Group together the elements of each pattern, forming another tree level.

Figure 9.5 The segmentation algorithm for logical tree generation

margin and *paragraph-start* $\succeq_R$ *right-margin left-margin*. The representations of the paragraphs in Figure 9.6 are given in Figure 9.7. They do not match directly, but the subsumption relation matches them, as shown in Figure 9.8.

```
        The retrieval of information from conceptually-specified
queries has become one of the grand challenges of computer science
due to the proliferation of information in electronic form, the
development of high-speed networking, and the evolution of digit-
ized audio and video.
        Users will require tools for filtering information from large
distributed repositories.  The challenge as a whole is posed as
the Multimedia Information Capture and Access problem:  given an
electronic environment, capture it by acquiring partial models and
access the data according to users' requests.
```

Figure 9.6 Two paragraphs

We consider indentation alphabets that include the special symbols *start-block* and *end-block*. These symbols begin and end each block description, and they simplify the characterization of the type of patterns we seek (*i.e.*, those which include only complete blocks). Different choices of indentation alphabets yield different results; the alphabet may be adjusted for different goals without affecting the algorithm. Similarly, the method of deriving blocks and sub-blocks may be altered without affecting the indentation alphabet. This modularity increases the power and ease of use of both elements of the document divider.

Paragraph 1	Paragraph 2
Centered	*Right-Margin*
Left-Margin	*Left-Margin*
Left-Margin	*Left-Margin*
Left-Margin	*Left-Margin*
Left-Margin	*Left-Margin*

Figure 9.7 Representations of the paragraphs

Paragraph 1	Paragraph 2	Subsuming Pattern	
Centered	*Right-Margin*		
Left-Margin	*Left-Margin*		
Left-Margin	*Left-Margin*		$\Longrightarrow$
Left-Margin	*Left-Margin*		
Left-Margin	*Left-Margin*		

Paragraph 1	Paragraph 2	Subsuming Pattern	
		Paragraph-Start	
Left-Margin	*Left-Margin*		$\Longrightarrow \ldots$
Left-Margin	*Left-Margin*		
Left-Margin	*Left-Margin*		

Paragraph 1	Paragraph 2	Subsuming Pattern
		Paragraph-Start
		Left-Margin
		Left-Margin
		Left-Margin

Figure 9.8 Matching the paragraphs

Useful Subsumption Relation Types

We consider indentation alphabets whose subsumption relations have special properties that aid their computational use. We define a set of such properties that will enable us to find the least upper bound of two strings by comparing one symbol at a time, without backtracking.

First, we require that the least upper bound of two strings be derivable from the least upper bounds of their substrings.

Definition 9.2.3 *The subsumption relation of an indentation alphabet* $\langle \Sigma, D, R \rangle$, *is* normal *if*
$$(\alpha \succeq_R \beta \wedge \gamma \succeq_R \delta) \Longrightarrow (\alpha\gamma \succeq_R \beta\delta).$$

That is, in a normal subsumption relation, concatenation does not invalidate subsumption. In order for substring subsumption to fully control string subsumption, though, we need the following stronger condition.

Definition 9.2.4 *A normal subsumption relation R of an indentation alphabet $\langle \Sigma, D, R \rangle$ is divisible if*
$$(\text{lub}(\alpha, \beta) = \gamma) \Longrightarrow (\forall \delta, \eta \in \Sigma^* : \text{lub}(\alpha\delta, \beta\eta) = \gamma\text{lub}(\delta, \eta)).$$

This indicates that a pattern found by looking at the beginning of a sequence will not be invalidated by symbols later in the sequence. In pattern matching based on a divisible subsumption relation, substrings may be considered from left to right, without requiring backtracking. We define a new lattice, made up of the substrings that will need to be considered.

Definition 9.2.5 *The* minimal subsumption relation $R_{\min}$ *of an indentation alphabet $\langle \Sigma, D, R \rangle$ with a divisible R is the lattice over a subset of $\Sigma^* \cup \top$ such that*
$$(\alpha \succeq_{R_{\min}} \beta) \Longleftrightarrow$$
$$((\alpha \succeq_R \beta) \wedge$$
$$(\forall \alpha', \beta' \in \Sigma^* :$$
$$(\exists \gamma, \eta \in \Sigma^* : (\gamma \neq \varepsilon \vee \delta \neq \varepsilon) \wedge (\alpha = \alpha'\gamma \wedge \beta = \beta'\eta)) \Rightarrow \neg(\alpha' \succeq_R \beta'))).$$

Thus, α subsumes β in $R_{\min}$ if in R, α subsumes β, but no proper prefixes of α and β bear this relationship. The rules of $R_{\min}$ may be used for pattern matching according to a divisible R. For matching to proceed based on individual symbols, we need to constrain the form of $R_{\min}$.

Definition 9.2.6 *A divisible subsumption relation R of an indentation alphabet $\langle \Sigma, D, R \rangle$ is symbol-oriented if*
$$\forall \alpha, \beta \in \Sigma^* : ((\alpha \succeq_{R_{\min}} \beta) \Longrightarrow |\beta| = 1).$$

With a symbol-oriented subsumption relation, we can perform matches on one character at a time, in a manner based on the following definitions.

Definition 9.2.7 *The symbol lattice, R', of an indentation alphabet $\langle \Sigma, D, R \rangle$ with a symbol-oriented R is given by:*
$$\forall x, y \in \Sigma : ((x \succeq_{R'} y) \Longleftrightarrow$$
$$(\exists x_1, \ldots x_n \in \Sigma, \alpha_0, \ldots, \alpha_n \in \Sigma^* :$$
$$(x\alpha_0 \succeq_{R_{\min}} x_1) \wedge (x_1\alpha_1 \succeq_{R_{\min}} x_2) \wedge (x_2\alpha_2 \succeq_{R_{\min}} x_3) \wedge \ldots \wedge (x_n\alpha_n \succeq_{R\min} y)),$$
and $\forall x \in \Sigma : \top \succeq_{R'} x$.
The sequence $\alpha_0\alpha_1 \ldots \alpha_n$ is called the y-x addition.

Then, a pair of sequences to be matched according to a symbol-oriented subsumption relation can be thought of as a pair of stacks of symbols. At each step in the match, a symbol is popped off of each stack. Suppose these symbols are x and y. If the least upper bound z of x and y in the symbol lattice is not $\top$, then the match (so far) succeeds; z is appended to the subsuming pattern formed so far, the x-z addition is pushed onto x's stack, and the y-z addition is pushed onto y's stack.

The least upper bounds and additions can be calculated in advance, leading to an alternative representation of these subsumption relations as pairs of the form $\langle (x, y, z), (\alpha, \beta) \rangle$, where α is the x-z addition, and β is the y-z addition.

Our Indentation Alphabet

We use the following indentation alphabet. When characterizing the first sub-block in a block, the left and right margins of the document serve as the left and right edges of the "preceding sub-block."

- $\Sigma = \{$ *Start-Block, End-Block, Both-Justified, Left-Justified, ⟨Centered-In, m⟩, ⟨Centered-Out, n⟩, Centered, Left-In, Left-Out, ⟨Blank, h⟩}*, where m, n and h range over the positive integers.

- $D =$

  Start-Block Represents the beginning of a new block; does not correspond to a sub-block.

  End-Block Represents the end of the current block; does not correspond to a sub-block.

  Both-Justified A set of one or more consecutive sub-blocks, not all of which are blank, in which the text sub-blocks are both left-justified and right-justified with respect to the preceding sub-block.

  Left-Justified A set of one or more consecutive sub-blocks, not all of which are blank, in which the text sub-blocks are left-justified but not right-justified with respect to the preceding sub-block.

  ⟨ Centered-In, m ⟩ A set of sub-blocks containing m text sub-blocks, which are centered with respect to the preceding sub-block. The left edge of each of the m sub-blocks lies to the right of the left edge of its predecessor.

  ⟨ Centered-Out, n ⟩ A set of sub-blocks containing n text sub-blocks, which are centered with respect to the preceding text sub-block. The left edge of each of the n sub-blocks lies to the left of the left edge of its predecessor.

  Centered A set of one or more consecutive sub-blocks, not all of which are blank, in which the text sub-blocks are centered with respect to the preceding sub-block and cannot be represented as a sequence of the symbols ⟨ Centered-In, m ⟩ and ⟨ Centered-Out, n ⟩.

  Left In A non-centered text sub-block whose left edge lies to the right of the left edge of the preceding sub-block.

  Left Out A non-centered text sub-block whose left edge lies to the left of the left edge of the preceding sub-block.

  ⟨ Blank, h ⟩ A set of one or more completely blank sub-blocks, of total height h.

- $R_{\min}$ is given by:
  Left-Justified $\succeq_{R_{\min}}$ *Both-Justified,*
  Centered $\succeq_{R_{\min}}$ *Both-Justified,*
  Centered $\succeq_{R_{\min}}$ *⟨Centered-In, m⟩,*

$Centered \succeq_{R_{\min}} \langle Centered\text{-}Out,\ n \rangle,$

$Left\text{-}In \succeq_{R_{\min}} \langle Centered\text{-}In,\ 1 \rangle,$

$Left\text{-}Out \succeq_{R_{\min}} \langle Centered\text{-}Out,\ 1 \rangle,$

$\langle Centered\text{-}In,\ 1 \rangle \langle Centered\text{-}In,\ m \rangle \succeq_{R_{\min}} \langle Centered\text{-}In,\ m+1 \rangle$

$\langle Centered\text{-}Out,\ 1 \rangle \langle Centered\text{-}Out,\ m \rangle \succeq_{R_{\min}} \langle Centered\text{-}Out,\ m+1 \rangle$

R may also be expressed in our alternative form for symbol-oriented divisible subsumption relations as:

$\{ \langle (Left\text{-}Justified,\ Both\text{-}Justified,\ Left\text{-}Justified),\ (\varepsilon, \varepsilon) \rangle,$

$\langle (Centered,\ Both\text{-}Justified,\ Centered),\ (\varepsilon, \varepsilon) \rangle,$

$\langle (\langle Centered\text{-}In,\ m \rangle,\ \langle Centered\text{-}Out,\ n \rangle,\ Centered),\ (\varepsilon, \varepsilon) \rangle,$

$\langle (Centered,\ \langle\ Centered\text{-}In,\ m \rangle,\ Centered),\ (\varepsilon, \varepsilon) \rangle,$

$\langle (Centered,\ \langle Centered\text{-}Out,\ n \rangle,\ Centered)\ (\varepsilon, \varepsilon) \rangle,$

$\langle (\langle Centered\text{-}In,\ 1 \rangle, Left\text{-}In,\ Left\text{-}In),\ (\varepsilon, \varepsilon) \rangle,$

$\langle (\langle Centered\text{-}Out,\ 1 \rangle, Left\text{-}Out,\ Left\text{-}Out),\ (\varepsilon, \varepsilon) \rangle,$

$\langle (\langle Centered\text{-}In,\ m > 1 \rangle, Left\text{-}In,\ Left\text{-}In),\ (\langle Centered\text{-}In,\ m-1 \rangle, \varepsilon) \rangle,$

$\langle (\langle Centered\text{-}Out,\ n > 1 \rangle, Left\text{-}Out,\ Left\text{-}Out)\ (\langle Centered\text{-}Out,\ n-1 \rangle, \varepsilon) \rangle \}$

In this alphabet, no sub-block is ever initially identified as *Centered*; this symbol exists for its role in the subsumption relation. Sub-blocks may be determined to follow a pattern that includes the symbol *Centered*, at which point, an instance of $\langle Centered\text{-}In,\ m \rangle$ or $\langle\ Centered\text{-}Out,\ m \rangle$, or *Both-Justified* becomes subsumed by the symbol *Centered*.

The height of blank sub-blocks provides a distinction between sections and subsections, as well as other nested structures in which the divisions are indicated in part by vertical white space. Since section headings and subsection headings are typically represented in different font sizes, the space surrounding these types of headings differs. Thus, a section heading and its surrounding blank lines will not match the pattern formed by a set of subsections; the subsections will be recognized as a structure at one level, and the section containing them will form part of a section structure at a higher level. Without considering font information directly, we take advantage of its effects to enable our logical structure trees to include the useful structures of sections and subsections.

9.2.3 The Indentation Pattern Language

We now provide a formal specification for the language of the indentation patterns found by our algorithm, called the *block indentation patterns*, using an indentation alphabet that includes the special symbols *Start-Block* and *End-Block*. (This indentation alphabet is presumed to be symbol-oriented.) In preparation for this definition and its analysis, we first define a notion of *fully distinguishable* symbols in an indentation alphabet and a useful relations E_R over the symbols of an indentation alphabet.

Definition 9.2.8 *Given an indentation alphabet* $\langle \Sigma, D, R \rangle$, *with R symbol oriented, and* $x, y \in \Sigma$, *x and y are said to be* fully distinguishable *if, in the symbol lattice* $\text{lub}(x, y) = \top$.

Intuitively, x and y are fully distinguishable if they can never be considered a match, regardless of what follows them.

Definition 9.2.9 *Given an indentation alphabet* $\langle \Sigma, D, R \rangle$, *with R symbol-oriented, and* $\alpha \in \Sigma^*$, *the* R-Extension *of* α, *written* $E_R(\alpha)$, *is given by* $\{\beta | \alpha \succeq_R \beta\}$.

The R-Extension of α thus consists of everything α subsumes, *i.e.*, the set of sequences that may match a pattern of α.

Definition 9.2.10 *An indentation alphabet* $\langle \Sigma, D, R, \rangle$ *is said to be* block-oriented *if the following are true:*

- *R is symbol-oriented.*

- *Σ contains the symbols Start-Block and End-Block, which are fully distinguishable from all other symbols in Σ.*

- *$\Sigma - \{Start\text{-}Block, End\text{-}Block\}$ contains at least one pair of fully distinguishable symbols.*

This describes the kind of indentation alphabets we use. We seek patterns that include only whole blocks, by requiring that they begin with *Start-Block* and end with *End-Block*. This leads to the following definition of the patterns to be found.

Definition 9.2.11 *Given a block-oriented indentation alphabet* $I = \langle \Sigma, D, R \rangle$ *the language of its* block indentation patterns *P_I is given by:*
$$P_I = \{\alpha_1 \alpha_2 \ldots \alpha_n \mid (n > 1) \wedge$$
$$(\exists \beta \in Start\text{-}Block \; (\Sigma - \{Start\text{-}Block, End\text{-}Block\})^* \; End\text{-}Block:$$
$$(\forall i, 1 \leq i \leq n : \; (\alpha_i \in E_R(\beta))))\}$$

At first glance, parsing might seem like a natural method of finding patterns in this language. Unfortunately, the following result leads us to reject this approach.

Theorem 9.2.1 *For any block-oriented indentation alphabet* $I = \langle \Sigma, D, R \rangle$, *$P_I$ is not a context-free language.*

Proof: Application of the pumping lemma for context-free languages to the string: *Start-Block* $(xy)^n$ *End-Block Start-Block* $(xy)^n$ *End-Block Start-Block* $(xy)^n$ *End-Block* in which x, y are fully distinguishable elements of $\Sigma - \{Start\text{-}Block, End\text{-}Block\}$. Consider pumping down once. $\square$

This language is, however, context-sensitive. This result has computational implications for the recognition of the indentation structures described here. Since context-sensitive parsing is not sufficiently efficient for use in the domain of large documents, we do not parse, but instead use a quadratic algorithm guaranteed to find repeated patterns if any exist.

9.2.4   A Logical Hierarchy Example

We now turn to an example application of the logical hierarchy generation algorithm. We apply this algorithm to the first section of the miniature document in Figure 9.2. This document contains no pattern interruptions, so we do not discuss the step of finding them. Its initial representation, based on a division into text blocks and blank blocks, is given in Figure 9.9.

On the first pass, two repeated patterns are found: a block of *⟨Blank, 1⟩* followed by a block of *Left-In, Left-In* and a block of *⟨Blank, 1⟩* followed by a block of *Left-In, Left-In, Left-Justified*. (These correspond to the two indented lists in the section.) The pattern elements each have a length of 1 block, so grouping their nodes yields no changes and is therefore skipped. Combining the elements of these patterns yields the set of divisions found on the second level (from the bottom) of the tree in Figure 9.3. For readability, in the presentation of this tree, each node that remains unchanged at various levels of the tree has been represented only once, at the highest level at which it appears. The document divisions we find now include such nodes at all their levels. Similarly, blank blocks have been removed in Figure 9.3.

Characterizing nodes at this level yields the representation in Figure 9.10. Now, a new repeated pattern appears: a block of *Left-Justified* followed by a block of *⟨Blank, 1⟩*, *Left-In*, *⟨Blank, 1⟩*, *Left-Justified* followed by a block of *⟨Blank, 1⟩*. (This corresponds to the section's observable repetition of a paragraph followed by an indented list.) Again, each pattern element has a length of 1 block, so we skip directly to grouping the nodes in the whole pattern; the divisions of the third level of Figure 9.3 are found.

A similar process takes place simultaneously within Section 2, and as these iterate, the representation tree in Figure 9.3 is built.

9.2.5   Future Extensions

The following areas are promising directions for further investigations.

- The document dividing algorithm occasionally creates trees with "extra" levels; for example, an itemized list may first be recognized as two or three smaller patterns, and only recognized as one cohesive pattern at a higher level in the tree. With a formalization of node descriptions, it should be possible to identify many, if not all, such extra levels and remove them from the tree.

- Logical document components sometimes consist of patterns that are interrupted. For example, a section may consist of a series of paragraphs, interrupted by a single indented list (all of which is set in from the left margin). The current version of the algorithm will not, in general, successfully recognize such a component; we are investigating a solution to this problem based on incorporating a coarser-grained indentation alphabet (such as one that distinguishes only text blocks and vertical white space of different heights), to be called upon in such instances. We need to find

Start-Block   Left-Justified   End-Block
Start-Block   ⟨ Blank, 2⟩   End-Block
Start-Block   Left-In   Left-Out   Left-Justified   End-Block
Start-Block   ⟨ Blank, 1⟩   End-Block
Start-Block   Left-In   Left-In   End-Block
Start-Block   ⟨ Blank, 1⟩   End-Block
Start-Block   Left-In   Left-In   End-Block
Start-Block   ⟨ Blank, 1⟩   End-Block
Start-Block   Left-In   Left-Out   Left-Justified   End-Block
Start-Block   ⟨ Blank, 1⟩   End-Block
Start-Block   Left-In   Left-In   Left-Justified   End-Block
Start-Block   ⟨ Blank, 1⟩   End-Block
Start-Block   Left-In   Left-In   Left-Justified   End-Block
Start-Block   ⟨ Blank, 1⟩   End-Block
Start-Block   Left-In   Left-Out   End-Block
Start-Block   ⟨ Blank, 3⟩

Figure 9.9 Representation of miniature document's Section 1

a specification of the appropriate situations in which to apply the coarser
alphabet.

- The indentation alphabet needs to incorporate further analysis of the role
  of the right margin. At the moment, the standards for both-justification
  and centering are very rigid; this may or may not prove to be a good choice.
  Furthermore, no information is currently derived from the length of lines
  that are neither centered nor both-justified. Very short lines do, however,
  seem significant; they either indicate paragraph breaks or the inclusion of
  some structure other than running text. We need a characterization of the
  situations in which the right edge of a text block or line is significant.

Start-Block   Left-Justified   End-Block
Start-Block   ⟨ Blank, 2⟩   End-Block
Start-Block   Left-Justified   End-Block
Start-Block   ⟨ Blank, 1⟩   Left-In   ⟨ Blank, 1⟩   Left-Justified   End-Block
Start-Block   ⟨ Blank, 1⟩   End-Block
Start-Block   Left-Justified   End-Block
Start-Block   ⟨ Blank, 1⟩   Left-In   ⟨ Blank, 1⟩   Left-Justified   End-Block
Start-Block   ⟨ Blank, 1⟩   End-Block
Start-Block   Left-Justified   End-Block
Start-Block   ⟨ Blank, 3⟩

Figure 9.10 Second level representation of miniature document's Section 1

- The indentation alphabet might benefit greatly from an extension including a consideration of font. Although we can usually detect changes in font size by the spacing between lines, this approach may not always prove reliable. We can only make this distinction when the changes in font are sufficiently large with respect to the granularity of the document representation. In the case of a scanned-in document, we are not assured that all significant font changes are readily identifiable in this manner. Furthermore, font types as well as sizes carry significant information. For example, the LaTeX environment `description` [155] includes a boldface heading at the beginning of each item. An indentation alphabet that included font type would be able to distinguish between a list of this kind and one without such headings.

9.3   Classification Algorithms

In this section we present algorithms for labeling the nodes in the layout tree. We focus on three types of high-level logical structures that occur in documents: tables, figures consisting of line drawings and function graphs, and itemized lists. Recognition of these document elements combined with a small amount of text analysis enables the execution of conceptually specified retrieval tasks, such as "find precision recall measures for the CACM collection," "find performance graphs of the Byzantine agreement protocol," and "find a list of assumptions in this chapter" [8]. In the future, we would like to create a comprehensive library of structure detectors with performance guarantees.

9.3.1   A Classifier for Tables

Webster's Seventh Dictionary defines a table as a *systematic arrangement of data usually in rows and columns for ready reference.* Implicit in this definition is a *layout* component and a *semantic* component: the data is organized in columns of similar information. For instance, the table in Figure 9.11 has a marked 3-column layout with uniform structure (*date, —, Cassini Mission event*). The table in Figure 9.11 is completely regular: the columns line up perfectly, the entries stay within their allotted space, and each record has the same format. Furthermore, the content similarities of the column entries are reflected lexically. Not all tables are this regular. Consider the example in Figure 9.12: the records are two lines long, the columns in the second line of a record do not align with the columns in the first, some columns extend into adjacent ones, and there are lexical irregularities in its records. The layout and lexical structures are still clear. Our goal is to check for column and content structure while tolerating irregularities to within specified error bounds. Note that, in this we differ from [202], where the goal is to find the grid structure in a text component known to be a table.

‖This section is based on [161].

08/22/96 - Titan IV/Centaur Launch
03/29/97 - 66 Maja Asteroid Flyby
06/08/98 - Earth Gravity Assist
02/06/00 - Jupiter Gravity Assist
12/06/02 - Saturn Arrival
03/27/03 - Titan Probe Release
03/29/03 - Orbiter Deflection Maneuver
04/18/03 - Titan Probe Entry
06/30/03 - Iapetus Flyby
05/20/04 - Dione Flyby
09/12/04 - Enceladus Flyby
08/14/05 - Iapetus Flyby
12/31/06 - End of Primary Mission

Figure 9.11 Table of Key Scheduled Dates for the Cassini Mission

The Table Recognition Algorithm

The measure for the column layout of a block of text is given in terms of a data structure called the *white space density graph* and denoted by WDG. (It corresponds to the inverse of the vertical character projection.) Let B be a block of text of n rows and m columns and $w : \{c|c$ is a character $\} \rightarrow \{0, 1\}$ with $w(\text{" "}) = 1$ and $\forall c \neq \text{" "}, w(c) = 0$.

Definition 9.3.1 Vertical structure: *The* white space density graph *of B is the polygonal line* WDG $: [0, m] \rightarrow [0, 1]$ *defined by the points* WDG$(i) = \frac{1}{n} \sum_{j=0}^{n} w(B_{i,j})$, $\forall i \in N \cap [0, m]$.

Figure 9.14 shows the WDG associated with the table in Figure 9.12.

Definition 9.3.2 Deviations in vertical structure: *Given an error tolerance ϵ_v, a block of text has* column structure *if it occurs between two successive local maxima in the* WDG *above* $(100 - \epsilon)\%$.

Each local maximum is a candidate column separator. A candidate column is a real table column only if it has corresponding horizontal lexical structure. We are far from being able to identify row structure based on semantic content, but semantic uniformity in rows is highly correlated with lexical uniformity. We exploit this correlation in the design of a robust table detector.

The process of discerning lexical structure is facilitated by the presence of non-alphabetic characters. For example, it is easy to recognize that the entries of the first column in Figure 9.11 represent similar information, since they have a very regular and distinct lexical pattern. In distinguishing lexical structure, we identify the following equivalence classes of characters: alphabetic, numeric, and special (each special character is in its own class). Let $c_0, c_1, \ldots c_n$ denote the columns of a text block. We use regular expressions for generalizing the contents of a column. In Table 9.11, all items in the first column (the mission dates) can be described by the conjunctive regular expression $NN/NN/NN$, where N is a symbol denoting a number and $/$ is a special character.

The *lexical description* of a column c_i is a regular expression r_i that describes the smallest possible language that includes all elements of c_i, subject to the requirement that r_i is a non-trivial generalization of these elements. The regular expression $r_1 + \ldots + r_n$ is a *trivial* generalization of a given set of elements $r_1, \ldots, r_n$; all other generalizations are *non-trivial*.

Definition 9.3.3 Horizontal structure: *Consider the columns $c_1 \ldots c_n$ of a block of text satisfying Definition 9.3.2, and consider the lexical descriptions $r_1 \ldots r_n$ of these columns. This text also has* row structure *if and only if the language described by $r_1 r_2 \ldots r_n$ is non-trivial.*

100a	Introduction to Computer Programming	4	Lec1 TR	9:05	Ives	120
	Wagner		Lec2 TR	11:15	Ives	120
100b	Introduction to Computer Programming	4	Lec1 TR	9:05	Olin	255
	Van Loan		Lec2 TR	11:15	Ives	110
101	The Computer Age	3	TR	1:25	Upson	B17
	Segre					
102	Intro Microcomputer Applications	3	Lec1 TR	10:10	RR	105
	Hillman (Ag. Engr.)		Lec2 TR	12:20	RR	105
108	A Taste of UNIX and C	1(4wk)	MWF	3:35	Olin	255
	Glade	su				

Figure 9.12 A Schedule of the Introductory Computer Science Courses

Now consider Figure 9.12. This table lacks the lexical regularity of Table 9.11, because there are small irregularities in the lexical structure of the columns. To express this more rigorously, let M be a metric for string comparison (we use the Levenstein metric [218].) Given $\epsilon > 0$, two strings a and b are ϵ-similar if $M(a, b) \leq \epsilon$. We use ϵ_h-typings, defined below, of the regular expressions that correspond to the entries of a column in order to control the imperfections we allow in lexical structure.

Definition 9.3.4 Deviations in horizontal structure: *Given $\epsilon_h > 0$ and a set of strings, an ϵ_h-typing is a division of the set into disjoint subsets such that any two strings in the same subset are ϵ_h-similar.*

Lexical typing for a table is done in three parts. First, an ϵ_h-typing is performed on the candidate column elements. This generates an alphabet of types, to be used in the next step. Then, each candidate column is analyzed to determine a regular expression for its type (over the newly formed type alphabet). Finally, the lexical type of the table is obtained by computing the minimum regular expression over the column types. The ϵ_h-typing in the first step allows for the occurrence of multi-line records in a table and for ϵ_h tolerance in the record units. Note that a minimal ϵ_h typing partitions the elements of the column in the coarsest possible way; unfortunately, as shown in 9.3.1, finding such a typing is NP-complete. We instead find a useful typing that may not be minimal, as described in 9.3.1.

1. Form the WDG of the text block.

2. Find column separators of height $(100 - \epsilon_v)\%$ blanks. If none exist, the text is not a table, so quit; otherwise continue.

3. Perform an ϵ_h-typing on the regular expression representations of the entries of each column.

4. Find the lexical structure these typings imply, if any. If such a structure is found, the text is a table; otherwise, it is not a table.

Figure 9.13 The Table Detection Algorithm

Figure 9.13 describes the table detection algorithm. An example application of this algorithm to the table in Figure 9.12 follows. The first step in the algorithm is to create the WDG associated with it, by calculating the percentage of blank spaces in each column of the block. Figure 9.14 shows the WDG associated with the text in Figure 9.12. The second step is to look for column separators, *i.e.*, peaks in the graph of height at least $1 - \frac{\epsilon_v}{100}$. This graph has six high peaks, which are associated with the rivers of white space flowing between the seven columns in Figure 9.12. In the third step, each candidate column is analyzed for lexical structure. If the column description patterns can be combined into a regular expression across the entire table, the block of text is a table. Otherwise it is not.

Details and Analysis

We now analyze the robustness of the algorithm. Computing peaks in the WDG is quite easy. What is not obvious is how to determine a reasonable threshold value ϵ_v that robustly and efficiently filters columns from basic text. We measure efficiency as the cost of the actual computation, and the probability that base text is passed through unnecessary lexical analysis. One approach is to require the user to specify the value of ϵ_v using his knowledge about the data environment. Another approach is to have the algorithm statistically learn the value of ϵ_v by analyzing the WDG of tables identified by the user. A third solution does not rely on user assistance, but rather makes use of a probabilistic analysis of WDGs of basic text. The question we ask is: for a high peak value in the WDG, what is the probability that it corresponds to a true table column rather than a random distribution of spaces in basic-text? From this analysis, we extract a tolerance parameter that can be used as an absolute lower bound on ϵ_v for detecting tables with irregularities in layout.

The analysis makes the following assumptions:

- The average word length that occurs in text is known. For English, [151] have determined that the average word length of distinct words is 8.1 characters, but of word occurrences in written text, it is 4.7 characters.

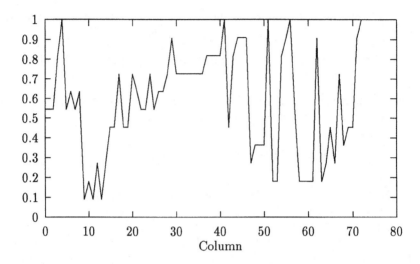

Figure 9.14 A White Space Density Graph for Table 2

For simplicity, we assume that in basic text, the average word length is 4 characters.

- The blank spaces in base text are distributed independently. This is due to the fact that the lengths of words and of the spacing between them are variable, and their occurrences in a line of text are random. We have tested the independence of the distribution of white space by extensive experiments with *Splus* [168]. This implies that the blank spaces of a line have a binomial distribution. Note that an interesting problem is to determine when the binomial distribution approaches a normal distribution; at present, we have no solution to this problem.

Let B be a block of text of n rows and m columns. Let p be the probability that a character c in a row is blank, and let $q = 1 - p$ be the probability that the character is non-blank. Note that an average word length of 4 characters yields $p = 0.2$ and $q = 0.8$. Let WDG be the white space density graph for B. Denote by WDG(k) the value for the kth column of B. Application of Chebyshev's theorem** yields

Corollary 9.3.1 *If the absolute value of a peak in the* WDG *is greater than* $np + h\sqrt{npq}$, *the probability that the peak is an occurrence of base-text is* $\frac{1}{h^2}$.

**For any distribution with standard deviation σ, at least a fraction $1 - \frac{1}{h^2}$ of the measurements differ from the mean by amounts at most $h\sigma$.

In other words, by setting the peak threshold to $np+h\sqrt{npq}$, with probability $\frac{1}{h^2}$ the presence of any value above the threshold is a candidate column separator in a table. The user can specify required confidence in identifying columns ($\frac{1}{h^2}$), and we can calculate the peak threshold, since n, p, q and h are all known.

Recall that the a block of text is a table if it has both vertical and horizontal structure. We now consider the complexity of lexical component analysis.

Theorem 9.3.2 *Finding the minimum ϵ-typing is NP-complete.*

Proof: Reduction of partitions into cliques. □

Although finding the minimum typing is a hard problem, a useful ϵ-typing can be found efficiently. An element is placed in a partition only if it is $\frac{\epsilon}{2}$-similar to the original element of that partition; when an element is encountered for which no such partition exists, it becomes the original element of a new partition.

The types of the entries of each column are assembled into the *type matrix*. A $m \times n$ type matrix is constructed for a block of text of m lines and n columns. If $t_{ij} = t_{i'j'}$ the data in row i and column j and the data in row i' and column j' are ϵ-similar. The type matrix for the table in Figure 9.12 is given in Figure 9.15. A GCD algorithm [146] can be used to determine the type, if any, of the overall matrix and thus to decide whether the matrix represents a table.

This efficient and robust table detector has been implemented and used to build information agents for retrieval tasks whose answers are found in tabular form [161].[††]

$$
\begin{bmatrix}
t_1 & t_2 & t_4 & t_6 & t_8 & t_9 & t_{10} \\
t_0 & t_3 & t_0 & t_6 & t_8 & t_9 & t_{10} \\
t_1 & t_2 & t_4 & t_6 & t_8 & t_9 & t_{10} \\
t_0 & t_3 & t_0 & t_6 & t_8 & t_9 & t_{10} \\
t_1 & t_2 & t_4 & t_0 & t_8 & t_9 & t_{10} \\
t_0 & t_3 & t_0 & t_0 & t_0 & t_0 & t_0 \\
t_1 & t_2 & t_4 & t_6 & t_8 & t_9 & t_{10} \\
t_0 & t_2 & t_0 & t_6 & t_8 & t_9 & t_{10} \\
t_1 & t_2 & t_4 & t_6 & t_8 & t_9 & t_{10} \\
t_0 & t_3 & t_5 & t_0 & t_0 & t_0 & t_0
\end{bmatrix}
$$

Figure 9.15 Type Matrix For Table 2

9.3.2   A Classifier for Line Drawings

The white space density graph can be used to determine far more about a document component than whether it is arranged in columns. In particular, graphs of

---

[††]Many thanks are due to Christopher Lewis and Matthew Scott for providing this implementation.

functions, convex polygons, and figures made up of multiple convex polygons all generate identifiable types of white space density graphs. Moreover, with respect to the WDG, closed curves and polygons lie in the same equivalence class.

Detecting polygonal structures has several applications. Given representations of the figures in a document, their WDGs can be generated, and the characterizations of these types of graphs can be used to gain information about the figures. This would enable a user to query a system based on a description of relevant figures. For example, a desired paper could be retrieved based on the recalled location of a function graph, or the section of a paper recalled to contain a convex polygon could be retrieved. This usage presumes prior knowledge of the portions of the document that constitute figures. In many cases, such an assumption is reasonable. For example, in a PostScript document representation, identifiable commands indicate the inclusion of figures; similarly in the XDOC format, generated by the ScanWorX optical character recognition software [50], figures are separated from text and represented differently. Nonetheless, this distinction may not always be readily available. An ASCII text file, such as an electronic news or mail message, will not provide such convenient separations. In this case characterizations of WDGs may aid in the attempt to distinguish figures from text; a portion of the document is especially likely to be a figure if its WDG has a shape that may describe a function, convex polygon, or combination of convex polygons.

Theorem 9.3.3 *For every closed curve there exists a polygon with the same number of line crossings and the same WDG.*

Proof: By construction. □

For example, consider the sketch of a snowman in Figure 9.16. Its WDG is identical to that of the polygon in Figure 9.16, and the two contain the same number of line crossings. In essence, the curves in the original figure have simply been "straightened" into lines. The WDG for these figures is given in Figure 9.17. The block containing exactly the figure has been divided into 53 lines of 142 characters.

The WDGs of this class of figures have special geometry that can be characterized in terms of their heights and slopes. An important special case is called a *plateau*.

Definition 9.3.5 *A segment of a WDG is a* plateau *if it has slope 0.*

Then, if the correct adjustments are made for the possible inclusion of axes and possible white space adjacent to the figure on the left and right, the following characterizations hold, so long as the granularity of the figure representation is sufficiently fine. The block under consideration is presumed to have been divided into n lines.

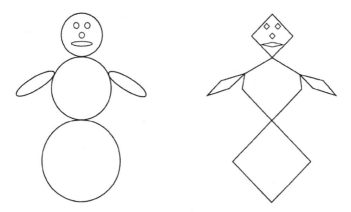

Figure 9.16 A curved figure and its polygonal equivalent

Theorem 9.3.4

- *The* WDG *of a continuous function consists of a plateau of height $\frac{n-1}{n}$.*

- *The* WDG *of a discontinuous function whose only discontinuities occur in its domain includes only heights of 1 and heights of $\frac{n-1}{n}$.*

- *The* WDG *of a convex polygon consists of two arbitrary endpoints, with a plateau of height $\frac{n-2}{n}$ between them.*

- *The* WDG *of a figure made up of convex polygons consists of a series of plateaux separated by transitions of length 2. The heights of the plateaux differ by multiples of $\frac{2}{n}$.*

For example, consider Figure 9.17, the WDG for Figure 9.16. In this case, $n = 53$. The graph consists of 13 plateaux, separated by transitions of length 2. (There are four plateaux of length exactly 2, at .88 and .84.) The height of each plateau differs from the height of its neighbors by .4, a rounding of .377, *i.e.*, $\frac{2}{53}$.

9.3.3   A Classifier for Itemized Lists

By itemized lists, we mean lists of the standard form generated by LaTeX list environments. Such lists have an easily characterized indentation structure: the first line is indented from the margin, and all subsequent lines are indented with respect to the first line but left-justified with respect to each other. This description yields the specification for the text elements of the pattern: *Left-In, Left-In, Left-Justified**. (The blank elements can be ignored, in this case.) The algorithm in Section 9.2 finds such patterns, and we characterize them as lists.

For example, consider again the first section of Figure 9.2. The early steps of the application of the logical hierarchy generation algorithm to this document portion appear in Subsection 9.2.4. In the first step, its lists are identified as patterns. The text portions of the patterns found are *Left-In, Left-In* and *Left-In, Left-In, Left-Justified*. These both match the above specification, so they are characterized as lists.

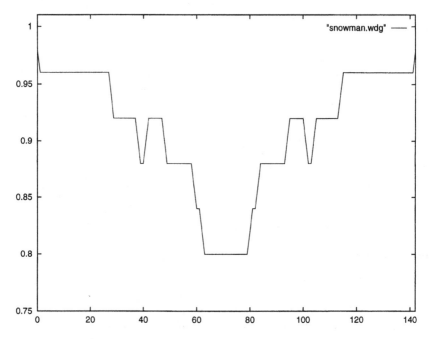

Figure 9.17 The WDG for the preceding figures

9.3.4   Future Extensions

The classification of logical hierarchy nodes requires additional exploration in at least the following areas.

- We would like to find a general characterization of the kinds of structures that can be identified using the WDG, as well as those that can be identified using any kind of white space aggregate. For structures of these types, we will seek algorithms that in fact rely on white space; for others, we will need to represent more complex information and consider symbols as well.

- The structures we classify at present are characterized by complete descriptions that must be precisely matched. Ideally, we envision a set of partial descriptions that may be matched by unforeseen patterns; classification would be performed by comparing the observed patterns to these partial descriptions. Some elements of this process will, of necessity, be heuristic. For example, distinguishing between a document's title and its author is not always possible without extensive cultural knowledge. Note that titles are usually printed in a larger size than authors' names or printed above them, but consider the novel *Daniel Deronda* by George Eliot. The cover to the paperback Oxford edition [72] contains two lines: one with the author's name, and one with the title. They are printed in the same font, and George Eliot's name appears above her novel's title. Formal investigation of the types of descriptions that can and should be provided is greatly needed.

9.4   Experiments

In this section we describe our implementation of the previous algorithms and give performance evaluations. Our data consists of the electronic library of computer science technical report at Cornell University, as well as the domain of newsgroups. The technical reports are represented as scanned-in bitmaps corresponding to pages. We discuss the performance of the segmentation algorithm on a random subset of 400 technical report pages. Finally, we present a sophisticated information access application that would be impossible without the tools discussed here.

9.4.1   Segmentation Experiments

The System

The system we use to segment technical report pages functions in the following manner. The pages are originally scanned in and represented as bitmaps. We then perform OCR on the pages, using the Xerox ScanWorX software, which returns a file in the XDOC format. We use a perl script to parse this file and return a file with the information needed by our algorithm[‡‡]: the page is divided into lines, the left and right edges of each line (with respect to the page margins) are given, and the height of the white space between lines is provided. (This space is considered significant only if it is greater than the page's minimum; thus the space between ordinary lines in a paragraph, for example, is not considered.) Then, the segmentation algorithm (implemented in Lisp) is run on this file. The version of the algorithm we use divides the document into blocks of one indentation value each for the initial level. It also includes a heuristic for handling titles: a sequence of centered lines at the top of a page is grouped by vertical distance, rather than by patterns. The output is a file that specifies the lines that are grouped together as blocks at each level of the tree. This file, together with one that specifies line positions, is read by a tcl script, which then displays the results (again, thanks to Jim Davis for providing the basis for this script).

9.4.2   The Results

We evaluated the algorithm's performance by looking at the blocks formed on each page and comparing these line groupings to the groupings that a human being considers logical. We counted the number of good (*i.e.*, logical) groupings, the number of bad groupings in the results, and the number of missing groupings (*i.e.*, those groupings that we considered to be required for a logical segmentation and were not in the results), keeping track of *input* errors that were due to

---

[‡‡]Many thanks to Jim Davis for providing the bulk of this script.

ScanWorX or the XDOC parser's interpretation of its information and those that were due to the algorithm. Since the algorithm works in a bottom-up fashion, errors at lower levels often generate errors at higher levels, and we separated these *propagated* errors from the *original* errors.

In evaluating the performance and errors, we rely on the ideas of precision and recall from information retrieval. In the realm of IR, these are defined as follows [215]:

$$Precision \quad = \quad \frac{Relevant \ retrieved}{Total \ retrieved}$$

$$Recall \quad = \quad \frac{Relevant \ retrieved}{Total \ relevant}$$

We analogize logical groupings to relevant documents and formed groupings to retrieved documents. This gives us:

$$Precision_{segment_{original}} \quad = \quad \frac{Good \ groups}{Good \ groups + Bad \ groups}$$

$$Recall_{segment_{original}} \quad = \quad \frac{Good \ groups}{Good \ groups + Missing \ groups}$$

These definitions specify a gross measure of precision and recall. They do not, however, take into account the difference between an original error and a propagated error. Since errors may be propagated by good behavior, this amounts to counting original errors multiple times. A more accurate and fair measure discards all propagated errors and all input errors. To understand the problem with propagated errors, suppose the final paragraph on a page is not recognized as a group because of an algorithmic failure. A propagated error might be to group all the other paragraphs that belong to its section together. This would be correct, if the final paragraph did not exist. We do not, of course, count these cases as good groupings. We also do not count them as incorrect (bad or missing); we simply remove them from consideration. The following measures reflect these observations:

$$Precision_{segment} \quad = \quad \frac{Good \ groups}{Good \ groups + Bad \ groups - Input \ bad - Propagated \ bad}$$

$$Recall_{segment} \quad = \quad \frac{Good \ groups}{Good \ groups + Missing \ groups - Input \ missing - Propagated \ missing}$$

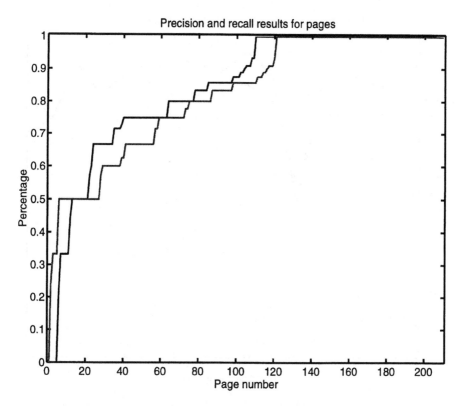

Figure 9.18: The solid graph shows the (sorted) precision statistics for a subset of the pages we analyzed. The shaded graph shows the recall statistics for the same subset of pages.

Results are shown in Figure 9.18 and Figure 9.19. We obtain over 75% precision and 65% recall for approximately 75% of our pages; this includes 100% precision on over 45% and 100% recall on over 40% of the pages. Overall, we obtain over 80% precision and 70% recall for 12 of our 15 technical reports. We reach these results without considering block classification; as the approach to classification matures, its results can be used to modify the segmentation results. This should improve performance substantially. We discuss the most common error types and their implications for future work below.

Two sample pages are shown in Figure 9.20; their results are shown in Figures 9.21 and 9.22. In the first example, a list is recognized and grouped, while sections are kept apart. The second example illustrates errors due to isolation and element length differences. The first full paragraph lies between two left-justified blocks, so it does not form part of a pattern; similarly, the two-line paragraph is not recognized as part of the pattern formed by the paragraphs that follow it. As a result, the algorithm halts too early.

A great many of the errors we found fall into a few general categories. These point the way for future work.

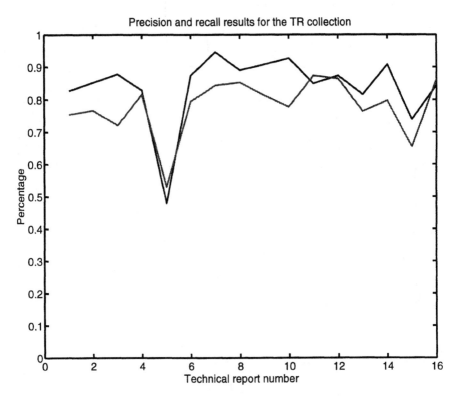

Figure 9.19: The solid graph shows the precision statistics for each of the technical reports we analyzed. The shaded graph shows the recall statistics for each of the technical reports we analyzed.

- *Isolated structures* This occurs most often with paragraphs. Paragraphs are recognized as elements of a repeating pattern, when two or more appear together. Sometimes, however, a page contains a paragraph surrounded by other kinds of blocks, such as left-justified theorems or headings. Since a standard paragraph contains no repetition, an isolated one is not found as a structure.

  This kind of special case requires some handling; perhaps a frequently occurring structure in a document should be recognized even when it is not currently part of a pattern. Also note that this case occurs more often in our page-by-page application than it would in an application applied to whole documents. Often, a paragraph is part of a pattern, but the rest of the pattern appears on the previous or following page.

- *Inconsistent element sizes* This occurs primarily with paragraphs and list items. Our indentation alphabet distinguishes between instances of

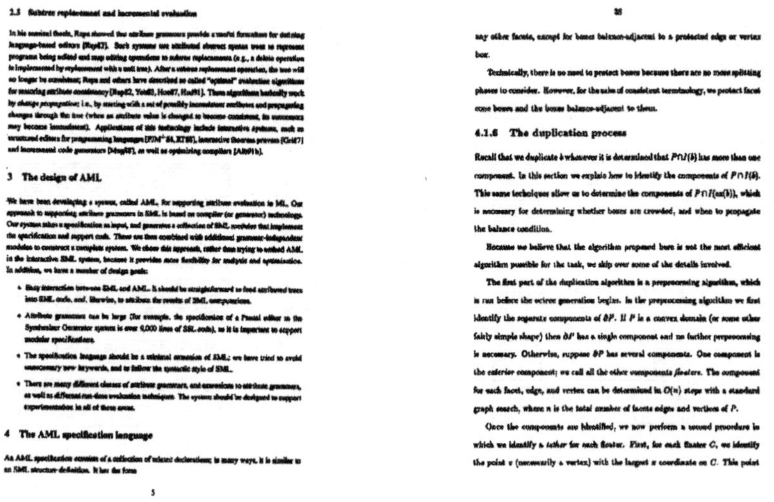

Figure 9.20: Two sample pages. The left page is grouped correctly by the algorithm. The right page is not.

these elements that have one line, instances with two lines, and instances with more than two lines. The difference between instances with two lines and with more than two comes from the inclusion of the *Left-Justified* character, as in the second list of our miniature document example. We would like to find an approach to determining when these kinds of observed differences should be considered significant.

- *Hanging indents*   In a page like a table of contents or some bibliographies, an indentation style is used that is the reverse of the usual paragraph indentation. When the entries are separated by blank lines, this does not pose a problem. When the entries are not so separated, the algorithm finds the wrong pattern. This is a limitation of the problem as we have posed it; with our set of observables, a page of hanging indents without blank lines is not distinguishable from a page of paragraphs (many of which may be one line long), beginning with some left-justified structure. Our indentation alphabet was chosen to prefer the latter interpretation, as this phenomenon is more common.

- *Spacing*   At times, the requirement that vertical white space be of equal height in pattern elements can prevent good patterns from being formed. For example, if elements of a list are found at different times (due to the size issue above), forming two or more list pieces, these should be combined. They are not combined, however, if the spacing within the list differs from the spacing surrounding the list.

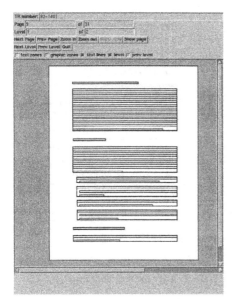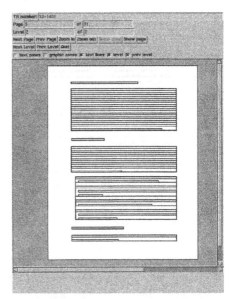

Figure 9.21: Correct groups for the left page of the prior figure. The left side shows level 1. On the right side, the heavy lines show level 2, and the divisions from level 1 are shown as dotted lines.

At other times, our consideration of spacing is insufficient to prevent bad groupings. This occurs because document layouts do not reserve one spacing distance for each kind of structure. For example, the spacing after a figure caption is often the same as the spacing after a heading. Thus, a left-justified caption and a left-justified heading are grouped together.

The information to be gleaned from the height of white space seems to depend on more context than our indentation alphabet considers. Characterizing this information and the relevant context warrants further investigation.

9.4.3 Application to Information Access

We now illustrate the use of automated segmentation and classification of non-textual components in information access. Starting from the data in the CS-TR collection, the goal is to support queries that are based on any non-textual structural unit that we can detect, along with keywords.

Imagine reading a FOCS paper that contains some cryptic definition. Starting from this definition, we would like to get a different version of the paper that explains the definition and perhaps even has figures illustrating the definition. This process can be automated by using a combination of algorithms for segmenting, classifying, indexing, and hyperlinking. We are able to execute this task with the following sequence of operations.

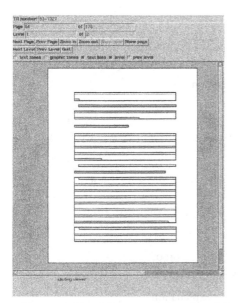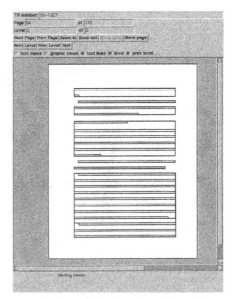

Figure 9.22: The groups for the right page of the earlier figure, with errors caused by the (upper) isolated paragraph and the (lower) two-line paragraph. The left side shows level 1. On the right side, the heavy lines show level 2, and the divisions from level 1 are shown as dotted lines.

Before a query comes in, each document is preprocessed by: (1) segmentation, to highlight the logical components; (2) classification, to associate types with the noded from the tree; and (3) using the nodes of the tree, the document can be automatically marked-up in an SGML-like fashion. We have implemented this by using our segmentation and classification algorithms on postscript file and by using the mark-up required by the Smart system for information retrieval (Smart indexes documents by keywords and uses a vector space model for retrieval) [215]. By restricting ourselves to the postscript files rather than generic, scanned-in images, we are able to label fully the nodes of our tree. That is, we are able to classify nodes as *sections, subsections, theorems, proofs, definitions, figures, figure captions, etc.* We achieve this by examining a combination of spacing and expected keywords. Although this implementation is not general, it illustrates the power of the approach we advocate for information access.

Preprocessing allows us to refer to words, as well as paragraphs, lists, tables, and other logical structures directly in a query. When a query comes in, all the logical structures from the documents being searched are sent to Smart as a collection of mini-documents. The system is then used to compute the hyper-links between logical pieces. Hyperlinks between the figures in the collection of documents are computed using the Hausdorff matching algorithm [211].

Figure 9.23 shows the results of this process to automatically find related pieces inside a document. The document is represented as a circular arc. Each

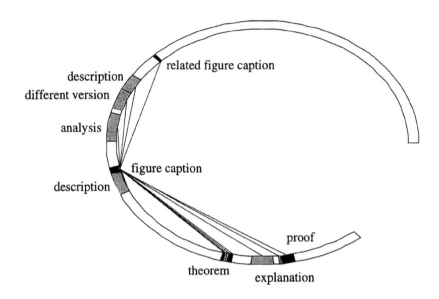

Figure 9.23: Structural hyperlinking for centralized information access. The circular arc represents a document. Various of its logical pieces are highlighted and edges are drawn between related parts.

logical piece at the granularity level of a paragraph is represented as a block within this circular arc. In figure 9.23 only the blocks that are found to be relevant are shown. Starting with a figure caption, the task is to find everything related to the figure within the document. This query is processed by organizing the logical pieces as a collection of documents. This collection is processed by the Smart system to find a related figure caption, some text describing it, as well as a theorem referring to the figure, its proof, and an application.

The example in Figure 9.23 is centralized, but nothing prevents it from working on a distributed collection. The obstacles in solving the FOCS query described in the beginning of this section are minor. We are currently working on building the necessary extensions.

9.5   Discussion

Our research agenda is to develop and prototype a methodology for conceptual retrieval tasks in large, heterogeneous, distributed electronic libraries. We consider the key question to be how to associate information with content. The natural language problem is still unsolved, but we can call upon other computational techniques to make progress. We believe that, in the environments we consider, content is partially encoded in extant underlying structures, which are found at varying levels of granularity. Hence, we seek to automatically discover structural hierarchies in documents. We believe that by developing efficient tools that allow users to specify tasks in visual terms we provide computational support for a search technique that people use naturally. At the same time, this approach enlarges the class of retrieval tasks supported by keyword-based systems.

The specific problem addressed in this chapter is the characterization of the logical structure of documents in terms of high-level geometric layout components. We have proposed a method for using the indentation contours to construct hierarchical layout representations and algorithms for classifying some of the nodes in the hierarchy. We have not solved the general problem of automatic document structuring, but we have obtained insights into how a simple notion of layout (namely, indentation) can be formalized and used to capture geometric content.

The algorithms presented in this chapter have implications for (1) creating rich, user-friendly browsing tools based on the automatic and on-line creation of indices and hyperlinks, *e.g.*, customizing the browsing of information by providing on-line automatic support for computing a variety of views; (2) distributed access of remote electronic repositories, by providing partial models of documents that essentially "compress" the data at a various levels of detail; (3) conceptualizing the search of electronic documents by providing support for retrieval with non-linguistic cues, an approach supported by our belief that the inherent structures in electronic repositories encode content in a task-specific way [213] and illustrated by examples throughout this chapter and in [8, 213]; and (4) uniformly marking-up generic documents for other retrieval purposes (for instance, an SGML mark-up for the Smart retrieval system [217]) by automatically recognizing the logical components of documents. This last would allow users the flexibility to create documents in the format of their choice; these could be automatically integrated with retrieval systems (like the Smart system) that usually rely on mark-up for indexing.

Acknowledgments

We are very grateful to John Hopcroft for proposing the problem and for his guidance and support. We thank Allen Back for many enlightening discussions on probability theory. Special thanks to James Allan, Jim Davis, Bruce Donald, Carl Lagoze, Dean Krafft, Matthew Morgenstern, T.V. Raman, and Devika Subramanian for many invaluable suggestions. Thanks also to Christopher Lewis, Matthew Scott, and Amit Singhal for useful comments and support.

Part IV

Classification And Indexing

Chapter 10

Corpus Linguistics for Establishing The Natural Language
Content of Digital Library Documents

Robert P. Futrelle[*],Xiaolan Zhang[†] and Yumiko Sekiya[‡]

10.1 Introduction

Any collection of information that is called a "library" must be an organized
collection, and the Digital Libraries of the future (DLs) are no exception [164,
220]. Access is not possible without organization. Some of this organization
is explicitly introduced at authoring time as the descriptive elements: source,
title, authors, affiliation, keywords, etc. A great deal more information is only
implicit, "encrypted" in the document's text. Thus, objects under discussion,
processes and events, the times and places of events, value judgments, etc., are
all useful in organizing the collection to guide prospective users of DLs to the
extent we have procedures for discovering the information.

The natural language methods discussed in this chapter are broadly referred
to as "Corpus Linguistics" methods. This denotes a variety of methods (parsing,
natural language understanding, semantic analysis, etc.) but as adapted to
work on very large corpora. See the two issues of *Computational Linguistics*
specifically devoted to using large corpora, for a good overview [48].

The structured information extracted from a corpus serves at least two purposes. The first is to improve the indexing of the collection, allowing the user
to access focused information, typically small parts of large documents that are
of the most interest. The second is to construct derivative objects which cod-
ify or summarize specific types of information from one or more documents.
These could be automatically constructed abstracts or tabular summaries of
data. The extraction of implicit information must be automated as much as

---

[*]Biological Knowledge Laboratory and Scientific Database Project, College of Computer Science, 161 Cullinane Hall, Northeastern University, Boston, MA 02115,
Email:futrelle@ccs.neu.edu

[†]Biological Knowledge Laboratory and Scientific Database Project, College of Computer Science, 161 Cullinane Hall, Northeastern University, Boston, MA 02115, Email:
xzhang@ccs.neu.edu

[‡]Biological Knowledge Laboratory and Scientific Database Project, College of Computer Science, 161 Cullinane Hall, Northeastern University, Boston, MA 02115, Email:
sekiya@ccs.neu.edu

possible, because the effort that would be required to do it manually is too large. It would be best if even the categories of information were discovered automatically, "bootstrapped" from the corpus itself. (For an excellent justification of the need for bootstrapping approaches, see [86].) When bootstrapping is used, the collection becomes self-organizing and, if done well, should produce consistent descriptions free of biases created by ad hoc organizational designs prescribed in advance. Self-organization, by its nature, is useful in characterizing specific knowledge domains, and genres, and their sublanguages, e.g., popular versus technical writing.

The challenge then, is to bootstrap from text to produce both structured categories and specific information. Bootstrapping can be done by correlating similar word sequences in text. For example, if a large number of sequences are seen in a corpus such as "big dog", "big cat", "old dog", "young cat", etc., then a bootstrapping classification system could create a category for the first word in each pair (commonly known as *adjective*) and a category for the second (commonly known as *noun*). In section 10.7, the largest portion of this chapter, we present results that demonstrate that such a classification strategy can distinguish both syntactic and semantic classes of words in the domain of microbiology, e.g., chemicals, species, mutants [99].

Our work focuses on the biological research literature, the largest single collection of scientific literature in the world, comprising half a million articles per year (3 billion words per year). Our first experiments used a 250,000 word collection of biological abstracts. Current work is focusing on a four million word corpus, the 1995 papers of the *Journal of Bacteriology*, taken from the American Society for Microbiology (ASM) CD-ROM. Some development and testing is being done on the Brown Corpus [96], one million words.

10.2   Information retrieval and browsing

In digital libraries, many modes of interaction will be supported. The two major ones will certainly be querying the collection to retrieve information, the classical information retrieval approach [215], and browsing by following various types of links. It is necessary to build organization into the collection to directly support these user modes.

10.3   Start-up and the steady state

To do linguistic analysis of text, the system must possess a basic vocabulary and knowledge of the structure of English. A corpus of many millions of words contains enough information so that the system should be able to induce the structure and relation of all the important elements of English using extensions of the current methods of corpus linguistics while needing very little human intervention [41]. The approach is most successful if a focused domain is used. This initial process of discovery constitutes the *start-up phase* [101]. The task is nothing short of bootstrapping the structure of natural language itself, which is daunting but not impossible. The results obtainable by corpus linguistics methods grow more impressive every year, so the goal is worth pursuing vigorously.

After the training corpus is analyzed and the various patterns of English have been induced, they can be used to analyze the new text entering the system. This is the *steady-state regime*. New items and structures will continue to appear in the steady-state, but at a greatly reduced frequency.

During the start-up phase, the types of information about language that need to be determined include:

- word and phrase disambiguation

- domain-specific word use

- domain-specific thesauri for query expansion

- translation of specialized markup (e.g., subscripts and superscripts in chemical nomenclature and numerical forms)

- ontological relations for knowledge frame building

In the steady-state, further information is extracted:

- analysis of internal contents (information distribution among sections and paragraphs)

- clustering of documents based on domain-specific information

- building knowledge frame instances by extracting the specific contents of documents

The corpus linguistic techniques used for these analyses combine statistical analysis and machine learning methods. In the building of frames, knowledge-based methods are needed.

10.4   The Linguistic Database

The information built up about words and language structure is stored in a linguistic database (fig. 10.1). This database becomes a permanent part of the digital library so that it can be used to analyze new items that are added to the collection as well as for on-line analysis of user queries and the production of derived objects.

One of the most important parts of the database is the lexicon, which contains statistical, morphological, syntactic, semantic and domain-related information about words. In section 10.7 we present results that can aid in the automatic building of lexicons and thesauri.

10.5   Domain and genre

One of the frustrating things about many current search and retrieval systems for documents is their lack of domain sensitivity; this can markedly reduce the precision of search. A simple example of this is when a word such as "date" is used in a query, information about fruits, times and social relationships is returned. "Date" is a polysemous word; it has multiple senses. Though more complex queries can help narrow the search, there is no direct way to tell such systems that a particular meaning of the word is the one intended. Even though such words are obviously ambiguous, most systems have no mechanism to store or use the different senses, and the texts that are indexed and searched do not distinguish senses either.

There are three aspects of the domain sensitivity problem. The first is to recognize multiple word senses and to tag the corpus text accordingly. The second is to bring together a collection of word senses, identifying them as the vocabulary of a knowledge domain. The third is to employ such knowledge in assisting a user in formulating queries and in executing those queries. For a discussion of three approaches to word sense disambiguation, see [104, 103].

Domains of knowledge are not crisply delimited, so it is necessary to use measures of appropriateness, not absolute inclusion or exclusion. Furthermore, the vocabulary used for one genre will differ from another, even in the same domain, e.g., an account of a breakthrough in genetics as reported in a newspaper versus a scientific journal. In addition to word senses, the entire style and organization of a document will vary in different genres [194].

10.6   Words

Language begins with words. There are a number of characteristics of words that can be usefully exploited in the analysis of corpora. Text presents us with a collection of homographs, words that can initially be distinguished only by their spelling (their orthography). It is useful to distinguish a word as *type*, which is a single entity, e.g., "DNA", versus a word *token* or occurrence, e.g., the many occurrences of the string "DNA" in a text [167].

Words have rich structure and interrelations, including,

Multiple senses: "stock" (cattle (n), fill larder (v))

Domain-specific senses: "clone" (computers vs. genes)

Synonyms/antonyms: "hot" and "cold"

Hyponyms/hypernyms: "collie" < "dog" < "animal"

Morphology/inflection: ("dog" and "dogs")

Morphology/derivation : ("filter" and "filtration")

Phrasal nouns/verbs: "New York City", "think up"

Capitalization, punctuation: "Gene", "gene", "gene," , "gene:"

Abbreviations, acronyms: "ACM", "VCR"

Complex structures: "[^{35}S]dATPαS,"

Etymology: history ("lasing" from "LASER")

Among the various types of information that can aid word classification, one is word morphology, especially for technical text. Stemming, or removing suffixes, is a simple morphological technique for relating words to a common form, approximately their root form. Stemming algorithms can never match the quality of a careful morphological analysis [208, 232]. Because of this, it is useful to expend a large one-time effort to properly compute the morphology of, say, the 500,000 most frequently met terms, build a database of these and never analyze any of them again. Since a good morphological analysis algorithm has a number of heuristics and special cases that it must consult in any event, e.g., relate "used" to "use" but not "need" to "nee", and "mutants" to "mutant" but not "whereas" to "wherea", this argues for the importance of a definitive database which is built, refined, and maintained over time. Similar analysis can be done for technical terms involving subscripts, superscripts, numbers and Greek letters [102]. What's more, morphological information can be smoothly integrated into our classification algorithms.

10.7   Word classification

One of the primary problems faced by all natural language analysis systems is the problem of resolving ambiguities among the various possible senses of a given word, the problem of lexical ambiguity resolution [9, 124]. This requires classifying tokens, because different occurrences may have different senses. The most useful classification of tokens separates them along syntactic and semantic dimensions. In the syntactic domain the primary classes are part-of-speech (noun, verb, adjective, ...) and syntactic category (subject, object, indirect object, ...). Part-of-speech classifiers, "taggers", have been developed to a high degree, both for supervised tagging, with training sets [47] or by guiding the tagging with lexical information [29, 62].

In the semantic domain the simplest relations are those between synonyms and between antonyms; other important relations include hyponymy (subclass, superclass) and meronymy (part, whole) [60]. Word classification is an important and useful analysis to do, because it assists in,

- Building focused browsing tools

- Developing thesaural expansion for querying

- Bootstrapping higher-order structures

- Query processing

The data presented in figures 10.2 and 10.3 are based on the analysis of a 227,408 word corpus composed of 1700 abstracts from a specialized field of biology [99]. The results shown are subtrees of the full classification tree for the 1,000 most frequent words. The 1,000 words covered 80% of all word occurrences in that corpus. A binary clustering algorithm is used, joining two subclusters at each step, where the simplest subcluster is a single word. The method is unsupervised, meaning that no training set of correctly classified items is needed in advance. The method, based on [85], is detailed in [99] and can be briefly described as follows:

1. The contexts of each word occurrence are used, the two words immediately preceding and following the word of interest, schematically, the pattern C1,C2,W,C3,C4. The 1,000 highest frequency Ws were studied.

2. The frequencies of the context words appearing in the four positions with respect to the tokens of a single word W are computed separately for each of the four positions. The only context words for which the frequencies are accumulated are the ones that had the 150 highest frequencies in the entire corpus. This results in a 4x150 = 600 element vector V of context word frequencies, 1,000 vectors in all. Since the data from every token of W are merged, the method is type-based.

3. Each element of each vector is rewritten in terms of its mutual information value instead of its raw frequency. This gives higher weight to context words that appeared at higher than their expected frequency, based on their overall frequency in the corpus.

4. The similarities S_{ij} of all pairs of vectors V_i and V_j are computed as the inner product of the mutual information vectors. In [85, 86], the raw frequencies were used, but the Spearman Rank Correlation Coefficient was used to compute similarities, another way of dealing with the widely varying word occurrence frequencies.

5. The resulting matrix of similarities is subjected to a hierarchical agglomerative clustering analysis. The two words with the greatest similarity are joined first, forming a subcluster. The vector representing the new subcluster is computed from the total frequencies of the context words in each subcluster. Then that subcluster and all other words or subclusters are compared and the most similar pair of items is joined, and so on, until the root is reached, containing all words in a binary tree. Portions of the resulting 1,000 node tree are shown in figures 10.2 and 10.3.

In figures 10.2 and 10.3, the similarities quoted refer to the similarities of the last two items joined together, unless otherwise noted. Each subcluster shown is reasonably homogeneous for part-of-speech, e.g., nouns tend to cluster with nouns, adjectives with adjectives, etc. So the system does achieve syntactic (part-of-speech) classification. The most striking thing about the data is the tight clustering of semantically related items. The method obviously does not cluster synonyms separately from antonyms, e.g., "higher" and "lower" are tightly clustered. A little reflection reveals why this must be so. The choice of "higher" or "lower" at a given point in the text is not determined by the syntactic context, but instead indicates some knowledge of the world placed there by the author to inform the reader. A reader cannot predict, on the basis of local syntactic context alone, which will occur and therefore there is no indication in the immediately surrounding text as to which will occur. Since there is no such distinguishing information and the local contexts are otherwise the same, the similarity analysis places the words together. For another discussion of this lack of pure synonym clusters (and the frequent occurrence of antonyms) see [115].

In figure 10.3A, the clustering of the -ed forms is obvious, and it might appear that the system was using the -ed suffix to aid the classification. In fact the algorithm has no information about word morphology. Convincing evidence for this is the inclusion of the irregular forms, "found" and "shown" in one of the early subclusters.

The clustering results demonstrate the ability of the approach to deal with domain-specific technical terms, e.g., terms for microorgansim behavior (chemotactic, sensory, and two-component) in figure 10.2A, terms for techniques, (microscopy, electrophoresis, and chromatography) in figure 10.3B and terms describing physical properties (pH, temperature, and concentration) in figure 10.3C. Other quite domain specific clusters (data not shown) group together species names (*coli, typhimurium,* etc.), names of sugars (maltose, galactose, ribose, etc.), and specific bacterial mutant loci (tar, tsr, cheB, etc.)

In our other work, we looked at the classification of single word occurrences [99]. When this is done, the statistical reliability of method drops, because data from multiple occurrences is not initially merged. To improve the reliability, context words were expanded by adding to them words that were found to be similar in the analysis described above. The set of words similar to a word, truncated at some minimal similarity, is called the *simset* of the word. Using simsets in this way, we successfully classified occurrences of some -ed forms as well as some words that occurred with frequency one.

Another approach to unsupervised word classification used a statistical analysis of the distribution of word pairs [29]. Only 30 word pairs deemed distributionally most similar according to their distributional probability vectors are extracted from the 300 most frequently occurring words in the Brown Corpus. Even the three most common articles, "the", "a" and "an" are not discovered in the classification.

The approach in [180] used co-occurrence frequencies in a five-word window (but ignored the exact positions relative to the word of interest). Only the 169 most frequently occurring nouns in Wall Street Journal articles were classified and the result depended very much on the selection of set of context words.

A vector space model with a very large context, a 1,000 character window, was used in another study [221]. The analysis focuses on finding significant directions in the high-dimensional context space and using these for word disambiguation.

The classification technique we used has some weaknesses:

- The method only works well with word types not tokens. Thus, every occurrence of a word such as "complex" is classified identically, even though some occurrences (in biology) are nouns referring to a coordinated aggregate of molecules and other occurrences are adjectives meaning "complicated".

- A large similarity matrix must be constructed and then modified as the algorithm executes. The matrix has N(N-1)/2 distinct elements. For N=1,000, this is a half a million elements. Because of this, the method could not be extended to cover all the distinct words in typical corpora which can be hundreds of thousands of items.

10.8   The Balanced Entropy Method

Because of the above difficulties, we have developed and are experimenting with a new approach to classification based on the principle of minimal complexity. The fundamental assumption of the method is that of Occam's Razor: subject to certain basic constraints, the simplest assignment of classes to word occurrences is the best assignment. There are a variety of measures of simplicity (or its converse, complexity) but one of the most useful is the information-theoretic or entropy measure [53]. An even more general approach is available via Kolmogorov complexity [162].

Our method proceeds by searching for class assignments that lead to the minimally complex structural description of the text. The first implementation of this approach is for part-of-speech tagging. In part-of-speech tagging, a specific class or "tag" is assigned to each word occurrence. The set of tagging patterns is chosen as either bigrams (all adjacent pairs of tags) or trigrams (all adjacent triples). Part-of-speech tagging is the first step towards more sophisticated semantic classification. It begins by assuming a fixed number of classes, $C_1, \ldots, C_n$, and attempts to satisfy the following three constraints simultaneously:

1. Class Use, C. Every class C_i should be used to an appreciable degree. (Using only one class would result in a trivial and vacuous description.)

2. Word Assignments, W. Each word should only be assigned to a few classes. (If every word occurrence could be assigned to any class freely, then the entire text could be described by a simple and clearly erroneous structure such as, $C_1, \ldots, C_n, C_1, \ldots, C_n, C_1, \ldots, C_n, \ldots$)

3. Pattern Use, P. The number of distinct patterns (bigrams or trigrams) should be as small as possible.

These three constraints are in conflict, so obviously the method has to achieve some balance between them. To do this, a measure is needed for each of the three components, one that is small when the distributions are simple and large when they are not. Given any normalized distribution p_i, such a measure is given by the entropy, $H = -\sum p_i log p_i$. $H \geq 0$ always. The entropy is zero when some $p_j = 1.0$ with all the rest zero. The entropy is maximal when all the p_i are equal to one another. Each of the three components, P, W and C involve distributions, so the complexity of each can be characterized by entropy functions, H_P, H_W, and H_C. (For W, we average across the H values for each word type.) The goal is to minimize H_P and H_W, but to maximize H_C at the same time, in a consistent way. That is, we want to *balance* the complexity of the pattern and word distributions against the complexity of the class distribution. This can be achieved by defining the *entropy balance function, B*, as:

$$B = H_P + wH_W - cH_C.$$

The coefficients c and w have to be chosen empirically, though we have some analytic results that suggest that $c = 2$ is a reasonable choice. (In practice, values of $c \approx 1.6$ have turned out to be optimal.) When types only are classified, the H_W term is omitted. In this case, if only bigrams are used for patterns, adjacent pairs of classes, then the choice of $c = 2$ converts B to minus the mutual information, I, which has been used by [174].

Computations based on the *balanced entropy principle* using B were done for simple text that was generated from a known grammar (30 word vocabulary, 10 grammar rules, 400 sentences), with classification accuracy > 99%. We should stress that the method is truly unsupervised so that no assignments of words to classes were necessary to start the computation. Work in progress is focused on the Brown Corpus of approximately one million words.

The method overcomes the limitations of the clustering method described earlier. Because the method is based on optimization of assigned patterns, a variety of approaches can be used to implement it. For one thing, it does not require that the text be processed sequentially, as the much-used Markov models do [41]. Those models have to assume that class assignments are based on the left context of a word or the right context, but not both simultaneously. The balanced entropy method also can be used in a supervised learning mode in which the assignments are made initially based on an already classified text (the training set) and subsequent assignments are made with those assignments "frozen" except for new words. The training phase can also be unsupervised, just as the clustering methods are. To jump-start the computations, one could assign class labels consistently to a few frequent and well-known common classes, e.g., placing the articles, "a", "an" and "the" in a single class.

One of the great strengths of the balanced entropy approach is that it can be used in a totally unsupervised mode, with no initial tagging assignments. In most studies, it is common to use lexical information (from a machine-readable dictionary) to restrict the set of classes that can be assigned to a given word type. Our method does this automatically via the wH_W term in B. Furthermore, the classes in the standard methods are picked in advance and subject to human choice and judgement (see the discussion in Appendix B of [109]). Our classes "flow" from the data itself and are constructed by the algorithm in a self-consistent way.

10.9   Word sense alignment between independent systems

In the future, there will undoubtedly be many independent digital libraries, all involved in analyzing corpora. When word classification analyses are done, a set of word senses for each word will be generated, so it is useful to have a simple way to find the correspondence between the word senses in the separate databases. For example, if we had two such distinct libraries, each would discover two distinct word senses for "train": train1(railroad) and train2 (educate) [258]. On its face, such classification offers no way to find which sense in one library corresponds to which sense in the other. However, if we exchanged simsets (section 10.7) of train1 and train2, then the four simsets could be aligned, pairwise, by looking at the overlap of the simsets (using homograph identity only).

10.10   Higher-order analysis of language

The multiple senses of individual words creates what is called the *lexical ambiguity* problem. At the sentence level, there are additional problems of *structural ambiguity*. The two primary causes of structural ambiguity in English are prepositional phrase attachment (PP-attachment) and conjunctions. A simple sentence such as, "She drove down the street in her car." is unambiguous for humans, because the prepositional phrase "in her car" is obviously attached to the verb "drove". But it can cause problems for automated systems because of another possible reading in which "street" is located "in her car". Similarly, conjunctions can create ambiguous structures, such as the preferred analysis, "[Pick up the phone and call] or [write a note]." versus "[Pick up the phone] and [call or write a note]."

Problems of structural ambiguity have been thought to be particularly difficult because they apparently depend on world knowledge, considerations that lie well beyond syntactic analysis and the methods of corpus linguistics. But given a large enough corpus, it may be possible to find examples of unambiguous structures to guide disambiguation algorithms. Thus, a number of constructions analogous to "She drove down the street." might be found, but none would be found of the general form, "The street in her car was wide." A similar approach has been used to guide the resolution of PP-attachment [123].

Determining the structure of sentences is the next level of problems beyond working with words. This is normally attacked by developing grammars that describe language and then using parsing to discover the actual structure of any given sentence. Stochastic grammars are grammars induced from text that embody the preferences found in real text [41]. The balanced entropy method we described earlier can be extended to the problem of discovering such grammars, to augment already existing techniques.

10.11 More complex needs — knowledge frames

Text is full of information. It would be best if the information could be so well analyzed that it could be reduced to a highly organized and schematic form that could be stored in a database. Then, instead of querying the text, the query could be directed toward the database, a well-structured object for which query methods are well-developed. In corpus linguistics, this process is described as knowledge frame-filling [126, 133, 204]. The great challenge of all this is that the potentially well-organized information is "encrypted" in natural language text, which must be "decrypted" to discover it. Extracting knowledge frames from text is a difficult problem that will be with us for a long time. It is at best, a method for expository text (not poetry!). We will not discuss this topic further, other than to give some examples of the types of knowledge frames that are of interest in the biological texts we study (figure 10.4). For more detailed discussion, see [117].

In most work in this field, knowledge frames are developed manually, but it is possible to develop them at least semi-automatically, once semantic word classes are available and some syntactic analysis of sentences is done. The reason that this is possible is because of the close correspondence between the predicate-argument structure of sentences and the knowledge frames that are ultimately desired. Thus, if we compare figure 10.3JA which contains semantically related terms such as "EXAMINED" and "STUDIED", we could analyze the structure of sentences that use either of them and develop a single frame such as the one in figure 10.4A, identifying "EXAMINED" with "B was done to", i.e., an examining act was performed.

10.12 Derivative objects

Now that full text sources are appearing online, it is desirable to build derivative objects from them. For single documents, there has been progress on automating the construction of abstracts [193, 194, 203]. But "data mining" techniques can be used to derive another type of derivative document or dataset from a number of related documents. In many information retrieval systems it is possible to rank the documents found in response to a query. On the other hand, suppose that a user of a system wants a list of all the zoos in the United states together with their locations and a brief description of each. Such a list may exist in some specialist publication, but assuming that this was not online, the list could be derived by analyzing a collection of more conventional sources. No ranking of the sources or resulting items in the derived object would be needed or even desired. Building derivative objects can be greatly aided by the corpus analysis approaches that we have described.

10.13   Diagrams — Contents and analysis

Diagrams form an important part of the contents of many documents. Important as they are, there is little work done on analyzing diagrams to extract information from them to aid in the structuring and retrieval of particular diagrams or the documents containing them. We have described some of these issues [98] and have more recently succeeded in efficiently analyzing some quite complex diagrams [100] [N. Nikolakis, thesis in preparation] by using *graphics constraint grammars*.

10.14   Multidatabases for natural language

In order to be fully integrated into a digital library, documents have to reside in databases of some type. There is a basic mismatch between documents, normally conceived of as flat text, and databases, which by nature are highly structured. There is some work on building text databases, but it is still in its infancy, surprisingly enough [113, 163]. In corpus linguistics a tradition has grown up that treats corpora as large character stream files, processing them with tools such as grep, lex and perl [17]. When text is processed in this way, it is often altered by adding in-line annotations that change the file positions of elements, making it impossible to build stable indexes pointing into the data. It makes sense to keep the text stable, making annotations to it in separate, updatable structures such as B-trees. Database techniques also allow incremental changes and annotations to be made to a corpus without having to process large files in their entirety. In our work [101] we have used multidatabases that employ indexed flat files as well as large persistent arrays in the spirit of relational databases, as well as persistent object stores [21]. The demands of large scale text processing are great, so often a new database structure has to be designed when a major new computation is to be done. However, every new structure is tied back to the original corpus through indexes, so the information is cumulative. Our work on databases for use in corpus linguistics analysis is shedding light on database needs for digital libraries, since there is obvious overlap between the two sets of requirements.

10.15   Authoring tools for capturing content

One of the problems with all information systems is that so much of what an author knows about a document is lost when the document is created. An author does know in fact, which sense of each word is intended, how ambiguous sentences are meant to be construed, what the components and relations are in a diagram, etc. The quality and organization of a collection in a digital library would clearly be enhanced if more of the author's knowledge could be captured at authoring time and included in the document. Currently, enormous efforts (such as we have been describing) have to be expended to recover the information lost at authoring time. Research is needed to develop ways to overcome this problem.

An author should not be required to write in a radically different "unambiguous" style or to explicitly specify which word senses are intended at each point in the document. Instead, the authoring application should attempt to capture and confirm the information while the author is present to verify the choices made. There are two challenges in building authoring tools that would aid in capturing more detailed information. The first is to make capturing the information as unobtrusive as possible, so as to not interfere with the author's goal of rapidly and flexibly creating a document in a non-distractive environment. The second challenge, and somewhat a corollary of the first, is to endow the authoring tools with enough intelligence to analyze the author's input and give feedback as to the system's interpretation of it, so the author can quickly confirm or alter the interpretation. As part of this, machine learning techniques can be used to identify favored word interpretations and modes of expression, so that the system would not have to constantly ask the author for verification. Alternatively, verification of the interpretation could be deferred, so as to not distract the author unduly.

Intelligent authoring tools are also needed for graphics and diagrammatic material in papers. In many ways, the graphics authoring problem is more tractable, because people are accustomed to using drawing applications that offer them a menu of system-defined choices such as lines, arrows, rectangles, ovals, etc. It is possible then to build graphics authoring applications with more semantically "loaded" choices.

Integrating intelligent authoring tools into digital libraries is non-trivial, because of representational issues. Thus, if a particular sense of a word is chosen, how is the chosen sense to be identified to one or more digital library systems which add the document to their collection? (One idea on how to do this was presented in the word sense alignment section earlier.) Representing the resolution of structural ambiguity in a portable format would be even more difficult, but still a worthy goal.

10.16 Conclusions

The methods of corpus linguistics can reveal a great deal of information about word use and language structure by careful processing of very large corpora. This information can be used for adding organizational structure to digital libraries both in terms of individual document content and inter-document relations. The structure discovered by corpus linguistics methods reflects the actual use of words and language style in particular domains and genres, rather than being constrained by pre-built categories. The data presented here has demonstrated the power of simple word classification methods for discovering semantically related word clusters. Work in progress based on the new balanced entropy principle overcomes a number of limitations of current classification methods and should discover more detailed and accurate information about word relations and text structure.

10.17   Acknowledgments

This work was supported in part by a grant from the National Science Foundation, IRI-9117030, the Department of Energy, DE-FG02-93ER61718, and by a Fulbright Senior Scholar grant (to RPF) for research in the United Kingdom, 1994.

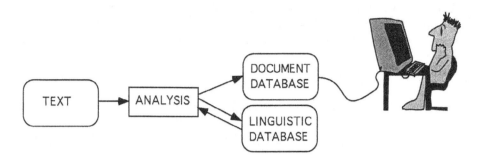

Figure 10.1: The linguistic database contains extensive information about words and language structure. In the start-up phase, the database is built from the initial text presented to the system. In the steady state, the database is augmented when new information is encountered and it is used to mediate user interaction. Some of the major uses of the database are to contribute to procedures which analyze the text to index it, derive secondary collections of information and build knowledge frames.

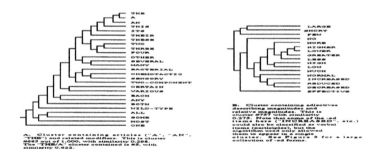

Figure 10.2: Excerpts from word classification results. The 1,000 highest frequency words in a biological corpus of about 200,000 words were clustered using a technique developed by [11,12]. Word similarity was computed using the similarity of their contexts, the immediately adjacent words, two on the left and two on the right. The similarity did not take into account any morphological properties of the words. Note the occurrence of some very high-frequency domain-specific terms (bacterial, etc.) in A. Details are discussed in the text and in [15].

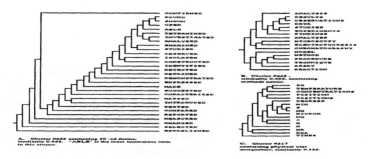

Figure 10.3: Additional clusters computed using the same techniques as in the preceding figure.

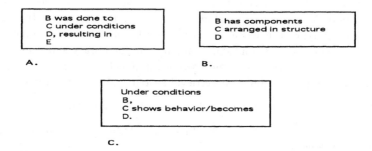

Figure 10.4: Three types of knowledge frames of particular use in biology. Knowledge extracted from the text would be used to fill instances of such frames

Chapter 11

Compression and Full-Text Indexing for Digital Libraries

Ian H. Witten[*], Alistair Moffat[†] and Timothy C. Bell[‡]

11.1 Introduction

This chapter argues that recent technological advances in compressing and indexing information have yielded a qualitative change in the feasibility of large-scale
full-text retrieval—not only of textual documents, but also of documents containing black-white, grayscale and color images, video clips, and sound bites.
To permit retrieval of textual and non-textual documents alike, we assume that
every document is described by a set of *representative terms*, or simply *terms*,
which are used to index it. The index is capable of identifying all documents
that contain combinations of specified terms or are in some other way judged
to be relevant to the set of query terms. In the case of textual documents, the
entire text is generally regarded as its own set of representative terms, so that
any words contained in the message can be used as query terms. Modern compression techniques make it quite feasible to index every single word in the text,
so no consideration need be given to selecting index terms when documents are
filed.

This kind of indexing provides full-text retrieval (FTR), which makes information immediately accessible to the end user without requiring that any
attention be paid to organizing or labeling it when it is filed. No manual indexing or keyword selection is necessary: the index terms are drawn from the
text itself. Nothing is missed: every single word is indexed. Information can be
retrieved either by specifying a boolean combination of words and seeking all
documents that include that combination, or alternatively by specifying a list of
words and applying a heuristic to gauge the relevance of each document to the
list. No special database, information-handling, or library skills are required:
this is an end-user technology, and users learn quickly through interacting with
a cheap and responsive full-text retrieval system. Moreover, exactly the same

---

[*]Department of Computer Science, University of Waikato, Hamilton, New Zealand,
ihw@waikato.ac.nz

[†]Department of Computer Science, The University of Melbourne, Victoria 3052, Australia,
alistair@cs.mu.oz.au

[‡]Department of Computer Science, University of Canterbury, Christchurch, New Zealand,
tim@cosc.canterbury.ac.nz

indexing mechanism can accommodate media other than machine-readable text, provided only that a textual description, or set of keywords, is available for every piece of information that is stored.

In the past, the chief drawback to full-text indexing has been its expense. There are three components to the cost: the space needed to store the document collection and index, the time required for retrieval, and the computational resources necessary to create the index in the first place. A word-level index, which records with each word of the vocabulary the exact locations where it appears in the text, is about the same size as the text itself, and this doubles the space requirement because both index and text must be stored. A large volume of text implies a huge index, and a huge index means that a great deal of time must be spent reading from disk when processing queries. Finally, the process of constructing an index essentially involves sorting a list that records each occurrence of every term, and this is a task that can take both a great deal of time and a large amount of space.

Recent advances in compression technology have had a dramatic impact on all three of these costs. Surprisingly, modern compression techniques mean that no extra space is required for the index; indeed, storage is saved because the text and index condense into significantly less space than was originally required by the text alone. A fully-indexed text collection can be stored in one third to one half of the space required for the uncompressed text, and the inclusion of image information increases the proportion saved because images are more compressible than text. Although answering queries incurs an overhead in decompression, a well-designed system can respond to reasonably simple queries in just one second—even for massive information bases containing gigabytes of text. In fact, the use of compression can actually reduce response time because less data must be transferred from disk. Finally, through the use of compressed internal data structures and careful algorithm design, the resources needed to create the index for a huge body of text can be dramatically reduced.

The net result of these advances in compression is a qualitative change in the feasibility of full-text indexing of large information bases. Full-text retrieval provides a fast, comprehensive, low-level access mechanism that can be obtained at essentially no cost. This chapter shows what recently-developed methods can offer in terms of access to large textual and pictorial information bases, and argues that full-text retrieval provides a much-needed strategy for deferring the organizational overhead associated with documents from filing time to retrieval time. It is based on the experience of designing, implementing, and using a compressed full-text retrieval system called MG that incorporates recently-developed state-of-the-art algorithms for compression and information retrieval (Witten *et al.* [257]), and all of the illustrations and examples in this chapter are taken from that system.[§]

[§]The MG system is public-domain software, and is available by anonymous ftp from munnari.oz.au [128.250.1.21] in the directory /pub/mg. A tutorial overview of the system appears in Witten *et al.* [257].

11.2 The information explosion

People have been complaining about the information explosion for years, but in reality it is only just beginning. It was estimated in 1975 that some fifty million books had been published up to that time [114], and the Library of Congress contains some twenty-two million volumes today. But the real problem is the rate of increase: it has also been estimated that the amount of information in the world doubles every twenty months [196]. These mind-boggling statistics may not be very accurate, but they do serve to underscore the problem that we all feel: information is getting out of control.

The amount of information that is kept on computers is growing at a much faster rate. As has often been observed, the real impact of computers is not so much in computation as in information and communication. The appearance of the personal computer a decade or two ago was a minor revolution. But what we are experiencing now, with the advent of technology such as the CD-ROM and the Internet, is a major revolution in information and the communication of information.

Personal information spaces. We all have our own personal document databases—large collections of books, magazines, and papers, of which, at any given time, we are only interested in a tiny fraction. As a very rough estimate, we might suppose that one printed page contains about four hundred words, or, including formatting and punctuation, about 2500 characters. This means that a 400-page book contains roughly one million characters. If we assume that the book is two centimeters thick, then a bookshelf stores information at the rate of fifty million characters per linear meter. An office wall of books might be five shelves high and four meters long, so it represents perhaps one *billion* characters, or, in computer terms, one gigabyte.¶

A personal information database should be able to hold more than just text. Images are an important part of many documents, usually taking the form of diagrams or photographs. The above rough estimate of the amount of storage needed for a document database conveniently ignores the cost of storing images. It is much more difficult to estimate the amount of space required for pictures than it is for text, but it is likely to be considerable. In a typical, well-illustrated book the pictures, when digitized, will certainly occupy several times as much space as the text.

Two gigabytes, equivalent to the text contained in perhaps just a few bookshelves if pictures are included, is commensurate in size with what one might expect to see on personal workstations today or in the very near future. The standard disk storage on a typical well-equipped workstation has grown from one megabyte to one gigabyte in just a few years. It is now far more cost-effective to purchase a new disk than to spend time tidying up, reviewing, and re-organizing

---

¶To be precise, one gigabyte $= 2^{30}$ bytes $= 1,073,741,824$ bytes, but it is convenient to approximate this number by $10^9 = 1,000,000,000$. Similarly, one megabyte $= 2^{20} \approx 10^6 = 1,000,000$ bytes.

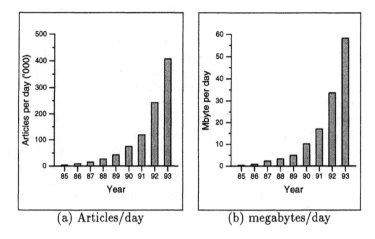

Figure 11.1 Growth of news on the Internet

one's collection of personal on-line information to create space for new data. Most personal computers are connected to networks and their users frequently download vast quantities of information. Consequently it is likely that many knowledge workers will very soon have personal on-line information bases that extend to a gigabyte or so.

Information availability.　The Internet is the world's largest computer network, and one of its most popular and widely-used services is the "Usenet" network news [148]. To give an idea of the information explosion on computer networks, Figure 11.1 shows how Usenet has grown over the years in terms of both the daily number of news articles and the number of megabytes they represent. Indexing, or rather the lack of it, is already a severe impediment to using the Internet as an information resource: serious networkers spend a large fraction of their day scanning through the news for information that is of interest to them. The volume of news has recently broken one hundred megabytes (roughly the equivalent of one hundred large printed books) *per day*. Even more alarming, though, is the rate of growth: the number of articles, newsgroups, users, and computers on the Internet have all been increasing exponentially since statistics began being collected in late 1984. As Figure 11.1 shows, the network news traffic almost doubles each year. In fact, the total Internet traffic is growing much faster: presently it rises by 12% each month, which corresponds to a doubling every six months. Clearly this cannot continue forever: there are limiting factors.‖

In 1937, the renowned science fiction author H.G. Wells was promoting the

---

‖For example, projecting the rate of growth of Internet users and the rate of growth of world population, the former will overtake the latter during the year 2000!

concept of a "world brain" based on a permanent world encyclopedia [255]. It is hard to resist pointing to the Internet as at least an augur of such a phenomenon. With nearly two million computers, each equipped with (let us say) five hundred megabytes of storage, it has been described as the world's largest library. If just 5% of this disk space were allocated for network use, the total space would amount to nearly fifty terabytes (fifty thousand gigabytes). According to a 1993 estimate, the disk space occupied worldwide by the Internet news is half this amount (twenty-two terabytes). Even the smaller figure is more than enough to accommodate a full-text database containing the text of the fifty million books estimated to have been published, if they are compressed using the techniques reviewed in this chapter. Of course, the problem then becomes that of access— being able to locate the right work at the right time; fortunately there is enough space to store a compressed full-text index along with the text to provide a base level of access to this universal library.

Example database. Throughout this chapter we use as an example a document database containing just over two gigabytes of text. Called *TREC* (the acronym stands for *text retrieval conference*), this large collection has been distributed to research groups worldwide for comparative information retrieval experiments. It includes documents taken from five sources: the Associated Press newswire; the U.S. Department of Energy; the U.S. Federal Register; the Wall Street Journal; and a selection of computer magazines and journals published by Ziff-Davis. Some statistics of the database are summarized in Table 11.1. It comprises nearly 750,000 documents averaging about 450 words each; the longest occupies over 2.5 megabytes. One document (selected because it matched the query *managing* AND *gigabytes*) is shown in Figure 11.2; like all documents in this collection it includes embedded mark-up commands enclosed in angle brackets. It is appropriate to strip out all the mark-up tags before any indexing takes place, and the values reported in Table 11.1 are exclusive of mark-up.

Documents	742,358
Number of words	333,856,749
Distinct words	538,244
Index pointers	136,010,026
Total size (megabyte)	2054.52

Table 11.1 The *TREC* document collection

11.3 Designing document databases

When designing a document database, several important decisions must be made that affect the way that items are retrieved. These include the unit in which items are retrieved, the manner in which queries can be couched, the accuracy to

```
<DOC>
<DOCNO> ZF07-781-012 </DOCNO>
<DOCID> 07 781 012.  </DOCID>
<JOURNAL> Government Computer News Oct 16 1989 v8 n21 p39(2)
Full Text COPYRIGHT Ziff-Davis Pub.  Co.  1989.  </JOURNAL>
<TITLE> Compressing data spurs growth of imaging.  </TITLE>
<AUTHOR> Hosinski, Joan M. </AUTHOR>
<DESCRIPTORS> Topic:  Data Compression, Data Communications, Optical
Disks, Imaging Technology.  Feature:  illustration chart.  Caption:
Path taken by image file.  (chart) </DESCRIPTORS>
<TEXT>
Compressing Data Spurs Growth of imaging

Data compression has spurred the growth of imaging applications, many
of which require users to send large amounts of data between two
locations, an Electronic Trend Publications report said.
    Data compression is an ''essential enabling technology'' and the
''importance of the compression step is comparable to the importance
of the optical disk as a cost-effective storage medium,'' the
Saratoga, Calif., company said in the report, Data Compression Impact
on Document and Image Processing Storage and Retrieval.

[Six paragraphs omitted]

</TEXT>
</DOC>
```

Figure 11.2 Sample text from *TREC*

which the index records positions in documents, and the lexical or morphological transformations that take place prior to indexing. All of these can be specified by the user at the time that the document collection is indexed, depending on the ways in which the collection is to be accessed. Here we examine them in turn.

Documents.   We suppose that an information base or *document database* can be treated as a set of indivisible atomic *documents*. A document is the unit of text that is returned in response to queries. For example, if the database consists of a collection of electronic office memoranda, each memo might be taken to be one document. In a list of names and addresses, each person's entry might be viewed as a separate document. When a printed work has been transcribed, each physical page might be a document. In the *TREC* database, each article is taken to be a document. There will also be situations in which it is sensible to choose a "document" in the database to be one paragraph or even just one sentence of a source document. This would allow paragraphs that meet some requirement to be extracted, independent of the text in which they are embedded.

   The components of an information base include natural language text; black-white, grayscale and color images; and images that are predominantly textual; as well as numerous other miscellaneous file types. The latter category includes such things as word-processed documents (e.g. RTF or "rich text format" files), structured pictures (e.g. PostScript files), address lists and bibliographies, computer programs in source and even binary form, video clips, and sound bites. We use the word *document* in a liberal sense: a picture or video clip is a document, and so is a source program or a binary program. Each individual file may well be treated as a document, although a PostScript file might be split into pages, an RTF file into sections, and a bibliography or address list into individual entries.

Representative terms. Every document is described by a set of *representative terms*, or simply *terms*, which are used to index it. The index must be capable of identifying all documents that contain combinations of specified terms or are in some other way judged to be relevant to the set of query terms. In the case of textual documents, the entire text is generally regarded as its own set of representative terms, so that any words contained in the message can be used as query terms. Modern compression techniques make it quite feasible to index every single word in the text—even common words like *and* and *the*—so that no thought need be given to selecting index terms when documents are filed.

In particular circumstances a more restricted set of representative terms may be appropriate. In an office mail system, the representative terms for each memo might be the recipient's name, the sender's name, the date, and the subject line. It would then be possible to issue queries such as *find memos from Jane to John on the subject of taxation.* However, a full index would allow memos to be retrieved whose body contained any given combination of words, and this additional power is likely to be useful in practice—particularly since the extra cost is small.

For other kinds of document, other techniques are necessary to derive the representative terms. The most appropriate terms are ones that are derived manually. If the documents are images, the terms to be indexed might be a few words describing each image, and a query might ask that all images containing an *elephant* be retrieved. This supposes that someone has studied the collection of images and decided in advance (by creating representative terms) which ones show elephants.

Although the task of taking an arbitrary image and deciding mechanically what objects are portrayed is a major research area in its own right, some features of images can be extracted automatically and used for indexing purposes [189]. It is relatively easy to index images on the basis of overall hue and intensity, so that queries like *retrieve all images that are predominantly greenish-blue* can be answered. Texture is another indexable attribute, with components such as coarseness, which measures the texture's scale or grain size; directionality, which measures whether or not it has a favored direction; and contrast. Texture can be specified either linguistically, using words or numbers to represent feature values, or visually, by selecting from a menu something that resembles the desired texture. Shape features, like area, circularity, eccentricity, and fractal dimension, can also be measured and used for indexing.

For many types of information, it is possible to glean at least some index terms automatically. The filename in which the information is stored provides a starting point. Text is easily extracted from a word-processed (e.g. RTF) document, and even in the case of structured pictures (e.g. PostScript), text strings—perhaps containing just a few words of labels—can be identified and used for indexing. Text strings extracted from binary programs, which generally contain prompts and error messages, will prove useful for indexing purposes. Optical character recognition (OCR) can be used to extract terms from images that are predominantly textual, such as faxes and other scanned text. Even if the document is stored in image form to guard against OCR errors, it may be acceptable to index it using automatically extracted, perhaps slightly garbled, text.

Index granularity.   The *granularity* of an index is the resolution to which term locations are recorded. Having decided for an office information system that a document will be a single memo, the system designer may still require that the index be capable of ascertaining a more exact location within the document of each term. Then, for example, documents in which the words *tax* and *avoidance* appear in the same sentence can be located using only the index.

In the limit, if the granularity of the index is taken to be one word, the index will record the exact location of every word in the collection, and so (with some considerable effort) the original text can be recovered from the index. When the granularity of the index is coarser—to the sentence or document level—the original text can no longer be recovered from the index, and a more economical representation becomes possible.

Word-level granularity has evident advantages over document-level granularity. For example, in an office memo system the query *find memos from Jane to John on the subject of taxation* cannot be answered directly from a document-level index, because any memos that mention Jane, John and taxation will be returned regardless of whether these words appear in the sender, recipient, and subject field respectively. With a word-level index the query could be answered by seeking memos that contain *From* and *Jane* as adjacent words, as well as the pairs *To* and *John*, and *Re* and *Taxation*. However, the same effect can be achieved using a document-level index if a post-retrieval scan is implemented. All memos containing the words *John*, *Jane*, and *taxation* are retrieved and then their text is linearly scanned looking for memos that contain the strings *From: Jane*, *To: John*, and *Re: Taxation*.

Index terms.   A more useful index is obtained if words are transformed before being included as representative terms. One transformation, *case-folding*, maps all upper-case letters to their lower-case equivalent (or vice versa). For example, if all upper-case letters are folded to lower-case, *ACT, Act,* and *act* are all indexed as *act,* and are regarded as equivalent at query time—regardless of which original version appeared in the source document. This transformation is carried out so that those querying the database can pose case-invariant queries and need not guess the case that has been used.

A second transformation is for words to be reduced to their morphological roots, that is, for all suffixes and other modifiers to be removed. For example, *compression, compressed,* and *compressor* all have the word *compress* as their root. This process is known as *stemming,* and it ensures that queries retrieve relevant documents even if the exact form of the word is different. If the representative terms are created using stemming, and all query terms are also stemmed, the query *data* AND *compression* would retrieve documents containing phrases such as *compressed data is* and *to compress the data.*

A third transformation that is sometimes applied (although we do not generally recommend it) is the omission of *stop words.* These are words that are deemed to be sufficiently common or of such low information content that their use in a query would be unlikely to eliminate many documents, since they are present in almost every document. If this really were the case, little would be lost by excluding them from the index. At the top of any stop word list for English is usually the word *the,* closely followed by *a, it,* and so on. Other terms might also be stopped in particular applications. In an on-line computer manual, appearances of the terms *options* and *usage* might not be indexed, and a financial archive might choose to stop words such as *dollar* and *stock,* and perhaps even *Dow* and *Jones.*

The omission of stop words places some restrictions on the use of the index. For example, Shakespeare's use of the verb *to do* has been studied, which would normally be treated as stop words. Klein *et al.* [145] mention a query of a French text collection for occurrences of the phrase *un de ces* ("one of these"). All three words were stop words, and so the index gave no help at all in locating them. It turns out that removing stop words yields little saving if an appropriate compression scheme is used, and we favor an approach in which every word in the database is regarded as a queryable term.

Finally, a further possible transformation is *thesaural substitution,* where synonyms—*fast* and *rapid,* for example—are identified and indexed under one or more class representatives. Multiple indexing is required in this case because *fast* should be represented in the class *starve* as well as the class *speedy.*

11.4   Storing the documents

This chapter argues that technological advances in compressing and indexing information have produced a qualitative change in the feasibility of large-scale full-text retrieval. A paradox of modern computer storage and communication systems is that despite a staggering increase in storage and transmission capacities, more and more effort has been put into using compression to increase the amount of data that can be handled. No matter how much storage space or transmission bandwidth is available, it invariably becomes full very quickly. We look briefly at the components of a document database to get a feel for how much compression today's technology can offer.

Text.   Text compression involves changing the representation of a file so that it takes less space to store, or less time to transmit, while allowing the original file to be reconstructed exactly from the compressed representation. Exact reproduction distinguishes text compression techniques from more general data compression methods. For some types of data other than text, such as sound or images, small changes, or *noise*, in the reconstructed data can be tolerated. However, with text it must be possible to reproduce the original file exactly.

The best text compression techniques achieve their power through the use of *adaptive* compression. All compression is relative to a model of the text being encoded—for example, the model may be a statistical characterization of the letter or word sequences that are expected. In adaptive compression the model is built up from the text that has just been coded and is continually adjusted as more text is processed. By basing the model on what has been seen so far, adaptive compression methods combine two key virtues: they are able to encode in a single pass through the input file, and they are able to compress a wide variety of inputs effectively rather than being fine-tuned for one particular type of data such as English text.

However, adaptive compression is inappropriate for full-text databases, because it is necessary to be able to decompress documents individually, rather than having to work through from the beginning of the database in order to determine what the model should be. A more appropriate compression system is obtained by building a *lexicon* that contains every word that appears in the text, along with the number of times it occurs. This can be used to derive a code that is used to represent the word each time it appears. Each word's code can be stored in the lexicon and used for decompression. However, a technique is available that avoids having to store the codes in the lexicon, and this saves considerable space.

The lexicon for the *TREC* example document database contains about half a million distinct words, as shown in Table 11.1. This is an extraordinarily large number, many more than are contained in English dictionaries. In our experience the number of distinct "words" in a text grows as an almost linear function of its size, without the tailing-off effect that one might predict. This is principally due to proper names, words appearing with different capitalization, acronyms, and so on, but also partially because new misspelt words appear at a reasonably constant rate. The result is that the lexicon continues to grow. Incidentally, it is important when splitting a document database into words to restrict the number of digits that may comprise a word. For example, we have worked with a database that contains 261,829 pages, numbered from 1 to 261829, and these numbers greatly inflated the word count until special precautions were taken to limit the number of numeric tokens to ten thousand by starting a new token every four digits (thus 261829 would be 2618 followed by 29).

The half-million-word example lexicon occupies just over 10 megabytes of storage, an amount which is excessive considering that decompression speed drops dramatically unless the lexicon is kept in main memory. Fortunately, it is possible to store a partial lexicon and "spell out" uncommon words whenever they appear in the text [177]. This reduces the lexicon size to 1 megabyte, with an almost imperceptible decrease in compression efficiency.

Using this coding technique, English text can generally be compressed to around 25% or 30% of its original size. The example collection compresses to 29%—not much worse than the best-known adaptive compression techniques, which compress it to 23%.

Images. In many circumstances it is necessary for a document database to store images. The images may be correspondence received by mail, or by facsimile, or they might be old records that had previously been stored on paper. Some organizations—such as the military—must store records for decades because they are required for pension purposes. Elsewhere it may be necessary to store images of a document for legal reasons. For example, an image of a check or credit card slip may be needed to settle a dispute, and the *way* in which the document is written may be as significant as *what* is written. Images of a text may also be important for historical reasons. Scholars retrieving a document may be interested in the original typeface, layout, alterations, or notes in the margin.

If the images that need to be stored in a full-text retrieval system can only be obtained from paper, they must be scanned into a computer, where they will be represented as a digital image of the page, made up of picture elements (or *pixels*). This sort of image is often referred to as a *document image*.

Pictures present a very different kind of compression problem from text. Whereas when compressing text it is essential that the decoded document is absolutely identical to the one that was encoded, for images this may be less important. Digital images are usually the result of converting a continuous range of shades or colors into a finite number of values. This means that a digital image is already an approximation to the original, and it does not necessarily make sense to store very fine details because they may have no physical counterpart in the source document. Substantial gains in compression can invariably be made if inexact reproduction is tolerated, and often the difference is so small that the human eye cannot detect it, or has great difficulty in doing so. Such methods are called *lossy*, since they lose some of the original document's detail. In contrast, methods for text compression are generally *lossless*—what is decompressed is supposed to be *exactly* the same as what was compressed.

There is a wide variety of kinds of image that information systems must accommodate. Depending on their content and purpose, different images tolerate different amounts of loss. Some are black and white, while in others each pixel can take on one of several shades of gray, and still others are reproduced in color. A further dimension of variation relates to how the image is to be decompressed and displayed: sometimes, particularly when browsing, it is nice to see an approximation to the final image as quickly as possible and have it gradually build up to the full level of detail—that way the user can interrupt and move to another image before the current one is complete. Because images can take considerable time to decompress, this provides a very real advantage.

All these possibilities mean that there are many different methods for dealing with images.

Most images are much more compressible than text. Reduction of an image to 10% of its original size or less is quite common, depending on the type of image, and for inexact reproduction compression figures of 1% or better are often achieved, depending on the reproduction quality desired.

Textual images.   Many images that are handled in daily life—particularly in the office environment—depict documents that contain mainly typed or typeset text. We call these *textual images*. For example, the digitized images used in facsimile transmission are generally business documents, and hence predominantly textual. Most office work deals with a mixture of machine-readable text and traditional paper documents, and serious problems arise from the fact that the documents are stored and transmitted in different physical forms. In document archiving, documents are scanned and stored electronically for later retrieval. While they sometimes contain line drawings or halftone pictures, more often they comprise text alone, or text mixed with a small assortment of other image types.

One possibility for textual image compression is to perform OCR on the text, and represent the document as a sequence of character codes in some standard alphabet. Depending on the document's layout, and the application, it may be necessary to include the position of characters on the page, as well as their sequential order. However, there are significant drawbacks to representing a document in this form. Optical character recognition is not completely reliable, particularly with poor-quality source documents. Imperfections in the original document, incorrect contrast settings when scanning, varying typefaces, and unusual characters, all conspire to produce high error rates. Stylized fonts, foreign languages, and mathematical expressions can be converted to nonsense. An obvious difficulty is the need to deal with many different typefaces and sizes—and in some ways the advent of computerized word processing has exacerbated the problem by vastly increasing the typographical repertoire of typical office documents. Finally, other ambiguities are caused by the nature of the letterforms themselves. For example, it can be difficult to distinguish between the letters *o*, *0*, *O*, *Q*, and *D*, and often context and linguistic knowledge must be used for disambiguation.

For these reasons, it is generally risky to subject documents to OCR, store the result as text, and discard the originals. In some circumstances, it is absolutely essential—for legal or historical reasons—to be able to reproduce documents in their original form. A database might include documents for which accurate facsimiles may be needed for legal purposes, although a textual version could be more useful for the purpose of routine consultation.

Special methods have been developed to store textual images effectively [256]. These involve segmenting an image into connected groups of pixels or *marks*, corresponding approximately to individual characters; constructing a library of the patterns seen in the image, so that each letterform is only stored once; and coding the marks in the image as a sequence of pattern numbers. From this information, along with the library itself and the offsets from one mark to the next, an approximate image can be reconstructed. This provides a very accurate, but not pixel-perfect, reproduction of the original image from between 0.5% and 7% of the information, depending on the resolution. Not surprisingly, higher resolution permits greater compression.

In cases where an exact reproduction of the original is necessary, a second stage can be applied to compress the *residue*, defined as those pixels that differ between the original and reconstructed image. This reduces the compression to between 2% and 15% of the original storage, again depending on resolution.

Other documents. Other document types include spreadsheet data files, word-processed documents, address lists and bibliographies, output from drawing packages, computer programs in source or binary form, and so on. While specialized compression methods may be able to produce slightly better performance, these all compress quite well using general text compression techniques. Note that documents which exhibit an unusually rich vocabulary—such as those containing many person or place names—are generally less compressible than natural language text.

Video and sound clips should be compressed using specialized tools such as the MPEG moving picture compression standard. Relatively poor compression results when these are processed with standard text compression techniques.

11.5   Indexing a document collection

The index is the data structure through which a document collection is queried. It is essential that the index be accessible quickly; moreover it is advantageous to minimize the space overhead incurred by the need to store an index. Here is a rare case in which one can eat one's cake and have it too: compressed index structures are not only much smaller than uncompressed ones, they are also faster to query because access time is usually dominated by the time needed for reading the index off disk. First we outline how indexes can be represented, then we discuss how the index can be created, and finally we summarize the computational resources required by the MG system to store and access a document database.

Index. A word-level index, which records with each word of the lexicon the exact locations in which it appears in the text, contains the same number of pointers as there are words in the text. Since the space required to store a pointer is not very different from that needed to store a word, an uncompressed index is about the same size as the text itself.

Three factors serve to significantly reduce the space occupied by the index. First, a document-level rather than a word-level index contains far fewer pointers, because whenever a word appears several times in the same document, only one pointer is needed. On typical collections this roughly halves the number of pointers to be stored. Second, the number of bits occupied by a pointer is smaller because each entry in the index points to a particular document rather than to an individual word. For a collection of a million documents and 300 million words, such a pointer takes twenty bits rather than twenty-nine. Finally, compression techniques can be used to reduce this to about six bits per pointer for typical document collections, a very worthwhile saving indeed.

The key to compression is the observation that each inverted file entry is an ascending sequence of integers. For example, suppose that some term *elephant* appears in 8 documents of a collection, those numbered 3, 5, 20, 21, 23, 76, 77, 78. Then this term is described in the inverted file by the entry

$$\langle elephant; 8; [3, 5, 20, 21, 23, 76, 77, 78] \rangle.$$

More generally, along with each term t is stored f_t, the number of documents it appears in, and a list of f_t document numbers:

$$\langle t; f_t; [d_1, d_2, \ldots, d_{f_t}] \rangle.$$

Because the document numbers within each inverted file entry are in ascending order, and all processing is sequential from the beginning of the entry, the list can be stored as an initial position followed by a list of *gaps*, the differences $d_{k+1} - d_k$. Thus the entry for the term above could just as easily be stored as

$$\langle elephant; 8; [3, 2, 15, 1, 2, 53, 1, 1] \rangle.$$

No information has been lost, since the original document numbers can be obtained by calculating cumulative sums of the gaps.

The two forms are equivalent, but it is not obvious that any significant saving has been achieved. However, several specific models have been proposed for describing the probability distribution of gap sizes. These can be grouped into two broad classes—*global* methods, in which every inverted file entry is compressed using the same common model; and *local* methods, where the compression model for each term's entries is adjusted according to some stored parameter, usually the frequency of the term. Local models tend to outperform global ones in terms of compression, and are no less efficient in terms of the processing time required during decoding, but they tend to be more complex to implement.

The actual size of the index for a particular collection depends on such factors as the average size of documents, the richness of the vocabulary, and the stemming algorithm that is used. As a rough rule of thumb, an index can be reduced to 15% of the original size of the text for a small collection, and 6% of the size for a large one like the example *TREC* database.

Building the index. Constructing the index is one of the most challenging tasks to be faced when a database is built. The process of building an index is known as *inverting* the database. Each document in the database contains some index terms, and each index term appears in some of the documents. This relationship can be expressed by a *frequency matrix*, in which each column corresponds to one term, each row corresponds to one document, and the number stored at any row and column is the frequency, in that document, of the term indicated by that column. To create an index the matrix must be transposed to form a new version in which the rows correspond to terms and the columns to documents.

Despite the apparent simplicity of this operation, inversion is in reality a very difficult task. The problem is the size of the frequency matrix. Suppose that the example collection is to be inverted. The matrix is daunting: approximately 500,000 index terms times 750,000 documents, or 1.5 *terabytes* if four-byte numbers are used. If this is stored on disk, each matrix access during inversion would require a seek, and this results in an inversion process that literally takes a lifetime.**

A different approach is to take an initial pass through the document database recording (index term, document) pairs, and sort the list of pairs. For the example collection this involves sorting a list of 136 million index term occurrences, and although this is feasible using external sorting techniques, it requires about 2.5 gigabytes of temporary file space.

Designing an algorithm to solve the problem in a practical sense becomes an intricate trade-off between disk storage, main memory size, and processing time. Simple algorithms place great demands upon one or other of these resources. One way that the problem has been solved is to make use of the index compression techniques, but applied in main memory. Using this method the example collection has been inverted in under five hours on a machine with 40 megabytes of main memory, and little more disk than is required to store the final compressed index.†† Estimates indicate that a five gigabyte collection could be inverted in about fifteen hours on the same machine.

Summary. The resources required by a compressed document database are as follows. Natural language text reduces to about 25–30% of its original size. Other textual material is likely to reduce to 25–50% of its original size. Images and textual images can generally be reduced considerably more than text, but much depends on the complexity of the image and on whether exact or approximate reproduction is required: figures range from 15% to well under 1%. For a collection of text documents the index takes about 5–15% of the original collection size, even when every word and number is indexed. For other types of documents, with manually produced index terms, the index will require even less space. Thus a fully-indexed text collection can be stored in one third to one half of the space required for the uncompressed text alone, and the inclusion of image information greatly increases the proportion saved.

The speed at which a document database can be compressed and inverted is approximately 4 megabytes/minute, or 250 megabytes/hour. Starting from scratch, it takes eight CPU-hours to build a retrieval database from a two giga-

---

** A closer estimate is 127 years, nearer to two lifetimes—and to make matters worse, disk lifetimes are much shorter than our alloted three score years and ten.

†† All processing times are measured on a Sun SPARC 10 Model 512, using one processor.

byte collection of text, and under two minutes to compress and index a small four megabyte collection (the verses of the King James Bible). A mid-range machine is required to create large document databases; for the *TREC* collection 40 megabytes of main memory is necessary. Image compression methods vary a great deal in execution time and it is hard to give an overall figure; however, the inclusion of images is likely to slow down database creation quite significantly.

On retrieval, text is decompressed at the rate of over 50 megabytes/minute, and can be done on a much smaller machine, with perhaps only one megabyte or so of main memory.

11.6 Querying a full-text information base

We now turn to the question of how best to use the index to locate information in the document database that it describes. There are two basically different types of query: *boolean* queries and *ranked* queries. Both are worth including (and both are implemented in the MG system) so that users can choose whichever suits their query best.

Boolean queries. A boolean query comprises a list of *terms*—words to be sought in the text—that are combined using the connectives AND, OR, and NOT. The *answers* to the query are those documents that satisfy the stipulated condition. For example, an appropriate query to search for material relevant to this chapter is

> *information* AND *compression* AND *retrieval.*

All three words (or variants considered equivalent by a stemming algorithm) must occur somewhere in every answer. They need not be adjacent, nor appear in any particular order. Documents containing phrases like *the compression of large amounts of information can speed its retrieval* will be returned as answers. Also returned would be a document containing *this gives information about the fractional distillation scavenging technique for retrieving argon from compressed air*—perhaps not quite what is sought, but nonetheless a correct answer to the query.

A problem with all retrieval systems is that invariably some (perhaps many) answers are returned that are not relevant, and these must be filtered out manually. A difficult choice must be made between casting a broad query to be sure of retrieving all relevant material, even if it is diluted with many irrelevant answers; and posing a narrow one that ensures that most documents retrieved are of interest, but risks eliminating others sight unseen. A broad search that identifies virtually all the relevant documents is said to have high *recall*, while one in which virtually all the retrieved documents are relevant has high *precision*. An enduring theme in information retrieval is the tension between these two virtues. One must choose in any particular application whether to prefer high precision or high recall, and cast the query appropriately.

Another problem with boolean retrieval systems is that small variations in a query can generate very different results. The query

> *data* AND *compression* AND *retrieval*

is likely to produce quite a different answer set from the previous query, yet the person issuing it probably sees it as very similar. To be sure of catching all the required documents, users become adept at adding extra terms, and learn to pose queries like

> *(information* OR *text* OR *data* OR *image)* AND
> *(compression* OR *compaction* OR *decompression)* AND
> *(archiving* OR *retrieval* OR *storage* OR *indexing)*

where the parentheses indicate operation order. This, coupled with the high cost of errors and poorly formed queries, is the reason why librarians guard access to the large international databases: formulating queries is something of an art, and librarians have the necessary experience and linguistic skills to guide a query very quickly toward an acceptable set of answers. However, when retrieval is cheap and immediate, end users can learn from their mistakes and quickly become proficient at formulating queries.

Despite these drawbacks, boolean retrieval systems have been the primary mechanism used to access on-line information over the last three decades, in both commercial and scientific applications.

Ranked queries. Rather than formulate a boolean query, it is sometimes easier to simply list words that are of interest and have the retrieval mechanism supply the documents that seem most relevant. For example, to locate material for this chapter, the query

> *text, data, image, compression, compaction, archiving, storage, re-*
> *trieval, indexing, document, database, searching, information*

is, to a person at least, probably a clearer description of the topic than the boolean query above.

Identifying documents relevant to a list of terms is not just a matter of converting the terms to a boolean query. It would be fruitless to connect these particular terms with AND operations, since vanishingly few documents are likely to match.[‡‡] It would be just as pointless to use OR connectives, since far too many documents will match and very few are likely to be useful answers.

The solution is to use a *ranked* query. This involves a heuristic that is applied to gauge the *similarity* of each document to the query. Based upon this numeric indicator, a specified number (say ten or a hundred) of most closely matching documents are returned as answers. If the heuristic is good, or the number specified is small, or (better still) both, there will be a predominance of relevant answers—high precision. If the heuristic is good and the number

---

[‡‡] We cannot, of course, say that no documents will match. This page certainly does.

specified is large, most of the documents in the collection that are relevant will fall within the set of documents returned—high recall. In practice, low precision invariably accompanies high recall, because many irrelevant documents will almost certainly crop up before the last of the relevant ones appears in the ranking. Conversely, when the precision is high, recall will probably be low, because precision will only be high near the beginning of the ranked list of documents, at which point only a few of the total set of relevant ones will have been encountered.

Great effort has been invested over the years in a quest for similarity measures and other ranking strategies that succeed in keeping both recall and precision reasonably high. Simple techniques just count the number of query terms that appear somewhere in the document: this is sometimes called *coordinate matching*. A document that contains five of the query terms will be ranked higher than one containing only three, and documents that match just one query term will be ranked lower still. An obvious drawback is that long documents are favored over short ones, since by virtue of size alone they are more likely to contain a wider selection of the query terms. Furthermore, common terms appearing in the query tend to discriminate unfairly against documents that do not happen to contain them, even ones that match on highly discriminatory words. For example, a query concerning *the, electronic, office* might rank a document containing *the office garbage can* ahead of one that discusses *an electronic workplace*. A word such as *the* in the query should probably not be given the same importance as *electronic*.

More sophisticated techniques take into account the length of the documents, and assign a numeric *weight* to each term. One commonly-used technique, the *cosine* measure, represents both documents and queries as vectors in n-dimensional space, n being the number of distinct terms in the collection [215]. The similarity measure is taken as the cosine of the angle between the document and query vector—the larger this cosine, the greater the similarity. For query Q and document D, this is given by

$$\frac{1}{W_q W_d} \sum_{t=1}^{n} w_{q,t} \cdot w_{d,t}.$$

Here, $w_{q,t}$ is the weight of the term t in the query, $w_{d,t}$ is the weight of the same term in the document, and

$$W_q = \left(\sum_{t=1}^{n} w_{q,t}^2 \right)^{1/2}, \quad W_d = \left(\sum_{t=1}^{n} w_{d,t}^2 \right)^{1/2}$$

are the lengths of the query and document vectors respectively. The weights of terms in the query and document are calculated from the frequencies with which the terms appear, for example by

$$w_{d,t} = -f_{d,t} \cdot \log_2 \frac{f_t}{N}$$

where $f_{d,t}$ is the frequency of the term in the document, f_t the number of documents that contain the term, and N the number of documents in the collection. It is usual to assume that $f_{q,t}$ is 1 for terms in the query and 0 for terms that are not.

Implementation and performance. It is relatively straightforward to process a boolean query using an inverted file index. The lexicon is searched for each term; each inverted file entry is retrieved and decoded; and the entries are merged, taking the intersection, the union, or the complement, as appropriate. Finally, the documents so indexed are retrieved and displayed to the user as the list of answers. On the example document database, for a typical boolean query of 5 to 10 terms, a second or so is spent reading and decoding inverted file entries, and then accessing, decoding, and writing the documents takes anything from tenths of a second to hundreds of seconds—depending on the number of answers. As noted earlier, text is decompressed at the rate of 55 megabytes/minute.

The cosine measure requires more information than boolean query processing because it is necessary to store within-document frequencies in the index. Furthermore, efficient evaluation of the formula is potentially very expensive, in terms of both processing time and memory requirements. Fortunately, approximate methods are available which significantly reduce these requirements [178]. The result is that ranked queries can be evaluated on large collections using not much more memory space and processing time than is required by boolean query evaluation. Ranked queries generally contain many more terms than boolean ones, and tests show that ranked queries of 40–50 terms are executed within 3–5 seconds—only slightly slower than boolean queries designed to retrieve the same set of answers.

It is interesting to consider how useful the cosine ranking method is. On a set of fifty queries applied to the example collection, it achieves an average precision exceeding 40% on the top one hundred answers to each query. In other words, when a ranked query was posed to *TREC*—which contains three-quarters of a million documents—forty of the top one hundred documents returned for each query were relevant. Such performance would be very difficult to achieve with a boolean query.

11.7 The problem of dynamic collections

An important issue that has not been addressed in this chapter—and is not addressed in the MG system—is the question of dynamic collections of documents. We have assumed that the entire database is available to be compressed and indexed at one time. However, it is rare for a database to be truly static. Even such collections as *The Complete Works of Shakespeare* undergo occasional expansion as new sonnets are discovered and authenticated, and dictionaries and encyclopedias are the subject of almost continual revision—as of course are personal information spaces.

A collection can be dynamic in one of two ways. First, it might provide an *insert* operation that appends a new document to an existing collection but does not change any of the current documents. More radically, it might also be necessary to support an *edit* operation that allows current documents to be altered and perhaps even removed.

It turns out that when compressing text, ten- or one hundred-fold expansion of the text can be tolerated using an incremental compression method without significant degradation in compression rates [177]. Adopting a conservative approach and rebuilding every time the collection has increased in size by a factor of ten means that just three recompressions will see a collection grow from one megabyte to one gigabyte, and a further three rebuildings will increase it to one terabyte. This latter quantity is so large that it seems safe to conclude that periodic recompression is an acceptable approach to the problem of maintaining a compression model in the face of document insertion, and that just 5–10 rebuildings will be more than sufficient during the life expectancy of a database.

More problematic is the effect that document insertion has upon the index. The simplest way to handle this is to accumulate updates in a "stop-press" file that is checked for each query issued. When the stop-press grows too large, or when the opportunity arises, the entire collection is rebuilt. The drawback of this approach is that it takes ever longer to reindex the data, and this operation has to be performed relatively frequently. Recompression of the text need only be carried out when the collection has doubled, but to defer reindexing until half of the data is in the stop-press is unthinkable. Fortunately, it is possible to design data structures that accommodate a more continuous approach to the problem of keeping the index up to date.

It becomes significantly harder to implement the cosine similarity measure in a dynamic collection, since the insertion of even one document might affect the weights of all others. The most practical way to handle this is to allow document weights to drift from their true values, and periodically rebuild the entire file of document weights. Since this can be done in a single pass over the inverted file, without involving the main text, it is not expensive.

A simple, brute force, solution to the whole question of dynamic collections is to ignore the problem and re-create the entire database at periodic intervals. Even a two gigabyte collection can be rebuilt overnight. Clearly, however, this is a stop-gap measure which, given the rate of information growth, cannot last very far into the future.

11.8 Conclusion

This chapter has demonstrated the feasibility of full-text indexing of large information bases. The use of modern compression techniques means that there is no space penalty: large document databases can be compressed and indexed in less than a third of the space required by the originals. Surprisingly, there is little or no time penalty either: querying can be faster because less information needs to be read from disk. Simple queries can be answered in a second; more complex ones with more query terms may take a few seconds. One important application is the creation of static databases on CD-ROM, and a 1.5 gigabyte document database can be compressed onto a standard 660 megabyte CD-ROM.

Creating a compressed and indexed document database containing hundreds of thousands of documents and gigabytes of data takes a few hours. Whereas retrieval can be done on ordinary workstations, creation requires a machine with a fair amount of main memory.

Acknowledgements

We would like to thank Neil Sharman and Stuart Inglis for their work on the implementation of MG. We have benefited from extremely helpful comments by Saul Greenberg on the structure of this chapter; from our long association with Justin Zobel in developing this line of research; and from assistance by Craig Nevill-Manning and Stuart Inglis with some of the details. This research was supported by the Australian Research Council.

Chapter 12

The Digital Library and The Home-based User

Andy Sloane*

12.1 Introduction

The move from paper-based information to a fully digitised form allows many new possibilities that open up the world of learning and education to a wider audience than ever before. The public library systems that have grown over the last few centuries are a wealth of information in an accessible form. To allow the same information to be accessible in a digital form is to allow both the current users of the information better access to it, and at the same time open up a broader range of information to more users who may be disadvantaged by locality or disability. The digital format enables a far greater range of delivery systems to be used for the information than was ever the case with paper-based information. It also allows the incorporation of different media types in a multimedia approach to information, thus allowing an appropriate form of information delivery and a more flexible approach to information storage. To take advantage of all these features digital libraries will inevitably be a networked distributed resource with all the attendant problems of such a complex configuration, but for the individual user to be able to take full advantage of these new possibilities the use of a communications-based approach to multimedia and digital libraries is required. Previous work has covered aspects of this already [226, 228] and is summarised below.

12.2 The digital library, multimedia and communications

The library is an information resource. The digital form of an information resource is a set of connected computers with a large amount of storage capacity to enable the encoded storage of different media types in a consistent addressable form. This is not the concern of this paper. What concerns the author is the access to information using some means of communication. This needs some

*Communications research group, University of Wolverhampton, WOLVERHAMPTON WV1 1SB, A.Sloane@wlv.ac.uk

software/hardware solution that will allow the user to navigate the network and/or connect to information resources and enable the required information to be downloaded or used as appropriate.

Indeed it may be that the actual use of information changes when the networks have matured and users find that they no longer need to keep book-like objects but can access information "bites" and link them to other "bites" or "chunks" to form a usable "document". Indeed this will probably be a preferred way of working for many network users as it enables a much more cost effective access to the systems than the digital analogy of taking some books out of the library! The future of the library, per se, is unsure. Digitisation of the contents of the library allows distribution in ways that are not necessarily controllable in the same way as books and other physical objects. This also requires us to ask if there is a need for a digital library or does the distribution of information in a networked form militate against the holding of large blocks of information in a single place.

The digitisation of the information also allows the use of multimedia. Whereas previously it was possible to access all media types in a library it was usual to keep them in different departments and cross-referencing was rare. The digitisation of information allows all media types to be used and communicated via networks to all users with the appropriate hardware/software to use the information. It can then be used in a multitude of different ways appropriate to the user. [228, 49]

Therefore, it can easily be seen that digital libraries are not necessarily a simple idea. They can take a number of different forms and provide different information and information types to different classes of user. Much will depend on the organisation of access to digital libraries for users to have the greatest benefit from these useful resources. It will also be noted that the conceptualisation of the 'library' will change when network distribution becomes a real alternative - in some ways it already is!

The rest of this paper will, therefore look at the ways in which networks and multimedia are organised to allow users' access to digital libraries of information, and the problems of the home based user in gaining access to the networks and the libraries.

12.3 Models of multimedia information provision

If the user requires access to all the multimedia facilities outlined above then there will be a marked increase in the complexity of library servers to deal with the increased complexity of storing and manipulating different types of object, and different combinations of multimedia objects. There are however a number of different scenarios or models that can provide for different types of user. These can be classified as three types (or two extremes and all points between!) and depend on the degree of processing power built into the server and/or client

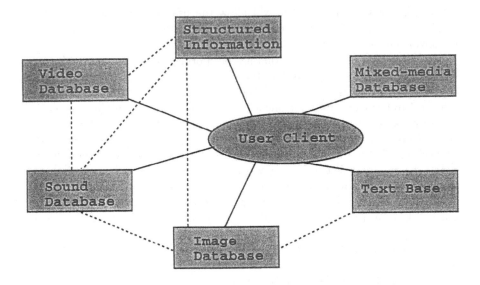

Figure 12.1 Media complex information provision

programs.

The three types can be classified as communications complex, media complex and a hybrid type that combines aspects of both the other two types. The essential difference lies in the way that information is stored and the amount of information that needs to be communicated between the server and the user's client.

A typical example of the media-complex model would be the CD-ROM where all the media are stored on one device and there is no need to communicate with other servers for information. While this model is interesting it does pose problems of distribution and update for users and libraries, although it also solves the problems of limiting access.

At the other extreme the individual network user without a specific multimedia storage device would be an example of the communications-complex model. Figure 1 shows this in more detail.

The user's client is linked via some connection method to the different types of information base as described above. These could be single types of media object or combinations of different objects to form mixed-media linked packages such as slide shows, audio-visual presentations etc.

The two extreme models present different problems to the user. The media-complex approach allows little freedom outside the provision of the information by the provider. So innovative use is unlikely since the information is fixed by the media used, especially in CD-ROM. The communications-complex approach allows a user access to any database of media to which they have access rights and presents the problem of "navigation". Without any aid to finding a way through the network of information the user can often spend many fruitless hours searching using valuable on-line time.

The hybrid approach is likely to be the way forward for the majority of applications, with CD-ROM playing a part in the areas of information provision that can permit the rigidity of such an approach or would prefer to remove communications from the ystem. A typical hybrid system would see a user's communication client brought in to resolve the query from a basic multimedia information system thus allowing the freedom to peruse remote databases of multimedia objects and providing a basic framework for the user.

To include this type of approach in a multimedia system would be a radical departure from the product-intensive systems that are currently on offer as multimedia machines. It would also allow users to access the information that they required to do the task they were attempting presuming that the information exists!

Also shown in figure 1 are the possible links between the various media types. Examples of these are the links between image and voice or text in a slide show or audio-video links or the links between a database structure and a flat file system storage of large data objects. These links will also produce an extra overhead which will depend on the degree of distribution of the data.

Figure 1 also shows a number of separate "libraries" of different information types. These are used in a logical sense and could easily be distributed in a different physical set-up to that shown in the diagram.

12.4   The home-based user

The use of digital forms for information allows access to that information by any connected user. The growth of the Internet and it's various resources and access mechanisms allows any user access from both their workplace and their home. This is where the power of digitisation empowers the user to access the information that they really need, when they need it, in a way that they can control. This contrasts sharply with the traditional approach of the library which has controlled the issue of books, some of which can only be consulted in the building, and only allowed access to limited numbers of the various resources at any one time.

The concept of borrowing and removal of books is not relevant to the digital approach since any number of users can have simultaneous access to the resources at once and copies can be made easily. It is only when viewing and printing documents that the difference in a personal system· gives the information a different aspect. The individual user can, if they want, alter the structure or layout of the information to conform to any personal preferences relatively easily.

The main benefit of the digital approach is, however, the ability for all users to access information from the home. This allows all users equal access (given that they have machine access) to the same information. This then allows isolated users the same access to information as those near to the library. Indeed distance is not really a relevant concept, especially if all users have the same type of communications access to the network resource. The consequences of this are that the isolated user , whether isolated by geography or disability has equal access to information.

There are, however, issues that need to be addressed for the home user to have useful access to the information stored in a digital library. Firstly, the problem of the speed of data transfer, or the available bandwidth of equipment used to access the resources. The current generation of fast modems is adequate for a large text transfer but even this can take some time for a large volume of information over a slow network (which can be slowed by multiple users). For highly data intensive forms of information such as video and high quality sound and graphics the time to transmit becomes a significant factor when assessing the usefulness of the home based approach to digital library access. Without the kind of technology currently available to the business user there are some compromises that will need to be made so that access is not denied to these users.

The use of ISDN is seen as the best route for the home user to gain access to the distributed services of digital libraries. [227] There are other options but none have yet either the base of equipment available at the right price for the home consumer or are not a universal solution available to a wide range of users. (Having said that, it should be noted that ISDN does not have universal coverage but this is more a matter of the economics of the telecommunications industry than any technical problems. This situation would change if more users need the facilities)

12.5 Navigation, classification, indexing and hypertext

Most of the other problems faced by the home user can be put into the categories of navigation and document referral. With the increasing use of digital storage and the inevitable distribution of the information held in a digital form the route to access has become much more difficult. The traditional means of book storage and classification no longer applies as there can be any number of indices referencing the various items in a digital library.

This also allows new possibilities that were not possible under the traditional regime. An example would be the resulting information from a query to the digital library. No longer would the user be given a stack of books but they could have the relevant information extracted and combined into a message to be transmitted to their workstation. This will not only cut down on network traffic but allow the library administration to be more responsive to the needs of the user than has been possible before.

The navigation problem is very real. With the distribution of information around the Internet the various tools available have an increasingly difficult task to locate specific information. There are also numerous copies of some information that do not give the user any new information but increase network access time and cost. The current use of classification systems for books soon becomes unwieldy in an electronic environment , due to the granularity of the classification system and it's application to whole books or other physical objects of information. A more rational approach would be the classification of individual "information nuggets", as determined by the author of whatever article is under consideration. For example, this paper could be considered a single nugget, or even a combination of two or more depending on the interest of the reader. Although due to its length it would probably be a single item in any such scheme. In other media it is easy to see how some video programmes can be formed from a number of information nuggets and others from a smaller number. Audio similarly has some obvious categorisations. These information nuggets can then all be cross-referenced and indexed by means of hypertext documents such as those used by World Wide Web Servers.

This then allows users access to those resources that they need as simply as possible. For the traditionalists it would still be possible to access the information in a form such as a book, but for the pioneers of cyberspace the possibilities are limitless.

12.6   Summary

The rapid digitisation of the information resource has led to a new set of possibilities for the digital storage and dissemination of information. The user of such information is no longer tied to the need to physically access the information resource or to access the information in the form that is pre-determined by the storer or author of the information. The use of network information systems to access libraries of information is set to revolutionise the way in which users access the resource and also as a by-product the way in which authors of information produce their work. Finally to cope with this new paradigm an alteration in the way that information is cplassified is also inevitable as the current systems based on physical objects have little relevance to the new information space of networked information systems.

Chapter 13

Integrating Natural Language With Large Dataspace Visualization*

Ira Smotroff[†], Lynette Hirschman[‡] and Samuel Bayer[§]

13.1 Information Overload

One of the most significant developments in society today is the rapid proliferation of information sources and the inability of existing tools to allow effective analysis of the large volume of information. A query to a large data repository can easily produce so many possible documents that the user's ability to ferret out the highest quality and most appropriate information is impaired. Most users of the Internet today will attest to the increasing difficulty of choosing information sources in a large, dynamic and constantly growing environment. The coming National Information Infrastructure (NII) promises to multiply these effects considerably.

Information Retrieval (IR) techniques are the primary general tools available for search in large information spaces today. While systems such as Smart[32], Inquery[54] and WAIS (Wide Area Information System)[137], are effective, they suffer from the fact that they use search engines that have an extremely limited treatment of document semantics. Standard techniques to restrict the number of document hits include Boolean keyword search, comparison of vectors based on word-frequency data, and use of relevance feedback to enhance retrieval.

Boolean operators (e.g., AND, NOT, OR) can be connected into logical expressions which can result in more focused queries. Boolean query composition has the advantage of being intuitive – the user controls what terms will cause a hit. But composing good Boolean search queries longer than a few terms turns out to be difficult for many humans, including computer scientists. Automatically derived vector-based techniques often provide more robust searches, but

*This work was funded by ARPA SISTO under contract DAAB07-94-C-H-601.

[†]Information Services Group, Digital Equipment Corporation, 334 South St., SHR3-1/P32 Shrewsbury, MA 01545; e-mail smotroff@mpgs.enet.com. Correspondence about this chapter should be directed to L. Hirschman at MITRE.

[‡]The MITRE Corporation MS K329, 202 Burlington Road, Bedford, MA 01730; e-mail: lynette@linus.mitre.org

[§]The MITRE Corporation, MS K329, 202 Burlington Road, Bedford, MA 01730; e-mail: sam@mitre.org

provide the user with little insight into why particular documents are retrieved or how the search can be effectively refocused or enlarged. Relevance feedback allows the user to select a document or some portion of a document that seems good, for use in defining further searches. This can improve retrieval, but still provides little insight into what documents will be collected, and which ones missed.

For example, a keyword search query which seeks to get all documents having the phrase *joint venture* could be structured to look for the word *joint* adjacent to the word *venture* in documents. This would miss a document which mentions a "venture between Toyota and GM". To capture all possibilities using keyword search, one would have to look at all the documents that have the word *joint* or the word *venture* or perhaps appropriate synonyms available from a thesaurus. Thus to get good *recall* using keyword search, the *precision* of the query is reduced, i.e., the effective number of false positive hits often has to be increased. Conversely, high *precision* in the query often requires reduced recall, which means that relevant documents are not retrieved. Similarly, if we wish to search for documents about joint ventures between Japan and Taiwan, there is no way to specify the particular relationship between Japan and Taiwan – we are not interested in joint ventures between Japanese partners that take place in Taiwan, for example. But these relationships are very difficult to capture without a richer semantic representation.

Given the difficulties in managing information overload while maintaining the quality of a search, we hypothesized that incorporation of visualization techniques integrated with the query process could enhance the user's ability to navigate a large document space. In addition, we wished to investigate how the query process could be closely coupled with natural language techniques to improve the user's ability to extract specific kinds of information from the document space. The remainder of the chapter discusses the experimental system we developed to explore these ideas.

13.2   The WAIS Information Exploration System

The WAIS (Wide Area Information Server) system is a popular information retrieval system on the Internet. Based on the Z39.50 protocol[188], WAIS allows the user to access relevant document collections distributed across the network; multiple servers can be accessed via a single query. The query can be phrased as a Boolean combination of keywords (*joint ADJ venture AND Japan AND Taiwan*) or as a natural language query (*Show joint ventures between Japan and Taiwan*), in which case the system forms keywords from a free text query by extracting stop words. WAIS provides a simple document retrieval rating calculated using metrics such as key word frequencies and proximity of keyword hits to the beginning of the document. Current interfaces to WAIS include one for TTY and one for the X window system. The latter provides scrollable lists

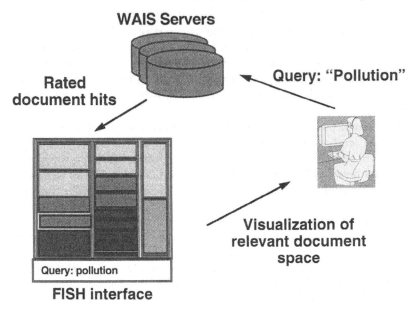

WAIS Servers

Rated document hits

Query: "Pollution"

Visualization of relevant document space

Query: pollution

FISH interface

Figure 13.1 Architecture for a Visualization Interface to WAIS Servers

which allow the user to select the desired databases to search and a scrollable window which displays the document hits in order of precision.

13.3   Visualization of Document Space

Our exploratory work on document space visualization was based on Shneiderman's Treemap system[223]. Treemap is designed to provide visualization and a means of exploring large hierarchies such as relational databases or file systems. It attempts to display as much information as possible by using all available screen space. It also allocates more screenspace to items that are more important. A fundamental design criterion for Treemap was that all interactions should be achievable through the use of mouse clicks. We have adapted Treemap to the information retrieval (and WAIS) environment.

13.3.1   Architecture for the Visualization Interface

To explore visualization of document spaces, we converted Treemap to work on dynamic data and integrated it with freeWAIS software.¶ After designating a list of servers, the user types in a query which is routed via Z39.50 to each of the designated servers (see Figure 13.1). When the search is completed, the visualization component builds the display based on the resulting document hits.

¶Using CNIDR's public domain WAIS client/server implementation.

13.3.2   The Visualizer

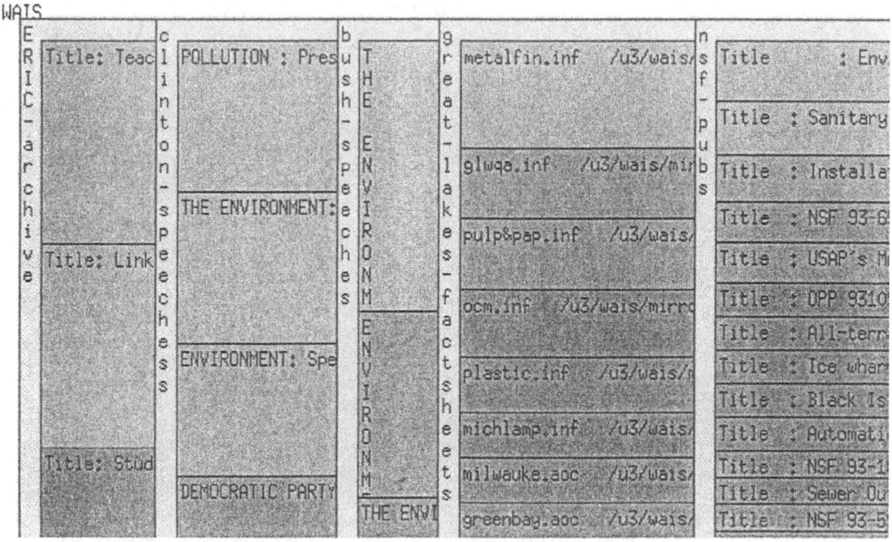

Figure 13.2 Visualization of Query for Keyword *pollution*

The graphical display of the information space allows the user to assess the quality and quantity of documents available for that query; this is illustrated in Figure 13.2. In our implementation, a flat hierarchy is used to model the space of WAIS servers and the associated document hits for each server. The columns of the display represent the servers queried about pollution. Servers (columns) with more document hits are deemed more important and are wider. For example, in Figure 13.2, the fourth column (titled "great lakes factsheets") represents a server with more hits than the servers in the first three columns ("ERIC archive", "clinton speeches" and "bush speeches"). The rows in each column of the display represent the document hits for the keyword *pollution*. There is a color key associated with the display which maps the WAIS retrieval rating of 125-1000 to the range of colors available. The higher ranked documents are lighter in color and are ordered closer to the top of the display. Documents with high ratings are also given more vertical space so that text and other information is more likely to be legible.

The current prototype displays only the title in a document's screen representation, but the entire document can be retrieved by clicking on a "Get Document" button. The document is retrieved via the usual Z39.50 protocol and displayed using X-Mosaic as a hypertext document viewer (Figure 13.10 below shows the interface for viewing documents).

With a visual representation of the information space, new possibilities for

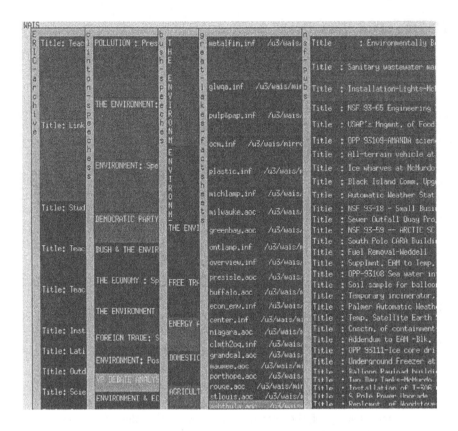

Figure 13.3 Color-based Refinement for Keyword *taxes*

query refinement become possible. For example, we can use color to selectively explore the information space. The results of a follow-up query using the keyword *taxes* is shown in Figure 13.3. Functionally, this is done by making an independent WAIS query on the new keyword and computing the intersection of the "taxes" documents with the original set of pollution documents. A joint color key combines a range of dark red to light red for taxes in the vertical dimension with a range of dark blue to light blue for pollution in the horizontal dimension. Thus, light purple in the color key represents the best possible joint rating. This appears in Figure 13.3 as lighter colored documents, particularly in the "clinton speeches" database towards the bottom of the figure. This technique can be readily extended to multiple attributes through the use of additional colors and textures.

13.3.3   Extensions to the Visualization Interface

In the current application, we make only limited use of the visualization capability, but it is easy to imagine useful extensions. For example, an abstract of the document could appear as the user zoomed in on the document's representation. If a document contained other media, various symbols could be shown indicating the types of media contained. Images or graphics could also be displayed, as well as information about document size, cost, etc. The system could support multi-level refinement, coupled with an ability to subset the search space for iterative probing and further refinement using mouse clicks or menu selections. Queries could be combined in various ways (union, intersection, elaboration of attributes) to support different kinds of views. As we discuss in the final section, we have implemented many of these features in a new visualization interface.

13.4   Integrating Natural Language With Visualization

To illustrate the benefits of combining visualization with more refined document semantics, we replaced the information retrieval system of WAIS with natural language processing, drawing on information extraction, natural language interface and text generation technologies.

We used natural language information extraction to extract the information in the documents and capture this information in a database. We then built a natural language interface to translate natural language queries into queries against the database created via information extraction. Finally, we used the underlying database to drive a summarization component which generated on-the-fly document summaries.

13.4.1   Information Extraction

Natural language information extraction focuses on identifying relevant information from free text and capturing this information in the form of "templates" (database records) that describe who did what to whom. Progress in this field has been fueled by the Message Understanding Conferences (MUCs). These conferences have been devoted to evaluating message understanding and information extraction systems[238, 44] in various application domains. We were able to leverage this work in producing a prototype natural language interface for a large document space.

To extract information in a given domain, a (domain-specific) template is defined for the application, e.g., if the subject matter is terrorism, the template will contain slots for terrorist event, intended target, organization, damage, etc. The automated system extracts information from the messages and builds the appropriate templates. For evaluation, the automatically generated templates are compared to manually generated templates, and the system is scored based on how well it matches the manually generated templates.

By choosing a domain from an earlier Message Understanding conference. (joint venture documents), we were able to use our existing information extraction technology to demonstrate natural language-based information processing. Specifically, we created WAIS databases from three sets of documents used to

General Electric Co. of the **U.S.** and **Taiwan's MITAC** International Corp. announced a joint venture to produce **advanced electronics** and **information-processing equipment** for defense use in Taiwan.

The partners will have equal stakes in the new company, dubbed **GETAC**. GE will take charge or technology transfer and foreign sales, while MITAC will be responsible for local management and sales, said Matthew Miau, MITAC Group chairman.

The venture will help improve the quality of Taiwan-made military products and promote the country's long-term goal of becoming a world-wide arms supplier, Mr. Miau said.

The partners expect to invest a total of **$6.6 million** in the project in the first year and to increase their investment to **$14 million** within the next five years.

Figure 13.4 Sample Document in the Joint Venture Domain

test the systems in MUC-5. This consisted of some 800 documents from three news wire services related to joint ventures. Figure 13.4 shows an actual document. There are a number of systems that generate such templates automatically given the text input, including one built at MITRE[1]. However, the recall and precision of these systems is typically in the 50-60% range. To illustrate the power of this approach, we chose to use the the best possible set of templates, namely the "answer keys" manually generated by experts (created for evaluation of the automated information extraction systems). The underlined text in Figure 13.4 shows information that must be mapped into the template to provide a description of the partners in the joint venture (General Electric and MITAC), the entity they are forming (GETAC) and their product (advanced electronics and information processing equipment).

The filled in template is shown in Figure 13.5. The template captures not only the key entities, but their relationships, e.g., the **TIE-UP RELATIONSHIP** indicates formation of a joint venture. The (normalized) names of companies forming the joint venture are entered in the **NAME** slots for **ENTITY 1** and **ENTITY 2** (General Electric and MITAC respectively), while the newly formed entity appears in the **NEW-ENTITY** slot (GETAC). Each of the entity slots has a location associated with it. The focus of the new joint venture is listed in the **INDUSTRY** slot, appropriately normalized. The processing to form the templates is done off-line, and the templates are collected to form the template database that includes pointers back to the original document. The use of the template database makes it possible to perform much more precise querying of documents, including queries about relationships among entities, e.g., the

General Electric Co. of the U.S. and Taiwan's MITAC
International Corp. announced a joint venture to
produce advanced electronics and information-
processing equipment for defense use in Taiwan.
   The partners will have equal stakes in the new
company, dubbed GETAC. GE will take charge or
technology
will be resp   **TEMPLATE**
said Matthe   **DATE 100889**
                         SOURCE Wall Street Journal
   The ventu   **TIE-UP RELATION**
made milita   **NEW-ENTITY: GETAC**
long-term   **ENTITY 1 NAME: General Electric Co**
supplier, Mr   **LOCATION: US**
   The partn   **ENTITY 2 NAME: MITAC**
in the proje   **LOCATION: Taiwan**
investment   **INDUSTRY Information processing**

Figure 13.5 Information Extraction in the Joint Venture Domain

partners in a joint venture, the product the new company manufactures, or the locations of the partners.

13.4.2 Natural Language Interface

Once the database is built from the templates, it can be queried via a natural language interface. To demonstrate this, we constructed a limited interface for this task, making use of a number of existing components. To parse the natural language input and construct a representation of its meaning (in terms of template categories), we used the Phoenix robust natural language parser from Carnegie Mellon University[249]. The Phoenix system allows the developer to write a flexible, robust phrase grammar that associates phrases with semantic descriptions that can, via additional processing, be associated with database (template) entries. Using this framework, we were able to write (in only several days) a limited grammar that could process queries about the joint venture domain. Figure 13.6 illustrates how the grammar assigns semantic structures to phrases and maps these to template slots. The phrase *joint ventures* indicates that this is a question about the **TIE-UP RELATIONSHIP**. The phrase *have a partner* maps into the **ENTITY*** relationships. The query is looking for a partner modified by *Nationality: Taiwanese*. This matches the **LOCATION** slot under **ENTITY-2** with value *Taiwan*, so there is a "hit" on this document for this query.

Query: What joint ventures have a Taiwanese partner

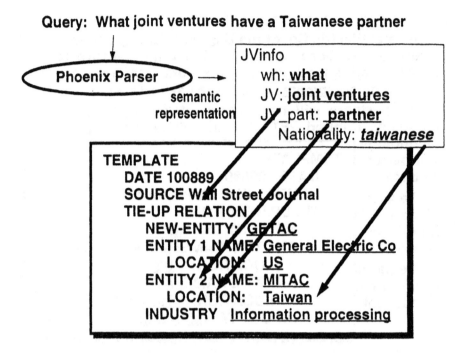

Figure 13.6 Mapping of an Input Sentence to a Template Query

13.4.3   Visualization with Natural Language Processing

We connected the prototype natural language system to the visualization system described earlier, operating on the 800 document joint venture database.[||] Figure 13.7 illustrates the case where the number of documents is so large (increasingly the normal case on the Internet) that all semantic information about the documents is effectively lost: in this display, each document is a raster line thick or less. In this case, the ability to identify a useful subset of documents for display is critical to making progress in retrieving useful information.

We can use a natural language query to retriev a subset of documents. For example, we can ask *Show me joint ventures with a Taiwanese partner?*, displayed in Figure 13.8. This limits the set of "interesting" documents to a smaller space that can be better viewed on the screen We can see that the server in the left-most column (the "Wall Street Journal") has two hits, the middle server ("Mead") has the most (some 30-40) and the remaining server (not shown) has just one hit. When we use natural language to identify document "hits", the

---

[||]In this case, the visualization component routed the query to the natural language interface, rather than to a set of WAIS servers via Z 39 50. However, once a document "hit" was identified, the document was accessed via the appropriate WAIS server.

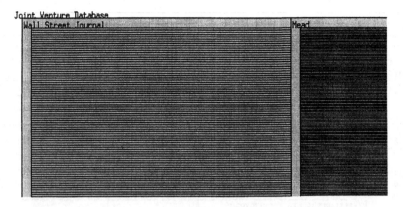

Figure 13.7: Display of the Joint Venture Servers with 800 Joint Venture Documents

template associated with the document either contains the desired information or it does not; there is no notion of relative retrieval scores, as there is with a normal WAIS retrieval. As a result, there is no color encoding: all documents are the same color.

We can now refine this query by asking a follow-up question, for example, *Which ones have an American partner?* The natural language system determines that the sentence contains an expression that refers to the previous query (*which ones*), so this query is treated as a restricting the set defined in the previous query. The result (three documents) is shown in Figure 13.9. We can further refine this query by asking, for example, *Which ones involve chemical manufacture?* which narrows the set of documents down to only two documents.

13.4.4   Document Summarization

Once we narrow down the number of documents, we need to be able to find out what the document says. There are two ways to do this. By clicking on the "Get Document" button in the interface, the Mosaic viewer is invoked to display the individual document. This is shown in Figure 13.10.

However, the full document can be long and the relevant section(s) may be buried in the text, making them difficult to locate – indeed, the relevant sections of the document in Figure 13.10 require scrolling down through several screens of text. To provide faster perusal of documents, we provided an additional "Summarize" button on the interface. Pushing the "Summarize" button activates the text generation system and produces a short document summary – compare the text generated in Figure 13.11 to the full text in Figure 13.10. Generation is done using the MITRE TEXPLAN[171] system which uses the associated database template to generate a short paragraph describing the relevant information. This process is illustrated in Figure 13.12.

Joint Venture Database

		Head	
W a l l	W a l l	FINANCIAL TIMES LIMITED, 09/18/90	
		KYODO NEWS SERVICE, 05/22/89	
		JIJI PRESS, 07/22/81	
S t r e e t	S t r e e t	JIJI PRESS, 05/15/80	
		KYODO NEWS SERVICE, 01/10/91	
		JIJI PRESS LTD., 11/06/90	
		JIJI PRESS LTD., 08/17/90	
		JIJI PRESS LTD., 11/10/89	
J o u r n a l	J o u r n a l	JIJI PRESS LTD., 06/22/89	
		JIJI PRESS LTD., 04/25/89	
		KYODO NEWS SERVICE, 01/17/89	
		JIJI PRESS LTD., 11/30/88	
		KYODO NEWS SERVICE, 11/07/88	
		KYODO NEWS SERVICE, 10/05/88	
,		JIJI PRESS LTD., 08/23/88	
0 8 / 1		KYODO NEWS SERVICE, 07/88/27	
		KYODO NEWS SERVICE, 06/15/88	
		THE FINANCIAL TIMES LIMITED, 04/29/88	
W a l		JIJI PRESS LTD., 04/27/88	
		KYODO NEWS SERVICE, 11/17/87	
		THE FINANCIAL TIMES LIMITED, 10/22/87	

Figure 13.8: Response to Query *Show me joint ventures with a Taiwanese part-ner?*

13.5 Future Directions

We have discussed several techniques that would be useful in navigating a larger information space, namely visualization and natural language processing. The visualization technology can be immediately deployed, while the natural language technology is not yet sufficiently robust or general to be deployed on a routine basis.[**]

We are now re-implementing the visualization component. Our goal is to provide greater flexibility and independence for the size, color and order attributes, to maximize the information that can be displayed about the set of documents retrieved. This tool, called FISH (Forager for the Information Super Highway), will serve as a general purpose WAIS front-end – or, with minor changes, to any search engine that can access multiple document collections and return a ranked list of documents and associated scores from each collection. FISH supports flexible recombination of successive queries, which can be displayed as unions or intersections. This flexibility will allow users to identify "information rich" servers by the density of good hits, to retain "working sets" of retrieved documents, and to extend or contract the scope of a query without having to do

---

[**]The technology, however, is robust enough to be used in special purpose applications, where a system can be hand-tailored to extract specific kinds of information from text sources.

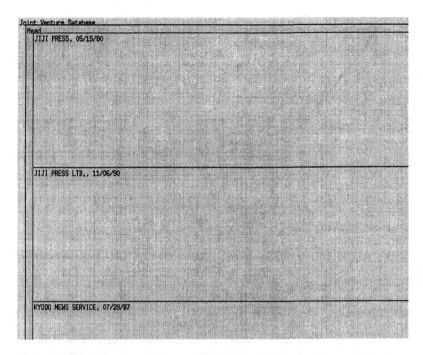

Figure 13.9 Response to Query *Which ones have an American partner?*

additional searches. Since the search of remote WAIS databases is the most time-consuming part of the query, we believe that the ability to recombine already retrieved information will be very useful. FISH currently runs under X on UNIX machines, and we have also developed an implementation using the Visix Gallaxy software, which runs on UNIX, Windows on the PC and the Mac.

There is also ongoing work on robust, general purpose natural language technology to provide additional semantic information. For example, we have internal research investigating the automatic generation of SGML semantic tags (location, date, person, organization) to provide richer indices for improved retrieval. Furthermore, current research in human language processing should improve the robustness and portability of natural language information extraction, interface, and generation systems. Promising directions include automatically trained parsing systems[28] as well as multi-lingual systems (see [238] for descriptions of information extraction systems that work on English and Japanese texts). This research will provide the next increment in robust, general information extraction and natural language query and generation technology.

0225
August 10, 1990, Friday
Copyright (c) 1990 The Financial Times Limited; Japan Although it is believed to be the country's largest foreign investor, principally in a broad selection of equities and government securities, the KIO's portfolio has traditionally been underweighted in Japan. In 1984, some 13 per cent of state funds invested in the industrialised countries were held there. The underweighting is partly due to the virtual absence of Japanese property among Kuwaiti holdings. 'We tried for years to do property in Japan and were totally unsuccessful,' says an insider. The emirate also met problems when attempting to invest in the Japanese oil sector. In 1984, its desire to buy Getty Oil's 50 per cent stake of Mitsubishi Oil was thwarted by the Ministry of International Trade and Industry. Spain The KIO's activities in Spain have tended to be more public than elsewhere, since it has bought controlling interests in a range of industrial companies. It controls assets worth Pta700bn (Pounds 3.9bn), of which it says Pta415bn are fixed assets. This makes it the country's biggest single foreign investor. Current stakes include 1.5 per cent of Banco Santander (which in turn controls 10 per cent of Royal Bank of Scotland) and 72.9 per cent of Grupo Torras Hostench, one of the country's largest industrial holding companies. Through Hostench it has 40 per cent of Erpo, an engineering consultancy, 50 per cent of Beta Capital, a stockbroker, 55 per cent of Seguros Amaya, a small insurer, and 24 per cent of Prima Inmobilaria, Spain's richest property developer. KIO also recently bought 25 per cent of Telecinco, a private television channel. Finally, there are three big industrial holdings: 39.5 per cent of Ebro Agricolas, the country's biggest sugar refiner, which has diversified into up-market canned foods; 100 per cent of Torras Papel, Spain's biggest paper company; and 39 per cent of Ercros, the largest chemicals company. All KIO investments in Spain are made through a company called Koolmees, registered in the Netherlands. West Germany In addition to the usual selection of non-disclosable equity stakes, Kuwait holds 14 per cent of Daimler-Benz (owned by the Kuwaiti Government rather than the KIO), 20 per cent of Hoechst (through KPC), and 20 per cent of Metallgesellschaft (through the KIO). A Kuwaiti was recently elected to the supervisory board of Asko, the retail company, although reports that Kuwait holds a 10 per cent stake have not been confirmed. Insiders say undisclosed investments include a substantial holding in Deutsche Bank. In terms of property, the KIO holds a lot of office space in central Frankfurt, according to the former

Figure 13.10 Full Document Retrieval

THE FINANCIAL TIMES LIMITED, 08/10/90

KPI and HUNGARIAN OIL & GAS TRUST have agreed to form a joint venture which will extract oil or gas and will provide electric, gas, or sanitary services. BERLINER BANK and KFTCIC have formed a joint venture which provides brokerage services. KIIC, SG WARBURG, and SONAI GROUP, have formed a joint venture called EFISA,.

Figure 13.11 Automatically Generated Document Summary

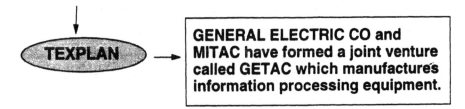

TEMPLATE
   DATE 100889
   SOURCE Wall Street Journal
   TIE-UP RELATION
      NEW-ENTITY: GETAC
      ENTITY 1 NAME: General Electric Co
         LOCATION: US
      ENTITY 2 NAME: MITAC
         LOCATION: Taiwan
      INDUSTRY Information processing

TEXPLAN →

GENERAL ELECTRIC CO and MITAC have formed a joint venture called GETAC which manufactures information processing equipment.

Figure 13.12 Generation of Text from Template Using TEXPLAN

13.6 Acknowledgements

Thanks to E. Haugsjaa, T. Howells and B. McCall for implementation support and useful discussions. Thanks to University of Maryland for Treemap and Carnegie Mellon University for Phoenix.

Chapter 14

The Automated Analysis, Cataloging,
and Searching of Digital Image Libraries:
A Machine Learning Approach

Usama M. Fayyad[*],Padhraic Smyth[†]

14.1   Introduction

In areas as diverse as Earth remote sensing, astronomy, and medical imaging,
image acquisition technology has undergone tremendous improvements in recent
years. The vast amounts of scientific data, stored in the form of digital image
libraries, are potential treasure-troves for scientific investigation and analysis.
Unfortunately, advances in our ability to deal with this volume of data in an
effective manner have not paralleled the hardware gains in storage technology
and data gathering instruments. While special-purpose tools for particular applications exist, no general-purpose software tools and algorithms which can
assist a scientist in exploring large scientific image libraries are available. This
chapter presents our recent progress in developing interactive semi-automated
image library exploration tools based on pattern recognition and machine learning techniques. Two successful applications at JPL will be used to ground the
discussion and point out the powerful impact the learning approach can have.
We then proceed to discuss the general problem of automated image library exploration, the particular aspects of image databases which distinguish them from
other databases, and how this impacts the application of off-the-shelf learning
algorithms to problems of this nature.

We are developing tools that can be trained by example to execute difficult
query-by-content type tasks on large image databases. Rather than developing
a dedicated tool for each specific problem, we are pursuing the development of a
tool that is *trainable* by scientists, using techniques from machine learning and
pattern recognition. A scientist provides training examples by locating candidate
targets within an image on the screen. The learning algorithms use the training
data to produce a classifier that will detect and identify other targets in a large

---

[*]Machine Learning Systems Group, Jet Propulsion Laboratory, California Institute of Technology, Pasadena, CA 91109, Email:fayyad@aig.jpl.nasa.gov

[†]Machine Learning Systems Group, Jet Propulsion Laboratory, California Institute of Technology, Pasadena, CA 91109, Email:pjs@aig.jpl.nasa.gov

library of similar images. The scientist can thus customize the tool to search for one type of visual feature versus another simply by providing positive and negative examples. This is a non-intrusive method in the sense that it will not require the scientists to perform anything different from what they do now: the task is simply to examine an image and determine objects of interest within it.

Such a tool can be used to navigate through large digital libraries to perform image analysis, cataloging of image contents, and browsing by specifying examples. In addition to automating laborious and visually-intensive tasks, it provides the means for an objective, examinable, and repeatable process for detecting and classifying objects in images.

14.1.1   The Query Formulation Problem

Work on techniques for digital libraries has focused mainly on digitization techniques, storage and retrieval mechanisms, and database issues dealing with efficient indexing and query execution. We believe there is an important and crucial problem that needs to be addressed before collections of digital images can be turned into *useful digital libraries*, namely the query formulation problem. Users would mainly like to be able to use a digital image library to search for particular patterns for cataloging or investigative purposes. A typical query would be something like: "in how many images does this pattern occur?" or "catalog all occurrences and sizes of objects in images satisfying certain conditions." Unfortunately, unlike dealing with a relational database or the text of a book, there is no easy way for the user to formulate the required query. This poses a potentially difficult bottleneck that stands in the way of making the notion of a digital image library a reality.

We propose an approach for developing a system that learns from examples. Hence, rather than issuing queries, the user simply provides training examples and asks the system to "find all objects that look like this." This approach promises to bypass a crucial bottleneck in the way humans currently interact with large databases: query formulation. For most interesting tasks of image analysis, formulating queries to specify a set of target objects/regions requires solving difficult problems that often involve effectively translating human visual intuition into pixel-level algorithmic constraints. This is a fairly challenging task in its own right. In many cases, formulating the query may be impractical for a user to perform. Querying a database by providing examples and counter-examples forms a novel and powerful basis for a new generation of intelligent database interface tools. These tools, capable of performing "query by content" type operations on large image databases, promise a fundamental paradigm shift of the interface between users and image databases and could enable orders of magnitude improvements in both the quantity and quality of analyses of digitized image libraries. The methods described in this chapter have general applications and can in principle be applied to industrial/commercial applications (e.g. product inspection in manufacturing) and medical image analysis problems (e.g. cell counting).

14.1.2 Overview of Chapter

We provide two illustrative examples of current projects at JPL involving the development of image exploration algorithms and tools with built-in classification learning components. We first introduce the SKICAT system which is used to automatically generate a large comprehensive sky object catalog from a set of sky survey images at a major astronomical observatory. The second system, called JARtool, is intended for use on the Magellan collection of over 30,000 SAR images of the surface of Venus. Both systems use machine learning techniques and are trained by scientists to perform the analysis work. The SKICAT results demonstrate how powerful a learning system can be, resulting in performance that exceeds that of human astronomers in recognizing faint sky objects.

When dealing with actual applications, many issues arise that are usually missed during the research stage. For example, the JARtool project demonstrates an important problem which occurs when applying machine learning to digital image libraries, especially when dealing with remote-sensing imagery. The users (scientists or domain experts) may not have access to ground truth, and thus training data obtained from the user may contain a high degree of "noise." By "noise" we mean disagreement on labelling objects between different users, and between different labellings by the same user. The learning methods need to account for such variance and need to be robust with respect to such problems. The latter part of the chapter deals specifically with this issue. The chapter concludes with a general discussion of learning in digital image libraries and the special advantages and challenges that image databases provide.

14.2 Case Study 1: The SKICAT System

The Sky Image Cataloging and Analysis Tool (SKICAT) has been developed for use on the images resulting from the 2nd Palomar Observatory Sky Survey (POSS-II) conducted by the California Institute of Technology (Caltech). The photographic plates are being digitized at the Space Telescope Science Institute, resulting in about 3,000 digital images of $23,040 \times 23,040$ pixels each, totalling over three terabytes of data. When complete, the survey will cover the entire northern sky in three colors, detecting virtually every sky object down to a B magnitude of 22 (a normalized measure of object brightness). This is at least one magnitude fainter than previous comparable photographic surveys. We estimate that at least 5×10^7 galaxies and 2×10^9 stellar objects (including over 10^5 quasars) will be detected. This data set will be the most comprehensive large-scale imaging survey produced to date.

The purpose of SKICAT is to facilitate the extraction of meaningful information from this large data set in an efficient and timely manner. The first step in analyzing the results of a sky survey is to identify, measure, and catalog the detected objects in the image into their respective classes. Once the objects have been classified, further scientific analysis can proceed. For example, the resulting catalog may be used to test models of the formation of large-scale structure in the universe, probe Galactic structure from star counts, perform automatic identifications of radio or infrared sources, and so forth [67, 252, 253]. Reducing the images to catalog entries is an overwhelming task which inherently requires an automated approach. The goal of this project is to automate this process, providing a consistent and uniform methodology for reducing the data sets. This will provide the means for objectively performing tasks that formerly required subjective and visually intensive manual analysis.

An important goal of this work is to classify objects whose intensity (isophotal magnitude) is too faint for recognition by visual inspection, hence requiring an automated classification procedure. Faint objects constitute the majority of objects on any given plate. We target the classification of objects that are at least one magnitude fainter than objects classified in previous surveys using comparable photographic material. We shall briefly give a general, high-level description of the application domain and report on the successful results which exceeded our initial accuracy goals.

14.2.1 Classifying Sky Objects

SKICAT provides an integrated environment for the construction, classification, management, and analysis of catalogs from large-scale imaging surveys. Due to the large amounts of data being collected, a manual approach to detecting and classifying sky objects in the images is infeasible: it would require on the order of tens of man years. Existing computational methods for classifying the images would preclude the identification of the majority of objects in each image since they are at levels too faint for traditional recognition algorithms or even manual inspection/analysis approaches. A principal goal of SKICAT is to provide an effective, objective, and examinable basis for classifying sky objects at levels beyond the limits of existing technology.

Figure 14.1 depicts the overall architecture of the SKICAT plate catalog construction and classification process. Each of the 3,000 digital images, consisting of $23,040^2$ 16-bit pixels, is subdivided into a set of partially overlapping frames. Low-level image processing and object separation is performed by a modified version of the FOCAS image processing software [135, 247]. The image processing steps detect contiguous pixels in the image that are to be grouped as one object. Attributes are then measured based on this segmentation. The total number of attributes measured for each object by SKICAT is 40, including magnitudes, areas, sky brightness, peak values, and intensity weighted and unweighted pixel moments.

Once all attributes, including normalized and non-linear combinations of these attributes, are measured for each object, final classification is performed on the catalog. Our current goal is to classify objects into four major categories, following the original scheme in FOCAS: *star, star with fuzz, galaxy,* and *artifact*[‡]. We may later refine the classification into more classes, however, clas-

---

[‡]The category *artifact* represents detected regions that are not sky objects, e.g. satellite trail, emulsion problem, etc.

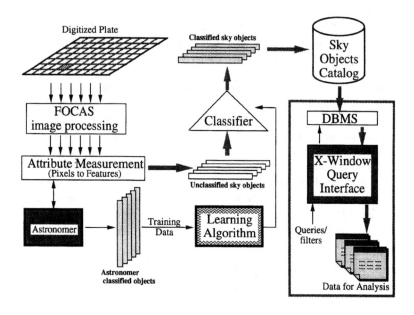

Figure 14.1: Architecture of the SKICAT Cataloging and Classification Process

sification into one of these four classes represents adequate discrimination for primary astronomical analyses of the catalogs.

14.2.2 Classifying Faint Objects

In addition to the scanned photographic plates, we have access to CCD images that span several small regions in some of the frames. The main advantage of a CCD image is higher resolution and signal-to-noise ratio at fainter levels. Hence, many of the objects that are too faint to be classified by inspection on a photographic plate are easily classifiable in a CCD image. In addition to using these images for photometric calibration of the photographic plates, we make use of CCD images for two machine learning purposes: (1) us to obtain class labels for faint objects in the photographic plates, and (2) to accurately assess our classification results.

In order to produce a classifier that classifies faint objects correctly, the learning algorithm needs training data consisting of faint objects labelled with the appropriate class. The class label is therefore obtained by examining the CCD frames. Once trained on properly labelled objects, the learning algorithm produces a classifier that is capable of properly classifying objects based on the values of the attributes measured from the lower resolution digitized plates. Hence, in principle, the classifier will be able to classify objects in the photographic image that are too faint for an astronomer to classify by inspection.

Using the class labels, the learning algorithms are being used to solve the difficult problem of separating the classes in the multi-dimensional space defined by the set of attributes derived via image processing. We target the classification of sky objects that are at least one magnitude fainter than objects classified in photographic all-sky surveys to date.

14.2.3 Summary of Results

The training and test data consisted of objects collected from four different plates from regions for which we had CCD image coverage (since this is data for which accurate classification is available). The learning algorithms are trained on a data set from 3 plates and tested on data from the remaining plate for cross validation. This estimates our accuracy in classifying objects across plates. Note that the plates cover different regions of the sky and that CCD frames cover multiple, very small portions of each plate. The training data consisted of 1,688 objects that were classified manually by an astronomer by examining the corresponding CCD frames. It is noteworthy that for the majority of these objects, the astronomer would not be able to reliably determine the classes by examining the corresponding survey (digitized photographic) images. All attributes used by the learning algorithms are derived from the survey images and *not* from the higher resolution CCD frames.

The learning algorithms used are based on efficiently generating decision trees or rules from the training data. It is beyond the scope of this chapter to cover the algorithms (interested readers are referred to [83, 254]). The classification results may be summarized as follows: Decision tree learning algorithms GID3* [80] and O-Btree [81, 82] performed in the range of 91% prediction accuracy. For a detailed exposition of decision tree classification learning, see [245]. By using RULER [83], a program that generates many decision trees and optimizes them by extracting a robust set of classification rules via cross-validation, statistical pruning, and greedy covering, a stable result of 94% accuracy has been achieved. For comparison, a commercially available decision tree learning algorithm called ID3 (or C4.5) [200] achieves only about 76% accuracy on average.

Note that such high classification accuracy results could only be obtained after expending significant effort on defining robust attributes that capture sufficient invariances between various plates. When the same experiments were conducted using only the base-level attributes measured by FOCAS, the results were significantly worse. The error rates jumped above 20% for O-BTree, above 25% for GID3*, and above 30% for ID3. The respective sizes of the trees grew significantly as well [83].

14.2.4 Summary of Benefits

The SKICAT project represents a step towards the development of an objective, reliable automated sky object classification method. The initial results of our effort to automate sky object classification in order to automatically reduce the POSS-II images to sky catalogs are indeed very encouraging. Using machine learning techniques, SKICAT classifies objects that are at least one magnitude fainter than objects cataloged in previous surveys. This results in a 200% increase in the number of classified sky objects available for scientific analysis in the resulting sky catalog database. Furthermore, we have exceeded our initial accuracy target of 90%. This level of accuracy is required for the data to be useful in testing or refuting theories on the formation of large structure in the universe and on other phenomena of interest to astronomers. SKICAT is now being employed to both reduce and analyze the survey images as they arrive from the digitization instrument. We are also beginning to explore the application of SKICAT to the analysis of other surveys planned by NASA and other institutions.

A consequence of the SKICAT work is a fundamental change in the notion of a sky catalog from the classical static entity "in print", to a dynamic, ever growing, ever improving, on-line database. An important feature of the survey analysis system will be to facilitate such detailed interactions with the catalogs. The catalog generated by SKICAT will eventually contain about a billion entries representing hundreds of millions of sky objects. We view our effort as targeting the development of a new generation of intelligent scientific analysis tools [253, 67]. Without the availability of these tools for the first Palomar survey conducted over four decades ago, no objective and comprehensive analysis of the data was possible. In contrast, we are targeting a comprehensive sky catalog that will be available on-line for the use of the scientific community.

14.3   Case Study 2: The Search for Volcanoes

The Magellan spacecraft transmitted back to earth a data set consisting of over 30,000 high resolution radar images of the surface of the planet Venus. The Magellan-Venus data set constitutes yet another example of the large volumes of data that modern remote-sensing instruments can collect, providing more detail of Venus than was previously available from Pioneer Venus, Venera 15/16, or ground-based radar observations put together [222]. Planetary scientists are literally swamped by data.

The study of volcanic processes is essential to an understanding of the geologic evolution of Venus [76]. Central to volcanic studies is the cataloging of each volcano location and its size and characteristics. It is estimated, based on extrapolating from previous studies and knowledge of the underlying geologic processes, that there should be on the order of 10^6 of these volcanoes visible in the Magellan data [16, 77] which are scattered throughout the 30,000 images. Furthermore, it has been estimated that manually locating all of these volcanoes would require on the order of 10 man-years of a planetary geologist's time to carry out. Hence, we have undertaken the development of techniques to partially automate this task. We are initially targeting the automated detection of the "small-shield" volcanoes (less than 15km in diameter) that constitute the most abundant visible geologic feature [75]. An example image showing volcanoes is given in Section 14.4.1

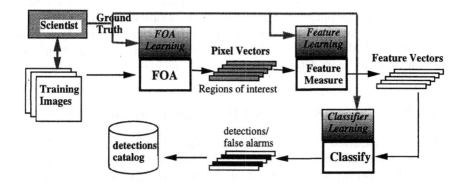

Figure 14.2 Block Diagram of the JARtool System

14.3.1   The Approach

There has been little prior work on detecting naturally occurring objects in remotely-sensed images. Most pattern recognition algorithms are geared towards detecting straight edges or large changes in texture or reflectivity. While this works well for detecting *man-made* objects, approaches such as edge detection and Hough transforms deal poorly with the variability and noise present in typical remotely sensed data [59, 199].

We are developing a system called JARtool (JPL Adaptive Recognition Tool) that consists of three distinct components: focus of attention, feature learning/extraction, and classification learning. Figure 14.2 gives a block diagram of the approach.

Our initial work in this problem has relied on the concept of using a focus of attention (FOA) method to detect regions of interest followed by local classification of regions of interest into volcano and non-volcano categories. The focus of attention component is designed primarily for computational efficiency. Its function is to quickly scan an input image and roughly determine regions of interest (regions potentially containing objects similar to those specified by the scientist). For this purpose we have used a matched filter which is automatically constructed from the training data by taking a normalized average of all volcanoes in the training set [36]. This approach detects the majority of volcanoes (including all of the volcanoes for which the scientists are most confident in their labelling). False alarms are caused by craters, grabens, other bright features, and SAR noise.

Given a set of detected regions of interest, one must then discriminate between the volcanoes and the false alarms. A current focus of the research is to find a useful feature-representation space — a representation based purely on pixels will tend to generalize poorly. For the purposes of incorporating prior knowledge the ideal feature set would be expressed in the form of expected sizes, shapes, and relative geometry of slopes and pits, namely, the same features as used by the scientists to describe the volcanoes. However, due to the low signal-to-noise ratio of the image, it is quite difficult to accurately estimate these features, effectively precluding their use at present. The current focus of our work is on a method which automatically derives robust feature representations (see Section 14.5.1 for more details).

14.3.2 Current Status and Preliminary Results

We have constructed several training sets using 75m/pixel resolution images labelled by the collaborating geologists at Brown University to get an initial estimate of the performance of the system. The FOA component typically detects more than 85% of all the volcanoes. Since it is designed to act as an aggressive filter whose function is to detect as many possible candidate targets as possible, the FOA component generates 5 to 6 times as many false alarms as true detections. Using a maximum-likelihood Gaussian classifier [69] we can classify the regions of interest into volcanoes and false alarms with an estimated independent test accuracy that is comparable to that of a scientist [36]. The Gaussian classifier uses the features derived from the principal components method (see Section 14.5.1). It is important to clarify that these are initial results and with further effort we hope to be able to improve the accuracy.

14.4 Uncertainty in Ground Truth Labelling

We now turn our attention to one of the problems that need to be addressed when one takes a machine learning approach to digital image library analysis. In image analysis, the labelling is often not in fact "ground truth," where ground truth is taken to mean that the object of interest has had its identity ascertained by a separate image-independent measurement with near-zero ambiguity. Instead, objects of interest are labelled in a *subjective* manner by a scientist. If the signal-to-noise ratio (SNR) of the images is high enough then the subjective estimates may be accepted as near enough to ground-truth for practical purposes. This is the case with the SKICAT data, especially with the use of higher resolution CCD images to obtain training data. However for the Magellan-Venus data, with low SNR, there can be some variability between different scientists (and the same scientist at different times) in labelling a particular image. Treating subjective estimates as ground truth is to ignore a potentially important source of noise in the data.

It is important to point out that, in the absence of absolute ground truth, the goal of our work is to be as comparable in performance as possible to the scientists in terms of labelling accuracy. Absolute accuracy is not measurable for this problem. Hence, the best the algorithm can do is to emulate the scientist's performance — this point will become clearer when we discuss performance metrics.

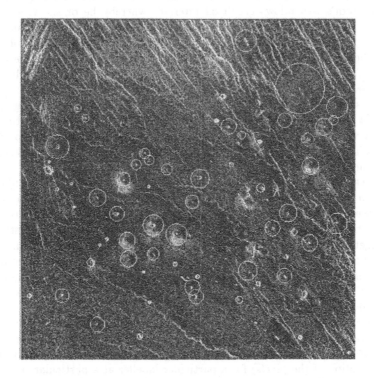

Figure 14.3: Magellan SAR image of Venus with consensus ground truth showing size and locations of small volcanoes.

14.4.1 Collecting Labelled Data

A standard Magellan image consists of 1000 × 1000 pixels, where the pixels are 75m in resolution for the results referred to in this chapter. Small volcano diameters are typically in the 2–3km range, i.e., 30 to 50 pixels wide. Volcanoes are often spatially clustered in volcano fields. As a consequence, most of the volcanoes are expected to be found in about 10-20% of the total number of images, and within these images there may number as many as 100 or more volcanoes, although typically the number is in the 10-50 range.

The standard manner in which we obtain labels is to have a labeller interact with Jartool's X-windows graphical interface whereby he or she uses mouse-clicks to locate candidate volcanoes. Starting with an initially blank image, the labeller proceeds to sequentially click on the estimated centers of the volcanoes. The labeller is then prompted to provide a subjective label estimate from a choice of categories 1–4 (described in more detail below) — by default, locations which are not labelled are considered to have label "0" (non-volcano). Clearly it is possible that based on the visual evidence, for the same local image patch, different labels may be provided by different labellers, or indeed by the same labeller at different times. In addition to labels, the labeller can also provide a fitted diameter estimate by fitting a circle to the feature. Figure 14.3 shows a typical image labelled in this manner.

Given that the scientists cannot classify each object with 100% confidence, how can we assess how well our algorithms are performing? The basic idea is to measure the performance of individual scientists with respect to a "consensus ground truth", where the consensus data is generated by several scientists working together discussing the merits of each candidate volcano (see Figure 14.3). The performance of an algorithm is considered to be satisfactory if, compared to consensus ground truth, its performance is as good as that of an individual scientist. The philosophy here is that if a single scientist is qualified to perform the analysis, then it is sufficient if our algorithms perform comparably.

After completing the labelling, the result is an annotation of that image which can be stored in standard database format — the unique key to the image is a label event, which corresponds to a particular latitude/longitude (to the resolution of the pixels) for a particular labeller at a particular time (since the same labeller may relabel an image multiple times). It is this database which provides the basic reference framework for deriving estimates of geologic parameters: training data for the learning algorithms and reference data for performance evaluation. A simple form of spatial clustering is used to determine which label events (from different labellers) actually correspond to the same geologic feature (volcano).

The scientists label training examples into quantized probability bins or "types", where the probability bins correspond to visually distinguishable sub-categories of volcanoes. In particular, we have used 5 types:

1. summit pits, bright-dark radar pair, and apparent topographic slope, all clearly visible, probability 0.98,
2. only 2 of the 3 criteria in category 1 are visible, probability 0.80,

3. no summit pit visible, evidence of flanks or circular outline, probability 0.60,

4. only a summit pit visible, probability 0.50, and

5. no volcano-like features visible, probability 0.0.

The probabilities correspond to the mean probability for a particular type (the probability that a volcano exists at a particular location given that it belongs to a particular type) and were elicited after considerable discussions with the planetary geologists. The use of quantized probability bins to attach levels of certainty to subjective image labelling is not new: the same approach is routinely used in the evaluation of radiographic image displays to generate subjective ROC (receiver operating characteristic) curves [43].

14.4.2   Modeling Multiple Expert Labellings

We have explored the use of statistical inference techniques to infer how likely it is that a volcano exists at a given pixel site given a particular set of labellings. In particular, the labels are the *observed data* from which one can infer the *hidden* true "type" of the volcano, where the type may be one of the 5 known categories described earlier. We have hypothesized a simple model for the labelling of images, and used an iterative maximum-likelihood technique known as the EM algorithm to infer the parameters of the model given the data. First we provide some details for our method of reconciling multiple inconsistent labellings of the same data, then present the results obtained in the following section.

The basic idea is that labels to training volcanoes are treated as estimates by scientists to an underlying *volcano type* variable. Since we have no ground truth, we cannot directly observe the *type*. Let N be the number of local regions of interest (ROI's) in the database (these are 15×15 pixel square image patches for the volcano application), and let T be the number of types and labels. For simplicity we consider the case of just a single labeller who labels a given set of regions of interest (ROI'S) a number of times — the extension to multiple labellers is straightforward. Let n_{il} be the number of times that ROI i is labelled with label l. Let Y_{it} denote a binary variable which takes value 1 if the true type of volcano i is t^*, and is 0 otherwise. We assume that labels are assigned independently to a given ROI from one labelling to the next, given that the type is known. If the true type t^* is known then

$$p(\text{observed labels}|t^*, i) \propto \prod_{l=1}^{T} p(l|t)^{n_{il}}. \tag{14.1}$$

Thus, unconditionally, we have

$$p(\text{observed labels}, t^*|i) \propto \prod_{t=1}^{T} \left(p(t) \prod_{l=1}^{T} p(l|t)^{n_{il}} \right)^{Y_{it}}, \tag{14.2}$$

where $Y_{it} = 1$ if $t = t^*$ and 0 otherwise. Assuming that each ROI is labelled independently of the others,

$$p(\text{observed labels}, t_i^*) \propto \prod_{i}^{N} \prod_{t=1}^{T} \left(p(t) \prod_{l=1}^{T} p(l|t)^{n_{il}} \right)^{Y_{it}}. \qquad (14.3)$$

Still assuming that the types t for each ROI are known (the Y_{it}), the maximum likelihood estimators of $p(l|t)$ and $p(t)$ are

$$\hat{p}(l|t) = \frac{\sum_{i} Y_{it} n_{il}}{\sum_{l}^{T} \sum_{i} Y_{it} n_{il}} \qquad (14.4)$$

and

$$\hat{p}(t) = \frac{1}{N} \sum_{i} Y_{it}. \qquad (14.5)$$

¿From Bayes' rule one can then show that

$$p(Y_{it} = 1 | \text{observed data}) = \frac{1}{C} \prod_{l}^{T} p(l|t)^{n_{il}} p(t) \qquad (14.6)$$

where C is a normalization constant. Thus, given the parameters $p(t|l)$ and $p(t)$ one can infer the posterior probabilities for the type variable via Equation 6 (and, thus, the posterior probability that a particular ROI is a volcano given that the "type-volcano" probabilities are known).

However, without knowing the Y_{it} values we cannot infer the parameters. In [63] it was noted that one could treat the Y_{it} as a hidden variable and thus apply the well-known EM procedure to find a local maximum of the likelihood function. The EM procedure is an iterative approach which proceeds as follows:

1. Obtain some initial estimates of the expected values of Y_{it}, e.g.,

$$E[Y_{it}] = \frac{n_{il}}{\sum_{l} n_{il}} \qquad (14.7)$$

2. M-step: choose the values of $p(l|t)$ and $p(t)$ which **maximize** the likelihood function (according to Equations 4 and 5), using $E[Y_{it}]$ in place of Y_{it}.

3. E-step: calculate the conditional **expectation** of Y_{it}, $E[Y_{it}|\text{data}] = p(Y_{it} = 1|\text{data})$ (Equation 6).

4. Return to Step 2 until convergence is achieved.

The extension to multiple labellers is straightforward (the interested reader is referred to [63] and was not presented above in the interest of keeping the notation manageable.

14.4.3   Experimental Results

For the purposes of the experiments described here, labellings from 4 planetary geologists on the same set of 4 images were obtained. In total, the geologists found 269 distinct regions, i.e., at least 1 of the 4 labelled each such region as belonging to one of the volcano types.

Applying the EM algorithm to this data resulted in the transition matrices for $p(l|t)$ shown in Table 14.1(a) (Scientist A) and Table 14.1(b) (Scientist C) — scientists B and D are not shown here but are qualitatively similar. From the marginal label probabilities it is clear that scientists A and C have quite different labelling patterns: A finds roughly equal numbers (17%) of types 1 and 4, while C only labels 2.6% as type 1's but 41.6% as type 4's. In terms of accuracy, if C provides a label 1 then it is certain to be of type 1, but a label 3 has a 66.7% chance of being type 2. Label 1 from scientist A has an 86.3% chance of not being of type 1, including a 2% chance of not being a volcano at all (type 5). The derived transition matrices provide a quantitative basis for comparing the accuracy and biases of different labellers.

Table 14.2 shows the estimated probabilities of each type, $p(Y_{it} = 1)$, along with the original labels for each of the first 30 ROI'S in the data. Note that the posterior type probabilities can often not be guessed based on simple averaging or voting as a function of the labels. For example, ROI 5 is most likely to be a type 2 according to the posterior probabilities even though none of the labellers classified it as label 2 — this is due (in part at least) to the fact that on average, a label "3" from labeller C is actually most likely to be a type "2" (see Table 14.1(b)). In [63] the method was applied to the problem of rating anesthetists. The resulting posterior probabilities were almost entirely 0 or 1 reflecting the fact that there was relatively good agreement between the experts. In the voicano problem there is a relatively high level of *disagreement*, and consequently less certainty in the posterior probabilities due to the underlying difficulty of the detection problem (significant variability of volcano shape and relatively low signal-to-noise ratio).   The determination of posterior probabilities for each of the ROI'S is a fundamental step in any quantitative analysis of the volcano data. Given the type probabilities we can simply estimate the probability of a volcano in a given ROI as $p(v) = \sum_t^T p(v|t)p(t)$ where the $p(t)$ terms are the posterior probabilities provided by the EM algorithm, and the $p(v|t)$ terms are the subjective volcano-type probabilities discussed earlier. In the next section we will discuss the use of receiver-operating characteristic (ROC) plots for performance comparison.

14.4.4   Performance Evaluation using ROC Curves

In its simplest form an ROC curve plots detections (the system/human detects a volcano at a location where a volcano exists) versus false alarms (the system/human declares a volcano where none exists). For a detection system such as the SVD-Gaussian classifier (see Section 14.5.1) which produces posterior probabilities, a sequence of detection/false-alarm points can be plotted from the

Table 14.1: (a,b): Scientist-dependent probabilities as estimated by EM procedure.
Scientist A:

Marginal Label Probabilities

Label 1	Label 2	Label 3	Label 4	Label 5
0.171	0.149	0.234	0.175	0.271

Probability(type|label)

	Type 1	Type 2	Type 3	Type 4	Type 5
Label 1	0.137	0.635	0.058	0.150	0.021
Label 2	0.025	0.378	0.169	0.382	0.046
Label 3	0.000	0.034	0.462	0.287	0.217
Label 4	0.000	0.000	0.000	0.883	0.117
Label 5	0.000	0.040	0.103	0.039	0.817

Scientist C:

Marginal Label Probabilities

Label 1	Label 2	Label 3	Label 4	Label 5
0.026	0.056	0.193	0.416	0.309

Probability(type|label)

	Type 1	Type 2	Type 3	Type 4	Type 5
Label 1	1.000	0.000	0.000	0.000	0.000
Label 2	0.019	0.977	0.004	0.000	0.000
Label 3	0.000	0.667	0.175	0.065	0.094
Label 4	0.000	0.000	0.042	0.725	0.233
Label 5	0.000	0.000	0.389	0.000	0.611

Table 14.2: First 30 ROI's in database: scientist labels and posterior probability estimates provided y the EM procedure

ROI	Scientist Labels				Posterior Probabilities (EM)				
	A	B	C	D	Type 1	Type 2	Type 3	Type 4	Type5
1	4	4	4	5	0.000	0.000	0.000	0.816	0.184
2	1	4	4	2	0.000	0.000	0.000	0.991	0.009
3	1	1	2	2	0.023	0.977	0.000	0.000	0.000
4	3	1	5	3	0.000	0.000	1.000	0.000	0.000
5	3	1	3	3	0.000	0.536	0.452	0.012	0.000
6	2	2	2	4	0.000	1.000	0.000	0.000	0.000
7	3	1	5	5	0.000	0.000	1.000	0.000	0.000
8	2	1	4	4	0.000	0.000	0.000	0.999	0.000
9	2	1	4	4	0.000	0.000	0.000	0.999	0.000
10	4	4	4	4	0.000	0.000	0.000	0.996	0.004
11	2	2	3	1	0.000	1.000	0.000	0.000	0.000
12	1	1	3	2	0.000	1.000	0.000	0.000	0.000
13	2	1	3	2	0.000	1.000	0.000	0.000	0.000
14	1	1	1	1	1.000	0.000	0.000	0.000	0.000
15	1	2	2	2	0.000	1.000	0.000	0.000	0.000
16	1	1	2	3	0.000	1.000	0.000	0.000	0.000
17	1	1	1	1	1.000	0.000	0.000	0.000	0.000
18	1	1	2	3	0.000	1.000	0.000	0.000	0.000
19	3	2	5	3	0.000	0.000	0.992	0.000	0.008
20	4	4	4	4	0.000	0.000	0.000	0.996	0.004
21	2	2	4	3	0.000	0.001	0.073	0.926	0.001
22	1	2	4	5	0.000	0.000	0.120	0.812	0.068
23	1	2	3	2	0.000	1.000	0.000	0.000	0.000
24	1	1	2	2	0.023	0.977	0.000	0.000	0.000
25	5	3	5	5	0.000	0.000	0.129	0.000	0.871
26	3	3	3	5	0.000	0.003	0.873	0.004	0.120
27	4	5	4	5	0.000	0.000	0.000	0.498	0.502
28	5	3	5	5	0.000	0.000	0.129	0.000	0.871
29	2	1	3	2	0.000	1.000	0.000	0.000	0.000
30	3	2	5	5	0.000	0.000	0.826	0.000	0.174

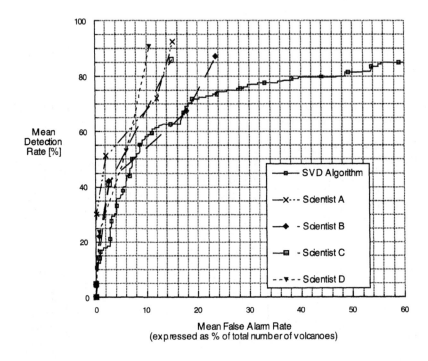

Figure 14.4: Probabilistic ROC curves for scientists and algorithms: estimation noise only

test data by varying the probability at which a test ROI is classified as a volcano. If a human categorizes his/her detections according to T distinct labels/types, then by ranking the detections according to the labels one can generate T points on the ROC plot [34, 43].

A complication in our application of course is that there is no "true" detection list with which to compare a given system or human. We proceed as follows; for each human or system, we estimate based on the EM procedure a probabilistic detection list using the labels from all of the other labellers. For example, with 4 labellers, each is compared with the EM-derived consensus of the other 3: the algorithm is compared with the EM-derived consensus of all 4. Since the EM-derived detection list is probabilistic, each detection or false alarm is weighted: for example, if the EM posterior probability estimate of a particular ROI is $p(v) = 0.8$, then a human or algorithm which detects this ROI has a probability of 0.8 of a true detection and 0.2 of a false alarm (this is how detections and false alarms are scored). This results in "probabilistic ROCs" and is the appropriate way to generate ROCs in the absence of ground truth.

The performance of the algorithms is determined as the cumulative ROC performance over each of the 4 images, where for each test image the algorithm

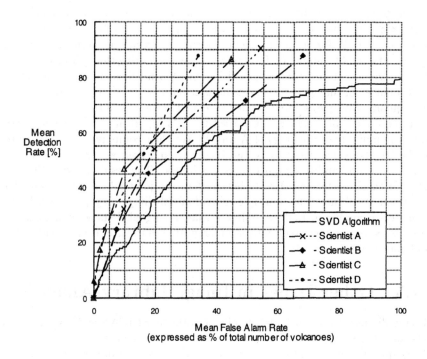

Figure 14.5: Probabilistic ROC curves for scientists and algorithms: estimation+type noise

was trained on the other 3 images. Figure 14.4 shows the probabilistic ROC when the type noise is ignored (the probability of a volcano is 1.0 given types 1 to 4) but the estimation noise is taken into account, whereas Figure 14.5 shows the full model. Clearly there is a substantial difference between the two plots (note that the x-axis scale is slightly different in each): scientists and algorithms are much less accurate when all of the uncertainty is modelled (Figure 14.5). In Figure 14.4, the SVD algorithm appears to be competitive with one of the scientists. However in Figure 14.5, the SVD algorithm curve has shifted further away from the scientists. On closer examination of the data it turns out that the SVD algorithm is doing particularly poorly in terms of approximating posterior probabilities and the more accurate model (Figure 14.5) is more sensitive to this fact. The poor probability approximation properties of the SVD method appears to be a function of the fact that the subspace projection destroys the implicit probabilistic information present in the labels, i.e., label 1's, 2's, etc. are jumbled up in the projected space without any particular structure.

We also note from the plots that there is a definite ordering in terms of accuracy among the scientists, namely, D, C, A, B. For example, B (the worst) typically generates twice as many false alarms as D (the best) for a given detection rate. None of the scientists are particularly accurate, the best being at about 88% detection for 36% false alarms. This reinforces the notion that the best one can hope for on this problem in terms of algorithmic performance, is to emulate the fallible human performance. It is worth noting that our probabilistic ROC curves are of direct interest to the scientists (independent of the algorithm performance) in that it is the first time that human detection capabilities have been quantitatively evaluated in the context of volcano counting.

In another experiment we have used the EM algorithm to derive estimates from the individual labellings of A and B. We then compared these estimates to the labellings generated by A and B jointly, and used as a reference set the EM-derived probabilities from C and D's labels. The result showed that the EM consensus performed slightly better than the joint labels, suggesting that a mathematical model for multiple individual labellings may provide a better approach to combining multiple opinions than having labellers work in a team — this observation is consistent with results reported in the literature on subjective probability assessment [139].

14.5 Other Issues in Image Library Analysis

Having discussed the particular details of both the SKICAT and JARtool data sets and the particular solutions which we have implemented, the remainder of the chapter will focus on the general issues which arise in problems of this nature. In particular, the focus will be on the interaction between image analysis and learning algorithms.

14.5.1 The Role of Prior Information

In general, prior information about an image exploration problem can be specified in two ways. The first is in terms of relatively high-level knowledge specifying expectations and constraints regarding certain characteristics of the objects of interest. For example, in the Magellan-Venus problem the incidence angle of the synthetic aperture radar instrument to the planet's surface is known, which in turn strongly influences the relative positions of bright and dark slope and summit regions for a given volcano [195]. The second type of prior information is the information which is implicitly specified by the labelled data, i.e., the data which has been examined by the domain expert and annotated in some manner.

One must determine the utility of each type of information in designing an image exploration algorithm. For example, in the SKICAT project, the prior knowledge was quite precise and helped a great deal in terms of determining the optimal features to use for the problem. In contrast, for the Magellan-Venus problem, the prior knowledge is quite general in nature and is not easily translatable into algorithmic constraints, leaving us only with the labelled training examples provided by the scientists.

Below we consider two important aspects of prior information. The first addresses the issue of deriving suitable higher-level representations from the raw pixels. The second issue concerns the nature of the labelled data provided by the domain expert.

Pixel Data versus Feature Data

Raw pixel data rarely provide a good basis for learning — appropriate pixel-derived *features* can typically provide a much more robust representation. In scientific data analysis, where the user typically knows the data well and has a list of defined features, selecting the appropriate features to present to the learning algorithm can be straightforward. SKICAT provides an excellent example of this. Not only was the segmentation problem (locating objects) easy to perform, but we had access to a host of defined attributes that we made use of effectively. Having the proper representation made the difference between success and failure.

In order for SKICAT to achieve stable classification accuracy results on classifying data from different plates, we had to spend some effort defining normalized attributes that are less sensitive to plate-to-plate variation. These attributes are computed automatically from the data and are defined such that their values would be normalized within and across images and plates. Many of these quantities (although not all) have physical interpretations. Other quantities we measured involved fitting a template to a set of "sure-stars" selected by the astronomer for each image, and then measuring the rest of the objects with respect to this template. In order to automate the measurement of such attributes, we automated the "sure-star" selection problem by treating it as a learning subproblem and building decision trees for selecting "sure-stars" in an arbitrary image. Fortunately, this turned out to be a relatively easy learning task: our accuracy on this subproblem exceeds 98%. This allowed us to automate the measurement of the needed and more sophisticated attributes.

The point is that in this case a wealth of knowledge was available to us in terms of attributes (measurements), while astronomers found it *difficult to use* these attributes to classify objects. The machine learning algorithms were able to produce a classifier that used many (as many as eight) dimensions. No projection of the data onto two or three dimensions would have allowed as accurate a classification, explaining the difficulty humans found in designing the classifier.

On the other hand, in the case of JARtool, the feature extraction problem is significantly more difficult to address. One approach we have been experimenting with is the use of principal component analysis [244]. Each training example (a subimage containing a positive example) can be turned into a vector of pixel values. The entire training set on n examples, each of which consists of a $k \times k$ pixel subimage, will thus form a $k^2 \times n$ matrix which can subsequently be decomposed into a set of orthonormal eigenvectors using singular value decomposition (SVD). An eigenvalue is associated with each of the vectors indicating its relative importance. When the eigenvectors (eigenvolcanoes) are viewed as images again, we note that each represents a "basic" feature of a volcano. Figure 14.6 shows 20 associated eigenvolcano features (those corresponding to the largest eigenvectors) ordered left to right by decreasing eigenvalues. Note that

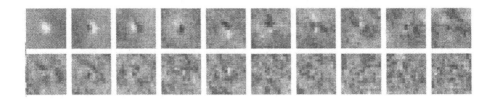

Figure 14.6 Eigenvolcanoes Derived from Training Data.

the eigenvectors become relatively less coherent starting with the sixth or seventh feature. Each block in the figure corresponds to a 225-component eigenvector that was re-translated into a 15×15 image and redisplayed as a block in the figure.

The eigenvolcanoes can be viewed as general features that can be used to encode each detected candidate volcano for classification purposes. This is an example of an automatic template (matched filter) generation procedure which can easily be augmented by other features provided by the expert user. However, the drawbacks of the SVD approach are worth mentioning: in general, the method can be sensitive to scale, rotation, and translation distortions (although these are not significant problems for the volcano problem) and it is difficult to encode prior knowledge about the domain into the model.

14.5.2   Modelling Spatial Context

Most learning algorithms implicitly assume that the training data consists of independent randomly chosen samples from the population of interest, e.g., a set of medical records for a hospital. Hence, such algorithms may not be directly suited to the task of learning from image data where there may be significant inter-pixel and inter-object spatial correlation present. To handle such correlation one can impose spatial smoothness constraints on both the labels and the pixel intensities. Models such as Markov random fields (MRF's) were developed for this purpose in the mid to late 1980's [110, 207]. While the theoretical basis of MRF's is well-founded it is important to remember that they are primarily used as a computational convenience rather than a realistic model of spatial interaction. Other, more global, models of spatial context have also been proposed [10, 45], again with a sound mathematical basis. In any of these approaches there is little theory on how to reconcile prior knowledge regarding spatial constraints with one's choice of model parameters, so that considerable experimentation and tuning is often necessary for a given application.

14.5.3   Online Learning and Adaptation

Another aspect of the image exploration problem is that one would ideally like to have an algorithm which could gradually improve its performance as it explores a particular database. This type of *incremental learning* has largely been ignored by researchers in learning and pattern recognition in favour of the simpler approach of "one-shot" batch learning. The particular type of model representation being used critically influences whether the model is easily adaptable or not. For example, neither discriminative models (such as the decision trees used in SKICAT) or PCA feature generation methods (as used in JARtool) are well-suited for online adaptation. In each case, to update the model to include new data, the training algorithm must be run in batch mode on *all* of the data which has been collected to that point. Memory and prototype-based models (including parametric density models, non-parametric density estimators, mixture models, nearest-neighbour models, etc.) are more suited to online adaptation — however, they typically suffer from poor approximation properties in high dimensions [230].

Given a particular adaptive algorithm, a unique feature of image analysis problems is the fact that the human visual system of the domain expert offers an excellent opportunity for supervised feedback to improve adaptation. This is in marked contrast to other domains, such as the analysis of "flat" medical data for example, where there is no intuitive way for a domain expert to visualize and quickly evaluate high-dimensional vectors for the purpose of labelling them. Hence, in principle, online image exploration algorithms could operate by iterative interaction with the human user, sequentially selecting examples from the database for labelling. While such algorithms have significant potential for changing the way in which scientists interact with image databases, it is also clear that until various fundamental representational issues are solved (c.f. learning mappings from pixels to meaningful categories), such adaptive algorithms will remain beyond our reach.

14.5.4   Multi-Sensor and Derived Map Data

A common feature in remote-imaging applications is the illumination of the same target area in different ways (e.g., at multiple wavelengths), thus obtaining a vector of intensities at each pixel site rather than just a single intensity. For example, in SKICAT, the data was collected in three optical color bands. In the Magellan-Venus data, many parts of the planet were imaged from different angles and at different resolutions. In addition, low-resolution altimeter data was also measured. This results in several different data sets being available for the same surface regions. Similarly, after data has been acquired and archived, different research groups will typically analyze the data and produce thematic maps and catalogs (either by manual or automated means) for different quantities of interest [37, 169]. For example, in the Magellan-Venus database, catalogs have already been produced for large volcanic structures and for the location of many of the large volcanic fields (but not the volcanoes within the fields).

Hence, in the general sense, each pixel can have a vector of associated attributes, whether these are data from another sensor, or derived qualitative categories (such as a map). In principle, such additional data should be particularly useful for computer-aided detection since it is often difficult for a human user to visualize such multi-dimensional representations. However, certain technical difficulties must be overcome for the additional data to be useful. For multi-sensor data, the different data sets must usually be *registered* so that the pixel measurements are somehow aligned to reference the same surface point — this can be an imprecise process. Similarly, subjectively derived thematic maps may be subject to various biases or systematic errors. Hence, methodologies for determining the relative reliability of different sources of information are highly desirable, although not always available in practice. At a minimum, automated cataloging systems and thematic mappers should provide a calibrated estimate of the reliability of the decision at each pixel or region of interest ("spatial error bars"). Although not a feature of the first-generation SKICAT or JARtool systems, probabilistic models for assessing model reliability are currently being pursued.

14.6   Discussion

Natural object detection and characterization in large digital image libraries is a generic task which poses many challenges to current pattern recognition and machine learning methods. This chapter has briefly touched on a number of relevant issues in problems of this nature. There are many other issues which impact the integration of learning and image analysis algorithms which were not discussed here due to space constraints, including the use of physical noise models for imaging processes at various wavelengths, the integration of multiple images of the same surface area taken at different times, and the use of multi-resolution and parallel algorithms to speed computation.

The SKICAT and JARtool projects are typical examples of the types of large-scale image database applications which will become increasingly common — for example, the NASA Earth Observing System Synthetic Aperture Radar (EOS SAR) satellite will generate on the order of 50 GBytes of remote sensing data per hour when operational [251]. In order for scientists to be able to effectively utilize these extremely large amounts of data, basic digital image library navigation tools will be essential.

Our existing JPL projects have so far demonstrated that efficient and accurate tools for natural object detection are a realistic goal provided there is strong prior knowledge about how pixels can be turned into features and from there to class categories. With the astronomy problem there was sufficient strong knowledge for this to be the case. With the volcano data, the knowledge is much less precise and consequently the design of effective object detection and recognition tools is considerably more difficult.

The common thread across the various issues would appear to be the problem of how to combine both prior knowledge and data. Much of the prior knowledge of a domain scientist is vague and imprecise and cannot be translated easily into pixel-level constraints. However, scientists find it significantly easier to provide attributes to measure on a given region than to specify the method they use to classify the region. This is an important aspect that can be exploited to solve significant problems as was done with the SKICAT system. This appears to be a good solution to the query formulation problem, which would be a major hurdle standing in the way of turning a large image database into a digital library: be it via data reduction (as in SKICAT cataloging) or object detection and recognition as in JARtool. The latter appears to be an essential problem to solve if the goal of a realistic query-by-content type capability is to be achieved.

Dealing with image data is uniquely appropriate for interactive tools since results can immediately be visualized and judged by inspection. This makes obtaining feedback and training data from users much easier. Since humans find it particularly difficult to express *how* they perform visual detection and classification, using a "learning from examples" approach becomes particularly appropriate. The fact that the image databases are becoming increasingly common and unmanageably large makes the need for the type of approaches advocated in this chapter particularly pressing.

14.7   Summary and Conclusion

Image databases are growing rapidly and constitute a large part of human stored knowledge, especially in scientific fields. We argue that work towards the establishment of useful digital image libraries cannot ignore a fundamental problem standing in the way of automatically indexing images (by content) as well as performing on-line searches and query-by-content type operations. We refer to this as the query formulation problem. It results from the fact that translating visual patterns into database queries is, for most cases, too difficult for users to perform. Querying a database by providing examples and counter-examples forms a novel and powerful basis for a new generation of intelligent analysis tools that can circumvent this problem in a natural and intuitive manner.

This chapter aims at clarifying some of the important issues that need to be addressed when targeting the general problem of performing object recognition in digital image libraries. Two major issues arise in this context: 1. transforming (reducing) the data from pixels to meaningful or useful features, and 2. recognizing (classifying) the detected objects in feature space. Rather than requiring the user to design and implement a classification algorithm to achieve the second step, a machine learning approach may be used to automatically construct the classifier based on training examples provided by the user. Not only does this alleviate the burden of programming from the user, it also provides a mechanism for tackling the often difficult problem of recognizing objects in feature space.

In addition to presenting the encouraging results achieved with the SKICAT system, the chapter examines the application of pattern recognition and machine learning technology to the general problem of image library exploration. In particular, it is argued that image libraries possess unique characteristics which impact the direct application of standard learning methods. Feature extraction from pixels, spatial context modeling, limited ground truth, the availability of prior knowledge, and the use of supervised feedback during learning are all common aspects of the problem which need addressing before the query-by-content problem is to be effectively dealt with. Finally, another major focus of this chapter was on the problem of accounting for and dealing with uncertain ground truth in training data. This is an important practical issue that needs significant attention.

We argue that without the development of a new generation of intelligent trainable tools, most data in large digital libraries will lie dormant, inaccessible and unexploited. Part of the effort of developing digital libraries must include the development and fielding of the types of tools we are developing. In our opinion, they constitute a major step towards turning large collection of images into true digital libraries.

Acknowledgments

The SKICAT work is a collaboration between U. Fayyad (JPL) and N. Weir, S. Djorgovski (Caltech Astronomy). The authors would like to thank Jayne Aubele and Larry Crumpler of the Department of Geological Sciences, Brown University, for their assistance in labelling Venus images, and Maureen Burl (JPL) for assistance in obtaining the experimental results described in this chapter. The work on JARtool is a collaboration between U. Fayyad, P. Smyth (JPL) and M. Burl, P. Perona (Caltech's E.E. Department). The work described in this chapter was carried out in part by the Jet Propulsion Laboratory, California Institute of Technology, under a contract with the National Aeronautics and Space Administration.

Part V

Prototypes/Applications

Chapter 15

A Video Database System for Digital Libraries

HongJiang Zhang[*],Stephen W. Smoliar[†],Jian Hua Wu[‡],Chien Yong Low [§] and Atreyi Kankanhalli[¶]

15.1   Introduction

With rapid advances in electronic imaging, data storage, data compression, and telecommunications, our libraries are becoming digital and multimedia. As more and more multimedia data are acquired, managing and manipulating them becomes an important issue to be resolved before we can take full advantage of their information content. Video is the most difficult of all the media resources to manage. Only an indexed video can effectively support retrieval and distribution in digital library and multimedia information systems; and that index must be based explicitly on the different media contents, rather than on attempts to summarize those contents through text descriptions [116]. Thus, constructing an effective video library will require a set of power tools whose functionality will support the tasks of parsing, indexing, retrieval, and browsing for video source material [260]. We have developed tools for all of these tasks which will be discussed in this chapter. Case studies have provided the primary means for testing our results, and we shall concentrate on one case study involving the construction of a database of video source material intended for use in news and documentary production.

The following Section discusses the tools we have developed to support the task of parsing video source material. This discussion will focus on the image portion of a video, although we are planning to expand our tool set to accommodate sound-track information as well. The next Section discusses the index

[*]Institute of Systems Science, National University of Singapore, Heng Mui Keng Terrace, Kent Ridge, Singapore 0511, Email: zhj@iss.nus.sg

[†]Institute of Systems Science, National University of Singapore, Heng Mui Keng Terrace, Kent Ridge, Singapore 0511, Email: smoliar@iss.nus.sg

[‡]Institute of Systems Science, National University of Singapore, Heng Mui Keng Terrace, Kent Ridge, Singapore 0511, Email: jhwu@iss.nus.sg

[§]Institute of Systems Science, National University of Singapore, Heng Mui Keng Terrace, Kent Ridge, Singapore 0511, Email: cylow@iss.nus.sg

[¶]Institute of Systems Science, National University of Singapore, Heng Mui Keng Terrace, Kent Ridge, Singapore 0511, Email: atreyi@iss.nus.sg

structure we have developed which is based on previous attempts to apply an object-oriented approach to accommodate the different media which must be managed [156]. Tools for retrieval and browsing are then discussed in a single Section, since we view these tasks as closely related means for interacting with the index structure.

15.2   Video Parsing

The first task in video parsing is to partition a video program into *generic clips*, which serve as the elemental units for indexing the database. There is no universal standard for defining these units; but the current consensus is that a generic clip should be a single *camera shot*, consisting of one or more contiguous frames representing a continuous action in time and space [185]. We have developed a set of video partitioning algorithms for this task which introduce a minor variation on this consensus. While most systems have concentrated on detecting simple breaks between camera shots, we have also incorporated a sophisticated approach which detects the sorts of gradual transitions between shots which are implemented by special effects such fades, wipes, and dissolves [259]. These transitional intervals are then identified as generic clips separate from those of the two camera shots being joined.

Once a given video has been partitioned, each clip must be analyzed for those *semantic primitives* which will form the basis for entries in an index structure [116]. While fully automatic content analysis of video source material is still not possible in general, we have developed a set of algorithms which make it easier for a user to detect and locate such semantic primitives. For example, we use motion analysis to classify a video clip automatically according to the camera operations which take place within that clip [259]. Such classification is useful in identifying or constructing a single image which may serve to represent an entire shot [242]. Furthermore, the decision of a director to zoom in is often an indication that the region of the zoom contains an object of interest.

In addition to exercising general-purpose tools based on camera operations, we have also been developing more specific *model-based* tools which can take advantage of any *a priori* knowledge of content. We have tested these tools with a system which can partition an entire news program and classify its clips into anchorperson shots, news shots, commercial break shots, and several highly specific content shots, such as financial news and weather forecasts [260]. These models can capture both the spatial structure of individual frames from a video and the temporal structure of either a camera shot or a contiguous sequence of such shots. Figure 1 is an example of the spatial structure of an anchorperson shot, while Figure 2 illustrates how the temporal structure of an entire news program may be modeled.

If storage space is limited, it may not be feasible to construct a database which contains digital representations of all videos in their entirety. Thus, identifying or constructing single representative images is not only important for content analysis: Those images may be the only material which may be readily

Figure 15.1 The spatial structure of a frame from an anchorperson shot.

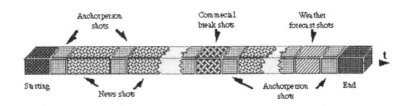

Figure 15.2 The temporal structure of a typical news program.

stored in the database. Fortunately, such images may be used as a type of visual index [185]; and content-based retrieval can be based on feature analysis of those images. We have developed a content-based approach to selecting such images which has been very successful in the test cases we have run to date. We have also been developing a repertoire of feature analysis algorithms which may be applied to indexing these images, once they have been selected [112].

15.3   Index Data Structure

A recent analysis of the queries which a user may wish to formulate in working with a video library [210] concluded that there are three basic types of indices which may be required to support those queries: bibliographic, structural, and content. Bibliographic indices resemble the sorts of indices we normally associate with library catalogs. Each entry would include a title, an abstract, keyword classifications of subject and genre, and the sort of information displayed in the opening and closing credits. Structural indices are based on the sort of structural parsing described in the preceding Section. This would include identifying units of both temporal and spatial structure, along with explicit representation of any models guiding the structural analysis. The sort of content indices envisaged by [210] are based on the *objects of content* in a video source, including the appearance and location of persons and physical objects which serve as scenery or properties. This type of index should accommodate objects which are both visual and auditory; and it should incorporate different levels of description, such as a dominant color in a scene or a sound effect designated in terms of the physical object which produced it. However, there is a second type of content index which is closer to the sorts of indices we normally associate with books. These are based on topical categories which reflect the subject matter of the source and will probably incorporate the keyword terms included in related bibliographic indices.

Queries based on the data in bibliographic indices can be handled by relatively conventional tools. Similarly, queries based on structural indices tend to be comparatively straightforward in nature, since they are driven by both general and specific models which drive the operations of structural parsing. The real challenge lies in dealing with queries based on content; and, given the multimedia nature of video source material, we believe it is important that the processing of such queries should be multimedia-based. Consequently, while any representation of topical categories can easily be based on text, when dealing with the objects of content, the actual *entries* in an index should be sorted according to their respective media. The index structure we are developing supports three such types: text, images, and sounds. Text data are still necessary for such things as transcripts of spoken material. Indexing based on image content is currently built on visual features such as color, texture, and shape of objects [112]. Our work on developing an audio index structure is still very preliminary, but we plan to proceed by analogy to the structure of our image index.

Our current plan is to integrate all three types of indices in a common frame-based knowledge base. This knowledge base will provide a foundational representation of all semantic objects, their attributes, and relations to their respective video and audio sources. These objects are assigned as instances in a hierarchical organization of categories which addresses the need for a topical approach to content. The hierarchical structure provides a varying granularity which may then be used to focus attention during both specific retrieval and browsing tasks. Let us now see how this structure serves all three types of queries.

Figure 3 shows a portion of the class-instance hierarchy constructed to support our model-based approach to the analysis of news video content. Note that, at one level, categories have been defined to correspond to the syntactic units of the temporal structure illustrated in Figure 2; but the actual content of the news items has been refined to represent different types of news stories. Furthermore, individual instances of news stories are structured to include both anchorperson shots and news shots. Thus, the framework which supports queries based on topical content also supports structural queries.

In addition to maintaining a class hierarchy of topical categories, frames are used to manage information about the objects of content which must also be indexed. For example, the image in Figure 1 can be used as a model for identifying similarly structured anchorperson shots. In this capacity it will be represented by a frame which is an instance of the `AnchorShotModel` class. The slot structure of this instance would take a form like the following:

```
Name:   Anchor_on_Left
Class:  AnchorShotModel
Objects:  #table[Left_Anchorperson
             Left_Anchorperson_name
             Right_News_icon
             Left_Background]
```

Each of the objects, in turn, is an instance of `ObjectModel` whose slot structure provides descriptive information to facilitate image-based retrieval. This slot structure may be illustrated with respect to the `Left_Anchorperson` frame:

```
Name:   Left_Anchorperson
Class:  ObjectModel
Location:
Size:
Color:
Shape:
```

Fillers for these last four slots are based on quantitative representations of location, size, color, and shape which have been discussed in greater detail in [112].

Bibliographic data are again represented in terms of slot structures for frames. For example, the **news3** instance in Figure 3 has the following more detailed slot structure:

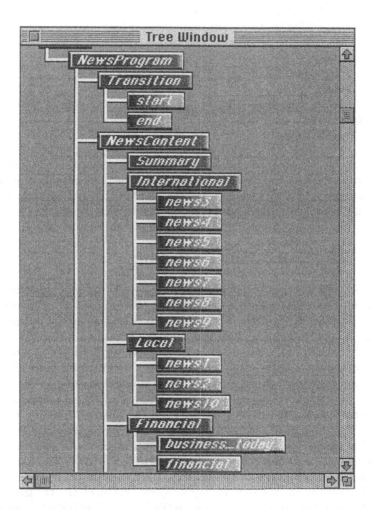

Figure 15.3: A portion of the class-instance hierarchy for a knowledge base of news videos.

```
Name:  news3
Class:  International
Shots:  #table[Korea_Intro
              Korea_Map
              Korea_Anchor_Transition
              Security_Council]
Description:  "North Korea nuclear inspection"
Time:  2100
Date:  261093
Source: Singapore_Broadcasting_Corporation
Video:  News3
Anchor:  Shobi_Pereira
Who:  Robert_Johnson
Where:  North_Korea
```

This representation provides both the structural information that the entire news story consists of four camera shots, each of which may be described in greater detail (for example, with a transcript of the spoken text), and a descriptive text string and several keys which are useful for bibliographic searches.

15.4 Retrieval and Browsing

The video library we are building should support bibliographic, structural, and content queries, where content must include the media of text, images, and sounds. However, to date we have only implemented support for queries based on text and visual features. Browsing tools are provided for inspection of the results of retrieval from a query and for refining queries. We feel it is particularly important that both retrieval and browsing appeal to the user's visual intuitions.

Our prototype system can accommodate text searches based on the contents of frame slots which contain either strings or the names of other frames. Given a text-based query, the system first extracts the relevant terms by removing the non-functional words and stemming the remainder. After this, the query is checked against a domain-specific thesaurus, where similarity measures are used to compare the text descriptions with the query terms [260]. The frame-based representation can be used to focus search either in terms of specific categories or with respect to specific slots of frame objects. Furthermore, the tree display of the hierarchy of categories, as shown in Figure 3, allows for interaction with the user for purposes of either browsing or retrieving an entire collection of video clips assigned to a given topic. For example, Figure 4 illustrates a display known as a *clip window* which presents of collection of video clips as a window of image icons, following the approach of [241]. This particular clip window is for browsing the instances of the entire **NewsContent** class.

Search and retrieval of video clips based on the visual features of their representative images is also supported in our system. Techniques for such an approach have been developed and implemented, including: computation of image features that support indexing and provide useful query functionality,

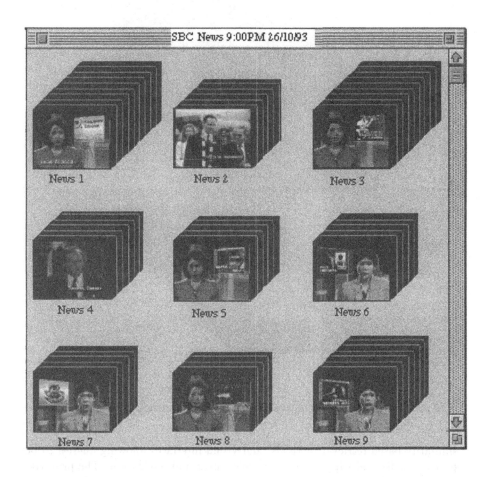

Figure 15.4 A clip window illustrating instances of the **NewsContent** class.

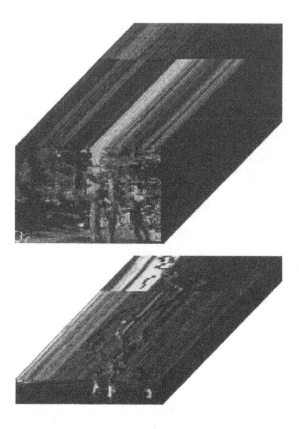

Figure 15.5 A spatiotemporal image illustrating traces of dancers' legs.

similarity-based retrieval methods, and visual interfaces allowing queries to be posed visually and supporting query refinement and navigation. The primitive image properties which we are currently investigating include color histograms, shapes, sizes, and locations of objects; and the objects are identified by a color segmentation algorithm. Search is facilitated through the use of numerical index keys which are generated automatically when images are analyzed prior to insertion in the database [112]. We have also developed a user-friendly visual interface to allow flexible user definition and refinement of visual queries. Experiments have shown that this approach achieves fast and accurate retrieval.

Image-based retrieval is, by its nature, based on static data; and our techniques have been applied to representative images which have been extracted from individual camera shots by either an automated technique or manual selection. However, video is distinguished from static images by virtue of the significance of the time dimension. We are currently working on utilizing temporal visual features which will extend our current capabilities by providing an *event*-based approach to indexing and retrieval. These features may be identified through the examination of sequences of frames from a video; but it is also possible to construct a *spatiotemporal image* [24] from an entire camera shot. This is a rectangular array, one of whose dimensions is the time duration of the shot; and the other dimension is a spatial "slice" through the array of a frame image. We have observed that it is often easier to identify events in these spatiotemporal images than it is to detect them by analysis of successive frame images. Figure 5 illustrates an example of such a spatiotemporal image. It is constructed by taking a horizontal slice through a micon (movie icon) which represents two consecutive camera shots as a rectangular solid of pixels [241]. These shots were taken from *Changing Steps*, a "dance for television" conceived by choreographer Merce Cunningham and video designer Elliot Caplan. Because the dancers all wear uniformly-colored leotards, the movements of their legs leave traces of colored lines in the spatiotemporal image which are very easy to detect and trace.

The retrieval system we are building behaves less like a traditional database and more like an information filter based on similarity matching, especially when queries are constructed from image or auditory features [112]. To support this, effective interactive visual interfaces are crucial and are the major access tools to the database. The query process is still iterative, with the system accepting feedback to narrow or reformulate searches or change its link-following behavior, and to refine any queries that are given.

Query results may be presented as text (based on the contents of slots of instance frames), images (such as the clip window illustrated in Figure 4), or a combination of the two. The task of retrieval is further facilitated by browsing tools of two levels of temporal granularity, overview and detail; and the user may easily move between these two levels. One may move from the overview browsing provided by clip windows to the greater detail of a "soft" video player. This player has the additional feature of being able to display selected representative images in their temporal order as if they were a video. The user may employ usual video player controls to view these images in forward or reverse, either "played" as a video or examined one frame at a time. This provides a significant improvement over VCR-style fast-forward and fast-reverse scanning, because the user is regularly advanced to the next display of new content.

There is also a hierarchical viewer which enables *non-linear* browsing; this viewer allows a user to examine a lengthy video source rapidly by arranging its frames into a temporal resolution hierarchy which may be easily scanned in a limited display space. This approach is based on the Hierarchical Video Magnifier of [175]; but we have subsequently refined the architecture to take advantage of knowledge of camera shot boundaries and representative images within each shot [229]. Figure 6 illustrates how this viewer facilitates browsing of a lengthy videotape of stock footage used in documentary production. The first two levels display temporal intervals of consecutive camera shots. The third level displays individual shots within one of these intervals, and the fourth level displays five representative images extracted from one of those shots.

Figure 15.6 A hierarchical browser of a full-length video.

15.5 Summary

The digital libraries of the future must be able to accommodate multimedia source material as readily as current libraries accommodate text. Our effort to achieve this goal has concentrated on the development of a prototype video library system. We have implemented software tools for parsing the content of video sources, generating index structures, and enabling both focused query retrieval and casual browsing. These tools are being enhanced as we apply them to case studies based on different video sources. Curently, our most active case study is concerned with the management of several hundred hours of stock footage which is available for documentary production.

15.6 Acknowledgements

Images from video sources in this chapter were provided through the courtesy of the Television Corporation of Singapore (formerly Singapore Broadcasting Corporation) and the Cunningham Dance Foundation.

Chapter 16

Developing The Scientific-Technical Digital Library At A National Laboratory

Laurie E. Stackpole*,Roderick D. Atkinson[†] and John Yokley[‡]

16.1 Introduction

The Ruth H. Hooker Research Library and Technical Information Center addresses the information needs of the Naval Research Laboratory's (NRL) research community, consisting of about 3,500 Federal staff and about 1,500 contractors at the Washington, D.C. facility. NRL occupies a 130-acre campus of 152 buildings located on the Potomac River in Southwest Washington, D.C. Research facilities are also located in Orlando, FL; Bay St. Louis, MS; and Monterey, CA. The research efforts of the Laboratory are concentrated in 17 broad areas: acoustics, advanced space sensing, artificial intelligence, astrophysics, biotechnology, chemistry, condensed matter science, information technology, materials research, optical sciences, plasma physics, radar and electronics, radiation technology, remote sensing, space science, space systems, and structural dynamics. In addition, the Library also serves NRL's parent organization, the Office of Naval Research, in nearby Arlington, VA.The Library is at the forefront in implementing services and systems to help researchers successfully adopt new technologies that support information access. Among its innovative services are: a campus-wide information system, the InfoNet, that provides end users with access to a broad spectrum of local and remote information sources from their in-office desktop computers or terminals; [12, 14] an optical imaging system, seamlessly linked to a pre-existing online catalog, for the storage, retrieval, online display, and printing of materials from the library's collection; [26, 92] and TORPEDO (The Optical Retrieval Project: Electronic Documents Online), an experimental effort to provide researchers with desktop access to the library's repository of over 100,000 reports stored as 5 million page images. The library is also working with the American Physical Society to test the feasibility of providing network access to two current journals in electronic formats. Recent

---

*U.S. Naval Research Laboratory
†U.S. Naval Research Laboratory
‡Kestrel Associates, Inc.

articles in Science [150], InternetWorld [149] and Government Computer News [172] have cited NRL as an example of the "virtual library" in action.

There are three initiatives that set the stage for the electronic age. Each is discussed below.

16.2   The InfoNet

16.2.1   Impetus for Developing a Campus-wide Information System

Since 1983, end users have been able to search the library's online catalog both on site and remotely over the campus-wide network, known as NICEnet. However, all other online searching continued to be performed by library reference staff, primarily using DIALOG, STN and DTIC. This situation began to change in 1988 when the library introduced CD-ROM databases for end-user searching in both its reference area and its Microcomputer SoftwareSupport Center. Users responded favorably to the CD-ROM products, enjoying the freedom to explore that comes with performing their own searches

In 1990, the library conducted a user needs analysis to develop specifications for a replacement automated library system. This analysis was instrumental in establishing support for the development of a campus-wide information system (CWIS) for in-office access to library-based CD-ROMs and other in-library and external resources. As a result of interviews with 46 individuals representing a cross section of research interests, the library was able to demonstrate that scientists throughout the laboratory wanted access to information resources from their own computers and workstations. Several key findings emerged, namely that the library should implement a system to: Provide subject and author access to journal articles as well as books;Allow users to request materials as part of an online search;Offer access to multiple databases, both bibliographic and informational;Store full text files, such as journal articles or handbooks, for downloading;Provide access to the catalogs of other libraries and to external databases; andOffer electronic document delivery from libraries or information providers.

While proceeding with plans to meet some of these objectives by identifying and procuring a state-of-the-art library system, the library began to look at other approaches that could complement the capabilities of existing commercial library systems. Added support for these efforts came from the involvement of the Library in the working group tasked withplanning for a fiber optic upgrade to the existing campus network backbone. The working group endorsed the concept of a library-provided information utility to: Provide researchers with access to local computer systems;Act as a gateway to remote systems;Integrate these functions with library materials and services; andMake scientific, technical, administrative and reference materials available to researchers at their computers or workstations.

16.2.2   Design and Development of the InfoNet

The InfoNet was introduced in August 1992. It allows users to query local and remote information systems and enables them to request library materials and services without leaving their offices. InfoNet users access a single menu to select from a wide variety of information resources including: library-mounted CD-ROM databases; electronic books downloaded from the Internet; other laboratory databases, including the library catalog; and resources located throughout the world through pre-programmed access to selected Internet hosts. The InfoNet has succeeded in demonstrating that end users in their offices, using any computing platform, can directly use a single menu-driven interface to access a wide spectrum of information resources.

The InfoNet system consists entirely of commercial off-the-shelf software and hardware. It uses a TCP/IP terminal server and a Novell Access Server (NAS) in tandem to permit complete end-user to host connectivity. Researchers from across the network access the library-based TCP/NAS host system using free terminal emulation software and are presented with a hierarchical menu-driven system. The CD-ROMs themselves are housed on a Novell NetWare 3.11 server and the MS-DOS-based search software runs on the NAS. The CD-ROMs are attached to the Novell Server and are mounted using SCSI Express software for NetWare. Each CD-ROM database resides in its own unique CD-ROM drive for optimal performance. Networked CD-ROMs generally perform much faster than stand-aloneCD-ROMs due to network data caching.[15]

In addition to offering end users a selection of 18 CD-ROM databases, InfoNet menus provide access to several NRL information systems (a SUN UNIX-based library catalog and VAX Cluster-based MIS databases) and a small selection of electronic books, as well as information systems found on the world-wide Internet through the use of Gopher, USENET news reader, and Telnet interfaces. All external information systems are accessed by the InfoNet through the NAS using the TCP/IP suite of protocols and are based on freely distributable client TCP/IP applicationswhich conform to the packet driver specifications. Since the system is based on TCP/IP protocols and COTS (commercial off-the-shelf) distributed systems architecture, end-user connectivity to the InfoNet both via modems and across the Internet to NRL Orlando, FL, and ONR, Arlington, VA, is easily achieved.[13] Dial-in access, to permit users to use the InfoNet from home or while on travel is also available.

16.2.3   How the InfoNet Impacts Research Productivity

To analyze usage of the InfoNet two main tools are used:

1. metering software which records actual accesses to applications, storing information such as who used what products, when, and for how long; and

2. surveys of researchers, including an online InfoNet user registration program which asks users about the impact of the InfoNet on their research.

Recent data taken from the metering reports show over 3,000 end-user accesses to InfoNet databases per month. Moreover, over seventy-fivepercent of end-user InfoNet accesses are coming from researchers across the network in their offices and laboratories, outside the library. In addition, almost twentypercent of InfoNet access is during times that the library is closed – on holidays, weekends, or either before or after working hours. Metering data also shows that end users log over 500 hours searching the InfoNet each month.

Although the InfoNet has been available since August 1992, until February of this year researchers initially logged into the system under a generic "guest" account. To improve InfoNet services by permitting dial-in access from home, InfoNet users are now required to fill out an online user registration program and use their own unique account names and passwords to access the InfoNet. Over 700 researchers have currently requested and obtained InfoNet accounts. In addition to the standard identification information, such as name, telephone number, and e-mail address, researchers are asked to provide the following information on how the InfoNet has affected their use of the library:

1. "How much time does the InfoNet save you in your research (compared to another method of gathering information, e.g. walking to the Library and browsing the shelves)?" and

2. "Do you go to the Library more frequently or less frequently now that the InfoNet is available?"

In response to question one, over 85 percent of the respondents stated that the InfoNet had saved them time. The answers ranged from 0 to 16 hours, with 2 hours/week being the average. This question was an optional question and it was answered by roughly two-thirds of all users who registered.

In response to the second question, over fifty percent of respondents said that they went to the library less frequently now that the InfoNet was available, and only six percent said that they visited the library more frequently. While the InfoNet can improve research productivity by meeting many needs of the NRL research community for convenient and reliable access to scientific and technical information, it currently handles only text files. This limitation precludes the InfoNet from providing information such as equations, graphs and charts, which are often stored as images. Expanding the InfoNet to handle images is a high-priority effort, as the Library believes this would dramatically improve researcher productivity as much of needed data are in the form of graphs and equations.

16.3   Research Reports Imaging System

16.3.1   Impetus for Optical Storage

Like many libraries, the Ruth H. Hooker Research Library and Technical Information Center is faced with a space problem. Its research reports collection was created in 1945 when it was thought that the end of World War II meant the end of the production of reports by government agencies and their contractors. The reports then at NRL were gathered together to form an archive that, it was believed, would not continue to grow. However, the oppositeproved to be true; in 1988 over 300,000 paper reports filled the library's shelves. These reports are both technically and historically valuable, but many were deteriorating due to the ravages of time and poor environmental conditions. Additionally they were occupying space that was badly needed for other purposes.

16.3.2 Design Considerations for NRL's Prototype Imaging System

In August of 1987, the library implemented an on-line reports catalog using Cuadra Star as its automated system. Star provides for a very large number of fields, so that a report can be thoroughly indexed. Fields may be searched in full or by individual words and the results can be combined by Boolean operators. The system is flexible enough to allow the addition of a field or sub-field if the need for a new one materializes. Global changes permit sweeping revisions in indexing if that should be necessary. In Star, the library had an automated reports catalog that library staff found to be well suited to their needs.

When the library began planning for optical storage, it decided to take a direct, straightforward approach to accomplish its conversion from paper to optical storage. A key decision was that the library would continue to use the Star system as the search and retrieval engine for reports. This meant that the optical storage system would be developed as a stand-alone system. This approach not only allowed the library to build on the capability it had already developed, it afforded maximum flexibility going into a new technology, allowing the library to change its search engine or its optical storage software independently. To keep the system as simple as possible, optical storage was considered as an alternative to physical storage on the shelf: the librarian or user searched the catalog from a computer terminal, located the appropriate reports record, and noted the accession number; then, instead of going to the shelf to find the report itself, the user moved to a second workstation, entered the accessionnumber, brought up the report image, and could view the document online or print it out, in whole or in part, on a high-speed printer.

16.3.3 Design and Implementation of a Reports Catalog That Displays the Full Document

In 1992, this custom-designed prototype optical system, operational since May 1989, was replaced with a system composed entirely of off-the-shelf components. The new system uses the Genesys Information Systems Corporation's ImagExtender software to create a seamless link between the Star catalog and the imaging system. Database searches and image retrieval are now accomplished at a single workstation. The two systems, still entirely separate, appear to the end user as one.

Major portions of the NRL research collection are stored as images retrievable at workstations in the Library. Almost 100,000 reports, 5 million pages, are stored as TIFF (Tagged Image File Format) files on 12-inch optical disks in a Sony Writable Optical Disk Autochanger Model WDA-610. One 12-inch "write once read many" (WORM) optical disk can hold 6.55 gigabytes (GB) of digital data, enough to store the contents of 130,000 typewritten pages. Housing 50 disks, one autochanger provides the equivalent storage space of 500 file cabinets. Autochangers can be daisy-chained to expand storage capacity.

The reports are scanned and their images compressed using a TDC 4530 scanner. This scanner is equipped with a sheet feeder and a monitor. It is capable of sustained scanning at a rate of 40 sheets a minute and can scan both sides of a sheet at the same time. Scanning is being done at 300 dpi. After enhancing the image electronically, the scanner compresses the image into the industry standard CCITT Group IV format.

Images are retrieved at the viewing stations, 486 PCs equipped with dual-page monitors, by first searching the Cuadra Star database resident on an Alpha micro minicomputer. Once a desired report is identified, and the report's unique accession number is displayed, the image is viewed by entering a single key stroke. The report can then be displayed page by page on the screen or the user can skim through the report or page forward or back at any desired pace. A page can be enlarged for detail or reduced in size to allow other pages to be displayed on the screen. More than one report can be viewed on a screen and the same report can be viewed simultaneously at more than one workstation at the same time. All or part of the report can be printed out on an HP Laser-Jet printer at 17 pages per minute. All equipment is networked internally on a Novell 3.11 LAN.

16.4 TORPEDO (The Optical Retrieval Project: Electronic Documents Online)

16.4.1 Impetus for Delivery of Images to Researchers

To respond to the needs of remote users for all the information contained in a document, the Library plans to develop an imaging capability that can be networked and integrated with the InfoNet. Since scientific journals are the most important information source for the researcher, a major thrust of this networked imaging system will be to provide access to core journals that appeal to a broad segment of the NRL community. The desire for such a capability has been strongly expressed by the scientific staff. In addition, the NRL Director of Research has taken an active interest in advancing this cause and is funding the first of what are planned as several Library-publisher cooperative projects.

The development of a networked information capability has implications that extend beyond improved service to NRL employees. For example, the reports collection that the Library has currently stored electronically consists entirely of government and government-sponsored publications, which for the most part are not protected by copyright. Although some reports may have security restrictions or other limitations on distribution,most can be freely disseminated. By providing network access to portions of this electronic documents collection through state-of-the-art retrieval tools, NRL can help in the realization of the "Digital Library."

16.4.2 Network Dissemination of Current Journals and Reports

The Library has recently signed a cooperative agreement with the American Physical Society (\PS) to disseminate to NRL/ONR employees two journals, Physical Review Letters and Physical Review E, in page-image format. This project is planned in three phases over a two-year period, with phase one making the two journal titles available within the Library, phase two providing network access to the D.C. campus, and phase three disseminating information to NRL remote sites and ONR over the Internet. The project has been named TORPEDO (The Optical Retrieval Project: Electronic Documents Online).

The Library also plans to make over 13,000 NRL-produced reports available through Internetaccess to TORPEDO and is negotiating to incorporate material originating in other organizations available as well.

16.4.3 Design and Development Considerations

The Genesys ImagExtender software used to link documents to the Star online catalog has proved to be an effective means of linking images to an existing database in a small networked environment. In the case of TORPEDO, however, NRL's multiplatform wide-area networking requirements are considerably more demanding. The Library serves a research community with a myriad of computing platforms, network connectivity configurations, and geographic locations; TORPEDO must be flexible enough to overcome all of these formidable demands. The system requirements for the TORPEDO project are:End user cost: End users must not be required to pay for client software to connect to TORPEDO;Ease of Use: The client software must provide the same functionality on the network as it would when running on a dedicated workstation within the Library;Adherence to wide-area network protocol standards: The client software must use the TCP/IP suite of protocols (required for both campus network and Internet connectivity);Multiplatform support: The imaging system must have client software support for X-Window/UNIX systems, PCs, and Macintosh computers;Full-text searching: The imaging system must be capable of building its own database using ASCII text files obtained through optical character recognition (OCR) software and permit field searching of bibliographic data;Software support and maintenance: The imaging system must to the extent possible use off-the-shelf software maintained by a third party and require little if any custom development; andSingle point of access to all information resources: TORPEDO must eventually coexist within the framework of a more advanced InfoNet system, that is the single point of entry menuing system on the InfoNet that has proven so successful in helping researchers find electronic information resources must be a design consideration in developing TORPEDO as well.

16.4.4   Software Evaluation

To evaluate the feasibility of a number of promising software alternatives, the Library assembled a testbed system consisting of a SUN SPARCserver 490 with 32MB RAM, 4.8GB hard disk storage, and two 5.25" multifunction optical disk near-line storage jukeboxes with three optical readers and a capacity of 62GB. The server was configured with SUN Solaris 1.0x as its operating system and SCSI Express for Solaris as the jukebox control software. The testbed itself was connected to the campus-wide network and was accessible to an assortment of computer configurations (Macintoshes, PCs, and SUN Workstations) within the Library and across the campus network. With the testbed constructed, the Library was ready to evaluate the potential of such freely distributable Internet search tools as WWW (World-Wide Web) and WAIS (Wide Area Information Server), as well as any commercial products that appeared to meet the design specifications.

Non-Commercial Search and Retrieval Products

1. **NCSA Mosaic and HTTP Server** One of the most promising products evaluated was NCSA's (National Center for Supercomputing Applications) Mosaic application. Mosaic is freely distributable but copyrighted client software developed and distributed by NCSA as a hypermedia tool for browsing the global Internet. As a semi-integrated package Mosaic essentially incorporates a collection of standard applications, concepts, and protocols that are already in use on the Internet. From NCSA's FTP server in Champaign, IL, the Mosaic client package is available for many kinds of computers, including Macintoshes, PCs (MS Windows), and most types of X-Window based UNIX workstations (such as SUN, SGI, IBM, HP), and also in X-Window source code. As its transport protocol, Mosaic uses native TCP/IP software already built into UNIX platforms, or in the case of Macintosh clients, the commonly site-licensed MacTCP distributed by Apple. For PCs, which have long been lacking any kind of standard for TCP/IP support, NCSA makes Trumpet, a shareware Winsock-compliant TCP/IP DLL (Dynamic Link Library), available, although almost any commercial Winsock compliant TCP/IP stack can be used in its place.

   Mosaic functions as a browsing tool that connects to a number of standard servers on the Internet, including native HTTP (HyperText Transport Protocol), Gopher, FTP (File Transfer Protocol), and NNTP (Network News Transfer Protocol). Once connected, information contained within the HyperText field allows Mosaic to determine what, if any, application it needs to launch (i.e., what additional application it needs to execute, such as a third party sound application) to support the incoming file type. Mosaic features that the Library finds advantageous are: its user-friendly graphical shell with HyperText features; cross platform availability; adherence to TCP/IP networking standards; and the ability to launch external applications.

The native protocol used by the NCSA Mosaic application is the HTTP server. The HTTP protocol provides fast search and retrieval capability of ASCII text over a Telnet-style internet protocol. There are several varieties of HTTP servers, including NCSA, CERN, and PERL servers, with software distributed freely on the Internet. The Library chose to evaluate the NCSA HTTP server because of its popularity, compatibility with Library hardware, and ease of installation.

The basic Mosaic software clearly lived up to its promise as friendly and readily navigable with extensive browsing features and adherence to existing Internet standards. The Library was favorably impressed by its broad acceptance by the research community, its freely distributable licensing policy, and support for multiple computing platforms. Moreover, the HTTP server released by NCSA was easy to configure and maintain. The HTML (HyperText Markup Language) files required for end-user navigation of the HTTP server were simple to write and update. However, there are some serious drawbacks:

Mosaic does not support the Library's CCITT Group IV TIFF files in its native in-line display. While GIF images could be used for thumbnails, this would require extensive file conversion. Moreover, GIF images are extremely slow in retrieval to the Mosaic Home Page;Image decompression does not take place at the Mosaic client and therefore in-line images are time-consuming to display and require extensive network bandwidth; and HTML does not support sub-script, super-script, or non-ASCII characters or mathematical expressions except as image formats. In addition, the concept of columns does not exist in HTML.

To display images on client workstations, NCSA distributes several third-party contributed viewers that can be launched by the Mosaic client software. Because Mosaic runs on multiple computing platforms, third-party products vary depending on the flavor of Mosaic software in use by the end user. NCSA distributes third party viewers for MS-Windows (Lview), for Macintosh systems (JPEGView), and for UNIX workstations (XV). Unfortunately all of these applications lack image display capabilities for CCITT Group IV TIFF images. Without the use of another imaging product, this poses a particular problem for the development of TORPEDO as all of the current archived materials (5 million pages) are black and white and are stored using CCITT Group IV TIFF data compression. To allow the Library to distribute the images, a CCITT Group IV TIFF viewer is required for each computing platform. Fortunately Mosaic is flexible enough to launch any third party application the Library chooses to distribute for viewing its images.

Inspite of its flaws, none of the problems in the basic Mosaic software is acute enough to rule out its use as a front-end interface. Therefore, it has been determined that scanned research reports and journal articles will be available through Mosaic using a hyper-text link to a third-party image database.

2. **WAIS** The first software that the Library evaluated for search and retrieval of text and images was FreeWAIS-0.202. WAIS (Wide Area Information Server) is a full-text client/server information storage and retrieval system designed to retrieve information over TCP/IP networks. The server database software itself is compatible with a variety of UNIX systems, including the Library's SUN server hardware. The WAIS client/server environment allows keyword searching of ASCII text and, with the purchase of commercial WAIS server software, field searching can also be made an option.

WAIS servers can be set up to provide access to multiple ASCII text databases across the Internet. Moreover, WAIS servers offer file linking that permits end users to retrieve both ASCII text files and associated images. WAIS clients can therefore retrieve a wide range of file formats, including ASCII text, sound files and images. Client WAIS software, both free and commercial, is available for most computing platforms, including PCs, Macintoshes, and UNIX workstations. In addition, WAIS can also be used as a back-end server for the NCSA Mosaic application. Over 500 WAIS servers are currently in operation on the Internet.

Initial testing of FreeWAIS indicated that WAIS would not provide the search and retrieval capabilities required by the Library. Although WAIS allows the linking of text files to image files, and the search engine provides the user with a list of titles in response to a keyword search, WAIS does not highlight the search string in the document after a hit is actually found; the user must therefore page through the entire document, which may consist of hundreds of pages, to find the object of the search. WAIS also does not allow a fuzzy search, an important requirement when searching text that has been generated by OCR. The WAIS client/serverthat was tested did not have native WAIS support for many Mosaic clients. For instance, Mosaic clients for both Macintosh and MS Windows were required to use a WAIS gateway. Furthermore, FreeWAIS does not provide field search capabilities, which the Library believed to be requirement for the effective retrieval of technical reports and journal articles. However, the most serious difficulty with using a WAIS/Mosaic system for journal imaging is in devising a method for displaying and printing retrieved images.

The major drawback that the Library found with a WAIS/Mosaic system is in how the two programs interact. Once an end user searched WAIS and selected an article for viewing, each page of the document is displayed within Mosaic as a GIF file. NCSA Mosaic and its third-party distributed viewers do not support the CCITT Group IV TIFF format currently in use in the Library's Research Reports imaging system. The difference between GIF and CCITT Group IV formatted files presents several problems for the Library. The first problem is that GIF formatted files are typically 3 to 4 times as large as CCITT Group IV TIFF files. A collection of GIF files would therefore require significantly more optical disk storage than the Library can currently support. The second problem is that in terms of performance a networked imaging system based on GIF files versus CCITT Group IV TIFF files would be 300 to 400 percent slower in transferring and displaying full-page images due to file size differences.Lastly, printing a document using a WAIS/Mosaic system is unwieldy. Using the third-party imaging software distributed by NCSA, end users of a WAIS/Mosaic system would be required to select, display, and print each page of a document one at a time.

Commercial Search and Retrieval Products – Excalibur EFS

After investigating non-commercial products it became clear that none was robust enough to support the requirements of the TORPEDO project on its own. Rather than attempting to program its own solution, the Library decided to investigate commercial imaging options. Drawing on the imaging experience of the Library's contractor, Kestrel Associates, incorporated,and a survey of recent product reviews and evaluations in computer and imaging journals, the Library identified only one product that appeared to meet all its requirements: Excalibur EFS.

To overcome many of the retrieval problems inherent in most full-text search software, ExcaliburEFS uses a fuzzy search retrieval concept called Adaptive Pattern Recognition Processing (APRP). Using APRP the retrieval software searches documents by recognizing data patterns at the binary level. As a result, the data automatically direct the creation of indexes that are highly fault tolerant and thus can accurately retrieve information based on an approximation of query terms or phrases. Because the retrieval software seeks patterns rather than exact words or phrases, users can accurately search "dirty" ASCII (raw OCR-processed text) without the need for ASCII clean-up or re-keying. Moreover, APRP indexes require considerably less memory overhead than conventional indexes – typically 30 percent as compared to overhead of 100 to 300 percent or more for many indexes. In addition, Excalibur full-text search and retrieval is fast. Excalibur's search software is capable of searching 200,000 pages of information in as little as ten seconds on most workstations.[79]

Excalibur EFS searching is not without its limitations however. The Library has found two significant drawbacks with Excalibur's searching capabilities:Field Searching: The only variable length field available in Excalibur EFS is the full text retrieval field. Excalibur EFS permits additional predefined search fields, but these fields are limited to 256 characters. This means that database entries with more than about three lines of text, as is commonly the case with the abstract field and sometimes the case with title and author fields, must be truncated.Lack of stop words: The Excalibur EFS retrieval software does to permit the creation of a stop word index to eliminate common retrieval words, such as "and" and "the" that seldom retrieve meaningful results. While some might argue that stop words make it difficult to search for certain articles and entries, as is stated in the Excalibur EFS marketing literaturealong with examples, stop-word indexes are a fundamental part of many search and retrieval systems and would have been desirable in the TORPEDO project.

16.4.5 Selected Software for Image Networking

A Hybrid Solution

Based on the evaluation of commercial and non-commercial products, a hybrid solution was selected to meet the Library's needs. NCSA Mosaic was chosen as the primary interface to TORPEDO and Excalibur EFS was chosen as the major imaging component for the project. The NRL Mosaic/Excalibur design will not display images imbedded in HTML, but instead will use Mosaic to launch the EFS software which provides native CCITT Group IV TIFF viewers for all computer platforms and was specifically designed for high performance imaging applications.

Scanning, OCR, and Storage Options

One common feature that became evident from the Library's investigation of commercial and non-commercial products was that OCR has become a required process for most unstructured document imaging applications. OCR is required to obtain the ASCII text from bit-mapped scanned page images for use with full-text retrieval databases. These ASCII text pages themselves are typically linked to document images, which may or may not be displayed along with the images themselves.

While OCR technology has become extremely reliable with high quality paper documents,no OCR software or hardware vendor can guarantee perfect accuracy and output. There are only two methods to provide a reliable unstructured (full-text) search and retrieval document imaging system if the text is obtained from the OCR process:

1. manual cleanup using clerical workers to compare ASCII files with the original text; or

2. use of a full text search engine which incorporates some type of fuzzy search logic in combination with highly accurate OCR software.

1. **Avatar Production Document Batch Capture and Conversion Software**[§] To scan and OCR the APS journals the Library plans to use a duplex scanner and a 486 Windows PC. The scanner is capable of converting dual sided paper at a rate of about 35 pages per minute. Avatar Document Batch Capture and Conversion Software and its bundled Calera

---

[§]Avatar Technologies,Inc., Enmasse! Product Description

OCR software will be used for this process. The existing report images will also be imported into Avatar for OCR.

Avatar batch software provides scanning, digitizing, and compression of hard copy images. The software was designed for high volume production OCR needs and can handle over 10,000 pages per day. The Avatar software can even be run on more than one computer concurrently. Moreover, Avatar software allows images to be saved in multiple image formats, but for the Library's purposes, all pages will be stored in CCITT Group IV TIFF format. The software also provides a method to perform field indexing with export capabilities to many different databases and imaging systems. Avatar runs on PCs and operates in the MS Windows 3.1 environment, but its batch output can go into any number of databases on many different platforms. In addition, Avatar is fully compatible with Novell networks. To import Avatar images into the TORPEDO imaging system on the Library's SUN SPARCserver 490, the Library's Novell network and beta software under development by Kestrel will be used.

One advantage of choosing Avatar is its image quality control and verification options. Avatar uses a split screen editor that automatically displays textual characters in synchronizationwith the associated images through "hot links". This allows easy comparison of OCR output text against the actual image for purposes of editing by an operator, if desired. In addition, Avatar performs automatic image deskew, despeckle, and sampling. The images can be verified in Avatar before they are imported into the Excalibur EFS image retrieval system for use with TORPEDO.

The OCR software used by Avatar is a bundled third party product from Calera Recognition Systems, Inc. In a University of Nevada-Las Vegas (UNLV) Information Science Research Institute [129] survey comparing eight OCR software vendor packages, the Calera product had the fewest misrecognized words from a 460-page sample with 119,497 characters. The UNLV study was the first publicly available study detail recognition accuracy based on the quality of the documents recognized. Calera OCR software addresses the variance in document quality and provides more consistent performance across a wide range of degraded documents. Findings of the UNLV study show that while products from Calera, Caere Corporation, ExperVision and Xerox Kurzweil all achieved average accuracy rates around 99.7 percent on high-quality documents, only Calera's technology maintained accuracy rates above 97 percent on the worst quality documents included in the test set.

2. **Storage Considerations** TORPEDO must incorporate some type of highly reliable, permanent, affordable large mass storage system. Optical disks combined with near-line storage juke boxes are currently the storage option of choice at most organizations. However, the problem with optical disk juke boxes from a multi-user perspective is that they have relatively slow access time and all the data are not truly online (unless they are ac-

tually in a drive bay) at any one time. When many users attempt to gain access to information in a juke box, the data cannot be transmitted over the network until the optical platter has been robotically moved to the optical disk drive and spun up to operating speed. If a second user asks for information on another disk, that disk must be physically moved to the drive, replacing the first users disk before the second user can obtain the information. Disk swapping time ranges from 3 to 20 seconds depending upon the juke box used. Increased demands for information from users will eventually cause a juke box system to thrash. Thrashing is where more time is spent swapping optical disks than sending information to the user with the result being very long queues for retrieval of image information.

The solution to this potential problem is use of multiple optical drives in each juke box and intelligent operating software called juke box management software. Until recently UNIX-based juke box management software has been very costly, with costs often exceeding $50,000 for each system. After performing a market search for an affordable solution to this problem, the Library has chosen Tracer Technologies software for juke box management. Tracer's Optical Drive and Juke Robotics device drivers are specifically designed for the devices they operate; they are optimized for maximum throughput and device functionality. Once a document page is requested the Tracer product prefetches the entire document to the server's hard disk and thereby minimizes platter swapping, thrashing and hogging.

16.5   CONCLUSION

The NRL Library is well on the way to providing its research community with access to a "digital library." Through its InfoNet Campus-Wide Information System it provides researchers with menu- driven desktop access to a large number of local and remote information resources. With its Research Reports Imaging System the Library turned its online reports catalog into an information retrieval tool instead of a pointer, enabling the user to view entire documents online or print them on demand. When completed, TORPEDO will combine the capabilities of both; through the use of powerful search and retrieval tools, it will disseminate electronic images, enabling end users seated at their computers or workstations to search, view and print the contents of large collections of library materials. The system, consisting of a Mosaic front end and a commercial imaging/indexing system, will be accessible via the campus network and the Internet.

TORPEDO is being designed for expansion and will permit the addition of multiple scanning subsystems and optical storage juke box devices. The initial system will permit NRL campus access to the information using the SUN workstation and associated optical storage hardware and software. The SUN will provide magnetic storage for the Excalibur text database and will host the

Mosaic software and the Excalibur retrieval engine. Initially TORPEDO will handle one million image pages which will occupy roughly 60GB of optical disk storage.

Chapter 17

DL-Raid: An Environment for Supporting Digital Library Services

Bharat Bhargava[*], Melliyal Annamalai[*], Shalab Goel[*], Shunge Li[*],
Evaggelia Pitoura[*], Aidong Zhang[†], Yongguang Zhang[‡]

17.1 Introduction

With rapid advances in electronic imaging, data storage, data compression, and telecommunication technologies, the demand for on-line access to digital library [95, 118] information has soared. For instance, NASA has terabytes of digital library data for exploration of Space Science, Atmospheric Science, Flight Dynamics, Life Sciences, and other related fields of science. This data is available in electronic and other forms. It becomes important for scientists and the general public to be able to utilize this information in their learning processes and scientific research. The task of accessing this data can be made simple by using a variety of user interfaces and the notion of digital libraries.

We consider a digital library as a facility which makes use of a large amount of data accessed over a wide area network [88]. A digital library will contain text, images, and sound in an integrated document repository and will provide a uniform interface for users' (local/remote) access to a vast amount of varied kinds of data. The concept of digital libraries can be realized by enhancing and integrating technologies in databases, communication networks, user interfaces, knowledge management, and information retrievals.

One of the main problems in digital libraries is retrieving this data efficiently [78]. Data in the digital library environment is large and unstructured in nature. Thus, the design of a data model for its representation and placement is an important step towards the design of successful retrieval schemes. In general, the data retrieval in digital libraries will have a great diversity. While some of this data can be retrieved based on its contents as the image data, the keyword

[*]Department of Computer Sciences, Purdue University, West Lafayette, IN 47907
{bb,man,sgoel,lis,pitoura}@cs.purdue.edu
  [†]Department of Computer Science, SUNY at Buffalo, Buffalo, NY 14260,
azhang@cs.buffalo.edu
  [‡]Hughes System Research Laboratories, Malibu, CA 90265,
ygz@isl.hrl.hac.com

based retrieval schemes are more suited to the document data. As the users may not have the exact knowledge on what to retrieve, retrieval schemes based on keyword matching alone will be too rigid. Furthermore, an exact match based on user's specification will not be always possible and fuzzy retrieval methods will have to be used. We propose the partial content-based schemes to match the user queries with some portion of data (e.g., portions of actual image of the Saturn) rather than just keywords associated with that data (e.g., the Saturn). This approach increases retrieval effectiveness and thus is promising. Moreover, these interactions will make the partial content-based schemes very communications intensive as such fuzzy retrieval queries may require multiple rounds of data transmission to narrow down the range of queries and to finally find the target information. Thus, the amount of data that is actually transferred to complete a user query may often be magnitudes larger than expected. As a result, the communication delays and packet losses in WAN may have significant impact on the efficiency and the effectiveness of a retrieval scheme in distributed environments. In addition, digital libraries must support a very large number of users for the concurrently access to the information base. This may lead to localized network congestion problem. Thus, the study of specific communication performance in the digital library environment becomes critically important.

The objective of our research is to develop a prototype digital library (DL-Raid) on top of an existing distributed database system called Raid. The architecture of the DL-Raid has six layers, with new features built on top of the Raid. The system will allow persistent storage, retrievals and communications of digital library data. A sophisticated retrieval approach, termed *partial content-based retrieval*, is supported in the system. This approach allow users to retrieve the data in various degrees. Relevant data can be located without searching the entire information repository. Communication experiments are conducted to study the communication delays for large unstructured data objects and to evaluate their impact on content-based retrieval schemes. We use the WANCE tool [261], developed in the Raid laboratory at Purdue University, for our communication experiments. Our experiments help us to categorize the retrieval methods based on how communication intensive they are. This characterization includes factors such as the number of messages interchanged, the size of query and the data retrieved, and the rate at which data is generated.

The remainder of this chapter is organized as follows. Sections 2 and 3 introduce the digital library data model and DL-Raid architecture. In Section 4, we present the partial content-based retrieval approaches. Section 5 presents the results of our communication experiments. Concluding remarks and future work are presented in Section 6.

17.2   Digital Library Data Model

This section proposes a new data model for the digital library environment. The formulation of a data model lies at the heart of the construction of a digital library system. The digital library systems are characterized by the involvement of multiple types of data and the existence of complex relationships among these data. Traditional data models, such as network model or hierarchical model, are simply not equipped to handle these data types and relationships.

17.2.1 A Typology of Digital Library Data

A careful analysis and classification of digital library data will provide insights that aid the development of the digital library data model. Digital library data is a broad concept which encompasses alphanumerical data (formatted data), text, image, audio, and video. Associated with each type of data is its corresponding administration information, such as identifiers, names, creation dates, physical storage locations (including site IP address). Usually, they are used as internal indices to digital library objects, and are transparent to users. For users to quickly and efficiently locate digital library objects in a large digital library repository, various types of external indices must be established.

The types of external indices are determined by the possible forms of queries asked by users, including traditional keyword-based query, content-based query, visual query, and fuzzy query. Therefore, the external indices in digital libraries can be classified as follows:

- **Bibliographic data:** This category contains keywords and other information *about* digital library objects.

- **Structural data:** These data characterize the structure of digital library objects, such as how many entities are contained in the objects and what spatio-temporal relationships exist among these entities.

- **Content descriptive data:** This is the information *of* digital library objects in symbolic forms. It describes the meaning of the digital library objects in question. To make the description more concise, it allows pointers to some application-dependent digital library objects predefined in knowledge base, in which attributes and operations of these predefined objects can therefore be re-used.

- **Visual data:** This is a non-symbolic, but an iconic representation of digital library objects. Like the raw digital library data, it is unstructured. It is useful when it is hard to provide symbolic description of content of digital library objects.

Due to the diversity of data types of these external indices and the semantic nature of content descriptive data, it is logical to incorporate such semantic data model as object-oriented data model into the framework of our proposed digital library prototype system design.

There are several strategies to implement an object-oriented system. The development of an object-oriented system from scratch for this purpose may carry certain advantages, but it would be highly time-consuming. On the other hand, it can be argued that the extension of an existing relational database into an object-oriented database to support digital library applications also carries its own advantages:

- The rapid development of a prototype of an experimental digital library system would permit direct encouragement in further research. Using an evolutionary approach allows such rapid prototyping.

- Alphanumerical data, which occurs commonly in digital library systems, administration data, and bibliographic data, are well handled by the relational data model. The resulting system should be able to use facilities provided by the relational model to handle these types of data efficiently.

- Much ongoing research on temporal databases, including the standardization of TSQL2 [231], an extension of SQL-92, is based on the relational data model [197]. To be consistent with future standards, a relational aspect should be included within any digital library data model.

17.2.2 Features of Object-Oriented Paradigm

- **Encapsulation:** The data describing the states and attributes of an entity and the operations describing its behavior are encapsulated in an integrated parcel, called an object. Encapsulation provides information hiding and clean interactive interfaces between objects.

- **Abstraction:** Relations between objects in a traditional object-oriented data model can be abstracted into three classes:

  - **Aggregation** indicates the *part_of* relations of objects. Objects can be aggregated as a composite object.
  - **Generalization** indicates the *is_a* or *a_kind_of* relations of objects. Objects can be conceptually generalized as a class with common attributes and/or operations. A member of the class is an instance of that class.
  - **Association** indicates *any other* relationships among objects in addition to aggregation and generalization.

  It is these abstractions that lend the object-oriented model greater power than the relational data model. In the relational model, all relationships among objects must be represented associations, even if they might more closely conform to an aggregation or generalization. In the object model, the relationships among objects are precisely classified into one of three abstractions, bringing the representation of the relationships among objects closer to reality.

- **Inheritance:** Classes of objects with common attributes and behaviors form during generalization. By recursively proceeding this process, a class hierarchy is formed. By construction, the properties of a class can be inherited by its members or subclasses. This mechanism allows members of a class to reuse the properties of the class and to overwrite them when necessary.

- **Polymorphism (Dynamic binding):** In object-oriented model, communication among objects is accomplished through message passing. When an object receives a message, it dynamically selects a method that is suitable for certain operations. This is different from the traditional system, where the binding between operations and the data on which the operations are executed is statically determined. The object-oriented model thus permits the overloading of various methods.

17.2.3 Additional Features of Distributed Object-Oriented Systems

- **Federation:** In a distributed environment, a complex object may be stored in different physical locations and accessed simultaneously by multiple users. The logical integrity of such an object must therefore be maintained to permit operations upon it.

- **Replication:** In order to decrease the communication cost, several copies of a database may be simultaneously maintained in different sites. In the object model, data as well as operations might be partially replicated. The methods of an object may therefore be remotely invoked by other objects.

- **Concurrency Control:** In a distributed environment, an object may be accessed concurrently by multiple users. Since the object in question may be a composite object, user updates to the object will permit any composite objects of which it is a part to be accessed simultaneously by other users even if those composite objects seem to be quite irrelevant.

17.2.4 Digital Library Data Description - Layered Approach

It is not straightforward to establish external indices for digital library objects, excluding the alphanumerical data. In particular, the construction of content descriptive data is extremely difficult not only because it is application dependent but also because it is *contained within* the original raw data. To address the discontinuity between the data, its semantics, and domain knowledge in typical digital library applications, we propose the following layered scheme to represent complex digital library data.

Figure 17.1 illustrates the extraction of content (semantic) information from digital library data. This semantic information can only be gleaned from the physical digital library data itself. The logical data extracted specifies the objects contained in the physical data and the spatio-temporal relationships among them. The contents of digital library data can then be extracted from this logical data, together with the domain knowledge base, which contains information and properties regarding all objects in the domain, along with their uses and interrelationships.

It is assumed that the transformation from the physical to the logical data layers is performed elsewhere, since this topic is beyond the scope of this chapter. Ideally, this mapping should be automatic, perhaps using pattern recognition and image processing (in case of image data) techniques, but such an approach is currently very time-consuming and rather inaccurate. Since real-time transformation is therefore not realistic at this time, it is preferable to perform these transformations off-line and in a semi-automatic fashion. Alternatively, users may specify the logical data, perhaps through authoring systems and specification languages.

The layered approach to data representation places objects from different levels in different layers of increasing abstraction. In the physical data layer, the digital library data is unstructured. This layer is the least abstract in that it provides no semantic representation for the digital library raw data. The logical data layer is more abstract than the physical data layer. It has, to some extent, the content information of digital library objects, such as the spatio-temporal relationships among its component entities. But it does not provide thorough information about the semantics of the digital library object in question, such as what its component entities and their properties really are. The content data layer has the complete representation of the digital library object semantics, thus has the highest abstraction level. It is in general very difficult and sometimes even impossible to extract thorough information about a complex digital library object without the aid of an intermediate layer and an application-dependent knowledge base. This approach simplifies the whole tasks by transforming or mapping the data from one layer to another.

Sometimes, it is very hard or cumbersome for users to represent and manipulate content data to retrieve information needed. Visual representation of content data provides an easy way to deal with this situation in digital libraries. One of the popular forms of visual data is icon, frequently seen in modern user interfaces.

It is natural to construct a class for each digital library data type. Each instance of a class has attributes corresponding to physical data, logical data (structural information), content data (semantic information), visual data (exterior representation), and operations on these attributes, including storage, editing, display, retrieval, transmission, and manipulation (update, insertion, and deletion) of data.

These components may be illustrated through image objects. The physical data is the image data itself, whether compressed or not. The logical data is made up of those entities within the images and the spatial relationships among those entities which reflect the structural information of the images. The semantic data is the symbolic description of the images, while the visual data consists of icons for interactive user manipulation. The operations include the procedures of accessing, retrieving, displaying, compressing/decompressing, transferring, and manipulating image data.

17.3   DL-Raid System Model

In this section, we will introduce a six-layered system model. This system, called DL-Raid, is built on top of O-Raid [19].

17.3.1   The Architecture of DL-Raid

Raid (Robust, Adaptable, Interoperable, and Distributed) is a distributed database system based on the relational model built at Purdue. The system has complete support for transaction processing, concurrency control, replication control, atomicity control, access control and persistency of data in the system [22]. The communication package in Raid is a location-transparent module built on top of the UDP/IP and can model local and wide area networks. O-Raid is an extension of the Raid system and supports distributed complex data objects [66]. It is an extension of the relational implementation and supports the defining and managing of classes and their objects. DL-Raid is a prototype system being implemented on top of O-Raid. Figures 17.2 and 17.3 show the layered architecture of O-Raid and DL-Raid respectively.

Using an incremental approach to build DL-Raid, traditional Raid applications will still be supported without modifications. All the features dedicated to digital library applications are constructed as an extension upon the O-Raid system, which is itself left intact. Furthermore, the functions supported by O-Raid, such as object composition, class definition, indexing [136], user-defined functions, and communications facilities, can be reused by DL-Raid.

The DL-Raid system will allow storage, retrieval, and transmission of digital library objects. The six layers of DL-Raid have the following functions:

- Layer 1 is the physical organization of data, including the digital library data itself and metadata databases. Digital library data consists of audio/video data, image data, documents, and alphanumerical data. Metadata databases contain class definitions, administration data, bibliographic data, structural data, semantic data (content descriptive data), and visual data for digital library objects. The raw digital library data is stored in a compressed form.

- Layer 2 is the Raid relational distributed database management system, combined with the communication facility. The Raid system supports transaction processing over local area and geographically distributed (WAN) environments. To improve the performance of data retrieval, Raid permits the replication of databases on different sites. Consistency among the replicas is automatically maintained by the system. The communication facility will be enhanced to support the transferring of large volume of data. This layer is the physical interface to the Internet.

- Layer 3 is the object layer of the DL-Raid system. It consists of two major parts: the O-Raid module and the object manager. The O-Raid module allows the definition of the user-defined classes and the composition of complex objects. The object manager is responsible for object definition, manipulation, and access. Inheritance, object migration, and classification are also supported. For digital library applications, the object manager directly accesses databases for metadata, descriptive data, and compressed digital library data without going through the Raid module (see the dash line in the figure), thus improving performance and compatibility.

- Layer 4 consists of toolkits, such as the MPEG encoder and decoder, which are necessary for the compression and decompression of digital library data. This layer performs conversions among data formats appropriate for storage, transmission, presentation, and editing.

- Layer 5 consists of several modules: digital library presentation and editing toolkits, and a digital library query processor. It allows users to define and manipulate digital library data. With these modules, users are allowed to play, browse, and edit digital library data selectively. The query processor transforms higher-level user queries, such as fuzzy or visual queries, into statements in the SQL++ language, which is the query language of O-Raid. Such queries may alternatively be transformed into internal object-oriented query statements to assist the object manager in finding targets. In general, digital library data is retrieved through the object manager by descriptions, contents, or bibliographic data. Of course, users may bypass the query processor and use SQL++ directly for retrieving digital library data.

- Layer 6 provides a uniform interactive graphical user interface that integrates underlying modules.

17.3.2 Extending O-Raid into DL-Raid

We propose an object-oriented framework for enumerating, classifying, and unifying the various structural and representational discrepancies. Some features of such a model have been designed and implemented in O-Raid, an object-oriented distributed database system. The object model of O-Raid contains basic constructs such as types, objects, and functions. These constructs are used to define unique names for objects, identify class of objects, and provide operations and mappings among objects. Based on this model, we plan to develop a uniform interface to access the underlying information bases.

Supporting both a relational and an object-oriented data model [233], O-Raid offers several potential advantages for the implementation of digital library systems. In DL-Raid, both alphanumerical data and some metadata (including bibliographic and descriptive data) are represented using a relational model, while other types of digital library data are best suited for the object model. O-Raid is thus suitable for the representation of digital library data.

In its extension to DL-Raid, inheritance must be fully supported. The concept of class hierarchy is useful in modeling user queries, in describing the contents of digital library data, and in organizing object storage in digital library systems. DL-Raid must also support object dynamics, especially object migrations and object classification, facilities which are often needed in digital library applications. For example, the editing of a document may cause a paragraph to migrate from body text into an appendix or figure caption, depending upon the constraints specified.

Improvements must also be made in the area of user interface. A truly object-oriented user interface should not only handle object definition and manipulation but also be equipped to display results in an object-based rather than a tuple-based fashion. The digital library graphical user interface to be supported by DL-Raid should have the ability to manipulate different types of data.

The extension of O-Raid into DL-Raid should incorporate the following steps:

Defining Abstract Data Types: It is desirable to define an abstract data type (ADT) for each digital library object, each entity extracted from the object, and each relation among objects. Practically, ADTs are implemented as objects.

Building Hierarchies Through Abstraction Two classes of abstraction discussed earlier form individual hierarchies. Generalization forms a class hierarchy, reflecting class-subclass relations; aggregation forms an object hierarchy, addressing object-subobject relations. Since classes are themselves higher-order objects, these categories of relations can be handled uniformly.

In order to gather information about a particular object and its relationships with other objects, all three hierarchies may be involved altogether. Each hierarchy has its own domain-independent properties which can be exploited by the object query language for retrieval. An object can also be fully represented with all three hierarchies, facilitating the content-based queries.

Combining Relational Model and Object-Oriented Model According to the object-oriented paradigm, relations can be viewed as a kind of objects. We can define a *relation* class to represent all such objects and their operations, thus bringing the relational model into the object-oriented model.

Enhancing Communication Facilities The communication facilities of the Raid system must be enhanced to support digital library data delivery. Currently, the Raid system uses UDP as the communication protocol to transmit data within a LAN/WAN environment. TCP or other new protocols may be considered as alternatives for the prototype system. The approach presented in [261] will be useful in conducting experiments over wide area networks within the LAN environment. Communication facilities may be further extended to the ATM network.

17.4   Partial Content-Based Retrievals in DL-Raid

We will now discuss the retrieval schemes that are to be supported in DL-Raid. We propose using partial content-based retrieval approach. This approach will allow users to locate relevant data in a flexible manner.

17.4.1   Retrieval Methods

Retrieval methods are in general classified into three categories: *keyword-based* , partial content-based and *full content-based* retrieval methods.

The keyword-based retrieval scheme provides the simplest mechanism for retrieving data. When data objects are added to the information base, a human expert has to provide a set of keywords to represent the object. The information retrieval system uses this information as an index to retrieve data. The data objects themselves are never inspected by the system. This scheme, though simple to implement, will not satisfy the needs of a digital library. It is inappropriate for retrieval of non-text data since it is not content-based. Content-based retrieval schemes use the matter contained in the object instead of just a representative piece of information. An example of a representative piece of information for an image is a name for the image. A name will not capture much of the semantic information in the image.

In contrast, the full content-based retrieval scheme provides a more flexible way for retrieving data but has more overheads associated with it. An index must contain all the information which is required by the retrieval algorithm including keyword frequencies or whatever else the algorithm might use. These methods use no access structures whatsoever. The entire data object can be used for retrieval. No information is omitted from the search. This is the ideal system but the costs can be prohibitive.

Both approaches cannot allow a variety of users to retrieve data in various degrees of detail and depth. In digital library environments, users should be able to locate relevant data without searching the entire information repository. Users may know approximately what data they need but might not be able to specify their needs precisely. They may not initially know exactly what data is available and needed. To help them, a retrieval based on content and imprecise queries should be supported and the system should interactively assist the users. Existing indexing schemes are too rigid and do not support retrieval based on semantic content of information. We propose to develop techniques that will allow the user to specify a query based on her partial knowledge of the content and route her query to the appropriate information base.

17.4.2   Supporting Image Classes

Our prototype will efficiently manage a large database of images. Each image will be represented by a set of text descriptors. These will be more than just image titles. They will capture the semantic content of the image. For example, consider the image of the snow-covered Rocky mountains in the winter. Its title would be exactly the same words - 'Snow-covered Rocky Mountains'. We will associate more words with the image. Since the image was taken in the winter, the word 'winter' should be included. The predominant color in the image, say 'white', will also be a descriptor. Other descriptors are 'north' to represent the hemisphere where the Rocky Mountains are located and 'cloud formations' to represent other significant characteristics of the image. We thus have the following text descriptors:

```
Color: White
Hemisphere: North
Season when the image was taken: Winter
What it was meant to capture: Cloud formations
```

In the above example, each text descriptor corresponds to one feature of the image. Each feature will have classes associated with it. Color is a feature of an image and so we need classes like 'blue', 'white' etc. Similarly, 'winter', 'summer' etc. are classes associated with the feature season.

Consider two classes *weather* and *mountain*. They share a common subclass *winter*. The image of the Rocky mountains and another of the Pacific Ocean taken in the winter will be stored under the same subclass winter (Figure 17.4). A meteorologist who is interested in winter images should be able to retrieve both though they are not related to each other in any other way. If he is studying cloud formations, he will want to retrieve the Rocky mountain image and if he is studying ocean currents he will want to retrieve the Pacific ocean image. Physical descriptions like color, shape, size will be used to filter out unwanted images.

This classification will be very tedious and time-consuming if done manually. Text descriptors can be generated in a semi-automatic fashion if the domain of images is limited [201]. NASA data, geographic information systems, data banks of research articles are all examples of information bases that can relate to a specific domain. Once a domain has been identified, we formulate the classification within the domain. A low-level image analysis module will recognize the basic objects in it and their associated distinguishing attributes [201].

An image can belong to more than one class. In a distributed system, different classes of images can be stored at different sites. Consider the following scenario. The weather bureau stores images under the class weather and this class receives new images every second. The Physics department at University of Kaiserslautern in Germany also stores the same images but under a different class. A researcher is searching for an image with some particular information. The query processor will direct the query to the Physics department site at this department. If the image itself is not stored there, the address of the weather bureau site will be stored there. This link can be traversed to retrieve the image. This retrieval thus has taken two steps. If retrieval is done often the time taken can be shortened by storing the image itself at the Physics Department site instead of the address of the weather bureau site. The communication delay and bandwidth limitations influence immediate updating of the images at the Physics Department.

17.4.3   Probability-Based Fuzzy Retrievals

We will support retrieval based on imprecise queries. This means that the user should be able to retrieve data even when the words he uses in his query do not exactly match those stored in the system. To implement this, special matching techniques are required. We will use fuzzy retrieval methods which are probability-based. Data objects are retrieved based on the estimate of the probability of their relevance to a query. Probability of relevance to a query is based on the degree of closeness between two words. For example,

```
Light: Sunshine (80%), Ray (55%), Bright (70%)
```

Let light be a text descriptor stored in the system. Sunshine, ray, and bright are words with semantics similar to the word light and which are likely to be used by the user instead of light in the context of retrieving images. With the word sunshine there is a 80% probability that the user meant light, with the word ray there is only a 55% probability that the user meant light and so on. We will compile a thesaurus and store it in the system. This thesaurus will contain the values for the degree of closeness. Whenever a user query does not find an exact match, the thesaurus will be checked to determine the value associated with their closeness. Based on such evaluation of closeness, one can compute $P(I|Object)$, which is the probability that a user's information need is satisfied given a particular object. The objects with high $P(I|Object)$ are retrieved for the user.

There are other parameters to be considered in a distributed environment. Communication delay is a parameter that can influence the scheme discussed above of retrieving the object with the highest $P(I|Object)$. Consider the following example. Let the Meteorological research center store images under the class climate. A user query with the word 'winter storm' may return a $P(I|Object)$ value of 65% from this site and a $P(I|Object)$ value of 80% from the Physics Department at the University of Kaiserslautern. Because of the communication delay in retrieving an image from this university, it might be cheaper with respect to time to retrieve the image from the Meteorological center and refine the query based on interactions with the user. After a few iterations of refining the query, the user might be able to get a 80% match and take less time than retrieving the image from the University of Kaiserslautern (Figure 17.5). We will incorporate communication delay as a parameter in computing $P(I|Object)$.

17.5   Communication Issues for Large Objects

In this section, we address the communication issues in the digital library environment. We observe that different data in the digital library environment have different characteristics and pose different data transfer requirements. A communication model, established on sound experimental and empirical study, must be provided for efficient retrieval of digital library data. We have conducted experiments to study the time to transfer various size of image data, voice data, text data, and database queries. The experimental results gives an insight into the feasibility and sensitivity of various retrieval schemes to the communications in the digital library environment. Since the user queries submitted to the information base can be often expected to be imprecise and will need to be incrementally improved by using an interactive dialogue between them, the impact of communication performance on access to the digital library data becomes all the more crucial and important.

17.5.1   WANCE Tool

The data objects in the digital library environment are large, unstructured, and often their sizes not known at the time of retrieval. It is our belief that accessing this data over the wide area network will affect the performance of user query significantly enough to motivate us in rethinking the digital library data organization and retrieval schemes. We use the WANCE (Wide Area Network Communication Emulation) tool [261], developed in Raid Laboratory at Purdue University, to conducting experiments for studying the performance of communication in transmitting large objects. We analyze the communication delays and packet losses in their transmission over the Internet.

The basic idea behind the WANCE tool is to *emulate* a remote Internet site with a local site (e.g. a host in Raid Laboratory), and thus achieve a real Internet communication environment in a local area network. The distributed software runs on the local hosts, but with the help of WANCE tool, the communication with actual remote Internet hosts is achieved. Since almost all Internet gateways support *source routing*, our experiments can be configured with different remote Internet hosts. The main advantage of the emulation approach is that no control (not even an account) on remote host is required, to obtain real communication results. Furthermore, virtually any site on Internet is available for experimentation using this approach. Compared with real experiments, measurements by emulation carries a mere 3% relative error [261].

17.5.2   Experimental Results

The communication experiments reveal a large variation in round trip time for data transmission with the size of data object, its format quality, and its location. We present below the details of the experimental results.

The left hand side graph in Figure 17.6 shows the round-trip time of sending an GIF image of 204KB using TCP/IP protocol to different sites. The average round-trip time between USA and Germany is about twice as much as that between two sites in USA (Purdue and Rutgers). The right hand side chart compares the transmission time for the same image in JPEG format as compression quality is varied.

Figure 17.7 shows the round-trip times it needs to send data of various size across the Internet. The communication protocol used affects the performance too. TCP/IP is more reliable than UDP/IP but takes longer time to transmit the same amount of data. In digital library environment, it will be required that some information be transmitted without any data loss whereas some others like images may be acceptable with a tolerable data loss. For example, when a user wants to browse a set of images retrieved from remote digital library, the quality of images may not be a concern if enough data is available to reconstruct the image at the user site. Thus, the system must be smart enough to make decision about the use of appropriate communication protocol form the suite of protocols available to it, to meet the user requirements. For example, faster but less reliable UDP may be more acceptable to an interactive-user than the much slower TCP.

In our previous empirical studies [261], we have shown that message delivery has an unbalanced performance across the wide area network. Although most of the hosts can be reached within 400ms, the variations in communication delays and packet losses are high. We have also observed that for small packets that can fit in an IP datagram without fragmentation, there is an approximate linear correlation between the transit time and the size of a packet.

The size of the digital library data to be retrieved may be many megabytes. This can be enough to congest the local host and the portions of the Internet during the busy hours of the day. Retransmitting of such large sized data may not guarantee the successful transmission, either. Based on the above observations, we propose that the system offload the work of transferring the non time-critical data to the idle hours of the Internet, based on precomputed information about their access patterns on local hosts.

17.5.3 Effects on DL Data Retrieval Strategies

The communication experiments help us to categorize the retrieval schemes based on their communication requirements. This categorization includes factors such as the number of messages exchanged (e.g. in interactive dialogues), the size of query and the amount of data retrieved, and the rate at which data is generated.

Fuzzy retrieval queries may require multiple rounds of data transmission to remote hosts to narrow down the range of queries and finally to find the specific targets. In general, the systems must be required to first search databases in the proximity to reduce the communication cost and improve the reliability. However, it is possible that because of the data organization at various distributed sites, the closer databases may require a larger number of rounds for interaction than those farther away.

The exceptions, shown in Figure 17.6, in which the round-trip time between Purdue and Rutgers is larger than that between Purdue and Germany, tells us that the decisions of whether to search closer databases or farther databases should be made based on not only static information such as average transmission rates between the two sites and the network topology, but also on the dynamic network behavior. The exceptions usually occur when the network is congested, or when some sites are not available. Thus, it is imperative that the system keep track of current network status such as traffic, site failure information, etc while making decision about the query execution.

17.6 Conclusions and Future Work

We have outlined our software prototype for supporting digital library services. This prototype supports a digital library data model which facilitates the specification of text, image, video, and sound data. Based on this model, partial content-based retrieval schemes are investigated to assist users in locating various data in a flexible manner. In addition, we have presented results of communication experiments with large data objects. We have discussed the impact of the communication performance on the design of various data retrieval schemes.

Our current research focus is to design and implement the proposed software prototype for a digital library. In order to test and evaluate the results of our research, we have selected the data available from NASA as an instance of our prototype. The NASA data has the types and characteristics that are common to a variety of digital library data. Hence, the results of our effort will be applicable to a wide variety of domains. The software prototype developed in this research will be utilized in developing software for digital libraries.

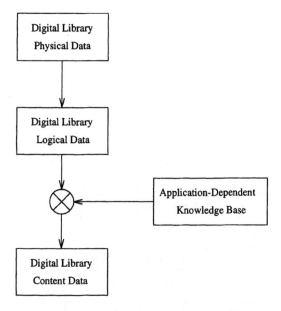

Figure 17.1 Layered Approach to Representing Digital Library Data

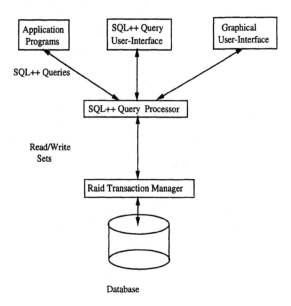

Figure 17.2 The Architecture of O-Raid

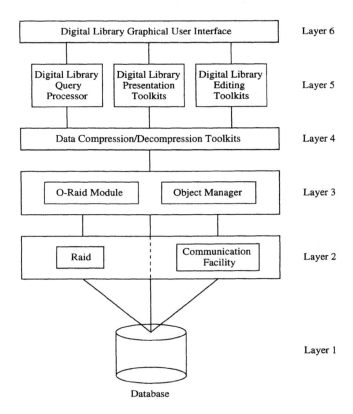

Figure 17.3 The Architecture of DL-Raid

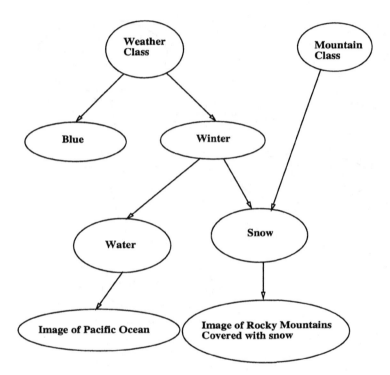

Figure 17.4 Example of relationship between image classes

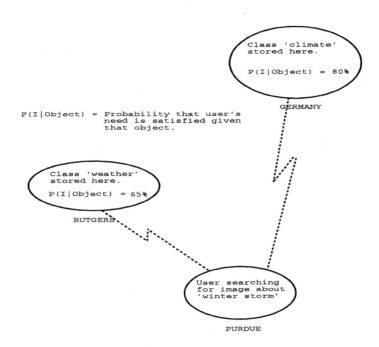

Figure 17.5 Fuzzy Retrieval based on P(I—Object) values

Average Round-Trip Time for Sending an Image of Size 204KB

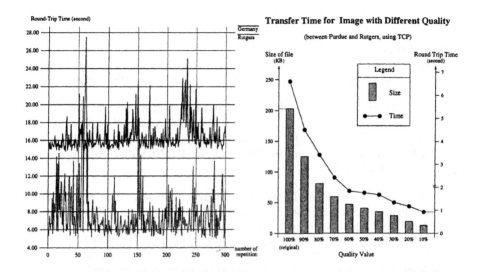

Figure 17.6 Round-trip times for Sending Images in WAN

Transfer Time for Large Data

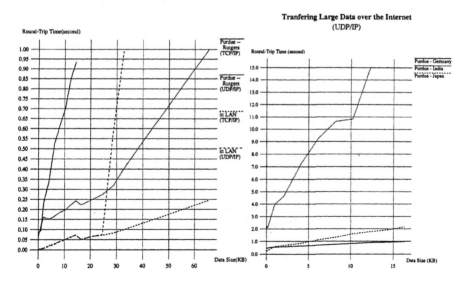

Figure 17.7 Communicating Large Data over the Internet

Bibliography

[1] J. Aberdeen, J. Burger, D. Connolly, S. Roberts, and M Vilain. Description of the *Alembic* System Used for MUC-5. In *Proc. of the Fifth Message Understanding Conference*, pages 137–146, Baltimore, Md., August 1993.

[2] K. Aberer. Demand-driven database integration for biomolecular applications. In *Electronic Proceedings of the Meeting on the Interconnection of Molecular Biology Databases, WWW page http://este.darmstadt.gmd.de:5000/ aberer/MIMBD.html*. Stanford University, August 1994.

[3] Karl Aberer, Klemens Böhm, and Christoph Hüser. The prospects of publishing using advanced database concepts. In Christoph Hüser, Wiebke Möhr, and Vincent Quint, editors, *Proceedings of Conference on Electronic Publishing*, pages 469–480. John Wiley & Sons, Ltd., April 1994.

[4] Karl Aberer and Gisela Fischer. Semantic query optimization for methods in object-oriented database systems. accepted for publication in Proceedings of International Conference on Data Engineering 1995, 1994.

[5] S. Abiteboul, S. Cluet, and T. Milo. Querying and updating the file. In R. Agrawal, S. Baker, and D. Bell, editors, *Proceedings of the International Conference on Very Large Data Bases*, pages 73–84. VLDB Endowment, 1993. Dublin, Ireland.

[6] Adobe Systems Incorporated. *pdfmark Reference Manual*, May 1993. Technical Note #LPS0172.

[7] E. Akpotsui and V. Quint. Type transformation in structured editing systems. In C. Vanoirbeek and G. Coray, editors, *Proceedings of Conference on Electronic Publishing*, pages 27–42. Cambridge University Press, 1992. Lausanne, Switzerland.

[8] J. Allan, J. Davis, D. Krafft, D. Rus, and D. Subramanian. Information agents for building hyperlinks, 1993.

[9] James Allen. *Natural Language Understanding*. Benjamin/Cummings Publishing Company, Menlo Park, CA, 2nd edition, 1994.

[10] Y. Amit, U. Grenander, and M. Piccioni. Structural image restoration through deformable templates. *J. American Statistical Association*, 86(414):376–387, 1991.

[11] Paula Angerstein. SGML queries, December 1992. Handout for the Session on SGML Query Languages at the SGML'92 Conference.

[12] Laurie E. Stackpole Atkinson, Roderick D. and John Yokley. Campus-wide Network Access to CD-ROM Databases. In *Proceedings of the Thirteenth National Online Meeting*, pages 379–385, New York, NY, May 5-7 1992. Learned Information, Inc.

[13] Roderick D. Atkinson. Wide Area CD-ROM Networking. In *Electronic Proceedings of the Ninth Annual Computers in Libraries Conference*, Arlington, VA, 28 February-4 March 1994.

[14] Roderick D. Atkinson and Daniel C. Curtiss. The InfoNet: Integrating Networked CD-ROM Databases and Internet Search Tools. In *Proceedings of the Fourteenth Annual Online Meeting*, pages 17–24, New York, NY, May 4-6 1993. Learned Information, Inc.

[15] Roderick D. Atkinson and John R. Yokley. Multiplatform CD-ROM Networking. *CD-ROM Professional*, pages 73–81, May 1993.

[16] J.C. Aubele and E.N. Slyuta. Small domes on venus: characteristics and origins. *Earth, Moon, and Planets*, 50/51:493–532, 1990.

[17] Ricardo A. Baeza-Yates. String searching methods. In William B. Frakes and Ricardo Baeza-Yates, editors, *Information Retrieval: Data Structures and Algorithms*, pages 219–240. Prentice Hall, Englewood Cliffs, New Jersey, 1992.

[18] J. Banerjee et al. Semantics and implementation of schema evolution in object-oriented databases. *Proceedings ACM SIGMOD*, 16(3):311–322, 1987.

[19] B.Bhargava, Y.Jiang, and J.Srinivasan. O-Raid: Experiences and Experiments. In *Proceedings of the International Conference on Intelligent and Cooperative Information Systems*, Rotterdam, Holland, May 1993.

[20] T. Berners-Lee, R. Cailliau, A. Luotonen, H. F. Nielsen, and A. Secret. The world-wide web. *Communications of the ACM*, 37(8):76–82, August 1994.

[21] Elisa Bertino and Lorenzo Martino. *Object-Oriented Database Systems*. Addison-Wesley, Reading, MA, 1993.

[22] B. Bhargava and J. Riedl. Communication in the Raid Distributed Database System. *IEEE Transactions on Software Engineering*, 16(6), June 1989.

[23] G.E. Blake et al. Text / relational database management systems: Harmonizing SQL and SGML. In *Proceedings of the First International Conference on Applications of Databases.* Lecture Notes in Computer Science, Springer Verlag, June 1994.

[24] R. C. Bolles, H. H. Baker, and D. H. Marimont. Epipolar-plane image analysis: An approach to determining structure from motion. *International Journal of Computer Vision*, 1(1):7–55, 1987.

[25] A. Bookstein. Fuzzy requests: An approach to weighted boolean searches. *Journal of the American Society for Information Science*, 30(4):240–247, 1980.

[26] Murray L. Bradley and Doris R. Folen. Retrieval of Optical Images Using Cuadra Star and Genesys in the Ruth H. Hooker Research Library and Technical Information Center. In *Proceedings of the Fourteenth National Online Meeting*, pages 43–49, New York, NY, May 4-6 1993. Learned Information, Inc.

[27] J. Brassil, S. Low, N. Maxemchuk, and L. O'Gorman. Marking of document images with codewords to deter illicit dissemination. *Proc. Rutgers Digital Library Workshop (to appear)*, 1994.

[28] E. Brill. Automatic grammar induction and parsing free text: A transformation-based approach. In *Proc. of the Human Language Technology Workshop*, pages 237–242. Morgan Kaufmann, March 1993.

[29] Eric Brill and Mitch Marcus. Tagging an unfamiliar text with minimal human supervision. In *AAAI Fall Symposium Series: Probabilistic Approaches to Natural Language (Working Notes)*, pages 10–16, Cambridge, MA, 1992.

[30] A. L. Brown, S. Mantha, and T. Wakayama. A formal specification of document processing. Xerox Corporation, Webster Research Center.

[31] A. L. Brown, T. Wakayma, and H. A. Blair. A reconstruction of context-dependent document processing in SGML. Xerox Corporation, Webster Research Center and Syracuse University, School of Computer and Information Science.

[32] C. Buckley, J. Allan, and G. Salton. Automatic Routing and Ad-hoc Retrieval Using SMART: TREC-2. In D. K. Harman, editor, *Proc. of the Second Text REtrieval Conference (TREC-2)*. NIST Special Publication 500-215, March 1994.

[33] D. A. Buell and D. H. Kraft. Threshold values and boolean retrieval system. *Information Processing and Management*, 17(3):127–136, 1981.

[34] P.C. Bunch, J.F. Hamilton, G.K. Sanderson, and A. H. Simmons. A free-response approach to the measurement and characterization of radiographic-observer performance. *J. Appl. Photo. Eng.*, 4(4):166–171, 1978.

[35] F.J. Burkowski. Retrieval activities in a database consisting of heterogeneous collections of structured text. In N. Belkin, P. Ingwersen, and A.M. Pejtersen, editors, *Proceedings of the Fifteenth Annual International ACM SIGIR Conference on Research and Development in Information Retrieval*, pages 112–125. ACM Press, 1992.

[36] M.C. Burl, U.M. Fayyad, P. Perona, P. Smyth, and M.P. Burl. Automating the hunt for volcanoes on venus. In *Proceedings of the 1994 Computer Vision and Pattern Recognition Conference ((CVPR-94)*, pages 302–309, Los Alamitos, CA, 1994. IEEE Computer Society Press.

[37] P.A. Burrough. *Principles of Geographic Information Systems for Land Resources Assessment*. Clarenden, Oxford, 1986.

[38] Butler. *How to Use the Internet - Join the Internet Revolution Today*. Ziff-Davis, 1994.

[39] J.P. Callan, W.B. Croft, and S.M. Hardig. The INQUERY retrieval system. In *Proceedings of the Third International Conference on Database and Expert Systems Application*, pages 78–83. Springer Verlag, 1992.

[40] Carey, M.J., Haas, L.M., Schwarz, P.M., et. al. Towards heterogeneous multimedia information systems: The Garlic approach. Technical report, IBM Technical Report, 1993.

[41] Eugene Charniak. *Statistical Language Learning*. MIT Press, Cambridge, MA, 1993.

[42] Y. Chenevoy and A. Belaid. Low-level structural recognition of documents. In *Third Annual Symposium on Document Analysis and Information Retrieval, April 11-13, 1994, Alexis Park Hotel, Las Vegas, Nevada*, pages 365–374. University of Nevada, Las Vegas, 1994.

[43] M.S. Chesters. Human visual perception and roc methodology in medical imaging. *Phys. Med. Biol.*, 37(7):1433–1476, 1992.

[44] N. Chinchor, L. Hirschman, and D. Lewis. Evaluating message understanding systems. *Computational Linguistics*, 19(3):409–450, September 1993.

[45] G. E. Christensen, R.D. Rabbitt, and M.I. Miller. 3d brain mapping using a deformable neuroanatomy. *Physics in Medicine and Biology*, 39(3):609–618, 1993.

[46] V. Christophides et al. From structured documents to novel query facilities. In *Proceedings ACM SIGMOD*. ACM Press, May 1994.

[47] K. W. Church. A stochastic parts program and noun parser for unrestricted text. In *Proc. 2nd Conf. on Applied Nat. Lang. Processing*, pages 136–143, Austin, TX, 1988.

[48] Kenneth W. Church and Robert L. Mercer. Introduction to the special issue on computational linguistics using large corpora. *Computational Linguistics*, 19(1):1–24, 1993.

[49] P Clark. The Role of Multimedia. In *Int. Conf. on Computer Communication ICCC 90, New Delhi*, pages 177–182, 1990.

[50] D. Conelly and B. Paddock. XDOC data format: Technical specification. Xerox Imaging Systems, Inc., Peabody, MA, 1993.

[51] J. Conklin. Hypertext: An introduction and survey. *IEEE Computer Magazine*, pages 17–41, September 1987.

[52] J. H. Coombs. Hypertext, full text, and automatic linking. In J.-L. Vidick, editor, *Proc. of the 13th Internat. Conf. on Research and Development in Information Retrieval, Brussels, Belgium, Sept. 5-7, 1990*, pages 83–98, 1990.

[53] Thomas M. Cover and Joy A. Thomas. *Elements of information theory*. Wiley, New York, 1991.

[54] W. Croft, J. Callan, and J. Broglio. TREC-2 Routing and Ad-Hoc Retrieval Evaluation Using the INQUERY System. In D. K. Harman, editor, *Proc. of the Second Text REtrieval Conference (TREC-2)*. NIST Special Publication 500-215, March 1994.

[55] W. B. Croft. Document representation in probablistic models in information retrieval. *Journal of the American Society for Information Science*, 31(6):451–457, 1981.

[56] W. B. Croft. Knowledge-based and statistical approaches to text retrieval. *IEEE EXPERT — Intelligent Systems & their Applications*, 8(2):8–12, April 1993.

[57] W.B. Croft, L.A. Smith, and H.R. Turtle. A loosely-coupled integration of a text retrieval system and an object-oriented database system. In N. Belkin, P. Ingwersen, and A.M. Pejtersen, editors, *Proceedings of the Fifteenth Annual International ACM SIGIR Conference on Research and Development in Information Retrieval*, pages 223–232. ACM Press, 1992.

[58] W.B. Croft and D.W. Stemple. Supporting office document architectures with constrained types. In *Proceedings ACM SIGMOD*. ACM Press, May 1987. San Francisco.

[59] A.M. Cross. Detection of circular geologic features using the hough transform. *Int. J. Remote Sensing*, 9(9):1519–1528, 1987.

[60] D. A. Cruse. *Lexical Semantics*. Cambridge U. Press, Cambridge, UK, 1986.

[61] D. Cutting, D. Karger, J. Pedersen, and J. Tukey. Scatter/gather: A cluster-based approach to browsing large document collections. In *Proceedings of the Fifteenth Annual International ACM/SIGIR Conference on Research and Development in Information Retrieval*, pages 318–329, Copenhagen, June 1992. ACM Press.

[62] D. Cutting, J. Kupiec, J. Pedersen, and P. Sibun. A practical part-of-speech tagger. In *Proc. 3rd Conf. on Applied Natural Language Processing*, pages 133–140, 1992.

[63] A.P. Dawid and A. M. Skene. Maximum likelihood estimation of observer error-rates using the em algorithm. *Applied Statistics*, 28(1):20–28, 1979.

[64] D'elie, G. The Role of the Public Libraries in Society. in collaboration with the University of Minnesota, Center for Survey Research and Gallop Poll Organization, July 1993. Prepared for the U.S. Department of Educational Research & Improvements, Library Program.

[65] A. Dengel. Anastasil: A system for low-level and high-level geometric analysis of printed documents. In H. S. Baird, H. Bunke, and K. Yamamoto, editors, *Structured Document Image Analysis*, pages 70–98. Springer-Verlag, 1992.

[66] P. Dewan, A. Vikram, and B. Bhargava. Engineering the Object-Relation Database Model in O-Raid. In *Proceedings of the International Conference on Foundations of Data Organization and Algorithms*, pages 389–403, June 1989.

[67] S. Djorgovski, N. Weir, and U. M. Fayyad. Processing and analysis of the palomar – stsci digital sky survey using a novel software technology. In D. Crabtree, J. Barnes, and R. Hanisch, editors, *Astronomical Data Analysis Software and Systems III*, page 39. A.S.P. Conf. Ser. 52, 1994.

[68] Doughherty and Koman. *The Mosaic Handbook for Microsoft Windows*. O'Reilly, 1994.

[69] R.O. Duda and P.E. Hart. *Pattern Classification and Scene Analysis*. John Wiley and Sons, Inc., 1973.

[70] J. Ebersole. Protecting Intellectual Property Rights on the Information Superhighways. *Information Industry Association Report*, March 1994.

[71] D. E. Egan, J. R. Remde, T. K. Landauer, C. C. Lochbaum, and L. M. Gomez. Behavioral evaluation and analysis of a hypertext browser. *Proc. CHI '89, Human Factors in Computing Systems*, pages 205–210, 1989.

[72] G. Eliot. *Daniel Deronda*. The World's Classics. Oxford University Press, Oxford, 1984.

[73] R. Elmasri and S. Navathe. *Fundamentals of Database Systems*. The Benjamin/Cummings Publishing Co., second edition, 1994.

[74] Engst, Low, and Simon. *The Internet Starter Kit for Windows*. Hayden books, 1994.

[75] J. E. Guest et al. Small volcanic edifices and volcanism in the plains of venus. *Journal Geophys. Res.*, 97(E10):15949, 1992.

[76] J. W. Head et al. Venus volcanic centers and their environmental settings: Recent data from magellan. *American Geophysical Union Spring meeting abstracts*, EOS 72:175, 1991.

[77] J. W. Head et al. Venus volcanism: classification of volcanic features and structures, associations, and global distribution from magellan data. *Journal Geophysical Res.*, 97(E8):13153–13197, 1992.

[78] Melia M. Hoffman et al. The RightPages Service: An Image-Based Electronic Library. *J. of the Am. Society for Information Science*, 44(8):446–452, 1993.

[79] Excalibur Technologies, Inc. Excalibur EFS White Paper: The Excalibur Advantage in Document Imaging. Technical report, Excalibur Technologies, Inc.

[80] U.M. Fayyad. Branching on attribute values in decision tree generation. In *Proc. of the Twelfth National Conference on Artificial Intelligence AAAI-94*, pages 601–606, Cambridge, MA, 1994. MIT Press.

[81] U.M. Fayyad and K.B. Irani. The attribute selection problem in decision tree generation. In *Proc. of the Tenth National Conference on Artificial Intelligence AAAI-92*, pages 104–110, Cambridge, MA, 1992. MIT Press.

[82] U.M. Fayyad and K.B. Irani. Multi-interval discretization of continuous-valued attributes for classification learning. In *Proc. of the Thirteenth Inter. Joint Conf. on Artificial Intelligence*, Chambery, France, 1993.

[83] U.M. Fayyad, N. Weir, and S. Djorgovski. Skicat: A machine learning system for the automated cataloging of large-scale sky surveys. In *Proc. of the Tenth International Conference on Machine Learning*, 1993.

[84] A. Feng and T. Wakayama. SIMON: A grammar based transformation system for structured documents. Xerox Corporation, Webster Research Center.

[85] S. Finch and N. Chater. Bootstrapping syntactic categories using statistical methods. In W. Daelemans and D. Powers, editors, *Proc. 1st SHOE Workshop*, pages 229–235, Tilburg U., The Netherlands, 1992.

[86] S. Finch and N. Chater. Learning syntactic categories: A statistical approach. In M. Oaksford and G. Brown, editors, *Neurodynamics and Psychology*, pages 295–319. Academic Press, San Diego, CA, 1993.

[87] G.M.C. Fisher, J.A. Young, C.M. Vest, T.E. Everhart, H.B. Schacht, and Sheinkman. Vision for a 21st Century Information Infrastructure. *Council on Competitiveness*, page iii, 1994.

[88] David W. Flater and Yelena Yesha. Issues for Bringing Digital Libraries into Public Use. Survey Report on Digital Libraries, 1993.

[89] D.W. Flater and Y. Yesha. Issues for bringing digital libraries into public use. In *Proceedings of the Third NASA GSFC Conference on Mass Storage and Technologies*, October 1993.

[90] D. Flavelle. Musician turns high-tech wizard. *The Toronto Star*, pages D1, D5, July 3 1994.

[91] D. Flavelle. Musician turns high-tech wizard. *The Toronto Star*, pages D1, D5, July 3 1994.

[92] Doris R. Folen and Laurie E. Stackpole. Optical Technology for Information Access at the NRL Library. *Microcomputers for Information Management*, December 1993.

[93] E. Fox, Q. Chen, and R. France. Integrating search and retrieval with hypertext. In E. Berk and J. Devlin, editors, *Hypertext/Hypermedia Handbook*, pages 329–355. McGraw-Hill, New York, 1991.

[94] E. A. Fox. Source book on digital libraries version 1.0. Technical report, National Science Foundation (CISE and IRIS), Virginia Tech, gopher://fox.cs.vt.edu/11/DL, December 1993.

[95] Edward A. Fox. Digital Libraries, Hot Topics. *IEEE Computer*, November 1993.

[96] W. Nelson Francis and Henry Kucera. *Frequency Analysis of English Usage*. Houghton Mifflin, Boston, MA, 1982.

[97] H. P. Frei and D. Stieger. Making use of hypertext links when retrieving information. In D. Lucarella, editor, *Proceedings of the ACM Conference on Hypertext, Milano, Italy, Nov. 30 - Dec. 4,1992*, pages 102–111, 1992.

[98] R. P. Futrelle, I. A. Kakadiaris, J. Alexander, C. M. Carriero, N. Nikolakis, and J. M. Futrelle. Understanding diagrams in technical documents. *IEEE Computer*, 25(7):75–78, 1992.

[99] Robert P. Futrelle and Susan Gauch. Experiments in syntactic and semantic classification and disambiguation using bootstrapping. In Branimir Boguraev and James Pustejovksy, editors, *Acquisition of Lexical Knowledge from Text*, pages 117–127, Columbus, OH, 1993. Assoc. Computational Linguistics.

[100] Robert P. Futrelle and Nikos Nikolakis. Efficient analysis of complex diagrams using constraint-based parsing. In *ICDAR'95*, Montreal, Canada, 1994. Submitted.

[101] Robert P. Futrelle and Xiaolan Zhang. Large-scale persistent object systems for corpus linguistics and information retrieval. In *Digital Libraries '94*, pages 80–87, College Station, Texas, 1994. Dept. of Computer Science, Texas A&M University.

[102] R.P. Futrelle, Chris C. Dunn, D.S. Ellis, and Maurice J. Jr. Pescitelli. Preprocessing and lexicon design for parsing technical text. In *Proc. 2nd Intern'l Workshop on Parsing Technologies*, pages 31–40, Morristown, New Jersey, 1991. ACL.

[103] William A. Gale, Kenneth W. Church, and David Yarowsky. A method for disambiguating word senses in a large corpus. *Computers and the Humanities*, 26(5):415–439, 1992.

[104] William A. Gale, Kenneth .W. Church, and David. Yarowsky. Work on statistical methods for word sense disambiguation. In *AAAI Fall Symposium Series: Probabilistic Approaches to Natural Language (Working Notes)*, pages 54–60, Cambridge, MA, 1992.

[105] J.R. Garrett. Digital libraries: The grand challenges. *Educom Review*, 28(4):17–21, July/August 1993.

[106] J.R. Garrett. Digital libraries: The grand challenges. *Educom Review*, 28(4):17–21, July/August 1993.

[107] J.R. Garrett. Digital libraries: The grand challenges. *Educom Review*, 28(4):17–21, July/August 1993.

[108] J.R. Garrett. Digital libraries: The grand challenges. *Educom Review*, 28(4):17–21, July/August 1993.

[109] Roger Garside, Geoffrey Leech, and Geoffrey Sampton. *The Computational Analysis of English, A-corpus-based approach.* Longman, 1987.

[110] S. Geman and D. Geman. Stochastic relaxation, gibbs distribution, and the bayesian restoration of images. *IEEE Trans. Patt. Anal. Mach. Int.*, 6(6):721–741, 1984.

[111] C. F. Goldfarb. *The SGML Handbook.* Clarendon Press, Oxford, 1990.

[112] Y. Gong et al. An image database system with content capturing and fast image indexing abilities. In *Proceedings of the International Conference on Multimedia Computing and Systems*, pages 121–130, Boston, MA, May 1994. IEEE.

[113] Gaston H. Gonnet, Ricardo A. Baeza-Yates, and Tim Snider. New indices for text: Pat trees and pat arrays. In Wiliam B. Frakes and Ricardo Baeza-Yates, editors, *Information Retrieval : Data Structures and Algorithms*, pages 66–82. Prentice Hall, Englewood Cliffs, New Jersey, 1992.

[114] D. Gore. Farewell to Alexandria: The theory of the no-growth, high-performance library. In D. Gore, editor, *Farewell to Alexandria*, pages 164–180. Greenwood Press, Westport, Connecticut, 1976.

[115] G. Grefenstette. Finding semantic similarity in raw text: the deese antonyms. In *AAAI Fall Symposium Series: Probabilistic Approaches to Natural Language (Working Notes)*, pages 61–66, Cambridge, MA, 1992.

[116] A. Gupta, T. Weymouth, and R. Jain. Semantic queries in image databases. In E. Knuth and L. M. Wegner, editors, *Visual Database Systems, II*, volume A-7 of *IFIP Transactions A: Computer Science and Technology*, pages 201–215. North-Holland, Amsterdam, THE NETHERLANDS, 1992.

[117] Carole Hafner, Kenneth Baclawski, Robert Futrelle, Natalya Fridman, and Shobana Sampath. Creating a knowledge base of biological research papers. In *2nd Inter'l Conf. on Intelligent Systems for Molecular Biology*, pages 147–155, Stanford, CA, 1994. AAAI Press.

[118] Milton Halem. Keynote Speech. In *Workshop on the Role of Digital Libraries in K-12 Education in Conjunction with the 2nd International Conference on Information and Knowledge Management (CIKM'93)*, Washington DC, November 1993.

[119] M. Halper et al. Integrating a part relationship into an open OODB system using metaclasses. In *Proceedings of Third International Conference on Information and Knowledge Management (CIKM'94)*. ACM Press, November 1994.

[120] M. A. Hearst. Contextualizing retrieval of full-length documents. Technical Report UCB/CSD-94-789, University of California, Berkeley, 1994.

[121] R. C. Heterick. The Blacksburg electronic village: A field of dreams. *Information Technology and Libraries*, pages 240–242, June 1993.

[122] R. C. Heterick. The Blacksburg electronic village: A field of dreams. *Information Technology and Libraries*, pages 240–242, June 1993.

[123] Donald Hindle and Mats Rooth. Structural ambiguity and lexical relations. *Computational Linguistics*, 19(1):103–120, 1993.

[124] Graeme Hirst. *Semantic interpretation and the resolution of ambiguity*. Cambridge University Press, Cambridge, 1987.

[125] T. K. Ho, J. J. Hull, and S. N. Srihari. A Word Shape Analysis Approach to Recognition of Degraded Word Images. In *USPS Advanced Technology Conference*, Washington D.C., November 1990.

[126] Jerry R. Hobbs, Mark E. Stickel, Douglas E. Appelt, and Paul Martin. Interpretation as abduction. *Artificial intelligence*, 63:69–142, 1993.

[127] M. M. Hoffman, L. O'Gorman, G. A. Story, J. Q. Arnold, and N. H. Macdonald. The RightPages service: an image-based electronic library. *J. Amer. Soc. for Inf. Science*, 44:446–452, 1993.

[128] M. Hofmann and S. Schmezko. Graphical structure–oriented search in a hypertext system. In *Database and Expert Systems Applications — Proceedings of the DEXA '92, Valencia, Spain, Sept. 2-4, 1992*, pages 179–184. Springer–Verlag, 1992.

[129] Information Science Research Institute. Annual Report on the Accuracy of OCR Devices: A follow on report to the 1992 Report. Technical report, University of Nevada Las Vegas, 4505 Maryland Parkway, Box 454021, Las Vegas, NV, 1993.

[130] Y. Ishitani. Document Skew Detection Based on Local Region Complexity. In *Second International Conference on Document Analysis and Recognition*, Tsukuba Science City, Japan, October 1993.

[131] Information technology - text and office systems - standardized generalized markup language (SGML), 1986. ISO 8879-1986 (E).

[132] Information technology - text and office systems - office document architecture (ODA) and interchange format, 1989. Part 2, Document Structures.

[133] Paul Jacobs and Lisa F. Rau. Innovations in text interpretation. *Artificial Intelligence*, 63:143–191, 1993.

[134] A. Jain and S. Bhattacharjee. Address block location on envelopes using gabor filters. *Pattern Recognition*, 25(12), 1992.

[135] J. Jarvis and A. Tyson. *SPIE Proc. on Instrumnetation and Astronomy*, 172:422, 1979.

[136] Y. Jiang, X. Liu, and B. Bhargava. Reevaluating indexing schemes for nested objects. In *Proceedings of the 3rd International Conference on Information and Knowledge Management*, November 1994.

[137] B. Kahle. An Information System for Corporate Users: Wide Area Information Servers. Technical Report Thinking Machines Technical Report TMC-199, Thinking Machines, 1991. also in *ONLINE Magazine*, August 1991.

[138] B. Kahle. Overview of wide area information servers, 1991. WAIS on-line documentation.

[139] D. Kahneman, P. Slovic, and A. Tversky. *Judgement under Uncertainty: Heuristics and Biases.* Cambridge University Press, Cambridge, 1982.

[140] B. W. Kernighan, M. E. Lesk, and J. F. Ossanna. Document preparation. *Bell Sys. Tech. J.*, 57(6):2115–2135, 1978.

[141] S. M. Kerpedjiev. Automatic extraction of information structures from documents. In *ICDAR 91*, pages 32–40, 1991.

[142] W. Klas, K. Aberer, and Erich J. Neuhold. Object-oriented modeling for hypermedia systems using the VODAK modeling language (VML). In A. Dogac, T. Ozsu, A. Biliris, and T. Sellis, editors, *Advances in Object-Oriented Database Management Systems*, NATO ASI Series. Springer Verlag Berlin Heidelberg, August 1994.

[143] W. Klas et al. *Object-Oriented Multidatabase Systems*, chapter Database Integration Using the Open Object-Oriented Database System VODAK. Prentice Hall, 1994.

[144] W. Klas et al. VML - The VODAK Model Language Version 4.0. Technical report, GMD-IPSI, October 1994.

[145] S.T. Klein, A. Bookstein, and S. Deerwester. Storing text retrieval systems on CD-ROM: Compression and encryption considerations. *ACM Transactions on Information Systems*, 7(3):230–245, July 1989.

[146] D. Kozen. *The Design and Analysis of Algorithms.* Springer-Verlag, New York, 1992.

[147] M. Kracker. A fuzzy concept network model and its application. Technical Report 585, GMD-IPSI, October 1991. St. Augustin.

[148] E. Krol. *The Whole Internet User's Guide and Catalog.* O'Reilly & Associates, Sebastopol, CA, 1992.

[149] Larry Krumenaker. How to Build a Library Without Walls. *Internet World*, 4(5):9–12, June/July/August 1993.

[150] Larry Krumenaker. Virtual Libraries Complete with Journals, Get Real. *Science*, 260(5111):1066–1067, May 21 1993.

[151] H. Kucera and W. Francis. *Computational Analysis of Presentday American English.* Brown University Press, Providence, RI, 1967.

[152] Y. Labrou and T. Finin, editors. *Intelligent Information Agents.* University of Maryland Baltimore County, 1994.

[153] S. W. Lam and S. N. Srihari. Frame-based Knowledge Representation for Multi-domain Document Layout Analysis. In *IEEE International Conference on Systems, Man, and Cybernetics*, Charlottesville, VA, October 1991.

[154] S. W. Lam and S. N. Srihari. Multi-domain Document Layout Understanding. In *First International Conference on Document Analysis and Recognition*, Saint-Malo, France, September 1991.

[155] L. Lamport. LaTeX: *A Document Preparation System*. Addison-Wesley, Reading, 1986.

[156] M.-K. Leong, S. Sam, and D. Narasimhalu. Towards a visual language for an object-oriented multi-media database system. In T. L. Kunii, editor, *Visual Database Systems*, pages 465–495. North-Holland, Amsterdam, THE NETHERLANDS, 1989.

[157] M. Lesk. Personal Communication, 1995.

[158] M. E. Lesk. Full text retrieval with graphics. *Bridging the Communication Gap (NATO AGARD Conference Preprint No. 487)*, pages 5-1 to 5-7, 1990.

[159] M. E. Lesk. The CORE electronic chemistry library. *Proc. 14th ACM SIGIR Conference*, pages 93–112, October 1991.

[160] V. I. Levenshtein. Binary codes capable of correcting deletions, insertions and reversals. *Soviet Physics Doklady*, 10(8):707–710, February 1966.

[161] C. Lewis, D. Rus, and M. Scott. A structure detector for tables. Forthcoming Technical Report.

[162] Ming Li and Paul Vitanyi. *An Introduction to Kolmogorov Complexity and Its Applications*. Springer-Verlag, New York, 1993.

[163] Arjan Loeffen. Text databases: A survey of text models and systems. *SIGMOD Record*, 23(1):97–106, 1994.

[164] Lois F. Lunin and Edward A. Fox. Perspectives on ... digital libraries: Introduction and overview. *Journal of American Society for Information Science*, 44(8):441–445, 1993.

[165] A. Luotonen and T. Berners-Lee. Cern httpd reference manual. URL: http://info.cern.ch/hypertext/WWW/Daemon/User/Guide.ps, May 1994.

[166] M. Stuart Lynn and committee. Consortium for university printing and information distribution (CUPID). protocols and services (version 1): An architectural overview. *Technological Strategies for Protecting Intellectual Property in the Networked Multimedia Environment*, 1(1):237–256, Jan. 1994.

[167] John Lyons. *Semantics*, volume 2. Cambridge University Press, 1977.

[168] Splus Reference Manual. Statistical Sciences, Inc., 1991.

[169] D.F. Marble and D.J. Peuquet. *Manual of Remote Sensing, 2nd ed., R.E. Colwell (Ed.)*, chapter Geographical information systems and remote sensing. Amer. Soc. Photogrammetry, Falls Church, VA, 1983.

[170] K. Matsui and K. Tanaka. Video-steganography: How to secretly embed a signature in a picture. *Technological Strategies for Protecting Intellectual Property in the Networked Multimedia Environment*, 1(1):187–206, Jan. 1994.

[171] Mark T. Maybury. *Generating Multisentential English Text Using Communicative Acts*. PhD thesis, Computer Laboratory, Cambridge University, England, 1991. also published as RADC Technical Report TR 90-411.

[172] Shawn McCarthy. Navy Lab Digitizes 600,000 (sic) Research Reports. *Government Computer News*, 12(16):51, August 2 1993.

[173] C. McKnight. Electronic journals-past, present. . .and future? *ASLIB Proc.*, 45:7–10, 1993.

[174] J. McMahon and F. J. Smith. Structural tags, annealing and automatic word classification. *cmp-lg@xxx.lanl.gov*, 9405029, 1994.

[175] M. Mills, J. Cohen, and Y. Y. Wong. A magnifier tool for video data. In *Proceedings: CHI'92*, pages 93–98, Monterey, CA, May 1992. ACM.

[176] M. Mizuno, Y. Tsuji, T. Tanaka, H. Tanaka, M. Iwashita, and T. Temma. Document recognition system with layout structure generator. *NEC Research and Development*, 32(2):430–437, July 1991.

[177] A. Moffat, N. Sharman, and J. Zobel. Static compression for dynamic texts. In J.A. Storer and M. Cohn, editors, *Proc. 4'th IEEE Data Compression Conference*, pages 126–135, Snowbird, Utah, March 1994. IEEE Computer Society Press, Los Alamitos, CA.

[178] A. Moffat and J. Zobel. Self-indexing inverted files for fast text retrieval. *ACM Transactions on Information Systems*. To appear.

[179] F. Moser and T.C. Rakow. Database support for the access towards an open and multimedia archive. In *GI-FG Databases, Fall Workshop*, September 1993. in German, Jena.

[180] S.H. Myaeng and M. Li. Building term clusters by acquiring lexical semantics from a corpus. In Y. Yesha, editor, *CIKM-92*, pages 130–137, Baltimore, MD, 1992.

[181] A. Myka. Putting paper documents in the world-wide web. In I. Goldstein, editor, *Proceedings of the 2nd International WWW Conference '94, Oct. 17-20, 1994, Chicago*, volume 1, pages 199–208, 1994.

[182] A. Myka, U. Güntzer, and F. Sarre. Monitoring user actions in the hypertext system "hyperman". In *Going Online — Conference Proceedings of the SIGDOC '92 (Oct. 13-16, 1992, Ottawa, Canada)*, pages 103–114. The Association for Computing Machinery, 1992.

[183] A. Myka, U. Güntzer, and J. Werner. An integrated approach to the electronic library of the future: Connecting a document retrieval with a hypertext system. In *Proceedings of the Hypermedia 94, Pretoria, March 23-25, 1994*, pages 149–160, 1994.

[184] A. Myka, M. Hüttl, and U. Güntzer. Hypertext conversion and representation of a printed manual. In *Proceedings of the RIAO '94, New York, Oct. 11-13, 1994*, pages 407–417. C.I.D.-C.A.S.I.S., 1994.

[185] A. Nagasaka and Y. Tanaka. Automatic video indexing and full-video search for object appearances. In E. Knuth and L. M. Wegner, editors, *Visual Database Systems, II*, volume A-7 of *IFIP Transactions A: Computer Science and Technology*, pages 113–127. North-Holland, Amsterdam, THE NETHERLANDS, 1992.

[186] G. Nagy. Towards a structured-document-image utility. In H. S. Baird, H. Bunke, and K. Yamamoto, editors, *Structured Document Image Analysis*, pages 54–69. Springer–Verlag, 1992.

[187] G. Nagy, S. Seth, and M. Vishwanathan. A prototype document image analysis system for technical journals. *Computer*, 25(7), 1992.

[188] National Information Standards Organization (Z39). Z39.50-1988: Information Retrieval Service Definition and Protocol Specification for Library Applications. Technical report, P.O. Box 1056, Bethesda, MD 20817, 1988.

[189] W. Niblack and M. Fletcher. Find me the pictures that look like this: IBM's image query project. *Advanced Imaging*, April 1993.

[190] NIST, U.S. Department of Commerce. A transformation of learning: Use of the NII for education and lifelong learning. In *Putting the Information Infrastructure to Work: Report of the Information Infrastructure Task Force Committee on Applications and Technology*, pages 61–62. U.S. Government Printing Office, 1994.

[191] NIST, U.S. Department of Commerce. A transformation of learning: Use of the NII for education and lifelong learning. In *Putting the Information Infrastructure to Work: Report of the Information Infrastructure Task Force Committee on Applications and Technology*, page 64. U.S. Government Printing Office, 1994.

[192] K. Obraczka, P.B. Danzig., and S.-H. Li. INTERNET resource discovery services. *IEEE Computer*, 26(9), 1993.

[193] Chris D. Paice. Constructing literature abstracts by computer: Techniques and prospects. *Information Processing & Management*, 26(1):171–186, 1990.

[194] Chris D. Paice and Paul A. Jones. The identification of important concepts in highly structured technical reports. In *SIGIR '93*, pages 69–78, Pittsburgh, PA, 1993. ACM.

[195] G.H. Pettengill, P.G. Ford, W.T.K. Johnson, R.K. Raney, and L.A. Soderblom. Magellan: radar performance and data products. *Science*, 252:260–265, 1991.

[196] G. Piatetsky-Shapiro and W.J. Frawley, editors. *Knowledge Discovery in Databases*. MIT Press, Cambridge, MA, 1991.

[197] N. Pissinou, R. T. Snodgrass, R. Elmasi, and etc. Towards an infrastructure for temporal databases: Report of an invitation arpa/nsf workshop. *ACM SIGMOD RECORD*, 23(1):35–51, 1994.

[198] G. Porter and E. Rainero. Document reconstruction: A system for recovering document structure from layout. In *Proceedings of the Conference on Electronic Publishing*, pages 127–141, 1992.

[199] S. Quegan, A.J., A. Hendry, J. Skingley, and C.J. Oddy-CJ. Automatic interpretation strategies for synthetic aperture radar images. *Trans. R. Soc. London*, A(324):409–421, 1988.

[200] J. R. Quinlan. The induction of decision trees. *Machine Learning*, 1(1), 1986.

[201] F. Rabitti and P. Savino. Automatic Image Indexation to Support Content-Based Retrieva. *Information Processing and Management*, 28(5):547–565, 1992.

[202] M. A. Rahgozar, Z. Fan, and E. V. Rainero. Tabular document recognition. In *SPIE Proceedings*, San Jose, February 1994.

[203] L. F. Rau, P. S. Jacobs, and U. Zernik. Information extraction and text summarization using linguistic knowledge acquisition. *Information Processing & Management*, 25(4):419–428, 1989.

[204] L.F. Rau and P.S. Jacobs. Creating segmented databases from free text for text retrieval. In A. Bookstein, Y. Chiaramella, G. Salton, and V. V. Raghavan, editors, *SIGIR '91*, pages 337–346, Chicago, IL, 1991. ACM.

[205] A. V. Rice, J. Kanai, and T. A. Nartker. The third annual test of ocr accuracy. In K. O. Grover, editor, *Information Science Research Institute — 1994 Annual Research Report*, pages 11–38. Information Science Research Institute, University of Nevada, Las Begas, 1994.

[206] D. Riecken, editor. *Intelligent Agents*, pages 18–147. ACM Press, 1994.

[207] B. D. Ripley. *Statistical Inference for Spatial Processes*. Cambridge University Press, Cambridge, 1988.

[208] G.D. Ritchie, G.J. Russell, A.W. Black, and S.G. Pulman. *Computational Morphology - Practical Mechanisms for the English Lexicon*. The MIT Press, Cambridge, MA, 1992.

[209] L. Rostek, W. Möhr, and D. Fischer. Weaving a web: the structure and creation of an object network representing an electronic reference work. *Electronic Publishing*, 6(4):495–505, 1994.

[210] L. A. Rowe, J. S. Boreczky, and C. A. Eads. Indexes for user access to large video databases. In *Symposium on Electronic Imaging Science and Technology: Storage and Retrieval for Image Video Databases II*, pages 150–161, San Jose, CA, February 1994. IS&T/SPIE.

[211] D. Rus and J. Allan. Image indexing using the hausdorff metric. Forthcoming Technical Report.

[212] D. Rus and D. Subramanian. Information retrieval, information structure, and information agents. Submitted to the *ACM Transactions on Information Systems*, 1993.

[213] D. Rus and D. Subramanian. Multi-media RISSC Informatics: Retrieving Information with Simple Structural Components. In *Proceedings of the ACM Conference on Information and Knowledge Management*, Washington DC, November 1993.

[214] O. Sacks. *The Man Who Mistook His Wife for a Hat and Other Clinical Tales*, chapter 9, pages 80–84. Harper & Row, New York, Perennial Library edition, 1987.

[215] G. Salton. *Automatic Text Processing: The Transformation, Analysis, and Retrieval of Information by Computer*. Addison-Wesley Pub. Co., Reading, MA, 1989.

[216] G. Salton and C. Buckley. Improving retrieval performance by relevance feedback. *Journal of American Society for Information Science*, 41(4):288–297, 1990.

[217] G. Salton and M. McGill. *Introduction to Modern Information Retrieval*. McGraw-Hill, New York, 1983.

[218] D. Sankoff and J. Kruskal. *Time warps, string edits, and macromolecules: the theory and practice of sequence comparison*. Addison-Wesley, 1983.

[219] F. Sarre and U. Güntzer. Automatic transformation of linear text into hypertext. In *Proceedings of the International Symposium on Database Systems for Advanced Applications (DASFAA '91), Tokyo, Japan, April 2-4, 1991*, pages 498–506, 1991.

[220] John L. Schnase, John J. Leggett, Richard K. Furuta, and Ted Metcalfe, editors. *Digital Libraries '94*. Dept. of Computer Science, Texas A&M University, College Station, Texas, 1994.

[221] H. Schutze. Context space. In *AAAI Fall Symposium Series: Probabilistic Approaches to Natural Language (Working Notes)*, pages 113–120, Cambridge, MA, 1992.

[222] Special issue on magellan data. *Science*, April 12, 1991.

[223] B. Shneiderman. Tree visualization with tree-maps: A 2-d space-filling approach. Technical Report Technical Report CAR-TR-548, CS-TR-2645, University of Maryland, College Park, 1990.

[224] K. Shoens et al. The rufus system: Information organization for semi-structured data. In R. Agrawal, S. Baker, and D. Bell, editors, *Proceedings of the International Conference on Very Large Data Bases*, pages 97–107. VLDB Endowment, 1993. Dublin, Ireland.

[225] R. Sinha, B. Prasade, G. Houle, and M. Sabourin. Hybrid contextual text recognition with string matching. *IEEE Transaction on Pattern Analysis and Machine Intelligence*, 15(9):915–925, September 1993.

[226] A Sloane. Aspects of multimedia database technology for teleteaching. In *Proc. 3rd IFIP Teleteaching conference, Trondheim, Norway*, pages 809–817, Aug. 1993.

[227] A Sloane. Homelink: A project to investigate computing and communications technology requirements in the home environment. In *Proc. IFIP 13th World Computer Congress, Hamburg*, pages 142–147, Aug. 1994.

[228] A Sloane. Multimedia and Communications: A quart into a pint pot? In *Proc. NDISD '94, University of Wolverhampton/BCS Seminar, Wolverhampton*, pages 25–32, April 1994.

[229] S. W. Smoliar and H. J. Zhang. Content-based video indexing and retrieval. *IEEE MultiMedia*, 1(2):62–72, Summer 1994.

[230] P. Smyth and J. Mellstrom. Detecting novel classes with applications to fault diagnosis. In *Proc. of the Ninth International Conference on Machine Learning*, pages 416–425, Los Altos, CA, 1992. Morgan Kaufmann.

[231] R. T. Snodgrass, I. Ahn, and etc. TSQL2 language specification. *ACM SIGMOD RECORD*, 23(1):65–86, 1994.

[232] R. Sproat. *Morphology and Computation*. The MIT Press, Cambridge, MA, 1992.

[233] J. Srinivasan. *Replication and Fragmentation of Composite Objects in Distributed database Systems*. PhD thesis, Purdue University, 1992.

[234] Barrie T. Stern. Adonis-a vision of the future. In G. P. Cornish and A. Gallico, editors, *Interlending and Document S upply*, pages 23–33. British Library, Boston Spa, 1990.

[235] G.A. Story, L. O'Gorman, D. Fox, L.L. Schaper, and H.V. Jagadish. The rightpages image–based electronic library for alerting and browsing. *IEEE Computer*, pages 17–26, September 1992.

[236] B. Subramanian et al. Querying lists and trees: A language and some optimizations. accepted for publication in Proceedings of International Conference on Data Engineering 1995, 1994.

[237] Klaus Süllow et al. MultiMedia Forum - an interactive online journal. In Christoph Hüser, Wiebke Möhr, and Vincent Quint, editors, *Proceedings of Conference on Electronic Publishing*, pages 413–422. John Wiley & Sons, Ltd., April 1994.

[238] B. Sundheim, editor. *Proceedings of the Fifth Message Understanding Conference*. Baltimore, MD, August 1993.

[239] K. Taghva, J. Borsack, B. Bullard, and A. Condit. Post–editing through approximation and global correction. In K. O. Grover, editor, *UNLV Information Science Research Institute 1993 Annual Report*, pages 57–70. Information Science Research Institute, Universtity of Nevada, Las Vegas, 1993.

[240] S. L. Thatte. InfoHarness. Internal Bellcore memorandum, 1995.

[241] Y. Tonomura. Video handling based on structured information for hypermedia systems. In *International Conference on Multimedia Information Systems '91*, pages 333–344, SINGAPORE, January 1991. ACM, McGraw Hill.

[242] Y. Tonomura et al. VideoMAP and VideoSpaceIcon: Tools for anatomizing video content. In *Proceedings: INTERCHI '93*, pages 131–136, 544, Amsterdam, NETHERLANDS, April 1993. ACM.

[243] S. Tsujimoto and H. Asada. Major components of a complete text reading system. In *Proceedings of the IEEE*, volume 80, 1992.

[244] M. Turk and A. Pentland. Eigenfaces for recognition. *J. of Cognitive Neurosci.*, 3:71–86, 1991.

[245] U.M.Fayyad. *On the Induction of Decision Trees for Multiple Concept Learning.* PhD thesis, Department of Electrical Engineering & Computer Science, The University of Michigan, Ann Arbor, 1991.

[246] Edward J. Valauskas. Ncsa mosaic on the macintosh. *Online,* 17(5):99–101, Sept. 1993.

[247] Valdes. In *Instrumentation in Astronomy IV,* volume 331:465, Bellingham, WA, 1994. SPIE.

[248] D. Wang and S. N. Srihari. Classification of newspaper image blocks using texture analysis. *Computer Vision, Graphics, and Image Processing,* 47:327–352, 1989.

[249] W. Ward and S. Issar. Recent Improvements in the CMU Spoken Language Understanding System. In *Proceedings of the ARPA Workshop on Human Language Technology,* Plainsboro, N.J., March 1994.

[250] J. Warmer and S. van Egmond. The implementation of the amsterdam SGML parser. Technical report, Faculteit Wiskunde en Informatica, Department of Mathematics and Computer Science, Vrije Universiteit Amsterdam, 1987.

[251] J. Way and E.A. Smith. The evolution of synthetic aperture radar systems and their progression to the eos sar. *IEEE Trans. on Geoscience and Remote Sensing,* 29(6):962–985, 1991.

[252] N. Weir, S. Djorgovski, and U.M. Fayyad. Skicat: A system for the scientific analysis of the palomar-stsci digital sky survey. In *Proc. of Astronomy from Large Databases II,* page 509, Munich, Germany: European Southern Observatory, 1993.

[253] N. Weir, S. Djorgovski, U.M. Fayyad, J.D. Smith, and J. Roden. Cataloging the northern sky using a new generation of software technology. In H. MacGillivray, editor, *Astronomy From Wide-Field Imaging, Proceedings of the IAU Symp. #161,* Dordrecht, 1994. Kluwer.

[254] N. Weir, U.M. Fayyad, and S. Djorgovski. Automated star/galaxy classification for digitized poss-ii. *to appear in The Astronomical Journal,* 1995. in press.

[255] H.G. Wells. *World Brain.* Doubleday, New York, 1938.

[256] I.H. Witten, T.C. Bell, H. Emberson, S. Inglis, and A. Moffat. Textual image compression: Two-stage lossy/lossless encoding of textual images. *Proceedings of the IEEE,* 82(6):878–888, June 1994.

[257] I.H. Witten, A. Moffat, and T.C. Bell. *Managing Gigabytes: Compressing and Indexing Documents and Images.* Van Nostrand Reinhold, New York, 1994.

[258] U. Zernik. Train1 vs. train2: Tagging word senses in corpus. In U. Zernik, editor, *Lexical Acquisition: Exploiting On-Line Resources to Build a Lexicon*, pages 97–112. Lawrence Erlbaum Associates, Publishers, Hillsdale, New Jersey, 1991.

[259] H. J. Zhang, A. Kankanhalli, and S. W. Smoliar. Automatic partitioning of full-motion video. *Multimedia Systems*, 1(1):10–28, 1993.

[260] H. J. Zhang and S. W. Smoliar. Developing power tools for video indexing and retrieval. In W. Niblack and R. Jain, editors, *Symposium on Electronic Imaging Science and Technology: Storage and Retrieval for Image Video Databases II*, pages 140–149, San Jose, CA, February 1994. IS&T/SPIE.

[261] Y. Zhang and B. Bhargava. A Facility for Experimenting Distributed Software in the Internet. submitted for publication, an early version appeared in the *Proceedings of IEEE workshop in Advances in Parallel and Distributed Systems*, Princeton, NJ, Oct. 1993, pp 40-45, 1994.

[262] J. Zobel, J.A. Thom, and R. Sacks-Davis. Efficiency of nested relational document database systems. In G.M. Lohmann, A. Sernadas, and R. Camps, editors, *Proceedings of the International Conference on Very Large Data Bases*, pages 91–102. VLDB Endowment, 1991. Barcelona, Spain.

Springer-Verlag and the Environment

We at Springer-Verlag firmly believe that an international science publisher has a special obligation to the environment, and our corporate policies consistently reflect this conviction.

We also expect our business partners – paper mills, printers, packaging manufacturers, etc. – to commit themselves to using environmentally friendly materials and production processes.

The paper in this book is made from low- or no-chlorine pulp and is acid free, in conformance with international standards for paper permanency.

Lecture Notes in Computer Science

For information about Vols. 1–835
please contact your bookseller or Springer-Verlag

Vol. 871: J. P. Lee, G. G. Grinstein (Eds.), Database Issues for Data Visualization. Proceedings, 1993. XIV, 229 pages. 1994.

Vol. 872: S Arikawa, K. P. Jantke (Eds.), Algorithmic Learning Theory. Proceedings, 1994. XIV, 575 pages. 1994.

Vol. 873: M. Naftalin, T. Denvir, M. Bertran (Eds.), FME '94: Industrial Benefit of Formal Methods. Proceedings, 1994. XI, 723 pages. 1994.

Vol. 874: A. Borning (Ed.), Principles and Practice of Constraint Programming. Proceedings, 1994. IX, 361 pages. 1994.

Vol. 875: D. Gollmann (Ed.), Computer Security – ESORICS 94. Proceedings, 1994. XI, 469 pages. 1994.

Vol. 876: B. Blumenthal, J. Gornostaev, C. Unger (Eds.), Human-Computer Interaction. Proceedings, 1994. IX, 239 pages. 1994.

Vol. 877: L. M. Adleman, M.-D. Huang (Eds.), Algorithmic Number Theory. Proceedings, 1994. IX, 323 pages. 1994.

Vol. 878: T. Ishida; Parallel, Distributed and Multiagent Production Systems. XVII, 166 pages. 1994. (Subseries LNAI).

Vol. 879: J. Dongarra, J. Waśniewski (Eds.), Parallel Scientific Computing. Proceedings, 1994. XI, 566 pages. 1994.

Vol. 880: P. S. Thiagarajan (Ed.), Foundations of Software Technology and Theoretical Computer Science. Proceedings, 1994. XI, 451 pages. 1994.

Vol. 881: P. Loucopoulos (Ed.), Entity-Relationship Approach – ER'94. Proceedings, 1994. XIII, 579 pages. 1994.

Vol. 882: D. Hutchison, A. Danthine, H. Leopold, G. Coulson (Eds.), Multimedia Transport and Teleservices. Proceedings, 1994. XI, 380 pages. 1994.

Vol. 883: L. Fribourg, F. Turini (Eds.), Logic Program Synthesis and Transformation – Meta-Programming in Logic. Proceedings, 1994. IX, 451 pages. 1994.

Vol. 884: J. Nievergelt, T. Roos, H.-J. Schek, P. Widmayer (Eds.), IGIS '94: Geographic Information Systems. Proceedings, 1994. VIII, 292 pages. 19944.

Vol. 885: R. C. Veltkamp, Closed Objects Boundaries from Scattered Points. VIII, 144 pages. 1994.

Vol. 886: M. M. Veloso, Planning and Learning by Analogical Reasoning. XIII, 181 pages. 1994. (Subseries LNAI).

Vol. 887: M. Toussaint (Ed.), Ada in Europe. Proceedings, 1994. XII, 521 pages. 1994.

Vol. 888: S. A. Andersson (Ed.), Analysis of Dynamical and Cognitive Systems. Proceedings, 1993. VII, 260 pages. 1995.

Vol. 889: H. P. Lubich, Towards a CSCW Framework for Scientific Cooperation in Europe. X, 268 pages. 1995.

Vol. 890: M. J. Wooldridge, N. R. Jennings (Eds.), Intelligent Agents. Proceedings, 1994. VIII, 407 pages. 1995. (Subseries LNAI).

Vol. 891: C. Lewerentz, T. Lindner (Eds.), Formal Development of Reactive Systems. XI, 394 pages. 1995.

Vol. 892: K. Pingali, U. Banerjee, D. Gelernter, A. Nicolau, D. Padua (Eds.), Languages and Compilers for Parallel Computing. Proceedings, 1994. XI, 496 pages. 1995.

Vol. 893: G. Gottlob, M. Y. Vardi (Eds.), Database Theory – ICDT '95. Proceedings, 1995. XI, 454 pages. 1995.

Vol. 894: R. Tamassia, I. G. Tollis (Eds.), Graph Drawing. Proceedings, 1994. X, 471 pages. 1995.

Vol. 895: R. L. Ibrahim (Ed.), Software Engineering Education. Proceedings, 1995. XII, 449 pages. 1995.

Vol. 896: R. N. Taylor, J. Coutaz (Eds.), Software Engineering and Human-Computer Interaction. Proceedings, 1994. X, 281 pages. 1995.

Vol. 897: M. Fisher, R. Owens (Eds.), Executable Modal and Temporal Logics. Proceedings, 1993. VII, 180 pages. 1995. (Subseries LNAI).

Vol. 898: P. Steffens (Ed.), Machine Translation and the Lexicon. Proceedings, 1993. X, 251 pages. 1995. (Subseries LNAI).

Vol. 899: W. Banzhaf, F. H. Eeckman (Eds.), Evolution and Biocomputation. VII, 277 pages. 1995.

Vol. 900: E. W. Mayr, C. Puech (Eds.), STACS 95. Proceedings, 1995. XIII, 654 pages. 1995.

Vol. 901: R. Kumar, T. Kropf (Eds.), Theorem Provers in Circuit Design. Proceedings, 1994. VIII, 303 pages. 1995.

Vol. 902: M. Dezani-Ciancaglini, G. Plotkin (Eds.), Typed Lambda Calculi and Applications. Proceedings, 1995. VIII, 443 pages. 1995.

Vol. 903: E. W. Mayr, G. Schmidt, G. Tinhofer (Eds.), Graph-Theoretic Concepts in Computer Science. Proceedings, 1994. IX, 414 pages. 1995.

Vol. 904: P. Vitányi (Ed.), Computational Learning Theory. EuroCOLT'95. Proceedings, 1995. XVII, 415 pages. 1995. (Subseries LNAI).

Vol. 905: N. Ayache (Ed.), Computer Vision, Virtual Reality and Robotics in Medicine. Proceedings, 1995. XIV, 567 pages. 1995.

Vol. 906: E. Astesiano, G. Reggio, A. Tarlecki (Eds.), Recent Trends in Data Type Specification. Proceedings, 1995. VIII, 523 pages. 1995.

Vol. 907: T. Ito, A. Yonezawa (Eds.), Theory and Practice of Parallel Programming. Proceedings, 1995. VIII, 485 pages. 1995.

Vol. 908: J. R. Rao Extensions of the UNITY Methodology: Compositionality, Fairness and Probability in Parallelism. XI, 178 pages. 1995.

Vol. 910: A. Podelski (Ed.), Constraint Programming: Basics and Trends. Proceedings, 1995. XI, 315 pages. 1995.

Vol. 911: R. Baeza-Yates, E. Goles, P. V. Poblete (Eds.), LATIN '95: Theoretical Informatics. Proceedings, 1995. IX, 525 pages. 1995.

Vol. 912: N. Lavrač, S. Wrobel (Eds.), Machine Learning: ECML – 95. Proceedings, 1995. XI, 370 pages. 1995. (Subseries LNAI).

Vol. 913: W. Schäfer (Ed.), Software Process Technology. Proceedings, 1995. IX, 261 pages. 1995.

Vol. 914: J. Hsiang (Ed.), Rewriting Techniques and Applications. Proceedings, 1995. XII, 473 pages. 1995.

Vol. 916: N. R. Adam, B. K. Bhargava, Y. Yesha (Eds.), Digital Libraries. Proceedings, 1994. XIII, 321 pages. 1995.